MEDIA RELATIONS IN SPORT

Other Titles in the Sport Management Library

— • —

Case Studies in Sport Marketing

— • —

Developing Successful Sport Marketing Plans, 2nd Edition

— • —

Developing Successful Sport Sponsorship Plans, 2nd Edition

— • —

Economics of Sport, 2nd Edition

— • —

Ethics and Morality in Sport Management

— • —

Financing Sport, 2nd Edition

— • —

Foundations of Sport Management

— • —

Fundamentals of Sport Marketing, 2nd Edition

— • —

Sport Facility Management: Organizing Events and Mitigating Risks

— • —

Sport Governance in the Global Community

— • —

Sport Management Field Experiences

MEDIA
RELATIONS
IN SPORT

SECOND EDITION

Allan Hall

William Nichols

Patrick Moynahan

Janis Taylor

Fitness Information Technology
a Division of the International Center
for Performance Excellence
262 Coliseum, WVU-PE, PO Box 6116
Morgantown, WV 26506-6116

Library of Congress Card Catalog Number: 2006938655

ISBN 13: 978-1-885693-74-7

Production Editor: Matt Brann
Cover Design: Craig Hines
Typesetter: Craig Hines
Copyeditor: Matt Brann
Proofreader: Maria E. denBoer
Indexer: Maria E. denBoer
Printed by: Sheridan Books
Cover Photo: Courtesy of John T. Greilick/ *The Detroit News*

10   9   8   7   6   5   4   3   2   1

Fitness Information Technology
A Division of the International Center for Performance Excellence
West Virginia University
262 Coliseum, WVU-PE
PO Box 6116
Morgantown, WV 26506-6116
800.477.4348 (toll free)
304.293.6888 (phone)
304.293.6658 (fax)
Email: icpe@mail.wvu.edu
Website: www.fitinfotech.com

Contents

Foreword

Creating an Image

In essence, that is the main objective of the sports public relations professional as he or she works together with other sports marketing personnel within a university athletic department or a professional sports organization.

On a daily basis—through the discipline of media relations—no one affects the image of an organization more than the public relations staff. Throughout the years, I have come to realize that the PR in sports public relations actually stands for *Planning Right*.

Creating an image encompasses many aspects of the sport business world, but on a consistent basis, it is the public relations staff who is challenged with the task of sharing that message through writing news releases; conducting press conferences; operating a press box; promoting executives, coaches, and players; planning special events, etc.

This second edition of *Media Relations in Sport* provides a wonderful understanding of the functions and workings of the sports media world. For those students who are planning careers in sports management or athletic administration, this guide is a must-read. It is a must-read because it provides you the foundation from which the basic skills of *Planning Right* are based.

Enjoy the book and good luck as you continue your education.

Sincerely,

Bob DiBiasio
Vice President, Public Relations
Cleveland Indians

Preface

The dramatic change brought about by television in the latter half of the 20th century led to a new relationship between the media and sports organizations. The electronic development took much of the personal relationship out of the sports information offices but brought a wealth of information and technical information into these offices.

Television began to dictate to sports organizations because they started to pay those organizations for production of their contests. The broadcast media quickly learned that advertisers were willing to pay substantial amounts of money to television and radio networks for the right to bring commercial messages into the breaks in sports action. Television networks began to offer significant amounts of money to sport organizations for exclusive broadcast rights to a sporting event. Television also dictated to sports organizations the dates and times when contests would be played.

This economic motive spurred a tremendous growth in television coverage of sports and expansion of athletic teams over the second half of the 20th century. Advances in technology and an increase in government deregulation of media ownership contributed to a corresponding explosion in the number of television and radio stations, which in turn created an intense competition among media companies for advertising revenues. The emergence of TV and the competition for audiences forced newspapers to seek new angles on news. They turned to more non-game stories, including investigations into finances, crime, and corruption in sport organizations. Competitive bidding drove broadcast rights to astronomical levels, providing significant revenues for sport organizations. These additional monies contributed to an increase in sport offerings at the high school and collegiate levels driven in part by federal Title IX legislation in the 1970s, which boosted athletic opportunities for women. Amateur and professional leagues enjoyed similar growth, propelled by TV coverage and by expansion into new cities across the country.

No longer were written and interpersonal skills sufficient to do the job of sport information management. The good sport information specialist now needed to know something about radio and television production, needed to understand finance and law, and needed to learn marketing and negotiations. They also needed to plan and organize game coverage to satisfy dozens of reporters with diverse technological support needs. Sports information directors even had to take care of print reporters, first with electronic word processors, then with computers connected to sports departments via telephone lines.

Sports organizations of every kind began to strengthen their sport information operations, both to accommodate the increasing number of media and to tap into the broadcast-generated revenue stream. Colleges and, to a lesser extent, high schools developed self-standing sports information or publicity departments to produce media guides, organize press conferences, and manage game coverage. They assigned sports information directors or athletic administrators to solicit and negotiate broadcast contracts. New athletic conferences were formed, broken apart, and reformed as athletic directors sought to find the proper mix of schools to attract the most lucrative broadcast bids. The institutions asked conference administrators to package deals for members and to provide league statistics, player profiles, and other data to the media. Amateur and professional leagues expanded into cities with large TV markets; developed revenue-sharing plans for affiliates; and created management-level, multi-faceted sport information/promotion units to disseminate information, oversee broadcast of events, and manage media relations.

This book lays a practical and conceptual foundation for individuals interested in careers in sports information management at any level. It attempts to provide the basic understanding of the formalized working relationships between the mass media and sports organizations including recreation centers and athletic clubs, high school and colleges, and amateur organization and professional leagues. The book is structured primarily for students majoring in sport management or minoring in journalism, public relations, or communications. Students pursuing careers as recreation directors, school athletic directors, sports information directors, conference athletic administrators, professional general managers, and administrative staff members also may benefit from the examination of media industries, operations, and practices.

The central focus of the book is the interaction among the people of, and the established operation conventions of, the organizations involved in the flow of information to the public. The objective is to introduce aspiring professionals to information and entertainment management principles demonstrated to be effective. The practical guidelines at the heart of the text are drawn from years of professional experience of the authors. The techniques included have also been tested in classroom settings. They will provide direction both in discerning what the public and the mass media expect from an organization and in devising strategies to meet those expectations effectively.

The text does not intend to provide a comprehensive exploration of mass communication theory as it relates to sports institutions. It does aim to acquaint readers with concepts essential to an understanding of the function of mass media in society and of the influence of sports information on social institutions. For example, the text explores how theoretical concepts relate to the work of sports journalists, media organizations, and sports information managers. Many of the practices presented are addressed in the "sports production complex." This model of sports communication was developed by Dr. Lawrence Wenner of the University of San Francisco and appeared in his book *Media, Sports, and Society*. Introduction to the model, based on Wenner's review of divergent mass communication theories will help readers understand the interdependent working relationship between media members and sports information specialists.

The principal players in the model are sport organizations, the media, and the public. The uniting factor that holds these participants together is sports information. Someone from the sport organization must manage the information about the athletic event, the team, the athletes, and the coaches, and must deliver that information to the media. The media interprets the information for the public. The public reads, hears, or views that interpretation by newspaper columns, radio talk shows, or television analysts. Each of the participants in the model influences and depends on the others to create and share this sports culture. The text will familiarize readers with the linkages in this interdependent relationship.

The sports information professional must recognize that the commercial underpinning of the sports culture influences the weave of the fabric. In one respect, the coverage of sports represents the selling of sport organizations and events to the public through the media. The sport organization sells broadcast rights to an event to the highest bidder; the media then sell the event to the advertisers. The events that draw the largest audiences command the highest prices.

The profit-driven nature of sports media industries raises a number of concerns for the aspiring sports journalist, such as the power of the mass media to influence individuals, organizations, and society at large. The media can create heroes and heroines; emphasize one sport over another; restructure the rules of the game, expose corruption; or evaluate an athlete, team, or institution to such mythical proportions that he, she, or it become an American tradition. The power of selection in coverage and interpretation of events rests with sports journalists and media organizations. The media can provide opportunities for increased public exposure, fan support, and revenues for a sport organization, but the sports information professional must accept that the profit motive is a factor in the equation.

This power to influence the sports culture heightens the degree of accountability and responsibility shouldered by all who pursue careers in organizations interlinked with sports information. The early chapters of this text address working relationships between journalists and sport organizations that have evolved from traditional coverage of sporting events such as professional football and men's college basketball games. The first section outlines interactional, informational, and financial dynamics of media organizations and their influence on sports culture. It emphasizes the dependency of both the mass media and the mass audience on the sports information professional in high-profile sports. However, the reader can relate this to low-profile sports by paying special attention to the concepts that define the relationships.

The sports information specialist must bear the same degree of responsibility as sports journalists and organizations. The latter chapters of the text offer aspiring information specialists an examination of their role within the sport culture. It is a tenuous position at best, because professionals must try to satisfy both the media organizations with which they deal and the sport organizations for which they work. From a practical standpoint sport information specialists must be conscious of the accuracy and truthfulness of the information which they disseminate to the media, while recognizing they cannot control the production or the interpretation of the message. They must also be aware that the content of the message influences the images of the sport organizations and the athletes they represent.

As indicated earlier, many of the technological advances examined have taken personal contacts out of the sports information director's hands. The wealth of information that can be stored and retrieved at a moments notice plus the speed with which information can be disseminated brings reliance of sports information directors on electronic capabilities rather than personal capabilities. Jim Wright of the National Collegiate Athletic Association has less personal contact with media and collegiate institutions than he did in the past. What he and his staff put on the website is now the important product. The type, quality, and amount of information supplied to the media may contribute to the media's interpretation of the athletic performance so sports information personnel must make a conscious effort to articulate their organization's philosophy of sport to the media and to combat misrepresentation of gender or ethnicity reflected in media content. Managing information entails managing concepts, themes, and representations of the organization and the individuals within the organization.

Following the introductory chapters, the text then defines the role and responsibilities of sports information specialists, along with the duties in disseminating information. This part provides practical guidelines on everything from writing press releases to preparing media guides to organizing and managing events such as news conference and media days. The text then moves into chapters that addresses the roles and responsibilities of sports information professionals in orchestrating events. It offers direction on game-coverage, organization and management, on promotion of special events ranging from awards banquets to tournaments, and on development of publicity campaigns. Those chapters collectively amount to a practical handbook on sport management operations.

In the closing chapters, the text examines the ethics of these formalized working relationships and the ideology they perpetuate. This section explores crisis management, the law and regulation of sports, and ethical constructs for media practitioners and sports management professionals. The text concludes by examining the integral introduction of the technological advances that have changed the dissemination of sports information. This advancement has altered methods of providing the media with easy access to essential sports information.

This text is designed to provide practical guidelines of how to perform the everyday duties of the profession. The text offers insight into the job responsibilities of and the constraints on sports writers, columnist, producers, announcers, and analysts and it also helps to explain the broader affect their working relationships have on sports information and the sports culture itself.

Acknowledgments

The authors extend a huge thank you to all of the professional help we received in preparing this second edition. With a text as comprehensive as this, many people contributed to its compilation over many years. This text has proven the mettle of those involved in interscholastic, intercollegiate, and professional sports administration. General managers, athletic directors, sports information directors, coaches, and athletic administrators all contributed heavily to this second edition. Jim Wright of the National Collegiate Athletic Association and Bob Goldring of the Ohio High School Athletic Association were particularly helpful in devoting hours with the lead author for the development of the chapter regarding technology, which is a growing topic in athletic communication and administration. The authors would also like to thank Andrew Ostrow and Matt Brann from Fitness Information Technology for their patience, support, and expertise in the publication of this second edition. I also thank my wife Pamela, daughter Beth, and son Dale for their tremendous help and support.

Dr. Allan W. Hall

Chapter One

MASS COMMUNICATION: THE PROCESS OF SPORT INFORMATION

The conference basketball championship is on the line. The top two teams will meet head to head for the title on campus tomorrow night. The winner will go to the National Collegiate Athletic Association playoffs; the loser will go to the sidelines.

Chapter 1 begins the first part of *Media Relations and Sport*, which examines the process of sport communication, the practices of sports journalists, and the connections between the two. Coverage choices are just some of hundreds of decisions made daily within the complex sports information culture in the United States. The decisions involve sports journalists, media industries, sport organizations, and the public. In the final analysis, media perceptions of values and emotions related to athletics in general and to a team in particular, the level of competition, the numbers and types of spectators or fans, the revenue a game will generate, and the amount and type of exposure by competitors all weigh in coverage decisions.

Part I reviews mass communication concepts that come into play in making coverage decisions in the business of sports information. Chapter 1 examines the links between the media and sport organizations in the process of communication—the participants, their practices and products, and their audiences. Chapters 2 and 3 look at the history, organization, and function of newspapers, radio, and broadcast and cable television. These chapters also explore competition among the media to capture advertising dollars and audience, and their influence on coverage decisions and content.

The arena has been sold out for weeks because the local team has not been in the hunt for a conference championship this late in the season for a decade. Newspaper, radio, and TV reporters have been crawling all over campus for days, hunting for fresh angles to the "big story." The star center's goldfish collection will do . . . if no one else has reported it.

Graduates have inundated the sports information office with calls, trying to use any possible connections they may have to obtain tickets. Every newspaper, radio, and TV station with a remote tie to either of the teams has requested press credentials. Some even have made outrageous demands for special favors involving electrical hookups, part-time help, and working space.

The *Associated Press* has asked for a call with the score and highlights as soon as the game ends. So has *ESPN*, the round-the-clock cable network that updates its scrolling sports scoreboard throughout the evening on its television networks and website. The network would also like taped video highlights, too, if you can supply them.

Where were all these media people last year when the team went 5-21? Where were they at midseason this year when the team stood 14-2 and started talking about playoff possibilities? Not a big story then? Not a playoff contender yet? If coverage decisions are based on a team's record, then where were the media when the women's volleyball team won 20 straight games and swept the conference tournament last month?

To those unfamiliar with the study of mass communication, the media serve as little more than information and entertainment sources. The major mass media— **The Mass Media**

newspapers, magazines, radio, broadcast and cable television, and now even the Internet—provide up-to-date news and weather, offer an escape from the stress of the work world, and pitch consumer products. Many people just accept the common belief that "what you see is what you get"—words, sounds, and pictures that inform, entertain, and persuade. They view the media from a functional perspective, giving little thought to the organizations that produce the media, the messages in their content, and their influence on readers, viewers, or listeners.

In fact, most of us do not pay much attention to such weighty matters at all, as long as we are satisfied with the services the media provide. We expect a newspaper delivered to the house every day, a wake-up call from the clock radio, and a quick update on the news from television before we go to work. We escape the demands of the workplace by listening to our favorite radio deejays or talk-show stars between home and work. Once the workday is done, we sit down to supper with the network or cable television newscasts within easy view. For relaxation later in the evening, we read a book, go to the movies, watch a videotape, listen to a new compact disc, browse the Internet, or return to television for a prime-time situation comedy or dramatic series.

The media have become such an omnipresent element of our daily lives that we simply take them for granted, yet researchers have discovered that by the time they are teenagers, American children have spent more hours watching television than engaging in any other activity except sleep—even more time than they have spent in school (Baran & Davis, 1995). Similarly, according to industry estimates, adults have spent more than half their waking lives in contact with the media.

In view of their pervasive presence in our lives, we might do well to look closer at the operation and influence of the business of mass communication, particularly as they relate to sports infor-

Consider the scope of four of the mass media in the United States:

- Research indicates that American adults spend 3 hours, 38 minutes a day with TV; 2 hours, 3 minutes with radio; 29 minutes with newspapers; and 17 minutes with magazines—i.e., more than one fourth of the day engaged by the media (TVB: TV Basics—Time Spent and Daily Reach by Major Media, 1999).

- Television reaches 88% of American adults daily; radio, 71%; newspapers, 56%; and magazines, 34% (TVB: TV Basics—Time Spent and Daily Reach by Major Media, 1999).

- U.S. advertisers spent $41 million on newspapers, $37 million on broadcast television, $13 million on radio, $10 million on magazines, and $5 million on cable television in 1997 (U.S. Advertising Expenditures, Newspaper Association of America, 1999).

- Nearly 96% of people 12 and older—that's 210 million Americans—listen to at least 15 minutes of radio per week (Statistical Research, Inc., 1998).

- By 1999, approximately 99.7% of the 100 million households in the United States had a television set; 75.6% had two or more TV sets (TVB: TV Basics—Multi-Set and Color Television Households, 1999).

- TV households in the United States averaged 7 hours, 15 minutes of viewing time a day in 1998 (TVB: TV Basics—Time Spent Viewing Per Television Home Per Day, 1999).

- The broadcast media counted among their family some 1,204 television stations and 10,532 radio stations ("Trends in Television," 1998).

- The United States produced 1,509 daily newspapers—705 morning papers and 816 evening papers—and 903 Sunday newspapers in 1997 (Number of U.S. Daily Newspapers, Newspaper Association of America, 1999).

- In 1997, daily circulation of newspapers—the number of copies printed and distributed—exceeded 56 million on weekdays and 60 million on Sundays (U.S. Daily Newspaper Circulation, Newspaper Association of America, 1999).

- Daily readership stood at 58.7% in 1997 and Sunday readership hit 68.5% (Facts About Newspapers, Newspaper Association of America, 1998).

mation. Newspapers, magazines, radio, and television represent the dominant avenues of sports communication in the United States. The print media, which deliver information through the written word, include everything from a neighborhood flyer to the *Associated Press*, the world's largest newsgathering agency. Print media also includes alternative publications of all kinds—fan publications, corporate newsletters, and special-interest magazines. Electronic media range from a single ham-operator at home to the local AM or FM station with regional reach, from the clear-channel 50,000-watt station to the powerful television network that beams sports around the world via cable and satellite.

Radio and television are the media of immediacy: They deliver sports information live as the event unfolds. They literally bring the game right into the living rooms of the world. Radio announcers use rich description to create verbal pictures of hits, runs, and errors as they occur. In television, the video monitor, the TV announcers, and the analysts offer both a description and an explanation of the live action as two thoroughbreds surge to the wire. Newspapers and magazines, on the other hand, are the media of depth and interpretation: They focus on how and why the contest turned out as it did. In addition to a detailed description of the game, they provide analysis and commentary; insights from the athletes, coaches, owners, and other participants; and features on the standout performers of the game.

Both the print and electronic media derive most of their revenue from the sale of advertising rather than from the sale of subscriptions or the sale of the product. The electronic media raise monies by selling the audience to advertisers. The print media also provide an audience of readers to advertisers—so the success of both media is tied in part to their ability to deliver a large audience to an advertiser. Consequently, each medium competes against the others for a share of the multibillion-dollar advertising revenues generated by the sport industry in the United States each year. The total market value of the four major professional leagues alone—the National Basketball Association, the National Football League, the National Hockey League, and Major League Baseball—amounts to $10 billion (Howard & Crompton, 1995).

Courtesy of John Reid/Cleveland Browns

The competition among sport media is intense in large cities where there are generally more than one daily newspaper and several TV and radio stations.

Much of the revenue that finances the expansion of sport organizations comes from advertising and from monies resulting from contracted agreements with the electronic media for exclusive broadcast rights. For example, broadcast fees contributed to a payout of $8.6 million each to the University of Nebraska and the University of Florida for participation in the 1996 Fiesta Bowl.

The competition among the media is intense because the financial stakes are so high. More than 2,200 journalists request credentials each year for a single event, the Super Bowl, because the NFL championship game generally attracts more than 100 million viewers. The major television networks bid millions of dollars for the rights to the Super Bowl because the large audience guarantees tremendous advertising revenues.

The financial successes of the media and of sport organizations are inseparably linked. The media provide sport organizations with substantial revenue, as well as opportunities for increased public exposure and fan support. The fan support, in turn, gives the media an audience base upon which to calculate advertising rates. This financial relationship has turned both parties into big businesses, often run by giant corporations, where profit-loss ledgers are as important as won-loss records. In some cases, they are parts of the same corporate enterprise. The Tribune Company owns a handful of newspapers across the country, including the *Chicago Tribune,* and also owns professional baseball's Chicago Cubs as well as the television networks the WB and WGN. Previously, the Disney Corporation owned professional hockey's Mighty Ducks of Anaheim and Major League Baseball's Los Angeles Angels of Anaheim before selling them in 2005 and 2003, respectively. Disney added ABC-TV to its holdings in 1995, and ABC-TV owns a share of ESPN. That means Disney, like the Tribune Company, were in the business of sports *and* sport communication.

The Evolution of Sports Journalism

Sport communication through the media is more than 200 years old. It began as a complement to the news and politics of the day in the daily newspaper, and it still is in the staid *New York Times.* However, most newspapers today devote a complete section to sports. Newspapers and magazines cover amateur and school sports of every kind, from local bowling results to college basketball's Final Four, and from figure skating to hunting and fishing. They also cover professional sports from every angle, from league play to stadium licenses, and from player performance to front-office finagling.

Newspapers and magazines dominated the delivery of sports information for more than 150 years, and coverage of games dominated the information delivered. The format changed little until the invention of wireless communication in the Industrial Revolution created a vehicle for the delivery of first the sound, then the sights of a sporting event. The new forms of communication transformed sports information from cottage industries to multibillion-dollar business conglomerates.

Print coverage of sports in the United States dates to May 5, 1773, when the *Boston Gazette* sent a reporter to England to cover a boxing match. Other newspapers followed suit in the 1830s when printers began to cater to mass audiences in the era of the Penny Press. Development of the rotary press made it possible to produce multiple copies inexpensively. A New York printer, Benjamin Day, started the *New York Sun* in 1833 and hired newsboys to hawk his paper on the streets for a penny, a nickel cheaper than competing newspapers. Day sold advertising to make up the difference. He also broadened the scope of coverage, offering news of interest to business people and to common laborers, including the news of sports.

By 1835 three other New York newspapers—the *Sun,* the *Transcript,* and the *Herald*—offered sports information. Coverage consisted mostly of contest results, a focus that continued for the next century. Prior to World War I, journalism concerned itself with a few athletic contests in baseball, college football, horse racing, and boxing. Most of the reporting focused on contests in the eastern part of the United States.

Joseph Pulitzer introduced a sports section in the *New York World* in 1896, and the public's appetite for sports news has grown steadily ever since (Hiebert, Unguarait, & Bohn, 1991). What historians call "The Golden Era" of print sports reporting came little more than two decades later, in the 1920s. After World War I, the quality of writing in general improved dramatically because of rapid increases in literacy resulting from the creation of a national system of public education. Hiring writers who possessed a knowledge of sports as well as a command of the English language, newspapers benefited from the increase. Colorful and entertaining writers helped to make national heroes of personalities such as Babe Ruth, Red Grange, Knute Rockne, and Jack Dempsey by dramatizing their athletic deeds. The game was the thing, and newspapers gave only a wink and veiled mention to off-field activities of players. They also shied away from the business of sports, unless it dealt with the salaries of players or the cost of tickets.

In the 1920s and 1930s, newspapers assigned "beat" reporters to baseball. Beat writers traveled with their city's Major League Baseball team. Some newspapers also assigned reporters to cover college football and prizefighting. They gathered information about other sports over the telephone from personnel who worked for the sport organizations—forerunners of the modern sport management professional.

The Golden Era also gave birth to sport communication via the electronic media. During the 1920s, radio stations began to offer live baseball broadcasts and clever re-creations of road games. Announcers read play-by-play off the Western Union telegraph wires and supplied their own sound effects to simulate live action. A station owned by the *Detroit News* broadcast the results of Major League Baseball's World Series in 1920, the same year a station in Texas carried a football game. KDKA in Pittsburgh, the first commercial radio station in the United States, presented prizefights as well as baseball games a year later. By the 1930s, all 16 Major League Baseball teams were on local radio.

As reader interest and sports coverage grew through the Great Depression and World War II, merchants found radio an inexpensive way to sell their products. Radio saw broadcasts of sporting events as a way to reach male audiences. Companies that manufactured products for men became regular sponsors of radio sports broadcasts.

The competition forced sportswriters to change their style, to try to offer readers something more than radio could give them. Radio provided the basic details of the game, including the score and highlights of the contest. Print reporters turned to digging up details not included in the radio broadcasts, to give readers something new when they opened their newspapers. Hence, stories became more comprehensive, with more explanation of key plays and players. Sports sections also supplemented game coverage with features on players and behind-the-scenes "notes" columns—tidbits of information about players and teams.

It was not until television added pictures to the broadcast package in the 1950s that newspaper writing and coverage styles changed dramatically. Television coverage drove sportswriters into locker rooms to get reactions and comments on the game from coaches, managers, and competitors.

Commercial Competition Changes the Media Game

In one sense, competition from TV precipitated a move to interpretive and investigative reporting by newspaper journalists. Television showed and told what happened. Sportswriters put greater emphasis on explaining how and why it happened and on offering the perspective of the competitors themselves. That gave print stories greater depth and perspective, but it put sports journalists in the position of interpreting the events.

Sports news now ranks as one of the primary reasons people purchase newspapers. The sports section is the second most heavily read part of the newspaper, after local news (Mencher, 1991). Consequently, the nation's metropolitan daily newspapers devote about 20% of their editorial space to sports, and they assign about 20% of their reporting staff to the sports department.

Television did not gain a foothold in sport communication until the 1950s. David Sarnoff, an electronic-media pioneer who became president of RCA records and NBC-TV, introduced 5-inch and 9-inch television sets at the 1939 World's Fair in New York City. Using a remote unit to present a new program each day, he broadcast a game between the Cincinnati Reds and the Brooklyn Dodgers at Ebbets Field. However, television did not offer sports programming to any significant degree until the end of World War II. The medium struggled initially because reception was poor and most of the sets were in bars and clubs, but improvements in picture quality and programming contributed to a jump in popularity in the early 1950s, when television began offering weekend coverage of Major League Baseball, college football, and professional football. The number of homes with television jumped from 15 million in 1952 to 45 million in 1960. Gross industry revenues increased from $300 million to $1.3 billion (Hiebert et al., 1991).

California State University media expert Shirley Biagi (1992) says the biggest single element in television's popularity over the past 30 years has been sports. Robert Wussler, a former president of CBS Sports, told *Newsweek* magazine in 1989 that sports provided the best way for a network to "shore up ratings, please affiliates, entice advertisers and allow heavy promotion of prime time shows" (1989, p. 66).

Thirteen of the top 25 network telecasts of all time have been sports programs (TVB: TV Basics—Top 25 Network Telecasts Ranked by Household Ratings, 1999).

By the late 1960s, the TV networks were broadcasting the major college football bowls, the World Series, and the professional football playoffs. They copied the format of radio—without need of sound effects—with announcers who described the game play-by-play and sprinkled in statistics and anecdotes about the players. The networks soon added "color commentators," many of them former athletes, who analyzed and explained plays, strategy, etc.

Sports coverage spread to weeknights in the 1970s with the advent of *Monday Night Football* on ABC-TV, and then moved on to cable when Ted Turner purchased the Atlanta Braves to supply programming for his struggling network, WTBS. Sport communication then went round-the-clock in 1979 with the debut of an all-sports cable channel, the Entertainment and Sports Programming Network (ESPN). Twenty-five years later, ESPN boasted 50 million households and offered more than 8,000 hours of televised sports (Biagi, 1995). It branched into a second all-sports cable channel, ESPN-2, in the mid-1990s. It has since added ESPN News and ESPNU to its stable of sports channels. The explosion of network and cable offerings means a sports fan can choose from among

The sport media industry has changed considerably since radio broadcasters like the late Jack Fleming, a legendary broadcaster for West Virginia University and the Pittsburgh Steelers, kept listeners glued to their radios.

10 college football games on a winter weekend, a couple of pro basketball or hockey games, a dozen pro football games, professional figure skating, and world-class gymnastics or tennis. Cable channels such as ESPN or Fox Sports Net even replay some games to pick up viewers who watched competing games earlier.

The advent of television forced radio to find a new approach to sport communication. Radio turned away from network programs and concentrated on local audience interests. During the 1980s and 1990s, radio responded to the mushrooming popularity of sports by initiating sports talk shows. The programs give fans an opportunity to second-guess coaches, make suggestions for improving their favorite teams, and generally offer their own interpretations or commentary on the games.

At the root of the rapid expansion of sports broadcasts is network affiliation. Because producing original programming is very expensive, most radio and TV stations affiliate with a network. William Paley, who launched the CBS radio network in 1929, came up with a way to make affiliation profitable for them. He persuaded sponsors to buy time, just as newspaper advertisers purchased space. He convinced sponsors that people who listened to radio programs would buy their products (Biagi, 1992). His sales pitch proved successful when CBS collected $16 million in advertising in 1932, during the Depression. Television advertising revenues have since climbed over the billion-dollar mark annually.

Paley introduced a commercial angle that revolutionized sport communication and forged a symbiotic relationship between media organizations and sport organizations that has generated enormous profits for both. Sport organizations initially paid television networks to present their games. The Orange Bowl Committee paid CBS $500 to put the game on radio in 1936. When television executives learned sports drew big audiences and corresponding advertising dollars, they began to offer substantial monies for exclusive rights to broadcast games. NBC paid $300,000 for the right to produce the Orange Bowl on TV for the first time, in 1964 (Hiebert et al., 1991).

Broadcast fees since have escalated at astronomical rates. In 1993, each of the 28 NFL teams got in excess of $32.5 million (Howard, 1995). ABC-TV won the rights to broadcast the 1972 Olympics for $13.5 million (Hiebert et al., 1991). NBC Sports agreed to pay the International Olympic Committee $3.6 billion for exclusive TV rights to five Olympic Games over an 8-year period, beginning in 1996.

In a very real sense, television has taken some sports events off the playing field and put them in the living room. The sports fan literally can purchase a "ticket" for a particular game, including paying for a season viewing packages sold by many satellite and cable providers. The fan can "attend" any number of games on any given weekend without leaving the couch. Home viewers can get replays of key plays, and other amenities, without the hassle of traffic tie-ups, cold weather, crowded restrooms, or other spectator travails. The TV cameras will take them right into the locker room—on some occasions, all the way to the boardrooms. The sport organization can make money even if no one attends the game, because attendance is secondary to the audience TV can deliver to advertisers. The important crowds are in bars and homes, in front of television sets—some of which are as large as movie screens and equipped with theater-quality sound systems.

In fact, it was possible as the 20th century came to a close for a person to follow a sport or team avidly for his or her entire life without ever stepping into a stadium, a coliseum, or a ballpark. Clearly, such audience members behave quite like fans at the fieldhouse, and some gain similar gratification. The unique difference between the fan in the fieldhouse and the fan at home is that, for the fan at home, technology has come between the game and the experience of the game. The media sports audience has given up the ambience of the game for an interpretation of the game via the printed words of a newspaper, the voice of radio, or the images of television.

To understand the implications of media-filtered sport information and entertainment, one must understand the complexities of mass communication, the technologies and people involved in the process, and the potential influence of their

The Mass Communication Process

work on the audience. Mass communication involves a process through which the media deliver written, aural, and visual messages to a large audience. The audience is diverse, invisible, and unknown in many respects. Feedback occurs much more slowly than in other forms of communication, which makes it difficult to know if all or most of the audience interpreted the message as it was intended.

That is what separates mass communication from other forms of communication. Interpersonal communication is a one-to-one process, and communicators can identify and clarify any misunderstanding or misinterpretation immediately. Group communication among individuals, within organizations, and between organizations also affords each party the opportunity to clear up any misconceptions rather quickly, regardless of the means of communication: informal conversations; speeches; audiovisual presentations; letters; memos; or reports via telephone, modems, and faxes. In contrast, sophisticated analytical studies are necessary to accurately assess the effectiveness and impact of mass communication.

Researchers agree that the large volume of information created, reproduced, and disseminated by the mass media daily contributes to the way people make sense of their immediate surroundings and the world in general. For example, King (1987) suggests that the media create a "paper reality" (p. 70). Instead of developing a picture of the world from personal experience, people base their view of what is real on an interpretation of information filtered by and through newspapers and broadcast scripts. Another researcher, Gerber, conducted a study that found that people who watch more television give more answers consistent with information drawn from TV broadcasts than with government data when asked about violent crime. He concluded that television creates a worldview upon which people base daily judgments, even if that view is inaccurate (Baran & Davis, 1995). The implications for the couch potato are obvious: What the fan believes to be real about sports may be shaped by the picture on the screen and may not be entirely true.

Not all researchers are ready to ascribe such great power to the media. Some believe that personal experience plays a larger role in one's perception of reality, and that the media tend to reinforce the personal view (Baran & Davis, 1995). The disagreement results from the diverse academic fields these researchers represent and the different analytical methods they employ. Studies by psychologists, social scientists, historians, philosophers, anthropologists, political scientists, journalists, and other scholars have generated a broad body of knowledge and a variety of theories on mass communication. Some scholars look at the process, such as how the media gather information and translate it into symbols that give meaning to the message. For example, what messages do the media send about race if they consistently credit former Boston Celtics great Larry Bird's success in basketball to hard work and former Los Angeles Lakers great Magic Johnson's to natural talent? Does that suggest that White, male athletes work harder than Black, male athletes? Other researchers look at the function of the media, how audience members use program content for their own gratification of needs. What pleasure do viewers get from screaming at referees, yelling insults at opponents, or simply rooting for the home team?

Although each study, each theory, adds clarity to the nature of human communication, none provides a universally accepted explanation of the social and cultural effects of mass communication (for an overview on communication theories see Baran & Davis, 1995; Infante, Rancer, & Womack, 1990; Littlejohn, 1989; and Trenholm, 1991).

The same perspectives for studying mass communication are applicable to sports information because it, too, involves transmission of a message to a large audience through the mass media. One of the few who have attempted a comprehensive study of the connection is Wenner (1989), a mass communication professor at the University of San Francisco. In his book, *Media, Sports and Society,* he identifies these key questions to ask about the process, function, and influence of sport communication:

- What is the nature of the relationship between media organizations and sport organizations?

- What does the sports contest mean to the audience and how do audience members consume it?

- How much power do sports journalists, media, and sport organizations wield in determining how audience members consume and interpret the sport?

To address Wenner's questions from a sports information perspective, one must define *mass communication.* Littlejohn (1989) offers a definition applicable to sport communication:

> Mass communication is the process whereby media organizations produce and transmit messages to large publics and the process by which those messages are sought, used and consumed by audiences. Central to any study of mass communication are the products or messages that affect and reflect the culture of the society. (p. 252)

The media industries of film, television, cable, radio, newspapers, books, magazines, and recordings compose the mass media in Littlejohn's definition.

McQuail (1987) identifies four elements of the mass media applicable to sport communication. The first element is their commercial nature. The profit motive is the driving force behind media organizations, and their content aims at attracting an audience for advertisers. The second element is the audience, a mass audience in the sense that it is large, heterogeneous, widely dispersed, and anonymous to the media organizations and other audience members. The third element is the content of the mass media—the words, sounds, and pictures. The final element is the media organization, the source of the content. Media companies are complex and formal organizations supported by sophisticated technology and specialized personnel that produce the content and thereby shape the message and influence interpretation by the audience, in McQuail's view.

> In his book, *Media, Sports and Society,* Wenner identifies these key questions to ask about the process, function, and influence of sport communication:
>
> - What is the nature of the relationship between media organizations and sport organizations?
>
> - What does the sports contest mean to the audience and how do audience members consume it?
>
> - How much power do sports journalists, media, and sport organizations wield in determining how audience members consume and interpret the sport?

McQuail identifies four elements of the mass media applicable to sport communication:

- commercial nature
- audience
- the content—the words, sounds, and pictures—of the mass media
- the media organization, the source of the content

Researchers typically examine these elements from three perspectives:

- the media practices
- the text
- the audience

Researchers typically examine these elements from three perspectives: (a) *media practices*, the decision making and production work of individual members of the media; (b) *text*, the product that results from media practices, such as a newspaper article or a television program; and (c) *audience*, the people who consume and interpret the product. However, the categories ignore sport organizations, which play a role in the process of sport communication. Not only do they interact with media practitioners and audience members at various steps in the process, but they also provide the content that is incorporated in the text. That means sport organizations are a factor in each perspective.

A Model of Sport Communication

Wenner (1989) offers a theoretical model that adapts readily to examination of sport communication because it incorporates sport organizations. It also attempts to bridge two major research directions in mass communication. Wenner calls his approach *a transactional model of sport communication* because he puts emphasis on *transactions*, the exchanges and relationships between the key individuals and organizations in the process. Wenner substitutes *sports production complex* for *media practices*, to address the work of sport organizations as well as of the mass media. He also considers how the media interpret content in his examination of the text and the audience. The principal people in Wenner's model are print and broadcast journalists, amateur and professional sport organizations, and the print and broadcast industries. Journalists include reporters, editors, TV sports directors, announcers, producers, and news anchors. Among his sport organizations are professional teams; college-sports information directors; and the leagues and conferences that regulate them, such as the National Football League, the National Collegiate Athletic Association, and the American Softball Association. Radio and television broadcasters, cable operations, and newspaper companies comprise Wenner's print and broadcast industries.

The foundation for Wenner's (1989) model comes from studies in sociology that explore the role of sport in society; the values of sport and sport participation; and the way children learn roles in society, including race and gender. He concludes that the media give us a shared sports culture; that is, they help to shape our picture of what sport is and means. The sports culture may reinforce existing expectations and stereotypes or contribute to changing them, depending on the way the media shape the message. The media may reinforce low expectations for women's sports by giving them little coverage, or they may increase coverage, giving readers the impression that women's sports represent a high priority and increasing expectations for high-caliber competition. This suggests that NBC's heavy coverage of women's events in the 1996, 2000, and 2004 Olympic Games—particularly of American successes—may help to change the perception of the skill level in women's sports.

Some of the consistent themes that surface in Wenner's (1989) treatise and other relevant research are instructive to those considering careers in the media or sport

organizations. Clearly, the practices of journalists and sports information specialists exercise considerable influence on the structure, popularity, and character of
sport in ways scholars are only beginning to discern.

Wenner (1989) looks at media practices (or transactions) at the organizational
and economic levels. He sees a symbiotic relationship between media industries
and sport organizations: Each needs the other to create
a large marketplace. The interdependence, of course, is
largely a result of the evolution of televised sports. Mass
media organizations profit from their distribution of
sports information and entertainment, primarily from
the high advertising rates that a large audience guarantees. Sport organizations
benefit from publicity and exposure (increased spectator interest), as well as the
money generated through broadcast license agreements.

> Wenner sees a symbiotic relationship between media
> industries and sport organizations: Each needs the
> other to create a large marketplace.

For example, consistently high TV ratings for Super Bowl broadcasts suggest to
advertisers that they can reach a large, worldwide audience through commercial
spots during the game. The network that wins the broadcast rights turns a huge
profit because of the high rate it can charge for each spot. The exposure of early
Super Bowls created additional audience interest that propelled the NFL title
game to the top of the sports world in popularity. The high fees resulting from
competitive network bidding for those ever-larger audiences brought enormous
financial benefits to pro football as well. It should follow, then, that the high ratings posted by NBC's Olympic coverage should generate increased advertiser and
media interest in women's sports. NBC Research estimated that more than 200
million people watched the first week of coverage (when American women enjoyed center stage in swimming and gymnastics), making the 1996 Games "the
most-watched ever" (Nelson, 1996, p. B6).

The Profit Motive

The influence of the profit motive on media organizations, sport organizations,
and sports themselves is one of the concerns raised by researchers. For instance,
why is it that television networks broadcast NCAA Division I men's basketball
games virtually every day of the week, yet Division I women's basketball receives
very little television coverage until the NCAA Tournament? For the same reason
that bidding for broadcast rights to professional football and baseball runs into the
millions of dollars. Television makes program decisions with audience and advertisers in mind: What audience can it deliver to advertisers, and how much are advertisers willing to pay for a 30-second mention during a time-out of a Duke-North
Carolina men's basketball game. The almost daily coverage of Division I men's basketball games is possible because the games draw the type of audience and the
numbers of viewers for which advertisers are willing to pay large sums of money.

Other researchers also view sports information as a product. From the perspective
of scholars of political economy, broadcasters select programs that deliver a specific audience to an advertiser. That makes the audience, not the information and
entertainment, the product. Programs serve as vehicles for advertising. In broadcasting and cable, sports programming enables the station or network to attain its

financial objectives. If a program fails to attract viewers, the lack of audience response jeopardizes the financial goals of the station or network. Sports programming ranks behind only prime-time dramas and situation comedies as a big-time money maker for TV (Biagi, 1992).

The makeup of the audience is a consideration, too. High-profile sports such as football, baseball, and men's basketball typically deliver a percentage of the male population to beer and automobile advertisers. Sports marketers for NASCAR (National Association of Stock Car Auto Racing) have been able to attract sponsors through surveys that show that spectators patronize them. NASCAR has attracted media coverage by adding seats to the tracks and selling out every event on the circuit. That every race now appears on television, and that three different networks bid for a share of each of them, is no coincidence.

The implications of these economic linkages between the media and sport organizations are far-reaching. The direct outcome of their profit-centered relationship is the evolution of a two-tiered class of sports. Those sports receiving consistent coverage by cable, broadcasting, and newspapers fit into a class of high-profile sports. Those sports not receiving extensive coverage fall into a group of low-profile sports. The defining element in the two classes is their ability to generate money. Examples of high-profile sports are professional sports—including the National Football League, the National Hockey League, the National Basketball Association, Major League Baseball, the American Tennis Professionals, the Professional Golfers' Association, NASCAR and the Indy Racing League—and such amateur sports as the Olympics, track and field, and NCAA Division I men's college basketball and football. Among the low-profile sports are the majority of the remainder of college and amateur sports, in addition to nearly all women's sports, except professional tennis and golf and amateur gymnastics and figure skating.

> The implications of these economic linkages between the media and sport organizations are far-reaching. The direct outcome of their profit-centered relationship is the evolution of a two-tiered class of sports. Those sports receiving consistent coverage by cable, broadcasting, and newspapers fit into a class of high-profile sports. Those sports not receiving extensive coverage fall into a group of low-profile sports. The defining element in the two classes is their ability to generate money.

The ability to generate television revenue also creates a disparity among sport organizations. A study by Bellamy (1988) found a concentration of economic power among a few teams in cities with a large, urban audience base and powerful television stations.

Like Wenner (1989), DeFluer and Ball-Rokeach (1989) attribute the two-class structure to the interdependent relationship between sport organizations and the media. Media organizations depend on each other for the resource of information, such as advertisers and broadcasters. Social institutions and media systems depend on each other for news, entertainment, and large numbers of audience members. High-profile sports deliver all three, so the media depend on high-profile sports for sports programming. Both high-profile sport organizations and media organizations depend on the public to provide the audience base they use to calculate advertising rates. In addition, advertisers depend on the mass media to deliver the audiences, just as the mass media depend on advertisers to purchase the audiences. In programming decisions for NCAA men's and women's basketball regular-season games, the dependent factors clearly favor men's basketball. That creates a formidable challenge for sport organizations trying to promote or "sell" women's basketball.

The economic underpinnings in these relationships create additional concerns. One concern is the increasing commercialization of sport, and its influence on the game. Min (1987) concluded that television networks persuaded organizers to reschedule some events of the 1984 Olympic Games to coincide with prime-time viewing hours in the United States. Min wonders if the increase in television rights for the Games has commercialized the Olympics to the extent that all parties lose sight of the spirit of the competition—and that the value of the Games suffers. The white elephant sale of professional football teams in late 1995 gives rise to similar concerns. Sports analysts estimated that as many as seven teams were considering moves to other cities. The size of the television market in a particular city figured as prominently in the debate over a particular team's plans as did the size of the crowds at the games.

Regulation of the market, antitrust laws in particular, is among the most discussed issues in the study of controls on the media and sport organizations. Antitrust laws deal with unfair trade practices. They most often come into play in response to protecting a market from competitors. One law under scholarly scrutiny is The Sports Broadcasting Act of 1961 (Public Law No. 87-331, Vol. 75, Page 31), which allows sports leagues to make deals jointly for all teams in the league and permits the NCAA to make deals for member schools. The legislation, in effect, sealed a monopolistic relationship between broadcasters and sports entities, thus giving increasing sums of money to sport organizations while providing programming for broadcasters (Altheide & Snow, 1978; Horowitz, 1978).

Beat reporters generally try to develop a good rapport with the coaches of teams they cover.

On the other side of the monopolistic coin is the 1922 U.S. Supreme Court decision that ruled that Major League Baseball is a sport, not a trade, and is therefore exempt from antitrust laws. The ruling, which gave baseball monopoly status, has been under renewed public scrutiny since a labor dispute that prematurely ended the 1994 Major League Baseball season and delayed the start of the 1995 season. Major League Baseball owners can restrict local television and radio broadcasts, enter into negotiations with broadcasting and cable networks for rights to the baseball season and playoffs, set their own prices, and determine the locations of new franchises.

Clearly, economics will be among the issues media members and sport organization administrators will have to address in the 21st century. Willis and Willis (1993) identified the major media-management concerns for the late 20th century as definition of mission, image and target audience, research strategies for assessing change in the marketplace and for predicting audience needs, marketing and promotions strategies, assessment of technological advances in delivery and distribution systems, and community involvement.

Other Theoretical Issues

Economics is not the only explanation for why NCAA Division I men's college basketball is so thoroughly televised and women's basketball is not, according to cultural researchers who look at the representation of society in the media. Male competition also dominates high-profile sports because of cultural roles and societal expectations created by the media—what the researchers call *media hegemony* and *dominant ideology*. Media hegemony refers to the ability of the media to construct and communicate a picture of reality that is accepted as natural and accurate by the public. In effect, the media perpetuate existing expectations and maintain social structure, roles, stability, and the status quo. Dominant ideology relates to social elements of power (Altheide, 1985). In practical terms, that means the media reinforce the common perception that men's competition is of a higher caliber, and media emphasis on high-profile sports keeps men's competition in the dominant position.

The result is a two-tiered class system based on gender and on social and psychological behaviors. Research into socialization, the way young people learn roles in society, indicates that people learn at an early age what is acceptable behavior. The media influence what they learn because young people spend so much time in contact with the media—more time than they spend in school. Thus, the dominance of men's competition subconsciously suggests to impressionable youngsters that men are better athletes. Simply put, the media persisted in portraying men's competition as superior even as women's college basketball became as competitive and exciting as men's. Competition in figure skating, swimming, golf, tennis, and other sports in which women have participated for decades may have received more coverage because it had already gained a measure of social acceptance. Basketball traditionally has been the domain of men since the emergence of television, and telecasts of women's games threaten that dominant ideology. It was not until 1995 that women's regular-season college basketball games began to appear more often on ESPN, but even today women's basketball is widely unseen unless it's on a cable station such as ESPN or Fox Sports Net.

Numerous studies on the representation of gender in the mass media support this troubling view. Groundbreaking research by Tuchman, Daniels, and Benet (1978) on women's images in the mass media identified ways in which media practices trivialized, ignored, or condemned women. McKay and Huber (1992) found that the media support a gender perspective that promotes the superiority of male athletes and marginalizes female athletes. The media do so, in part, through promotion of technical competency and physical skills in sports in which women do not compete, such as auto racing, sailing, motorcycling, and powerboating. During coverage of these sports, the media show women in supporting roles only, not in competitors' roles. Duncan and Hasbrook (1988) found conflicting messages in coverage of women athletes, some of which trivialized and neutralized the women's efforts. Other researchers found the same in commentaries on basketball games (Blinde, Greendorfer, & Shanker, 1991). A study by Lee (1992) concluded that Canadian and U.S. newspapers presented a more favorable portrayal of men than of women athletes in coverage of the summer 1984 and 1988 Olympic Games.

Media hegemony is not limited to gender. It has also been assessed for race issues. For example, Wonsek (1992) says the use of images of Black athletes for entertainment during competition exploited these athletes, as did their consistent exclusion from the commercials. In essence, the programmers and advertisers played to a White audience. In the mid-1990s, however, Black athletes began to appear more often in commercials.

Some researchers contend that sports audiences share a cultural experience, an experience influenced by the media. The structure and plot of a story, the length of a story, and its position on a page influence the audience's interpretation of the event or sport. A high school basketball coach once complained bitterly about a game story by one of the authors of this text; he insisted that the lead paragraph's focus on the losing team suggested they were more important or more valued than the winning team. In broadcasting, camera angles, framing, and editing all influence how the audience perceives the information. How many times have viewers changed their opinion about an official's call after watching a replay from a different angle?

Researchers who believe coverage primarily reinforces views of reality concede that the media help to set the public agenda and to confer status on people in the spotlight. They say that the media do not tell people what to think, but that they tell people what to think *about* (i.e., they set the agenda). McCombs and Shaw (1972) contend that story selection and emphasis play an important role in shaping public perception (Baran & Davis, 1972). They found that readers not only learned information about an issue, but also attached more importance to it if it appeared in a prominent spot on the page. From a sport communication perspective, fans may attach significance to the volume and position of stories on a newspaper page or newscast. Front-page stories and heavy broadcast focus on the debate over a coach's firing suggest the issue is important—more important, perhaps, than coverage of a murder trial mentioned briefly inside the paper or at the end of the newscast. Similarly, frequent coverage elevates the credibility of an athlete, or confers status on that individual. Media expert John Vivian (1995) says in *The Media of Mass Communication* that media attention "lends a legitimacy to events, individuals and issues that does not extend to issues that go uncovered" (p. 391). Status conferral is evident in the college polls and postseason awards. The schools that receive the most media attention wind up among the top-rated teams. Frequently, an "unknown" knocks off a couple of them in head-to-head competition in the NCAA tournament. Likewise, Heismann Trophy speculation each year focuses on the athletes at big-name schools appearing frequently on television, often ignoring the best players from the "mid-major" conferences.

The audience comes into play in two respects. From the standpoint of the media, programmers make coverage decisions, and advertisers purchase commercial time based on ratings. From the perspective of the audience, the ratings indicate how much an audience values a program, and how loyal audience members are to a sport. Ratings also help media industries determine the demographic makeup of an audience attracted to a particular sport.

Collectively, the research speaks to the immense power of the mass media to influence individuals, organizations, and society at large. The media have helped turn athletes into entertainment stars and sport organizations—particularly professional leagues—into lucrative corporations. This financial partnership also has ceded to the media a role in the structure of sporting events. At the lowest level, colleges routinely change starting times for basketball and football games to accommodate TV programming schedules. They also include "TV time-outs" to provide additional commercial breaks. The Chicago Cubs gave in to pressure from Major League Baseball and put up lights at Wrigley Field to make prime-time telecasts of games possible.

At the highest level, the media create a two-class system in professional sports. Teams in big-market cities (i.e., with large populations of viewers) make far more money from broadcast license fees than do those in small-market cities. As a result, the big-market teams can afford to pay more for high-caliber athletes, coaches, etc. Local media cited the disparity in broadcast revenues as one of the reasons Art Modell elected in 1995 to move his pro football franchise to Baltimore from Cleveland, which consistently packed a 78,000-seat stadium with fans.

The power of selecting the games/sports to cover and the interpretation for the audience rests with the media. Their choices empower some sports organizations and disenfranchise others, dividing them into "haves" and "have-nots" at every level of sport organization. NCAA Division III schools do not reap the monetary benefits that Division I schools collect. Telegenic coaches and players receive more airtime than do the dull or drab. Men's sports receive more newsprint than do women's sports, and professional teams receive more coverage than do amateur sports.

The manner in which the mass media cover teams and individuals is a factor in how the audience perceives them, also. They can turn unknowns into stars overnight. Witness the celebrity of mediocre boxer Peter McNeely, a nobody before a first-round knockout by Mike Tyson but a star in TV commercials afterwards. This ability to influence the audience's perception of a sports event as well as to describe it and the people involved puts the media in a powerful position of determining the value, the importance, and the legitimacy of sports.

Unfortunately, the criteria for selection and interpretation by the mass media are inseparable from profit motive and competition. The media view athletics in many respects from a monetary imperative, not from the altruistic image of healthy competition as defined by sports philosophers. At the same time, what appeals to the public, what is newsworthy to the public, often is conflict, whether in the context of a close game or in a controversy surrounding the sports event or participants.

That means it will not be the won-lost record or level of competition alone that determines whether the mass media cover the basketball team's march to the conference title game or the women's volleyball championships. The decision will depend on a number of interrelated criteria that collectively relate to the profit-loss ledger.

Summary

Sport communication is a process of mass communication—the transmission of information and entertainment to an audience through the mass media. The key groups in the process are sports journalists, sport organizations, media industries, and sports audiences. The media choose what games they will cover and what information they will supply, so they wield enormous power in the process of communication and in the performance of sport organizations.

Four aspects of the mass media are critical to an examination of the process. First, the mass media are commercial in nature; they sell a product. Second, the audience is large, heterogeneous, and anonymous. Third, the media shape the content or message, thereby presenting the audience with an interpretation of the information. Fourth, the media organizations that supply the content are complex businesses that shape the content through sophisticated technology and specially trained personnel.

From a practical standpoint, the media provide an avenue for the delivery of sports to an audience of fans. From a theoretical perspective, the process of sport communication plays a role in creating a uniquely American sports culture. Newspaper stories and broadcast programs contribute to how people understand sports; that is, they help create a picture in people's minds of what sports is all about in the United States.

Historically, newspapers dominated sport communication until the middle of the 20th century. The emphasis was on the players and the games, not business or nongame matters. The emergence of TV in the 1950s changed both media coverage and sport communication. Because TV offered coverage of the games as they unfolded, the print media shifted their emphasis in content to analysis, commentary, and investigation. The investigation turned the spotlight on financial matters, corruption, and other off-field concerns.

Television added an entertainment component and a financial imperative that changed the dynamics of the sport communication process. Theorists say the financial arrangement created an interdependent relationship between the mass media and sport organizations. The effect of the relationships between sport organizations, the media, and the public is the focus of ongoing study. Researchers in a variety of academic disciplines agree the profit motive is the driving force behind media organizations. Televised sports programs not only supply information and entertainment to an audience, but also deliver an audience to advertisers. The print media also deliver an audience to advertisers, though not as directly.

The financial relationship is profitable for sport organizations as well as for media industries. Sport organizations profit by auctioning off broadcast rights to the highest bidder. Broadcast companies benefit from selling commercial time to advertisers. The larger the audience each can deliver, the more money they can make. The bidding reached its highest level ever in 1995, when NBC negotiated a $3.55 billion deal with the International Olympic Committee for the broadcast of five Olympic Games.

Historically, the economic dynamics of the relationship raise serious ethical and cultural questions. The profit motive has created a two-tiered class of sport organizations. Those that generate revenue receive extensive coverage. Those that do not, receive little attention, if any. Furthermore, profit-driven programming has contributed to a two-tiered class of sports from a gender perspective: high-profile men's competition and low-profile women's sports. Some researchers believe the division is a result of the mass media's tendency to maintain stability and reinforce the status quo. Men's competition dominates sports information content because of the perception that it is superior. The disparity in coverage validates such assumptions. It also contributes to the way young people learn gender roles and perceive their place in sports.

The dominance of high-profile sports illustrates the media's power to influence sport organizations and the cultural perspectives of sports. Heavy media coverage lends importance to an issue and status or credibility to individuals and teams. That means the media can dictate, in many respects, how the audience understands the game and the realities of sports—even if the interpretation is inaccurate. It also means a spectator could follow sports for a lifetime without ever leaving the living room of the home. In such a case, the spectator's entire understanding of the game would be based on the way the media shape and interpret the content. This media-constructed content might be markedly different from reality.

Where does the sport management professional fit into this discussion? Understanding the process of mass communication will help the aspiring professional practice the art and science of sports information. Mass communication theory and the transactional model of sport communication provide insights into the dynamics of the relationships among the groups within the American sport culture and their role within it. By understanding the audience's makeup, the information manager is in a position to better determine what information to emphasize to the media. An awareness of the economic dynamics will aid in determining which sports and/or events offer the most potential to be revenue generating and selling points for those that do not promise financial gain. Knowledge of the ethical and theoretical issues raised by the symbiotic relationship between the principals in sport communication will help the professional affect positive change.

The professional familiar with ratings, demographics, and psychographics may be able to tap unmined fan support or loyalty in the community for a low-profile sport. A stronger fan base may enhance the marketability of the sport at most, or give the sport manager another selling point at least. In short, a working knowledge of media practices and mass communication may provide direction on how to take a low-profile sport such as volleyball and boost its revenue production. It also may provide answers on how to attract additional media interest in volleyball and basketball during the regular season, long before the league championship game in a high-profile sport.

DISCUSSION QUESTIONS

1. What are the political and economic relationships between sport organizations and the mass media? How have commercial practices changed the nature of sport and sport policy? How have licensing rights sold to broadcasting and cable increased franchise values of sport organizations?

2. What function do the mass media provide a sport organization in public relations, development of fans, and revenues? What function do sport organizations provide the mass media?

3. For what reasons (needs) do sports viewers attend some local games and watch others on television? What satisfaction do readers obtain from reading about a bench-emptying brawl? What are the different gratifications in the spectating experiences of a viewer of the game and a spectator at the game?

4. Are there psychological effects to consider if viewers become single-event or single-program watchers? With the demand for sports programs, what effect does the technology of cable have on the acquisition of sports rights and on exposure to a variety of sporting events?

5. What impact have cable sports networks had on network sports programming decisions? What types of advertisers purchase commercial time during sports programming?

SUGGESTED EXERCISES

1. Check with the local network television station and ask the news director to explain how story priority is established, with the most important story as the lead.

2. Ask your daily newspaper to define the demographics of its reading audience. Ask about age, income, race, gender, and location. Also, do the results have a bearing on what is printed in the sports section the next day?

Chapter Two

THE PRINT MEDIA: THE ORIGINAL MODEL OF SPORT INFORMATION

The tip-off for the 1996 NCAA Men's Basketball Championship was not until 9:22 P.M. EST, and newspaper reporters from the East and the South were in a surly mood.

Chapter 2 explores the evolution of the print media from its initial role as primary provider of sports news to its soul-searching secondary role in sports coverage. It examines the organizational structure, economic foundations, and editorial operation of newspapers. It also explores the interdependent relationship between print reporters and sports information personnel, with emphasis on factors that influence the working relationship and shape the content of stories in newspapers, magazines, and other publications.

Reporters for the "AM" newspapers, which hit the streets in early morning, have complained for years about executive decisions to set printing deadlines earlier and earlier. The earlier the paper rolls off the press, the easier to plop it on a customer's porch before the first pot of coffee perks—and before the first television newscast appears —in the morning.

Competition with TV makes it more and more difficult to do a decent job of sports coverage, sportswriters complain. A columnist for *The Courier-Journal* in Louisville, Kentucky, used to opine that he could foresee a day when he would have to finish and file his story before the end of the game and just guess at the outcome.

As if early deadlines did not pose enough of an irritation, the late start time in 1996 resulted from a concession to TV. NCAA officials agreed to the late start because it put the game in prime time on the East Coast and dinnertime on the West Coast, the ideal time to draw the largest viewing audience. The majority of subsequent championship games have also started at approximately 9:20 P.M. EST, including the 2006 finals between Florida and UCLA, which began at 9:21 P.M.

Such an arrangement puts the print media at a competitive disadvantage. While the 2006 NCAA final included a team, UCLA, from the West Coast, the 1996 NCAA final described above matched the University of Kentucky and Syracuse University, two teams in the Eastern time zone. The game did not end until 11:30 P.M., *after* the deadline for the first edition for some newspapers and *right on* the deadline for most of the other AM papers that covered the two teams in the championship.

How can a reporter with a deadline 30 minutes after the final buzzer compose a thorough and entertaining story on the most important game of the year for college basketball fans?

In such circumstances, reporters must rely on the resources of sport organizations and perhaps trade on their relationship with a sports information director (SID) for one of the teams. NCAA tournament workers will quickly provide play-by-play sheets and statistics. They also will assemble coaches and players for postgame press conferences, and a sympathetic SID might pull a key player out of the midcourt pile of celebrants or a proud parent out of the upper reaches of the arena for a quick comment.

The NCAA Men's Basketball Tournament illustrates not only the intensity of the competition among media today, but also the dynamics of the relationship between sports journalists and sports information personnel. Early deadlines and late games are the product of competitive pressures, driven by economic decisions at the highest level of media organizations. They create a dilemma for the individual at the lowest level who writes the article, the sports reporter. The reporter must deliver a thorough and entertaining story—the newspaper's product—to a large and demanding audience, under the most trying conditions. Therefore, the sports information specialist may play an integral role in gathering and delivering the information that shapes the product, that dictates the content of the message and the impressions it leaves with the audience.

Scope of Print Media

The printed word has served as the primary means of mass communication since the invention of movable type by Johann Gutenberg in Germany more than 500 years ago. Although the broadcast media have usurped newspapers' role as primary provider of breaking news, readership studies indicate the majority of the American public still depends on newspapers, magazines, and books for explanation and interpretation of issues and events.

In short, the majority of the American public still count on newspapers each day to keep them up to date on local, national, and international events—including sports events—or to put developments into a context they can understand. A study by a brewing company in the early 1980s found that nearly 70% of Americans watch, discuss, or read about sports daily (Wilcox, Ault, & Agee, 1992). A national survey commissioned by Gannet Co. in 1996 revealed that 71% of adults in the United States read at least one weekday edition of a local or regional newspaper. On a typical Sunday, 64% read a newspaper (*Editor and Publisher*, 1996).

The emergence of television and changes in lifestyle over the past two decades led to a stagnation in readership, but the newspaper industry is far from dead. The number of daily newspapers and their circulation have remained constant even though readership penetration has declined from 100% of homes in the 1970s to 70% in the 1990s (Hunt & Ruben, 1993). People still like to read the newspaper over the first cup of coffee or on the ride to work on the subway. However, they opt for television instead of news and entertainment when they return home in the evening. Afternoon or "PM" newspapers have nearly disappeared in the nation's major metropolitan markets, although they continue to flourish in smaller markets.

In contrast, morning newspapers, Sunday editions, suburban newspapers, and weekly newspapers are on the rise. Twenty-four dailies switched from PM to AM in

1995, increasing total morning circulation of newspapers in the United States by 928,674, according to the *Editor & Publisher International Yearbook* (1995). The number of Sunday newspapers increased by 50% between 1972 and 1992, from 600 to almost 900. In 1994, some 1,548 daily newspapers distributed 46 million copies, and 886 Sunday newspapers reached 66 million readers. Weekly newspapers sold another 50 million copies, reaching about 200 million people, according to the 1995 *Editor & Publisher International Yearbook* (Part 1). In addition, daily newspapers continued to lead all other United States media, with more than 26% of total advertising—a $32 billion share of a $125 billion pot.

> John Vivian (1994), a mass media researcher at Winona State University, concluded that "the newspaper industry dwarfs other news media by almost every measure" (p. 83).
>
> Except for brief downturns in the overall economy and an occasional exceptional situation, daily newspapers have been consistently profitable enterprises through the 20th century. Less than double-digit returns on investment are uncommon. As a mass medium, the newspaper is not to be underrated. (p. 84)

Sports news ranks near the top of reader interests in newspapers. The sports section is the second most heavily read part of the newspaper—after local news (Mencher, 1991). One reason is that sports competition is good drama, according to *Mass Communication Producers and Consumers* (Hunt & Ruben, 1993). Sports events provide a cultural bond among Americans by giving them something to talk about with family, friends, and coworkers. The more successful the team, the more the collective interest and the greater the likelihood of newspaper sales. For example, rack sales of the *Cincinnati Enquirer*, the *Cincinnati Post*, and the *Kentucky Post* jumped dramatically during the two weeks between the Cincinnati Bengals' victory in the 1987 American Football Conference championship and the Super Bowl game against the San Francisco 49ers.

From Heroes to Hard Investigations

Despite the explosion of televised sports events in the past decade, the print media still play a significant role in the delivery of sports information, particularly on the local level. Of all the media, the nation's print media provide the most thorough and consistent coverage of sports on a regular basis because of their high reader interest and entertainment value. Readers buy newspapers for scores and other information on their favorite teams, rivals, and leagues. More is better—more scores, more game coverage, more types of sports covered. Even the smallest weekly newspaper generally assigns a reporter to cover local sports.

Sports reporting in the United States has grown from the simple report of a professional fight in England by the *Boston Gazette* in 1773 to multifaceted coverage of dozens of sports on a daily basis. Today, the nation's newspapers and magazines routinely cover amateur and school sports of every kind, from local bowling to college basketball's Final Four, and from figure skating to hunting and fishing. They cover professional sports from every angle, from league play to stadium licenses, and from player performance to front-office operations. In addition, they produce special sections on major events, such as the opening of the baseball season and the selection of teams for the NCAA basketball tournaments.

The *American Farmer,* published in 1819, was the first publication devoted exclusively to sports in the United States. The magazine covered fishing, hunting, shooting, and bicycle racing. However, most sports magazines through the first half of the 20th century failed quickly. In fact, for every 100 magazines devoted to sports that fail, one or maybe two survive. The exception is *Sports Illustrated,* which celebrated its 50th anniversary in 2004 and ranked 15th in circulation among all magazines.

However, it was newspapers that gave sports its audience and its theater. Newspapers on the east coast—the *Sun,* the *Transcript,* and the *Herald* in New York, for example—offered reports on the results of contests as early as the 1830s, but sports coverage remained a minor part of daily newspaper reports until immigration and the Industrial Revolution provided the means and machines to sustain a national sports culture. Industrialization spawned company teams and fueled rivalries among local factories. Industrialists subsequently began to sponsor "professional" teams to send against the best of neighboring communities. The passenger train and motor vehicles made it possible to travel from community to community to play other teams or to follow the local team. Rapid population growth in the cities provided the spectators and financial support to field teams and to build bigger and bigger stadiums to hold more and more sports fans.

The blossoming of sports coincided with a significant rise in literacy, the result of a developing public school system. People of all ages began to read newspapers to keep up with events of the day and make sense of their rapidly changing world. The number of newspapers increased by more than 400 between 1900 and 1920, and national circulation increased by around 9 million from 1910 to 1920. Circulation has hovered between 55 and 63 million for the past 45 years (Daily Newspaper Circulation, Newspaper Association of America).

Into this milieu stepped a talented array of writers—or dramatists, to be more accurate. In the early 20th century, sports coverage concerned itself with recitation of a few athletic contests in baseball, college football, horse racing, and boxing. Most of the coverage focused on contests in the eastern part of the United States. Reporters primarily used a writing technique called the *inverted pyramid* (see Chapter 5). They provided a quick summary of the 5Ws and H (who, what, when, where, why, and how), then filled in the details in descending order of importance. The game was the thing, and newspapers gave only a wink and brief mention to off-field activities and scandals. The start of the grand jury investigation into allegations that gamblers paid eight members of the Chicago White Sox to throw the World Series in 1919 appeared on page 8 of the *New York Times* ("Baseball Chiefs,"

> After World War I, newspapers began hiring reporters such as Ring Lardner, Westbrook Pegler, Studs Terkel, and Grantland Rice, wordsmiths who used their literary acumen and dramatic instincts to pen narratives of the sports action. These writers employed a descriptive, literary style and spiced each story liberally with their own observations in addition to the statistical data and rundowns on the game action. Rice, one of the best known American sportswriters, majored in Greek and Latin at Vanderbilt University. A Phi Beta Kappa scholar, he was fond of using verse. Here is the start of a story he wrote in 1901; years later readers wondered why he never got around to giving the score:
>
> > Baker Was an Easy Mark
> > Pounded Hard Over Park
> > Selma's Infield is a Peach
> > But Nashville Now is Out of Reach
> > All of the Boys Go Out to Dine
> > And Some of Them Get Full of Wine
>
> After their long, successful trip the locals opened up against Selma yesterday afternoon at Athletic Park, and when the shades of night had settled on the land, the difference that separated the two teams had increased by some dozen points.
>
> Throughout the whole morning a dark, lead-colored sky overhung the city, and a steady rain dripped and drizzled, only stopping in time to play the game, but leaving the field soft and slow. . . . (Quoted in Itule & Anderson, 1987, p. 463)

1920). The story did not make the front pages until indisputable evidence turned accusations into the "Black Sox Scandal" in 1920.

Because all the games were played in the afternoon, sportswriting became almost a leisurely endeavor; reporters had plenty of time to craft their stories. Sports columnists evolved and began to shape public opinion in much the same way as their counterparts on the editorial pages. The most eloquent among them emerged as literary giants in the context of sport. They turned sports "actors" like Babe Ruth—celebrities on the order of film stars—into larger-than-life, tragic heroes and transformed highs and lows of athletic competition into the social dramas of the day.

Not coincidentally, perhaps, a University of Chicago philosopher named George Herbert Mead proposed in 1934 that baseball represented a microcosm of society, with team members learning their roles from interaction with others (Baran & Davis, 1995). Although Mead's theories on socialization no longer are in favor among those who study philosophy or mass communication, his work generated further inquiry into how mass media affect socialization and influence the national sports culture.

As reader interest in sports coverage grew through the Great Depression and World War II, an electronic competitor arose that could provide the drama instantly, not a day or more later. Advertisers flocked to sponsor radio broadcasts of baseball games in the late 1920s and early 1930s. By the time television added pictures to the drama in the 1950s, newspapers were desperately searching for alternatives.

They turned away from the field of play, without abandoning it. They continued to emphasize game coverage, but mixed player comments and analysis with the play-by-play. They focused on pivotal plays and the performers who produced them. They also supplemented game coverage with features on players, personal tidbits about them, and facts and figures about the team. Particularly popular were the "notes" columns—collections of short items about injuries, off-field activities, and player developments— that were not unlike the sports conversations around the watercooler at work.

Cultural developments in the 1960s and 1970s had a major impact on sports coverage heading into the last decade of the 20th century. The women's movement served as a catalyst for passage of the Education Amendment Acts of 1972. One section, commonly known as Title IX, called for all schools that receive federal funding to work toward gender equity in their athletics programs or risk financial penalties. A longitudinal study by Acosta and Carpenter (Vivian & Carpenter, 1994) found that substantial growth in women's sports began to occur around 1978, when compliance was required. In 1977, the average number of teams offered for girls and women was 5.61; in 1994, it was 7.22. In 1994, all three competitive divisions at the collegiate level showed increases in the number of sport offerings for female athletes.

A Supreme Court ruling in 1991 and the release of a Gender Equity Task Force report by the National Collegiate Athletic Association in 1993 spurred additional growth. The Supreme Court ruling on the Georgia case, *Franklin v. Gwinnett*

Public Schools (1991), made it clear that both punitive and compensatory damages could be collected for intentional discrimination. The decision enabled individuals who experienced gender discrimination to take legal action. The Gender Equity Task Force report raised questions about the proportional allocation of financial assistance and benefits between male and female athletes. The report recommended that NCAA schools adopt a proportional representation (i.e., sports participation ratios that match the proportion of men and women in the student body), meaning a school with equal numbers of men and women should have roughly the same number of men and women participating in varsity sports (National Collegiate Athletic Association [NCAA] Gender Equity Study, 1992).

In some cases in the 1970s, the number of girls' and women's sports teams increased dramatically. In 1973 the Kentucky High School Athletic Association ordered schools to field women's teams in every sport in which they sponsored men's teams (with the exception of football). The number of high school sports teams nearly doubled overnight. Other states added women's basketball, volleyball, soccer, and softball to their athletic offerings.

The size of newspaper sports staffs and sports space, dictated by advertising revenues, did not change significantly during the same period. That forced sports departments to try to cover more teams and cram more information into roughly the same amount of space as previously. For example, the *Evansville Sunday Courier & Press,* which covered 98 high schools in three states, found itself trying to cover 196 high school basketball teams with four reporters in 1983. The sports department also covered three local colleges—the University of Evansville, Indiana State University-Evansville (now University of Southern Indiana), and Kentucky Wesleyan. Although the number of women's sports at colleges did not multiply as rapidly, most were fielding 10-14 athletic teams by the mid-1980s. The *Courier & Press* resorted to hiring inexperienced writers in various communities to cover games when the basketball tournament overlap reached a peak in March.

At the same time school sports teams were expanding, newspapers were consolidating. Caught up in the takeover craze of the 1980s, large corporations such as Gannett Co. and Knight-Ridder began buying up dailies across the country. Small newspapers soon joined to form their own corporations for profit and for protection. By the mid-1990s, the large conglomerates were devouring the smaller chains. Some companies swallowed up as many as 75 weekly newspapers, according to The *New York Times* (Hunt, 1995). The *Sun* group had acquired 23 weeklies surrounding Cleveland by 1995.

The mergers and acquisitions resulted in a consolidation of power, cost cuts, and staff reductions. Critics contend that some corporations reduced staffs and trimmed news space to boost profits and satisfy shareholders. The result—fewer sportswriters and less space to accommodate all the news from an expanding sports industry. For example, a study of the *Courier-Journal* (Coulson & Hansen, 1995) following acquisition by Gannett showed less news coverage, less space devoted to local news, and fewer staff-written stories. The *Cleveland Plain Dealer,* on the other hand, actually added sports reporters to keep pace with the growing number of sports.

The *Cincinnati Post* and the *Kentucky Post*, sister newspapers in Greater Cincinnati owned by Scripps Howard, consolidated their graphics departments and trimmed more than 30 employees from their ranks in December 1995. Three months later, graphics editor Rick Millians found himself trying to juggle photographers to cover overlaps in high school basketball tournaments in three states, Northern Kentucky University in the Division II men's basketball tournament; the University of Kentucky and the University of Cincinnati in the Division I men's tournament; the NCAA Division I hockey finals in Cincinnati; opening day for the Cincinnati Reds; and a Kentucky Derby prep race at Turfway Park.

On the other hand, chain ownership can be an asset. Newspapers in the same chain can share stories of mutual interest and combine their efforts through a joint news service. In addition, chain ownership can lead to better pay, better training, and better sportswriting on some newspapers. The *Cincinnati Enquirer*, a Gannett newspaper, increased its coverage of the University of Kentucky basketball team in 1995–1996 by picking up columns and stories from the *Courier-Journal*. Likewise, stories and columns in the *News Herald* of Willoughby, Ohio, appear in other newspapers in the Journal Register Co. chain. The company owns 31 newspapers, each with its own publisher, yet the same stories, written by the same writers, often appear in multiple newspapers in the chain.

Types of Print Media

Sports information specialists likely will work regularly with reporters from state, regional, and local daily or weekly newspapers. However, newsgathering agencies of many kinds may come calling when a local player or team excels, or when the sport organization hosts a major event. Such objects of media scrutiny may be besieged by magazines, wire services, and specialty publications for fans of a specific team or a specific sport. National and international wire services serve more clients now than ever before as high-speed communication hookups shrink the world. The *Associated Press*, the world's largest newsgathering agency, and *Reuters*, headquartered in London, bring sports news from around the world to front porches and newsstands in a matter of hours.

Major Dailies

Metropolitan dailies, newspapers with 100,000-plus circulation, are most likely to cover professional and collegiate sports on a consistent basis. Each major city in the United States has at least one major daily newspaper.

Since the 1960s, the number of competing dailies has declined in the face of corporate mergers and competition from the electronic media. The number of major dailies in New York City has dropped from seven to three: the *Times, Post,* and *Daily News.* Cleveland had three daily newspapers in 1960; it now has one, the *Cleveland Plain Dealer.* Most of the surviving metropolitan dailies are morning newspapers.

Small Dailies

Small dailies, newspapers with less than 100,000 subscribers, go into much greater depth and breadth on local news, including their coverage of sports. They generally summarize national and international news, including sports, instead focusing most of their efforts on covering the area high schools and colleges. Because they exchange stories with the wire services, their stories sometimes make their way to larger newspapers via the *Associated Press* or news services created by newspaper corporations.

Weekly Newspapers

A sport administrator or sports information director will find weekly newspapers valuable allies in spreading the word about his or her school or organization. Community news, including sports, is the heart of the weekly newspaper. Weekly neighborhood newspapers began to flourish in the 1970s and quickly began to develop their own sports sections, similar to those in the daily papers. The number of weekly newspapers jumped 25% during the 1980s (Hunt & Ruben, 1993).

Most weeklies publish on Thursday, but some print on Tuesday or Wednesday. Because of staff limitations, they generally must prepare or "make up" their pages several days in advance. The sports information professional often can find a spot for a story that develops a couple of days after the event in a weekly, because of the time lapse between issues. Because of the production limitations, the professional cannot expect to get a story into print the day before publication.

National Newspapers

Since the demise of *The National,* an all-sports newspaper that lasted less than a year, *USA Today* has been the only national newspaper that has attempted to offer a comprehensive sports section every day. *USA Today* has succeeded in capturing a large national following

Press conferences make it much easier for print media to gather quotes and serve as a rich source of information for sports reporters.

with short, concise stories and an abundance of statistics and charts five mornings a week (Monday through Friday). However, some critics refer to it as "McNews," a play on McDonald's McNuggets, because of *USA Today*'s propensity for boiling stories down to the basic news nuggets.

The *New York Times,* although distributed nationally, is still in part geared to a New York City reading audience. The nation's most recognized "newspaper of record," the *Times* does send sports reporters to all major sporting events in the country.

Sports coverage also is not a staple of the *Washington Post,* the *Wall Street Journal* (*WSJ*), or the *Christian Science Monitor.* The *Wall Street Journal,* which has the largest circulation of any newspaper in the United States, concentrates on business or finance. *WSJ* will offer an occasional in-depth examination of a financial issue related to sports. For example, the *WSJ* might examine the economic dynamics that prompted "musical chairs" among teams in the National Football League in 1994 and 1995. The *Christian Science Monitor* will sometimes publish an in-depth feature on an athlete, coach, or team.

Wire Services

Wire services in print media provide words and pictures of news events throughout the world in a cooperative arrangement with members. Subscribers agree to provide stories to the wire service in exchange for stories written by news service reporters and stories picked up from other subscribers. Members of the cooperative pay a yearly fee for the service.

The largest cooperatives, the *Associated Press* and *Reuters*, maintain state, regional, national, and international bureaus. Staff members cover stories within the region and rewrite stories picked up from members for release on the wire or news services.

The wire services are the eyes and ears of publications that cannot afford to be everywhere. In fact, it is impossible for any single publication to cover more than a small percentage of what the wire services can offer through their cooperative arrangement with members/subscribers. Travel expenses alone prohibit small newspapers, and many large ones, from staffing events far from home. The wires provide this service.

The *Associated Press* maintains bureaus on every continent and in most countries in the world. *United Press International* has developed into the *Associated Press's* chief competition in South America and Asia since financial difficulties in the 1980s sapped its U.S. operations. *Reuters* primarily serves the world outside the United States, although it maintains a bureau in New York City.

In addition to a large staff of administrators, writers, and photographers, each of these wire services employs a multitude of part-time help, referred to as *stringers*. These contract workers send stories to the appropriate wire-service office electronically via computer. A story originating from anywhere in the world can be transmitted anywhere else in the world in approximately five minutes.

Wire-service personnel are important contacts for sports information professionals. The wire services reach an audience that may be local, statewide, regional, national, or international. In addition to game results, wire services provide features and columns written by nationally known sportswriters.

Conglomerate-owned news services such as the *Washington Post–Los Angeles Times*, *Knight-Ridder*, and the *New York Times* primarily provide feature stories, photographs, and columns. Each usually places a story or photograph on its services after it appears in a member publication.

Magazines

Sport magazine, which has a circulation of more than one million, first appeared after World War II. *Sports Illustrated* made its debut in 1954 and grew into the most widely circulated magazine on sports. *Sports Illustrated* features stories on the major national sports of the preceding week, as well as in-depth examinations of sports issues. *SI* produced a daily magazine in Atlanta during the 1996 Olympic Games.

Innumerable magazines devoted to specific sports, such as *Golf Digest* and *Field and Stream*, are also popular. The *Sporting News*, which began as a weekly newspaper devoted exclusively to baseball, has evolved into a diverse publication with a staff of freelance writers from coast to coast. The *Sporting News* offers a myriad of statistics, feature stories, and columns. *Baseball America* took over the role the *Sporting News* occupied for nearly four decades among baseball fans. *BA*, which is published biweekly, is top-heavy with information about minor league baseball and its target audience is what can be described as baseball junkies. A third national magazine that has emerged in hopes of competing with *Sports Illustrated* and the *Sporting News* is *ESPN The Magazine*, which is published biweekly, although it is still considered a distant third in the competition among the three publications.

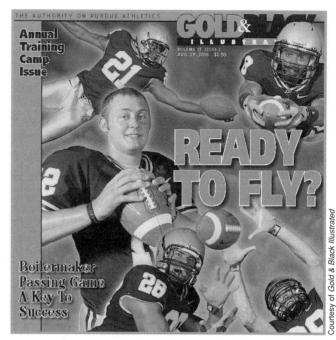

Fan magazines, such as Gold & Black Illustrated, *which covers Purdue University athletics, cater to the die-hard fans of a particular college or team.*

Specialty Magazines

A number of annual publications offer previews of upcoming football, basketball, and baseball seasons. They offer the sports information specialist a rich source of information as well as fertile ground for publicizing a team or a star player. For example, readers eagerly await the publication of each *Street and Smith* ranking of top players and teams in college and professional sports. The previews are geared toward rabid sports fans who consume stats and trivia with gusto. A story in one of these specialty publications can provide prestige for an organization and spark fan interest in a team. The emerging popularity of fantasy sports has also sparked a handful of specialty magazines devoted to giving fantasy "players" a statistical breakdown of professional players in the specific league in which the magazine focuses.

Another type of specialty publication is the fan magazine. Professional teams sponsor some of them; independent operators publish others. In every case, these magazines contain statistics, features, game previews and reviews, ticket information, promotions, and contests. Their editorial content is typically favorable to the team or organization. *Vine Line*, the official monthly magazine of the Chicago Cubs, is an example of a specialty magazine of a professional team. At the collegiate level, nearly every major university now has a fan magazine devoted entirely to covering that school's athletic endeavors.

Print Media Organization

The print media generally separate the business and the editorial (content) sides of production. The primary organizational units—advertising, editorial (news), production (printing), and circulation—function almost autonomously in a purposeful attempt to minimize commercial influence on content decisions and to maximize fair and objective news/sports coverage.

The separation is possible because the connection between advertising and content is markedly different in the print media from what it is in the broadcast media. Advertisers buy specific time slots for specific programs on radio and TV. The number of viewers dictates the advertising rate for the commercial time. No such direct connection exists between advertisers and specific stories in a newspaper. An advertiser may request placement in a specific section of a newspaper, but the ad may appear on any page. The advertiser, in effect, buys space in the newspaper or magazine with no strings attached to content or to a particular story. A formula based on production costs and circulation (audience) numbers—not the popularity of a program—dictates the advertising rate, because newspapers cannot measure the number of readers for a given story on a given day.

The volume of advertising each day determines the size of the newspaper. If advertising is light, the newspaper is small. If advertising is heavy, the paper is large. Consequently, advertising revenues *do* limit the *amount* of content. But they have little effect on the nature of coverage or content-selection decisions. Advertisers generally contract for space based on the size and makeup of the overall reading audience. Only on rare occasions does an advertising contract come with an agreement to publish a specific story.

One of the primary duties of a newspaper's beat reporters is to cover the games of the sport in which they are assigned.

Newspapers did not even sell advertising space until the 1830s, when they reduced the cost of single copies to one cent to reach mass audiences. Now advertising provides the bulk of newspaper and magazine profits. Income from subscription and newsstand prices barely covers the cost of the paper upon which the publication is printed (Hiebert, Ungurait, & Bohn, 1991). The notion that print media publish a particular story "just to sell newspapers" is a myth. Because the cost of a single copy covers only the price of the paper, there is no particular gain in publishing a story that sells more individual copies on a given day.

As the decade of the 1990s opened, roughly 40% of revenues came from the classified and personal ads; the rest, from the larger display ads scattered among the pages. To offset rising costs without raising rates, newspapers and magazines allot a higher percentage of space in a given issue to ads. Some newspapers currently devote more than 65% of the daily space to advertisements.

The chief operating officer in a newspaper or magazine generally is the publisher. The advertising department manager, the circula-

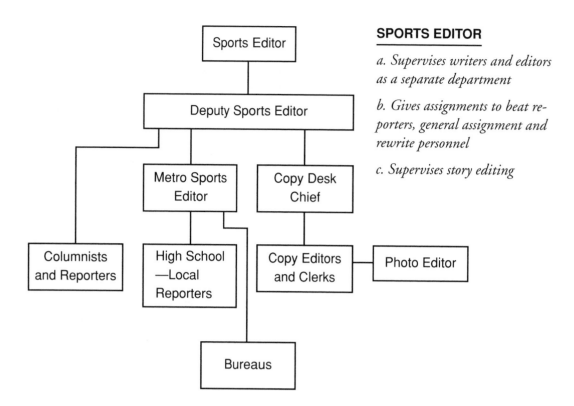

SPORTS EDITOR

a. Supervises writers and editors as a separate department

b. Gives assignments to beat reporters, general assignment and rewrite personnel

c. Supervises story editing

Figure 1. Plain Dealer organizational chart

tion manager, the editor, and the production manager function as vice presidents, overseeing largely independent operating units. The advertising department (sometimes a part of the business department) sells space and provides the editorial department with page "dummies" with ads already in place. The editorial units fill the space with stories and pictures. The production department handles the mechanical processes involved in printing, and the circulation department distributes the final product.

The number of editorial divisions—news, sports, business, feature, entertainment, etc.—depends on the nature and size of the publication. Department heads serve as mid-level managers.

Nearly all major dailies across the nation devote a complete section to the coverage of sports and fill it with a combination of local, national, and international sports. The sports editor manages a departmental budget, negotiated at the start of the year. The budget allotment likely will not increase during the year, even if coverage demands do, so heavy and unanticipated expenses for overtime, travel, etc., during the year also may limit coverage. The draw for the 64-team bracket for the NCAA Division I men's basketball tournament generates intense interest from sports editors because assignment of a local team to a region far away can seriously dent the budget. The same can be said for an NCAA Division I college football team that makes an unexpected appearance in a bowl game, as travel required to cover the event could also put an unexpected crunch on a yearly budget.

Staff reporters generally cover the local teams, and the sports department picks up regional, state, and national stories from news services to which the newspaper subscribes. A weekly may depend on one person to cover local sports as well as news assignments and leave the national and international sports to the dailies and the electronic media, yet nearly all assign someone to cover local recreation, high school, and college sports across the geographical area in which they circulate.

Depending on the size of the circulation area and the number needed to produce the section each day, the sports department on a daily newspaper will range from four or five people to as many as 75. (The number of sports or teams the newspaper covers has little influence on the size of the staff or increases in staff, as previously noted.) The *Plain Dealer* in Cleveland had a sports staff of 65 in 1996, one-sixth of the editorial staff. However, the sports department received only 1/64th of the $2-million operating budget. The average metropolitan daily has about 20 sports employees.

Sports magazines generally hire small staffs that put the product together in a central location. They assign selected reporters—*Sports Illustrated* calls them contributing editors—to cover one story per issue as events dictate.

A typical sports department on a major daily newspaper consists of a sports editor or executive sports editor, an assistant or deputy sports editor, a slot person, beat reporters, rewrite people, columnists, and feature writers. If one thinks of the sports section of a newspaper as a smorgasbord, the executive editor is the chef, whereas the writers and editors are the cooks. (See Figure 1 for a rundown on the organizational structure.)

Sports editor
Deputy sports editor
Slot person
Beat reporters
Rewrite people
Columnists
Feature writers

Sports Editor

The sports editor is the management executive in charge of the department. The editor oversees everything from budgeting to story assignment and coordination to daily production of the section. On smaller dailies, the sports editor also may double as a columnist or reporter.

Deputy Sports Editor

The deputy sports editor usually is responsible for scheduling reporters, coordinating assignments, and troubleshooting story and production problems on deadline.

Slot Person

The slot person is in charge of the copy desk, which handles production responsibilities such as designing pages, editing copy, and writing headlines. This person, generally the second in command on deadline, often sits in an area that resembles a slot in the desk or table, and functions much like a traffic cop to ensure a smooth flow of stories and page layouts to the makeup department, which puts the pages together and sends them to the printing department.

Beat Reporters

Beat reporters are the journalists who most often interact with sports information specialists. Sports departments assign specific reporters to cover a geographical or topical area, or *beat,* on an ongoing basis. For example, one sportswriter's beat might be the local university, and the reporter would be responsible for covering all sports at the university; or a reporter might be assigned to the basketball beat and would be responsible for coverage of basketball teams in a given conference or geographical area. Sports departments most often assign beats by region, by sport, or by sports level (high school, college, or professional).

Rewrite People

Rewrite people are office personnel who pull information into story form as deadlines approach. They may take information over the telephone from a beat reporter and fashion it into a story. They may combine local information and news-service information into a single story or pull information from several wire stories into one story.

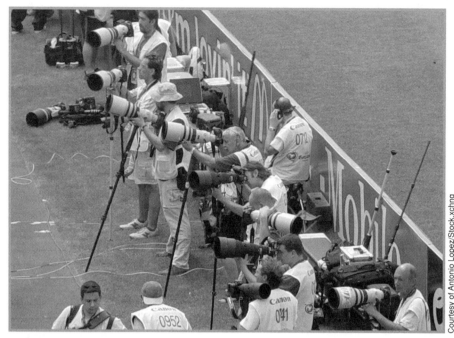

The work of sports photographers enhances the visual appeal of a newspaper's sports section or a sports magazine.

Courtesy of Antonio Lopez/Stock.xchng

Columnists

Sports columnists provide the commentary in the sports section. They generally are not assigned to a particular beat, but move among them all to provide comments on the "big story" of the day. They may contribute to the coverage of an Indiana-Ohio State basketball game one day, and a Cincinnati Bengals-Cleveland Browns game the next.

Feature Writers

Feature writers are the at-large reporters on daily newspapers, sometimes tied to a beat but more often assigned to specific stories as circumstances warrant. They generally write human-interest stories and personality profiles related to the news of the day. In the week prior to the championship game, a feature writer might write a personality profile of the coach who turned the conference doormat into a title contender.

On a typical day on an AM newspaper, the sports editor and deputy editors will collaborate with beat reporters, feature writers, and columnists on game-coverage schedules and other stories early in the day. The sports editor will adjust a floating schedule of stories, called a *story budget,* as the day unfolds and nongame stories develop or die.

When the page dummies arrive from advertising, department heads will meet to discuss options for the front page of the newspaper. A sports story may be among the selections and move from the sports to the news department. Editors and slot-desk personnel then go about the business of determining what stories go on which page, and the design, editing, and makeup of pages begins.

Editors "move" stories to the copy desk as the articles arrive. The earlier the reporter completes the story, the more attention it is likely to get from an editor, rewrite person, and headline writer on the copy desk, etc. Crunch time comes when games end close to deadline; all must move quickly. An editor quickly checks to make certain the story is accurate, fair, and complete. A rewrite person may incorporate information from other stories on the wire, write a headline, and trim the story to a specified length so that it fits the space allotted in the page design. Editors and rewrite people may juggle several "late" stories at the same time until the deadline arrives.

Time is, indeed, money. Miss the deadline, and you may have to pay overtime to reporters, desk personnel, and printers. Miss the deadline, and you may not beat the TV news to the customer's door . . . and you may lose a customer.

The Coverage Puzzle

Sports journalists typically make the major coverage and content decisions in newspapers and magazines, because they operate primarily as autonomous units. The publisher, editor, and managing editor seldom involve themselves in decision making in the department unless a significant problem or substantial complaints about coverage arise.

Sports journalists make coverage decisions based on a number of interrelated factors: size of staff, number of teams/sports in the coverage area, amount of space available, level of audience interest, and significance of the event. The decision-makers measure those factors against six principles of *news value* or *characteristics of news:* timeliness, proximity, prominence, importance or impact, oddities, and conflict. That means sports journalists and publications lean toward coverage of timely contests between prominent teams (or involving prominent sports) in their circulation area that promise to be hotly contested. Audience considerations figure significantly in the application of the criteria. For example, the sports staff may measure importance or impact according to their perceptions of how many of their readers have an interest in the team or sport. This method loads the coverage scale heavily in favor of high-profile sports at prominent institutions and reinforces the dominant ideology of sports. Such a decision also tips the scale toward winning teams (importance and prominence).

That is one reason success leads to more coverage. Kerry Lewin's pursuit of the national collegiate record for service aces propelled women's volleyball at Division II Northern Kentucky University onto the front page of Greater Cincinnati dailies for a couple of games in November 1995. Similarly, a drive to the championship game of the Division II tournament by the men's basketball team put NKU stories up front alongside coverage of the University of Cincinnati and the University of Kentucky.

Practically speaking, sports coverage is a product of joint decisions among beat reports and editors on which stories have the most news value for a given edition.

The daily coverage schedule results from individual and group meetings on how best to allot limited resources based on those news-value discussions. Most sports sections make some effort to include features on low-profile sports, and scores and highlights of all teams to at least touch all subaudiences as often as possible.

The growth of sports, along with coverage limitations, clearly has an impact on the work of sports information professionals. In the early 1990s, no media covered the John Carroll University Lady Blue Streaks' home game in an early round of the NCAA Division III volleyball playoffs, in part because the football team was playing its home finale against rival Baldwin-Wallace College at the same time. On another occasion, no media showed up for the Ohio Athletic Conference cross country championships at John Carroll because the meet coincided with a football game. The increasing number of sports events even overloads the sports information departments at times. The North Coast Athletic Conference cross country championships were once postponed a day because of a conflict in starting times with a Case Western Reserve University home football game against Allegheny College. The sports information staff could not handle two events at the same time.

A successful sports staff knows its audience, literally and figuratively. Editors and beat reporters know the pulse of their audiences—what readers want to see and expect to see—based on readership surveys, interaction with readers (telephone calls and letters), and association with teams they cover. All figure prominently in coverage decisions.

In a major league market, for example, the sports section most certainly will devote considerable resources and space to professional teams. If college sports command a large following, as they do in the Midwest, these teams also will receive high news priority. Most sports editors of daily newspapers realize the importance of high school coverage as well, particularly in the midwestern, southern, and southwestern areas of the United States. Conversely, New York City newspapers pay little attention to high school sports because of the prominence of professional and college teams.

In the early 1980s, the sports editor of the *Plain Dealer* believed no one cared about high school sports and reduced coverage drastically. Readers bombarded the newspaper with protests. Thousands of complaints arrived in the mail, and the telephone rang endlessly with more of the same. High school sports coverage increased immediately. By the mid-1990s, the *Plain Dealer* offered arguably the most complete coverage of high school sports in the Midwest. The newspaper divided distribution into four zones and editions, each with a different daily sports section, over a seven-county area of northeast Ohio. One of the four editions covered three counties, another covered two counties, and the other two covered a single county each, including Greater Cleveland with a population of more than 2 million people. The newspaper assigned 11 reporters to cover high school sports during the academic year, all coordinated by the metro sports editor.

Since the early 1980s, newspapers have offered additional opportunities to insert periodic mention of a specific team or athlete. In an effort to cover as much ground as possible in a limited amount of space, sports sections use a lot of statistical information, including charts, standings, averages, and polls.

The *Boston Globe*, annually rated among the top sports newspapers in the nation, popularized the designation of one entire page for statistics each day, often referred to as the "scoreboard" section of a newspaper. The comprehensive package of facts and statistics in *USA Today* is one of the major attractions of the paper's sports page. Nearly all dailies have followed this trend.

In addition to covering the news of sports, sports sections take stances with opinions by their own columnists. A good column is one that is well written, well timed, and thought provoking.

Sports departments traditionally built their reader bases on game stories, player profiles, and team features. Because coverage has shifted toward more in-depth reporting, sports articles also have encompassed the business of sports, and illegal and improper activities. Still, game stories and profiles remain the foundation. Readers want scores, details of the games, explanation of key plays and players, examination of the turning point, and comments and reactions from the participants. Those who attended the game, heard it on the radio, or saw it on television expect to find something new in the newspaper—not only what happened, but how and why.

Features on participants also rank high in reader interest. Readers want to learn more than just stats about the top players, the coaches, the stars of a particular game, or the player who rides the bench without complaint all season. Profiles put the players on the stage. Issues ranging from the role of money in sports to performance enhancing drug use among athletes to recruiting violations to inclusion of minorities and women in athletics have gained interest as newspapers have struggled to find alternatives to game coverage in the face of competition from the broadcast media.

Another well-read part of the modern sports pages is the notes column, which includes a variety of items written in sentence or paragraph form. Some notes columns cover the full gamut of sports, whereas others concentrate on a particular area, sport, or team.

| **Sports Information Concerns** | Sports information professionals must learn the personnel, organization, deadlines, and coverage philosophy of the print media that cover their organization on a regular basis. They also should be aware of the national newspapers, wire services, magazines, and specialty publications they might cultivate. |

More important, sports information specialists must learn how to work effectively with print reporters with different competitive needs and demands. The SID may have to deal with competitors from two or more daily newspapers in one city, large and small dailies in a region, or the broadcast media and the print media. Sports information directors must learn how to assist each without alienating any of the others. For example, they must be aware that giving an important story to one may hurt relationships with others.

Even more important, the sports information specialist must learn how to use the operation conventions and policies of each member of the print media effectively. The SID who understands the factors involved in coverage decisions may be able to get a picture, a story, or some small mention in the media. For example, the SID may strike a responsive chord by pitching a particular story to an editor or beat reporter based on one or more of the news value criteria: "You might want to cover our women's lacrosse match today, because our goalie has a chance to set the conference record for shutouts." The savvy professional also may improve the "play" of a story—bigger headline, more prominent location on the page, etc.—by addressing those criteria when calling in game results. Explaining how a story fulfills the criteria has a far greater chance of success than does whining about the poor coverage of a particular team or sport.

Kevin Ruple, SID at Baldwin-Wallace College in Berea, Ohio, found a way to get a story on a Division III athlete into *Sports Illustrated*. Ruple called *Sports Illustrated* in March, prior to publication of the *Sports Illustrated College Football Preview* edition, to tell them about John Koz, a standout quarterback at Baldwin-Wallace. As he talked to the tenth person, Ruple struck a responsive chord while discussing the rivalry between Koz and Jim Ballard of Mount Union, the favorite to win the Ohio Athletic Conference. Ballard, the Mount Union quarterback, was receiving lots of media attention, so Ruple decided to play off the rivalry between the two schools and the performances of their star quarterbacks.

"I decided to divide and conquer," he said. "First, I found the comparisons. Then I looked for the differences. Both had great numbers. They both played at NCAA Division III schools. They both played the same position and were the leaders of their teams. And, both transferred to their respective schools."

The differences between the two quarterbacks became Ruple's selling point. Koz was 6-foot-3 and 215 pounds. He was a business major with a 3.4 grade point average. He knew he was playing his last season of organized football (although he did get a tryout with the Cleveland Thunderbolts of the Arena Football League). He loved the cerebral part of the game, picking apart a defense with pinpoint passing. Ballard was about the same size as Koz but had professional potential. He could run and throw. He was a flashy, Division III hotshot who enjoyed the spotlight.

Ten calls after the first pitch, Ruple won over *Sports Illustrated*. The story appeared in the college football preview. *Sports Illustrated* also followed up with a story on the game at Baldwin-Wallace. The game attracted a record crowd of 9,100 to Finnie Stadium. Mount Union won, 35-7, and went on to win the NCAA Division III National Championship, but Baldwin-Wallace got two stories in *Sports Illustrated*, thanks to the efforts of Ruple.

Summary

The printed word and photographs remain powerful instruments of sports information in the United States. The print media are still the dominant media in almost every category of measurement, from daily circulation to advertising revenue.

The print media take various forms, from daily newspapers to wire services to specialty magazines. Advertising provides the bulk of their financial underpinning, but advertisers exert little influence on coverage decisions. The print media link advertising rates to subscription totals, not to fluctuating audience levels or specific stories or programs. Consequently, advertising has less influence on coverage decisions in the print media than in the broadcast media.

Game results and personality profiles remain the backbone of print media coverage, but competition from other media and changes in lifestyle have prompted some shifts. Coverage of business and sports issues now makes up a significant part of sports content as the print media seek to offer readers greater detail on "how" and "why" the sports world operates as it does. Explanation has replaced narration. Postgame interviews with players have replaced eloquent prose laced with the reporter's opinion.

Print media provide the most consistent coverage of local sports, because of their organization and mission. Nearly every newspaper, even the smallest weekly, assigns a reporter to cover local sports as a facet of local news. Dailies generally assign reporters to a specific beat, making them responsible for ongoing coverage of a geographic area, sport, or sports organization. The structure gives the sports information specialist innumerable outlets for stories about players, teams, and sporting events.

DISCUSSION QUESTIONS

1. Why has there been a decrease in afternoon newspapers since the mid-1970s?
2. What were the sports subjects and events in the United States prior to 1924?

SUGGESTED EXERCISES

1. Write a paper analyzing the influence that *USA Today* has on sports sections of major daily newspapers around the United States.
2. Write a paper analyzing a major daily newspaper's approach to covering a major event that will be nationally televised.

Chapter Three

THE BROADCAST MEDIA:
THE MOST POWERFUL SPORTS INFORMATION PROVIDERS

In 1983, the University of Evansville in Indiana (UE) submitted a bid to the NCAA to host first-round games of the Division I men's basketball championships.

University athletics officials desperately wanted to bring network TV cameras to Evansville because they hoped the national exposure would help resurrect a basketball program devastated by an airplane crash five years earlier. A charter flight headed for a game at Middle Tennessee State University on a rainy, wintry evening in February 1978 had crashed on takeoff and killed all aboard—members of the Purple Aces basketball team, the coaching staff, a radio broadcast team, and several prominent members of the athletics booster club.

The disaster occurred the same year UE had planned to jump to Division I from Division II, where the Aces had won five national titles. University officials felt a weekend of camera shots on those championship banners in venerable Roberts Stadium would help attract attention—and basketball recruits—to the Evansville campus.

Chapter 3 explores the rapid emergence of radio and TV as the most powerful sports media in the United States today. It looks at the news and entertainment functions of sports programming and how they relate to financial considerations. It also examines the connections between content decisions and the profit motive, and their influence on the nature of the relationship with sports information specialists and sporting events.

The NCAA awarded the bid to Evansville, but the jubilation was short-lived. ABC-TV, which owned the broadcast rights to the regional site, insisted on exclusive control over the arena Friday through Sunday. The Indiana high school boys' sectional basketball tournament, which Evansville had hosted for years, was scheduled for Saturday, the day between collegiate games.

Citing concerns about the security of thousands of dollars of broadcast equipment, ABC executives said the high school tournament had to go. The NCAA gave Evansville a choice: Drop the prep tournament or give up the bid.

UE officials suddenly found themselves in the middle of a controversy. College fans demanded the NCAA playoffs. High school fans lobbied to keep the sectional. Officials from UE, local high schools, and the city of Evansville asked the Indiana High School Athletic Association (IHSAA) for assurances the sectional would return in 1984 if Evansville gave it up for a year. IHSAA executives would make no promises.

City officials, who controlled the arena, eventually opted for the NCAA and vowed to fight to get the sectional back. But they fought an uphill battle, as the sectional was moved to Terre Haute and in future years did not return to Evansville, costing the city thousands of dollars in lost revenue as prep fans instead headed in droves to Terre Haute for the local sectional tournament.

The University of Evansville's experience demonstrates the unparalleled influence of the broadcast media on sport organizations. The broadcast media, particularly television, wield enormous power in sport management decisions because they help pay the bills for athletic programs and events. Through licensing agreements, they effectively become financial partners in the production of an event. Consequently, they enjoy a working relationship with sport organizations that their print media counterparts can only envy.

The economic linkages enable TV executives to dictate the time, the structure and, in some cases, the rules of the games. That power creates additional concerns for the sports information professional. The sports information specialist must play a role not only in gathering and disseminating information, but also in shaping the presentation of the product to the audience. In short, the sports information specialist often serves a dual function—providing information and producing entertainment—in dealing with the broadcast media.

Scope of the Broadcast Industry

Ever since Guglielmo Marconi invented wireless communication in the late 1800s, broadcast communication has kept the world entertained as well as informed. Among the biggest beneficiaries of the meteoric rise in broadcast communications are sports and sports fans.

Whereas the print media provide a second-hand, second-day rundown on sporting events, radio and television offer same-day coverage and a front-row seat at the game. Consequently, the broadcast media provide a more direct link to the action, the next best thing to being there. Maybe better, some say.

The ability to put the audience into the sports theater is one of the reasons television is among the most powerful and most popular media in the world. Thanks to the development of cable and satellite technology, sporting events can be brought right into the living rooms of Middle America from anywhere in the world. NBC-TV broadcast coverage of the 1992, 1996, 2000, and 2004 Summer Olympics almost around the clock. The 1992 Games were held in Barcelona, Spain, a six-hour difference in time zones from the eastern US, and nine hours between Spain and the western US. But despite the thousands of miles and many hours that separated Spain from the US, NBC's coverage presented visually stunning theater in its finest form. Sitting in a living room in a midwestern town or city and watching the Olympics, one could imagine the events were taking place just a few miles away.

Good theater attracts a big audience, and sport is good theater, as Hunt and Ruben note in Chapter 2. More than 98% of the households in the United States own at least one TV set, and that set is turned on seven hours a day. Nearly 56 million of the 92 million TV sets are equipped with cable capabilities, according to the *World Almanac*, and that figure continues to grow annually.

Radio and TV rapidly emerged as the most powerful sport media in the US.

The ability to draw big audiences gives television an enormous advantage over other media in attracting advertisers and generating revenue. According to the A. C. Nielsen Company, one of the nation's premier rating companies, advertisers indirectly influence the media through placement of their commercial messages. Nielsen conducts weekly surveys of TV—audience viewing habits based on a sample of households. Quick overnight ratings from New York, Chicago, and Los Angeles provide at least a barometer of viewer interests. High ratings guarantee financial success because the large audience appeals to advertisers who want to spread the word about their products. Low ratings mean almost certain death because of their lack of drawing power, that is, their inability to attract commercial "investors."

According to *Advertising Age,* a publication that monitors the financial realm of the media, commercial revenues first made television a billion-dollar industry in 1990. The number one advertiser was Proctor and Gamble. The Cincinnati-based firm spent over $2 million on television advertising, including $488,756 on network television, $285,118 on sport TV, and $31,000 on cable TV, according to the 1995 *World Almanac.* By the mid-1990s, cable advertising was running at $2.5 million a year (Dominick, 1996). By 1996, the Big Four broadcast networks alone—ABC, NBC, CBS, and FOX—took in $2.5 billion from sports broadcasts. Cable hauled in another $951 million ("TV Sport," 1996).

Because of the lucrative financial return on top-rated programs, broadcasters are willing to pay sport organizations handsomely for coverage rights. The popularity of men's college basketball prompted CBS to spend $1.7 billion for exclusive rights to the NCAA Division I men's basketball tournament through 2002, according to NCAA figures. The NCAA reported that the contract for the men's basketball tournament from 1995–2002 averaged $215.6 million per year, a 50% increase over the previous contract.

CBS Sports Vice President Len DeLuca, in a column by sportswriter Tom Hoffarth of the *Los Angeles Daily News,* said,

> The tournament is one of the great success stories in terms of continued growth, advertiser loyalty and fervor. This is our foundation, something we identified in the early '80s as a huge target, and we've grown with it. Some have a problem with the magnitude of 1.725 billion, but here's another number: 70 hours. That's how much of the tournament we have from March 10 to April 1 (1996). As the rights fees grow, so do the amount of hours and available (commercial) units. Thus far, there continues to be a growth and demand. (quoted in Hoffarth, p. P-2)

The growth and demand spurred the fledgling FOX Television Network to outbid CBS for rights to professional football games in an attempt to establish credibility as a network. In addition to network contracts and agreements with cable superstations, vast amounts of money are realized through local television on VHF, UHF, and cable systems. The money continues to grow and grow. *Broadcasting and Cable* magazine counted some 20 broadcast and cable networks among the major bidders for TV rights, including pay channels like HBO and pay-per-view cable companies that charge by the event ("TV Sports," 1996).

Several professional teams in baseball, football, and basketball survive only because of the vast amounts of money received from television. In 1993, national and local television, cable, and radio broadcasting garnered $2.46 billion in revenues for all leagues. In fact, author Shirley Biagi of California State University estimated that television fees fund "most of the cost of the nation's organized sports" (1992, p. 186).

Sport organizations negotiate contracts for broadcast rights in a number of ways. The leagues dictate the major national contracts; others are arranged by teams through competitive negotiations with local stations. The National Basketball Association, National Football League, National Collegiate Athletic Association, Major League Baseball, Major League Soccer, and Ladies Professional Golf Association sell their own national rights, according to *Broadcasting & Cable* magazine ("TV Sports," 1996). Each track on the NASCAR circuit negotiates its own rights, and promoters work out the deals for boxing matches.

Because of the lucrative financial return on top-rated programs, broadcasters are willing to pay sport organizations handsomely for coverage rights. CBS Sports Vice President Len DeLuca, in a column by sportswriter Tom Hoffarth of the *Los Angeles Daily News*, said,

The tournament is one of the great success stories in terms of continued growth, advertiser loyalty and fervor. This is our foundation, something we identified in the early '80s as a huge target, and we've grown with it. Some have a problem with the magnitude of 1.725 billion, but here's another number: 70 hours. That's how much of the tournament we have from March 10 to April 1 (1996). As the rights fees grow, so do the amount of hours and available (commercial) units. Thus far, there continues to be a growth and demand. (quoted in Hoffarth, p. P-2)

The sanctioning bodies in golf and tennis issue the rights for some events, whereas the host organization controls others. For example, Augusta National handles rights for the Masters.

The broadcasting director of the Cleveland Indians usually consults the senior executives at individual stations about local contracts. The team usually attempts to deal with the current partner first. If that fails, the broadcasting director will solicit offers from other stations, according to Indians Vice President Dennis Lehman (personal communication with Bill Nichols, March 2, 1995). The objective is to maximize revenues and arrange the most marketing support possible. The Indians do not have any direct involvement in the network deals. A committee made up of representatives from major league clubs conducts the negotiations and makes a recommendation after consultation with team executives. The national contracts give the network considerable leeway in selecting which games to broadcast—who's hot or which game offers the best competitive matchup. In pro basketball, the Cleveland Cavaliers maintain a local radio and television partnership. The arrangement enables the team to generate its own revenue. Channel 43, a Cleveland-area UHF station, allows the Cavs to purchase airtime and then sell it themselves; so does AM Radio WTAM (1100).

Television networks continue to increase their bid for the contract rights to broadcast live college and professional sporting events.

In contrast, regional network FOX Sports Ohio pays a rights fee, then sells the advertising. The Cavs retain the right to approve promotions and the announcers for the locally televised games.

The huge rights fees in the broadcast-television and cable industries created a two-tiered level of sports, or "big-market" and "small-market" teams, in the 1990s. National advertisers buy time on television stations according to market size (i.e., potential viewers in broadcast range). Teams in big cities promise big audiences and command bigger rights fees than do teams in cities with smaller audience potential. New York and Los Angeles obviously are big markets. Cities such as Pittsburgh, Cincinnati, and Cleveland are large, but they are small television markets. The teams in these three cities are unable to generate revenues anywhere close to what is earned in New York, Chicago, and Los Angeles. That's why the National Football League began maneuvering to put a team in Los Angeles after the departure of the Rams and the Raiders. When no one stepped up with an acceptable proposal, the NFL awarded a franchise to Houston, which lost its team to Nashville. The big-market teams also can attract the better and more high-profile athletes, so they have a chance to have the best teams. That may be unfair, but it is a fact of life in a professional sports world that derives substantial financial support from television.

A similar dynamic is at work in collegiate sport. High-profile sports such as basketball and football attract lots of broadcast suitors, particularly at schools with large fan support. Notre Dame, which boasts a nationwide following, can take its choice of suitors for broadcast of all its football games. For the past 15 years, the Fighting Irish have had an exclusive deal with NBC to broadcast its home games, and the two recently signed an extension that makes the deal, reportedly worth $9 million a year for Notre Dame, though the 2010 season. Unlike Notre Dame, small schools and low-profile sports prove a hard advertising sell because of the small audience they draw.

Given the increasing popularity of televised sports, the reservoir of advertising appears to be endless. The insatiable American sports public even appears willing to pay extra for special events. Prizefights and pro wrestling spectaculars command event prices of $30–$50 on pay-per-program TV; college football games, $8–$10. *Broadcasting & Cable* ("TV Sports," 1996) calls the sports "TV's $3.5 billion addiction" (p. 34). Also in 1996, *TV Sports Magazine* said,

> Many in the industry see alliances between broadcast and cable networks changing the competitive landscape in television sports. Observers see a new round of fierce bidding in the coming years for big-event sports by superpowers including NBC, ABC/ESPN and FOX/Liberty. ("TV Sports," 1996, p. 35)

History of the Broadcast Media

Radio was at the root of the development of the broadcast media, and growth evolved along two lines—news and entertainment. The broadcast media provide sports results and taped highlights on regular newscasts. They also offer sports programs as prime-time entertainment.

Live coverage of sports by radio blossomed in the 1920s. KDKA in Pittsburgh, the first commercial radio station in the United States, found an eager audience for prizefights and baseball games as early as 1921. The heavyweight championship fight between Jack Dempsey and George Carpenter on July 21, 1921, was the first boxing match to be broadcast on the radio. In 1927, Dempsey fought Gene Tunney, and one department store reportedly sold nearly $100,000 worth of radio equipment prior to the championship bout. Related industries benefited from the sudden popularity of radio as well.

By the 1930s, nearly 500 million radios were in use in the United States. Motion pictures and radio provided much of the nation's entertainment. All 16 Major League Baseball teams had their games broadcast to local audiences, and the financial structure to support programming had been established. That financial structure was the concept of advertising or "the purchase of time from a station for the presentation of commercial messages" (Sterling & Kittross, 1990, p. 70). In addition, commercial radio networks were in place to offer national advertising spots. In 1935, revenues generated from national spots were $14.9 million, and for local spots, $35 million (Sterling & Kittross, 1990). Sports programming was lumped into the programming category of talk programs, which included human-interest programs, news, public affairs, quiz shows, and religion. In 1938, sports play-by-play programming on commercial-network evening radio was two quarter hours (Sterling & Kittross, 1990).

In those days, radio play-by-play announcers did not accompany teams on the road. The announcers would re-create the away games using Western Union tapes for the play-by-play. These same announcers would read the tape and it would say, "Jones grounded out to third." The play-by-play announcer would create a ball-and-strike count, set the scene in the field, and more or less fabricate portions of the game. Announcers would also use sound effects, such as banging a wastebasket for a foul ball. It was all in fun, and baseball fans enjoyed it. The late president Ronald Reagan re-created Chicago Cubs games during a brief career as a sportscaster.

The airways belonged to radio from the 1920s to the 1940s. Three of the major networks—ABC, NBC, and CBS—arose in the late 1920s and changed both the financial and the program content of radio. The Radio Corporation of America launched the first network, the National Broadcasting Company (NBC), in 1926 by linking WJZ in Newark, New Jersey, with a station in Schenectady, New York. At the same time, American Telephone and Telegraph was putting together a 27-station network. NBC bought the network and ran both of them until the Federal Communications Commission ordered NBC to sell one. The new network became the American Broadcasting Company (ABC). William Paley bought an independent network a year later and called it the Columbia Broadcasting System (CBS).

The networks gave advertisers a national audience and based their rates, as they still do, on the number of potential listeners they could deliver though affiliated stations. They still give stations a share of the advertising dollar, as well as a ready source of programming. The networks originally offered sports, music, news, and variety shows. Dramatic presentations also were popular.

With the advent of television during the immediate post-World War II era, radio changed its marketing approach. Instead of large area audiences and network programming, radio offered news, sports talk shows, or music shows aimed at local audiences.

Television appeared on the broadcast scene in 1927. The first televised sporting event, a baseball game between Ivy League rivals Princeton and Columbia, took place on May 17, 1939. Legendary sports announcer Bill Stern did the play-by-play. At that time, there were fewer than 500 television sets in the nation, and the majority were owned by networks. Television screens ranged from 5 to 12 inches in diameter and cost around $600 each. Now, television screens are as large as a wall or nearly as small as the face of a wristwatch.

Some Americans can recall seeing a very rare television screen just prior to World War II, but commercial television as we know it today took a foothold in the late 1940s and early 1950s. The medium went transcontinental on September 4, 1951, with President Harry Truman's address at the Japanese Peace Treaty Conference in San Francisco.

The networks absorbed TV stations as well as radio stations. Two thirds of the 900 commercial stations in 1994 were affiliated with networks (Vivian, 1995). The networks offered local stations the kind of high-quality programming they could not afford to produce themselves. They also shared advertising revenues with affiliates, as they did with radio.

The networks attracted more than 90% of TV viewers until the 1980s brought cable and satellite technology. Visionaries like Ted Turner turned the new technology into a new way of delivering a national audience to advertisers. Turner bought satellite time in 1976 and persuaded cable operators to add WTBS to their offerings (Vivian, 1995). He subsequently bought the Atlanta Braves to boost the station's audience, and later started specialty channels such as Cable Network News (CNN) and Turner Network Television (TNT), which presents movies and sports. In 1996, WTBS and TNT owned the rights to 115 NBA games, 12 pro football games, 125 Atlanta Braves games, NASCAR races, NCAA football, and pro golf tournaments (*Broadcasting & Cable*, May 13, 1996, p. 38).

The 1990s have seen an explosion of cable channels and specialty stations that has pulled viewers away from the networks. The network share of the audience has dropped 30% since 1980 (Dominick, 1996). Cable subscribers may get 100 or more stations, most for a single monthly fee. What the networks get is more competition for audience and advertisers, which raises the stakes in bidding wars for sporting events.

Types of Broadcast Media

The sports information specialist may work with all kinds of broadcast journalists, from AM and FM radio disc jockeys who just want the scores to network TV executives seeking multi-game and multi-year licensing agreements. In between are radio and TV sports directors, announcers, and producers who make up the news and live-coverage teams.

The broadcast teams may want to conduct interviews with players, coaches, and others involved in the games. They may want to broadcast games or shoot a few highlights for the evening news. They may offer to produce a coach's show. They may need special equipment, electrical hookups, a place to park a rolling broadcast unit, and runners to relay statistics and other materials to a play-by-play team.

Here is a rundown of the different types of broadcast media:

Networks

There are four major television networks, including the three original American networks, NBC, ABC, and CBS. FOX Television Networks, which debuted in 1987, has moved up to major network status with a full schedule of prime-time entertainment programs and broadcast of major sporting events. Several smaller networks with limited entertainment programming arose in the late 1990s.

The four major networks offer nightly newscasts and they usually broadcast from studios in New York City or Washington, DC. Sports items appear on the newscasts only if the story has national interest and appeals to a broad audience, not just to sports enthusiasts.

Types of Broadcast Media

Networks

UHF channels

Superstations

Cable channels

Sport channels

Independent producers

Local TV stations

Cable franchises

Pay-per-view

Local radio

The networks also are among the primary bidders for sports broadcast rights. Because of the high-stakes bidding, the broadcast outlets for professional sports and major events are in constant flux.

UHF Channels

Ultra high frequency (UHF) channels are very popular in large television markets. They originally featured reruns and movies. However, in recent years, some have added nightly news shows to compete with their network counterparts.

UHF stations also have discovered that sports can increase viewers and, thus, increase revenues. Many major league games in baseball and basketball are carried locally by UHF stations.

Superstations

A number of independent stations have hooked up with cable companies and purchased satellite time to reach national audiences. The largest are WGN in Chicago and WTBS in Atlanta. WGN had broadcast rights to both the Chicago Cubs and White Sox, as well as the NBA Bulls, with WTBS airing games played by the Atlanta Braves. These stations provide powerful national exposure for their respective teams.

Cable Channels

The fastest growing companies in the television community are cable outlets, both national and local. Important national cable stations that offer major sports include TNT out of Atlanta and the USA Network in New York City. TNT is a cable flagship station for the NBA, whereas ABC has a contract with the NBA but coverage is spotty until the play-offs. USA Network's sports offerings are largely boxing, golf, and tennis. In some cases, the Thursday and Friday rounds of a PGA event will appear on USA Network and the Friday and Saturday rounds on NBC.

Sports Channels

ESPN, the Entertainment and Sports Programming Network, has developed into a cultural icon since launching the first all-sports channel. The game highlights and patter on the *SportsCenter* news show are must-see for all serious sports enthusiasts.

ESPN, now owned in part by ABC, offers everything from cheerleading contests to hunting and fishing shows to college and professional sports. The network also provides round-by-round coverage of the professional sports drafts. A spin-off channel, ESPN2, adds offbeat events like "extreme games" to the standard sports fare and runs scores across the bottom of the TV screen continuously. ESPN News was added to the network's family and included the scrolling ticker, as well as recaps and highlights of the

Courtesy of Stock.xchng

The domination of network and cable stations has forced local TV stations to focus more on coverage of small college athletics and other community-related sporting events.

day's sporting events, typically recycling and updating its news-format program every 30 minutes. Recently, the network also added ESPNU, which exclusively broadcasts college sports, including lower-profile college sports such as baseball, softball, and lacrosse that were rarely seen on ESPN or ESPN2.

Regional imitators include Fox Sports Net, which has localized stations in cities such as St. Louis, and Comcast. They offer a variety of professional games, college sports, and independently produced programs. The National Cable Television lists some 24 regional sports networks, such as Prime Network in Houston; Prism in Philadelphia; Fox Sports Net in various cities; and the Sunshine Network in Orlando, Florida.

Independent Producers

A number of independent producers contract to cover specific sports events and sell events for which they have obtained the rights to the highest cable or network bidder.

Local TV Stations

Local VHF broadcast affiliates now present multiple newscasts in the morning and early evening in addition to the standard 10 P.M. or 11 P.M. wrap-up at the end of the evening's prime-time lineup. Local sports directors generally are allotted 5–10 minutes for a combination of local scores, video highlights of local events, and network clips from major league games.

Some local stations in professional sports markets also purchase the rights to a package of Major League Baseball games. Additionally, they may broadcast selected games involving area colleges and produce a college coach's show or call-in program.

Independent stations generally do not maintain news departments, but they may bid on the rights for local college games or other popular local sporting events.

Cable Franchises

Local cable operators may provide coverage of high school sports, delayed broadcasts of collegiate sports, and call-in shows on public access channels. College and high school football and basketball sometimes are shown at different times during the week on tape.

Pay-Per-View

Pay-per-view is a subscription service available through cable franchises. Cable subscribers can order special events—sports, movies, etc.—by telephone or through the cable converter box. The viewer pays separately for each event, just as in purchasing a ticket. Everything from college sports events to major prizefights are offered on a pay-per-view basis.

Local Radio

Stations on the AM band (535 to 1,605 kilocycles) depend on talk shows and entertainment for programming because music has gravitated to FM stations (88 to 108 megacycles), which produce static-free transmission. Consequently, local commentary and call-in shows are popular fare on AM radio. Local stations in some cities have adopted all-sports formats, but round-the-clock sports radio has been largely unsuccessful.

Organization of Broadcast Media

Sports and the broadcast media, particularly TV, have enjoyed a long-standing love affair that has matured into a marriage. The relationship is often tumultuous, but never dull. For example, TV turned a ninth-inning home run in the 1988 World Series by Kirk Gibson of the Los Angeles Dodgers into a historic event. Using marvelous camera angles, NBC squeezed every ounce of drama out of the event. The game-winning hit is now remembered as "The Homer," an image forever etched by broadcaster Jack Buck in the minds of those who witnessed it.

It is that kind of drama that sport organizations covet—positive images that linger in the memory and bring spectators back to the stands. What sports information specialists soon learn is that generating that kind of television coverage is far more difficult and complex than arranging coverage with the print media.

First, unlike in the print media, there is a direct link in broadcasting between advertising sales and programming decisions. Broadcast programmers make content decisions on the basis of what sells. No matter how big the rivalry between two area colleges, the local TV station will not provide live coverage unless it can sell the advertising necessary to support the broadcast. The advertising pays the production costs. A network or cable operator is not likely to broadcast a local game unless it has widespread interest that will appeal to national advertisers. That is why all of Notre Dame's football games appear on television, and none of Division III Thomas More College's do (except on the local cable channel).

In addition, the popularity of the sport and the sports team influences the decisions. Ratings play a critical role in programming decisions because of the direct link between audience size, advertiser interest, and the cost of commercial spots during the broadcast of a specific program. Time is a factor in the decision, first because programs during prime time (8–11 P.M.) and on weekends draw more viewers than do those at times when most people are at work.

Second, time limits sports news coverage on television far more than space constricts stories in the print media. A typical 30-minute newscast consists of 24 minutes of noncommercial time. The amount of information a station can provide during that time is equivalent to roughly one page in a newspaper, and sports get only 5–8 minutes of the news time—a quarter of a page.

Third, broadcasting production requirements differ markedly from those of the print media. Because the networks provide 90–95% of local programming, local stations do not maintain large staffs of news reporters. Although a local daily newspaper may employ 8–10 people in the sports department, the television station in the same city may have only two sports reporters. The radio sports contact also may have to do the news,

> Time limits sports news coverage on television far more than space constricts stories in the print media.

weather, and commercials. Radio and TV reporters sometimes double as announcers on local games that a station broadcasts. Professional teams typically hire their own broadcast teams or approve the ones selected by the local rights holder.

Furthermore, broadcast news and local programming are team efforts—not a single endeavor by a reporter and photographer working individually. The reporters or play-by-play teams work in concert with producers and technical staff, who literally structure the coverage as it unfolds. The technical demands are such that engineering is a separate department of most broadcast organizations.

The typical broadcast operation divides its workforce into programming, sales, engineering, and management. Programming encompasses reporters, writers, graphic artists, videographers (camera people), audio and/or video editors, announcers, on-air personalities, directors, and producers. The sales department takes care of advertising and directs production of local commercials, which may utilize personnel from the programming department. Engineering provides the technical support, from the people who operate the cameras to those who maintain the equipment.

The top management person typically is a general manager, who oversees all departments. The programming department may include a news unit and a production unit that produces local shows, or it may combine them. Programming managers decide what events to broadcast live, what types of original shows to produce (such as a call-in program or coach's show), and what time to air them.

Here is a rundown on the personnel it takes to produce a typical television package:

Television Package Personnel
Director
Producer
Reporter
Writers
Videographer
Editor
Anchor

Director

Sports and program directors manage the budget, work schedules, and story assignments. On a small station, the news, sports, and program director may be rolled into one position. A director also may double as the assigning editor at a local station. Some stations assign a single person to decide where reporters and camera crews go on a given day.

Producer

The producer is in charge of the production of a program or newscast. For a newscast, the producer generally decides what stories will appear, in what order, and at what length. The producer oversees the work of reporters, camera operators, writers, and audiotape or videotape editors.

Reporter

The reporter plays the same role in radio or TV as in the print media. However, TV reporters often have to cover both news and sports events because of the small size of news staffs.

Writers

Stations in large- and medium-size markets also hire writers. They compose the lead-ins to stories for on-air anchors. They also may coordinate the preparation of a news "package"—words, pictures, and graphics.

Writers sometimes serve as in-house reporters and wire service editors. They gather local news via the telephone and convert stories that move on the wire services to broadcast style.

The primary wire services, the *Associated Press* and *Reuters*, provide news for the broadcast media as well as for the print media. The same information is provided for radio and television as is given to newspapers, but it is written much more concisely. The fewer words, the better when it comes to news and bulletins for radio and television. In fact, news for the electronic media that is provided by the wire services is filed on what is called a "radio wire." It is factual information, but is presented in a very concise manner.

Videographer

The videographer is the broadcast equivalent of a photojournalist. The video specialist works with the reporter in the field to determine what shots to take for a news assignment. The camera operator also may cover a specific area of the playing field or focus on a specific assignment during live coverage. For example, a videographer may follow the favorite horse from the starting gate to the finish line at the Kentucky Derby. The videographer also is a field technician of sorts, setting up the sound, lighting, etc., for live broadcasts or news reports.

Editor

The editor combines the reporter's words, video shots, and any art or graphics into a single package of words and pictures. Reporters often edit their own stories, particularly at small- and medium-market stations.

Anchor

The anchor is the on-air personality who reads copy or introduces news packages during the newscast. Anchors may or may not have journalism training. They are paid to present the news, not to gather it. At many stations, however, reporters move into anchor slots, which are the highest paid positions because of their high profile.

The anchor is not the person to call to request coverage of an event. Sports information specialists will be far more successful if they cultivate a positive relationship with reporters, just as they do with print journalists. They should approach the assigning editor, sports director, or producer about coverage concerns.

Given the proliferation of local stations and cable operations, the typical sports viewer is swamped with choices in a typical week—in a single hour on a given weekend. More than 10 games on average are available each weekend on either a regional, national, or tape-delay basis. On a Sunday in April, the couch potato with a remote may flip between an NBA playoff game, a pro golf event, a pro tennis tournament, a NASCAR or Indy car race, and a Major League Baseball game.

Local cable television and public television have become important vehicles for small-college and high school sports, particularly football and basketball. Some of the games are taped and shown at a later time or date. In Cincinnati and other large cities, broadcast teams scurry from one high school football game to another in a helicopter to provide video "clips" from as many games as possible for the late news. Colleges and high schools often provide network television affiliates with excerpts of a televised game. The stations run clips during their newscasts, often as a backdrop when they run the scores on the screen.

FM stations have supplemented AM radio, especially on college campuses. They often broadcast college football, basketball, and sometimes baseball games. The broadcasts provide a valuable training ground for students who hope to build careers in broadcast media sports or sports public relations. Public radio may broadcast high school games, but they require corporate sponsorship.

Content Decisions

Programming decisions and advertising sales are inseparable in the broadcast media. No direct link exists with newscasts, but TV sports news is little more than a flash of free highlights three or four times a day. The money, for both broadcast and sports organizations, is in entertainment programming—live or taped coverage of an event.

The quality and drama of television sports are improving almost daily as engineers learn how to mount tiny cameras in the asphalt of an auto race track, on a player's helmet, in the stands, on dollies above the goal, and in the Goodyear or Met Life blimps in the sky.

New technology and techniques take viewers right into the game, the huddles, the locker rooms, and, on occasion, the boardrooms. Not only did camera angles improve in the 1980s and early 1990s, but the use of tape to show replays from every conceivable angle also became an integral part of sports telecasts. The popularity of *SportsCenter* on ESPN relies on the combination of camera angles and clever dialogue. The improvements contribute to the ever-growing financial connections between audience, sport organization, and broadcast industry.

Television coverage of sporting events has become so intense that coaches are regularly approached by sideline reporters to do postgame interviews before even leaving the field of play.

The top-rated sports programs on television consistently are Monday Night Football, the Super Bowl, the World Series, professional basketball and baseball's all-star games, NBA playoff games, and college bowl games. It is no accident that these programs also command the highest prices for commercial spots.

Television ratings are much more than sets of seemingly disconnected numbers. They are the fuels that drive the commercial television industry (David Glasier,

The *NewsHerald*, Willoughby, OH). Ratings are used to set the rates for commercials that supply networks, local network affiliates, and independently owned stations with their financial lifeblood. Entertainment shows and newscasts rise and fall with their ratings, as do the careers of people on both sides of the cameras. ABC, number three in the network-rating race, used sports to climb out of the cellar as far back as 1960. ABC launched *Wide World of Sports*, which stimulated interest in a variety of athletic achievements, when the other networks were paying less attention to sports (Watkins, 1991).

So, what are ratings and whence do they come? Ratings are a measurement of audience size and composition based on the program choices of a relative handful of viewers. The business of compiling ratings is dominated by two companies, Arbitron and Nielsen. To compile these ratings, the companies rely on written diaries, electronic meters hooked to TV sets, or a combination of the two. Nielsen is responsible for the weekly ratings report of network TV shows. Arbitron leads the way in ratings reports for individual television markets such as New York, Chicago, and Cleveland. In addition to measuring performance of prime-time shows, Arbitron takes care of ratings for local newscasts, syndicated shows, and all other programs that air on local TV stations.

The ratings services provide radio and/or television stations with breakdowns on viewership in two categories. The *rating* represents the percentage of homes tuned to the station out of all the homes with receivers in the market area. The *share* amounts to the percentage of receivers that actually were in use and tuned to the station at the time. If a favorite network program last week finished second in its time period with a 12 rating and 20 share, this rating indicates 20% of the 91.8 million TV households tuned into that program. Share is the percentage of households using TV at that time of day tuned into a particular program. The base figure for ratings never changes, whereas HUT (households using TV) levels vary according to the time of day. For instance, many more people are watching television at prime time than are at 9 a.m.

The ratings services also supply breakdowns by demographic category. Of increasing importance to advertisers and network programmers are demographics or ratings for specific age groups (18–35 to 25–49). New developments in ratings technology include the so-called "passive" meter, which automatically determines which family members are using television and records what they are watching. The meters enable the ratings companies to break down the audience into age categories.

Ratings are of great importance at all times, but particularly so during the so-called "sweeps" months of November, February, May, and July. Results of ratings sweeps months are used to calibrate advertising rates for the next quarter. Thus, millions of dollars are riding on the outcome of sweeps at the network level and in smaller markets such as Cleveland, 16th largest in the United States as of 2005. Market size also is a factor in the advertising rate formula, because it relates to the number of potential viewers. Market size is determined by the number of viewers in each designated market area, according to Nielsen Media Research. Each county in the United States is designated in a specific TV market, following a standard called "significantly viewed." That means the majority of people in the market watch stations in that area. For example, counties designated to the Cleveland market are Ashtabula, Ashland, Carroll, Cuyahoga, Erie, Geauga, Holmes, Huron, Lake, Lorain, Medina, Portage, Richland, Stark, Summit, Tuscarawas, and Wayne. The seventeen counties encompass 1,541,780 homes with TV.

Sports Management Concerns

The dichotomy of broadcast sports represents a double-edged sword for sport administrators. Live coverage of a game may boost fan support, but it also may keep fans at home.

Television has redesigned sport to satisfy its needs, such as creating time-outs for commercial messages. It also has created a huge reservoir of relatively easy money for sport organizations. The size of the financial boon has created concern about the impact of greed on sports. Television has created so much money, it seems every university wants a larger share of the pie, and so do the athletes who provide the entertainment. College basketball and football players are leaving college early in significant numbers because of the huge salaries offered by NBA and NFL teams with fat wallets in large part from TV contracts.

The trend of leaving school early to enter the professional ranks even filtered down to the high school level, with Kobe Bryant and LeBron James being the most famous current NBA stars to make the jump directly from the prep ranks to the pros. In the 2004 NBA Draft, eight of the first 30 picks were high school players. But the NBA adopted a new rule in 2006, increasing the minimum draft age from 18 to 19 (plus being at least one year removed from high school).

Contract switching and complaints are common. Watkins (1991) showed how the friction between the National Collegiate Athletic Association and the College Football Association led to a Supreme Court decision ruling the NCAA's exclusive television rights to college football were anticompetitive. Critics contend the competition has pushed coaches to cheat in their recruiting in order to draw the talent to make the team attractive to television producers. Marketing is everything. College athletics have become "produced" just like toothpaste and automobiles.

> * Will fans show up for a local college game on a cold, rainy fall evening when the game will be broadcast on tape delay two hours after it ends?
>
> * Will the revenue from broadcast rights offset the loss of ticket sales and concession revenues?
>
> These are among the questions sport organizations are trying to answer. Is there a link between the empty stadiums around Major League Baseball and the proliferation of games broadcast on local stations, TV networks, cable stations, and sports channels?

These are among the issues sport administrators and sports information specialists face in attempting to manage the entertainment aspect of radio and television. The specialist who understands the links between audience, ratings, and broadcast function is better prepared to handle both the information and the entertainment functions of the job.

The sports information specialist's role in gathering and disseminating news is very much the same for both print and broadcast media. Sports information directors should make an effort to know the sportscasters in the area, their likes, dislikes, and particularly their deadlines. A sport administrator or sports information director should supply television outlets with feature ideas; a few will hit with a sports reporter on an off day with little breaking news.

More important, sports information professionals should provide results of athletic contests, and supportive information, as far in advance of news time as possible. A newscast develops on the run, because it is live; the earlier the score gets in, the more likely it will appear on the screen with comments from the reporter.

Because television is a live and visual medium, sports information specialists should think in terms of time and pictures. Does the SID want a story on the early or late news, or both? Early news shows do more sports feature stories, whereas the late shows concentrate on results of that night's action. Sports information specialists can suggest particular shots or scenes with drama or entertainment value. News conferences should be set up at a time when camera operators and reporters are available. Remember, editing words and pictures into a story takes time. The more time one can give the broadcast team to edit, the more likely it is they will produce a complete and high-quality package that will command a high priority in the story schedule.

Most sports anchors have to cram the sports of the day into a five-minute segment of a newscast, and commercials take up two minutes of the time. The sports information director or sport administrator competes with other schools, colleges, and amateur and professional organizations for 30 seconds of time at most, a score on the screen at least; but time on television may mean money and prestige for the organization. Telling a story well in a brief sportscast may be a struggle, but it is a battle worth fighting, because of the large general audience that may see or hear it.

Sports information specialists compete daily for coverage of their respective sport or team in a local TV station's three-minute sports newscast but the ability to reach a large audience is well worth the effort.

Live broadcasts complicate the equation. Televising an athletic event requires teamwork and the utmost in timing between crew and camera. Professional football broadcasts such as the Super Bowl may utilize nearly 20 cameras and 300 people in order to provide the best visual, as well as audio, presentation. Because of the limited playing areas, basketball, bowling, and tennis lend themselves best to television. Golf is extremely difficult to televise.

The sports information specialist gets involved with television and radio broadcasts of events in a number of ways. Merle Levin, retired sports information director at Cleveland State University, said in an interview with Bill Nichols,

> Long before the game, you will be on the phone with some facets of the TV crew. They will want to know when they can bring their trucks to the site, where they can park and what security will be provided, since the likelihood is they will arrive the day before or remain the night after the contest and at some time the trucks may be left unmanned on game day. They will also need to know when they can power up (connect and turn on their lines) and that an electrician from the site will be on hand to assist in this procedure. (February 16, 1996)

The producer usually shows up far in advance of the game, sometimes a day or two early, to check out camera locations and lighting. The advance person may want a lounge for the crew if the competition will last for a long period of time, as in a track or swim meet. The broadcast team also will need an interview room, and they might want to do a halftime interview. Often they will request a statistician and a couple of runners, people who can assist with whatever is needed during the broadcast.

In contrast, most radio stations are largely self-sufficient. Levin says they should be expected to make their own arrangements for broadcast lines because (a) their requirements vary greatly, and (b) it simplifies billing procedures. The sports information director can supply the name and telephone number of the person to call to order the lines. A radio station usually needs two or three telephones for use during an event. Often the school will provide them.

The sports information specialist can help the radio team by providing a media packet, with game notes, a media guide, and a timetable showing when the national anthem will be performed, when the starting lineups will be announced, and when the game will begin. Sometimes a radio station will also ask for a spotter, to help the play-by-play announcer identify specific players. The most important service the SID can provide is up-to-date statistics—and in a hurry. Remember, radio is live. "Being aware of the immediacy of radio is the biggest favor you can provide a radio broadcaster," says Levin. "Be doubly sure these people are the very first to receive halftime and postgame statistics. They need them pronto."

Radio can be a valuable asset to a sport organization. Radio is a very effective vehicle for announcements of events such as sports and community recreation and special events. Radio stations are required to allot a certain amount of time during a 24-hour day to free public service announcements. Schools and other non-profit organizations can use such announcements to highlight their activities. Most radio stations have a deadline, which is typically two weeks, for releases to be used in the public service area, so that should be taken into consideration when sending announcements to radio stations.

Summary

Television is unquestionably the most powerful form of media in the world. It also is the most effective communication tool for reaching a large general audience—both for advertisers and for sport organizations.

Profit motive drives the broadcast industry far more than it does the print media because of the direct links between advertising and programming content. Television sells an audience to an advertiser. The bigger the audience, the higher the advertising rate. As a result, sports programs are products the broadcast industry sells to an advertiser to make money.

Sports are among the most popular television products because the drama of athletic competition draws large audiences. That means television is willing to pay huge sums of money to gain exclusive rights to cover an event that guarantees large audiences.

The competition among the broadcast media has made financial partners out of broadcast media and sport organizations; both have profited enormously from the relationship. Sport organizations make millions of dollars from TV each year. A one-year contract for the best athletes runs in the millions of dollars, too, because of the huge take from TV.

The financial partnership has created a two-tiered class system among sports teams and sports events and has given the TV industry enormous power to control everything from starting times to postgame interviews. It also has added to the complexity of the responsibilities of sports information managers. A story tip, a news release, and a copy of statistics are not enough for the broadcast industry. Broadcast production takes a team with special equipment and transmission needs.

The proliferation of sports on television is transforming the sports audience into couch potatoes and channel surfers who flip with a remote from game to game and sport to sport on TV. In-house attendance still is important, but one day, fans in the stands may be both insignificant and invisible.

If current trends continue, sporting events will be strictly a product of television—a TV production. There may not be enough fans in attendance to ring the arena. The large crowds will be in the living rooms and sports bars across America.

DISCUSSION QUESTIONS

1. What value does a school's football or basketball team's playing on national television have in the institution's recruitment of student-athletes?
2. How important is it to an institution to have its basketball and football teams on radio play-by-play when its contests are nationally televised?

SUGGESTED EXERCISES

1. Write a critique of a television or radio coverage (play-by-play) of an athletic contest. Critique both audio and visual presentation. Is it effective? Why or why not? Give suggestions for improvement. Discuss the delivery and the knowledge of the broadcasters.
2. Conduct role-playing in which one student acts as a radio broadcaster and host on a sports talk show. The other students act as callers and create interactions between callers and host.
3. Write a critique of a game televised on cable. Critique both audio and visual presentation. Is it effective? Why or why not? Give suggestions for improvement. Also, discuss the delivery of the broadcasters.

Chapter Four

SPORTS INFORMATION SPECIALISTS: SPORT ORGANIZATION MANAGERS OF INFORMATION AND ENTERTAINMENT

The demand for interviews with players, coaches, and team officials each week of the National Football League season is overwhelming. As many as 20 sportswriters from 20 different area newspapers may hound team publicists for inside information and access to players. Local TV reporters want video footage as well as information and interviews.

The producers of pregame shows on network and cable TV want clips of last week's game or shots of the key plays and players. They also may want to set up cameras and conduct interviews during practice when the team is on a winning streak. In addition, they want access to teams, players, and coaches when something goes awry (i.e., when a player is suspended, a coach's job is on the line, or rumors of a move by the team to another city are in the air).

Writers for national magazines also may come calling, in the best of times and the worst of times for the team. They all want the *same* thing and a *different* thing. Each has a story, but each has different angles on what the best story of the moment is. Each is searching for an exclusive story to beat the competition.

Chapter 4 explains the complex balancing act the sports information specialist must perform. It examines the evolution of public relations and sports information departments in companies and sport organizations. It defines the responsibilities of various types of sports information specialists, their responsibilities in disseminating information and managing events, and their working relationships with members of the media.

When the Baltimore Ravens called Cleveland home (as the Cleveland Browns), they developed a system to give each reporter uninterrupted, one-on-one interviews with players. The reporter would have to contact the Browns' public relations staff a day or two in advance to request an interview with a particular player. At an agreed time, prior to practice, publicist Francine Lubera, the Ravens' assistant director of public relations, would put the reporter and the player into a small, private room with a desk and two chairs. Players were also available in the locker room briefly at a predetermined time, prior to practice, for short interviews. Some players might also grant interviews after practice, but most wanted to get home to rest following a hard workout.

Arranging interviews for a pack of competitive journalists is one of the most demanding tasks performed by sports publicists for professional teams and by sports information directors for colleges and universities. However, the hassle provides one of the best opportunities for the sports publicist or SID to subtly articulate the sport organization's philosophy and put the team and players in the most favorable light. For example, the sports publicist may suggest story ideas, chat about the team's position on an important issue, and further cultivate a positive working relationship.

The sports publicist or SID is the day-to-day voice of the organization, both in word and in action. Nurturing the image of the organization is a primary responsibility. The task may involve simply setting up interviews and pacifying reporters one day; on another, it may require withholding certain details, declining to discuss sensitive issues, or shielding players from pushy reporters. It may also demand massaging the bruised egos of competing sports journalists who get beat on a big story. The SID must try to maintain a positive relationship with all, even in times of controversy and conflict.

The daily responsibilities of the sports information specialist illustrate the dichotomy in the working relationship between the media and sport organizations in what Wenner calls the "sports production complex" in his transactional model of sport communication (1989). As Chapter 1 notes, Wenner's model suggests that both sport organizations and the media play a role in shaping the public's interpretation of a story or coverage of an event, that is, the public's perception of what it means. The sport organization tries to present the message in a way that increases the organization's exposure and enhances its image. The media try to package and present the information in a way that is appealing to both their advertisers and their audiences.

Sports information specialists, in effect, serve two masters in the process. On one hand, they provide the information the media want or need to present a story to the public. On the other hand, they decide what information to provide to best serve the interests of the organization, coaches, and players they represent. Economic factors complicate this precarious balancing act. Sport organizations depend on their information specialists to attract media coverage, in hopes the exposure will boost attendance and revenues. Broadcast media organizations make coverage decisions based largely on the size of audiences, to attract advertisers and increase revenues. The connection between a particular story or event and the audience and advertisers is not as direct in the print industry, but reader and advertiser appeals are also concerns typically expressed in news meetings at which coverage decisions are made. Therefore, the sports information specialist must convince the media a story or event holds wide audience appeal to ensure media coverage that will increase audience interest. Sports information specialists who handle the dual roles well can boost media exposure and attract more spectators, but not without considerable stress and occasional negative results.

Evolution of Sports Public Relations

The work of sports information specialists falls under the umbrella of *public relations,* a term that has come to describe the way businesses communicate their point of view to the media and to the public. The term embraces a broad range of jobs and responsibilities, from the recreation-center employee who writes press releases about league events to the public relations director of a professional team who coordinates the efforts of specialists in advertising, marketing, promotion, and publicity.

The size and mission of the organization determine the role and skills required of the public relations practitioner. In small organizations, one person may write publicity releases and deal with reporters and editors. In large organizations, the public relations director may write press releases and speeches; take pictures or supervise photographers; plan and package fliers, brochures, and newsletters; plan and manage press conferences, banquets, seminars, and other company-sponsored events; advise management on policy decisions; and devise campaigns that incorporate marketing research, advertising, publicity, and audience or client promotions. It has been estimated that the number of people working in the field in the United States ranges from 160,000 to 500,000.

Wilcox, Ault, and Agee (1992) note in *Public Relations: Strategies and Tactics* that the profession involves both management and technical skills. On one hand, public relations specialists act as advisers to company officials; on the other, they work as technicians, using oral, visual, and written-language skills. The authors define public relations as "the management of an organization's relationships with various publics (themselves discrete segments of the audience)" (p. 3). Some in the field of sports public relations define the business in more practical terms that relate to the practitioners' primary responsibility—getting the right facts to the right people at the right time and in the right way.

The lack of a precise definition arises from the disjointed evolution of the profession, which is less than a century old. Public relations grew out of the public's and the press's mistrust of big business during the Industrial Revolution. Investigative magazine reporters, called *muckrakers*, exposed abuses and corruption in the railroad, oil, meat-packing, patent medicine, and other industries. Among the more famous exposés was a 19-part series in *McClure's* magazine in 1902 that chronicled the monopoly created by the Standard Oil Company, owned by John D. Rockefeller, Jr. Big business responded by hiring journalists to deal with the press and attempt to present company efforts in a more positive light.

Two former journalists in particular, Ivy Ledbetter Lee and Edward L. Bernays, are credited with laying the foundation for the multifaceted nature of modern public relations. Lee, a former reporter for the *New York Times* and *New York Journal*, started a company to provide information about businesses to newspapers. Among his clients were the Pennsylvania Railroad, Standard Oil, the American Red Cross, and Harvard University. He urged his clients, who traditionally snubbed the media during times of conflict, to deal openly and honestly with reporters' questions. At one point, he issued a Declaration of Principles to both clients and the press on how his company would operate. He promised to give reporters complete and accurate information as quickly as possible (Hiebert, 1966, p. 48). Lee also played a key role in the transformation of the public image of John D. Rockefeller in the wake of an incident called the Ludlow Massacre at one of Rockefeller's mines in Colorado. Rockefeller was pilloried on newspaper editorial pages across the country when company guards at his mine opened fire on strikers, killing men, women, and children. Lee persuaded Rockefeller to go to Colorado and meet with the miners. Rockefeller not only spoke to the miners and their wives, but also danced with many of the women. Rockefeller later drew up a grievance process, which was ratified by the miners. Under Lee's guidance,

Rockefeller's image changed from cold-hearted businessman to caring owner and philanthropist (Vivian, 1995). Lee's honest approach—he offered to provide verification of all facts—moved the public relations profession a step away from the hype and puffery of people like P. T. Barnum and Hollywood press agents.

Bernays, a nephew of Sigmund Freud, started out as a press agent for singer Enrico Caruso. He later worked for the Creel Committee on Public Organization, which was headed by former reporter George Creel and was designed to recruit support for participation in World War I and to promote Liberty Bonds to help finance it. Bernays saw public relations as a way to influence public opinion as well as a method simply to provide information. In 1923, he wrote the first book on public relations, *Crystallizing Public Opinion*, which explained how to use press releases and other techniques to gain public support for a project. His approach led to the incorporation of opinion polls and market research in the process (Hiebert, Ungurait, & Ruben, 1993). Bernays also taught the first public relations course and, in 1952, wrote the first college textbook on the profession (*Public Relations*).

The evolution of public relations has created at least four possible models for the profession (see Hunt & Ruben, 1993, p. 343 and Hiebert et al., 1991, pp. 152–154). They range from simple publicity units to corporate management departments. Hunt and Ruben divide them according to the direction of information flow and the interaction with the public or audiences:

Publicity

The purpose is propaganda or promotion. The information flows in one direction, from the public relations practitioner to the public. Audience research is minimal, beyond counting the size of the audience. Publicity is used most often in sports, theatre, and product promotions.

Public Information

The purpose is dissemination of information. Information flows in one direction. There is little research, beyond readability or readership studies. Public information is used most often in government, nonprofit associations, and business.

Courtesy of Cleveland State University

News conferences are an important and effective way in which the sports information specialist can reach a large contingent of sport media.

Two-Way Asymmetric. The purpose is persuasion, through use of documented facts. Information is two-way, involving feedback from the public. Research on public attitudes prior to the release of information dictates the direction of the campaign. The reaction of consumer publics influences the campaign. The model is used most often in competitive businesses and agencies.

Two-Way Symmetric. The purpose is mutual understanding. Information is two-way, with balanced effects. Research measures public opinion on various ideas or options to determine the best course of action. This model is used most often by regulated businesses and agencies, including publicly funded institutions such as secondary schools and colleges.

Wilcox et al. (1992) say sports public relations comes closest to the publicity model because the emphasis is on drawing attention to stars and promoting entertainment. However, the other models also may have application in some circumstances, particularly for college sports information directors. For example, the typical sports information department produces reams of information about the school and its athletes, such as hometown releases on athletic achievements, that are not directly aimed at drawing spectators to an event. In addition, an SID may take an asymmetrical approach to winning support for an athlete for All-America or Heisman Trophy honors, or the sports information department may follow the two-way symmetric model to aid the university's deliberations on the addition of a new sport or a new season-ticket/seat-selection process. The aspiring sports information specialist must understand which approach in a given situation will best accomplish the sport organization's objectives.

Sports public relations aligns most closely to the publicity model in part because the profession grew out of teams' efforts to promote their sports and attract fans. It gained form and structure with the development of a sports division within the American College Public Relations Association in the mid-1940s. Wiles Hallock of the University of Wyoming headed the division, which was created through an alliance of college sports publicists. In 1957, the sports division broke away from the parent organization to form the College Sports Information Directors Association, or CoSIDA. The thinking of the nation's SIDs was that they had little in common with college public relations directors. The first president of the organization was C. Robert Paul, Jr., SID for the University of Pennsylvania.

CoSIDA stages a national convention every summer. Although the organization does not require members to follow a specific credo, ethical conduct is at the core of the principles the organization promotes. The essence is reflected in this simple objective: distinctive service and accomplishment on behalf of college athletics.

Roles and Responsibilities of Sports Information Specialists

A multifaceted public relations program is a necessity for any sports organization, whether amateur or professional. Effective public relations calls for efficient organization, sound planning, consistent and appropriate communication, and credible crisis management. Effective public relations for a sport organization also demands cooperation among administrators, public relations or sports information personnel, coaches, athletes, managers, and program directors. All perform public relations duties, either directly or indirectly.

Educator John Vivian (1995) identifies four steps essential to success in public relations:

1. Identifying relationships—Assessing the existing relationships with the organization's constituencies or publics. The publics for a university, for example, likely would include faculty, staff, students, alumni, financial supporters, professional academic organizations, the media, the community, and the state legislature.

2. Evaluating the relationships—Studying the relationships to see how well they are working. The relationship might be excellent with one group and poor with another. It also may change periodically. For example, the relationship with the community may be excellent when athletic teams are winning but abysmal when athletes get into trouble in the community.

3. Designing policies to improve the relationships—Recommending policies to school or company officials to improve the relationships. Policies may demand internal changes or may simply require fence-mending to soothe bruised egos or to erase misconceptions.

4. Implementing the policies—Using the tools of communication to put the policies into practice. Public relations specialists communicate to their publics personally or through the media.

These broad steps represent the philosophy of the entire sport organization, of course. The marketing department of a professional team or the development office of a university may assume primary responsibility for identifying publics and measuring the relationships. Advertising, promotion, and publicity people all may play roles in designing and implementing policies. Depending on the size of the organization, the public relations director or sports information director may oversee all four steps or simply fill the communication role in implementing the policies.

Realistically, the actions in public by any representative of an athletic department or team may influence the public impression of the institution or professional organization. That influence also may affect the relationship between various constituencies and the organization. Even part-time employees or support staff, such as parking-lot attendants, ushers, ticket takers, concessionaires, and press box/press table workers represent the organization in the overall public relations scheme. Customers who are mistreated by frontline personnel often will not return to the stadium or arena, so effective public relations involves communication not only with the media, but also with customers. A good sports information director or sport administrator will involve all members of the organization in a positive public relations strategy, from the visible to the not-so-visible personnel.

> **The Essential Steps of Public Relations**
>
> 1. Identify relationships
>
> 2. Evaluate the relationships
>
> 3. Design policies to improve the relationships
>
> 4. Implement the policies

Large organizations may divide specific public relations duties among several departments: advertising, marketing, promotion, publicity, and community relations. Smaller organizations may lump all advertising and promotional responsibilities into one division, all publicity and media/community relations into another. The smallest may assign a single person to take care of publicity and contact with the public and the media. Whatever the role, the sports information specialist must understand the organizational structure—who is responsible for each step, and the links between the steps. For example, the SID at a college must know the university's policy on release of information on athletes suspended or dismissed from the team in order to respond appropriately and effectively to inquiries from the media.

Regardless of the size of the organization, the sports information specialist is the linchpin in the organizational scheme. Good media relations can improve relationships with the community and exposure in the media, because public relations specialists and SIDs communicate the organization's message to the public through the media. Schulte and Dufresne, in *Getting the Story: An Advanced Reporting Guide to Beats, Records and Sources* (1994), cite studies that estimate 40% of all news content originates from public relations, including 75% of entertainment news. Furthermore, even a successful business is a failure in part if the public is not aware of its successes in the sports arena. Perkins (1985) says a sports information director who constructs a good public relations plan aids both the athletic department and the entire institution.

The effective program at any level is a combination of two types of public relations—direct and indirect. *Direct public relations* in sports ranges from one-on-one contact by an individual member with one of the organization's publics to organizational group work directly with another of the publics. A good illustration of individual contact is a public-speaking appearance in the community by an athlete, coach, athletics director, or general manager. A group approach might be a visit to a hospital, a collegiate conference media day, or an autograph-signing session involving several members of the organization.

Indirect public relations is simply publicity, the traditional responsibility of sports information specialists. News conferences, news releases, and photographs for print or broadcast are the most common examples. Live performances on television or radio talk shows, or an Internet chat session are a more recent spin-off of indirect public relations. Postgame interviews are direct public relations exercises with indirect results. One-on-one interviews and group question-answer sessions with large groups of reporters—"pack journalism"—result in stories delivered to the public through the print and broadcast media.

Sport organizations can control advertising and marketing promotions because they pay for them directly. They cannot control indirect public relations, which amounts to free advertising. Although they may attempt to convey the positive aspects of an athlete or event, the media package and present the information to the public; consequently, the media shape the content of the message generated by a news release, a postgame interview, or other form of indirect public relations.

Building relationships with newspaper beat reporters is a great way for a sports information specialist to penetrate the local print media in order to garner more coverage for a team or deserving athlete.

Interviews and news conferences are important to the effective implementation of the public relations policy, if the focus remains positive. Roger Valdiserri (1985), associate athletics director at the University of Notre Dame, suggests that an SID brief athletes so they understand what the media is seeking in the interview process. Administrators or athletes who are not good in interviews, for whatever reason, may inadvertently trigger a negative story, and one negative story can offset any number of positive stories.

Some public relations directors believe that anything said or written about the program or organization is good and that being ignored is the worst possible fate. Joe Jaggers, a football coach at Trigg County High School in western Kentucky, told a reporter for the *Paducah Sun* to write whatever he wanted because the public would only remember Jaggers's name six months later, not the context of the story. All may not agree with this philosophy. However, all do agree that the best of all worlds is media coverage that consistently puts the sport organization and its athletes and coaches in a positive context. A successful program, coupled with effective public relations management, usually results in an even more successful program.

Types of Jobs

The overall job responsibilities and specific duties of the sports information specialist will vary according to the size and organizational structure of the business or institution. However, the primary objective of all is the same: to publicize and gain support for the organization's athletics programs.

Wilcox et al. (1992) say that distributing news items about personalities and scheduling interviews are the major functions of sports public relations because the emphasis is on stars. Kobe Bryant draws large crowds in basketball; Barry Bonds draws large crowds in baseball. Exposure in print and broadcast media is essential to success in the highly competitive entertainment and sports fields, and exposure is built on stars and personalities, whether they be coaches or players. A personality such as men's basketball coach Bob Knight at Texas Tech University may be as much a part of the story as his team because of his antics at courtside and conflicts with reporters. A personality such as Mia Hamm in soccer may draw as much fan interest as the game itself does. Wilcox et al. (1992) note that professional and college sports must be sold like motion pictures, rock concerts, and other forms of entertainment. Consequently, sports information specialists must use the same techniques as other entertainment organizations to build crowds, maintain fan enthusiasm, and attract star athletes.

The focus of this text is on the sports information director, whose daily responsibilities typify the multifaceted nature of sports public relations. The SID at a large, Division I school coordinates efforts with several university departments and supervises the work of photographers, videographers, and writers. A good SID can attract more media attention to a college or university athletics program than perhaps any other area of the college. All institutions of higher learning pursue funds and students; the SID's primary purpose is to keep the institution's name in the public eye as part of the overall university effort to increase both funds and enrollment.

The responsibilities of SIDs at Division II or smaller institutions are no less important than those of their counterparts at Division I schools. The workload for the SID at a smaller school may be greater because of the need to work on several sports or projects simultaneously. The SIDs at small schools must work harder to "sell" their ideas to the media, whereas the media often initiate the contact at larger schools. The Lexington *Herald-Leader* and the Louisville *Courier-Journal* both assign beat reporters to the University of Kentucky. Reporters spend most of their time looking for and working on story angles. Each paper also assigns a single reporter to keep up with several junior colleges and community colleges in their respective area. Consequently, the SID at a community college might have to lobby hard for mention of a noteworthy achievement such as a cross country runner's high finish in a national event, particularly if the reporter is immersed with a noteworthy story at another college.

SIDs at Division II and III schools are not often blessed with a large staff of specialists. They make daily lists of assignments to complete and go about them in order of priority. They utilize volunteer student help and student interns to the fullest, which benefits both the students and the university. Not only do the students learn about the profession and gain valuable hands-on experience, but they also help the SID survive, and they contribute to the success of the sports program.

In professional sport organizations, the SID's responsibilities are assumed by a public relations director. Duties are much the same as those for college athletics, except that energy is spent on just one sport rather than on all the sports of a college athletic department. During the season, the PR director will work practically around-the-clock to complete the required tasks. In the off-season, there is time for renewal and planning for the next season.

At the secondary school level, the athletics director normally assumes responsibility for sports information. The job is more simplified at this level, but no less important. The same is true for the recreation center director, who must handle most of the public relations chores.

Regardless of the size of the organization or the type of job responsibilities, the sports information practitioner must possess strong writing skills. The news release is the basic informational tool in any public relations job, the link to publicity in both print and broadcast media as well as the lure for media coverage and spectator

---

Here is a list of characteristics essential to success in sports public relations:

1. *Strong writing skills.* News releases, brochures, broadcast announcements, newsletters, press kits, and advertising copy constitute the core of the sports information specialist's writing duties.

2. *Strong visual skills.* At the very least, the aspiring sports information practitioner should possess basic design and artistic composition skills. At best, the public relations professional will acquire photography, video editing, and other multimedia presentation training, including knowledge about website design and maintenance.

3. *Strong speaking skills.* The sports information specialist needs good public speaking skills, as well as the ability to sell an idea to management or the media.

4. *Effective problem-solving skills.* Policy development and event planning are key responsibilities for public relations directors in multifaceted operations. Problem-solving expertise is also valuable in crisis management.

5. *An understanding of economics.* Because of the financial partnership between media and sport organizations, a grounding in economics is a must. The sports information specialist at the highest levels also must understand budgeting, financial management, marketing, and advertising.

6. *A good sense of humor.* The job can become a bit tense when competition among media heats up or conflict management reaches crisis proportions.

7. *Strong interpersonal skills.* The aspiring sports information specialist cannot succeed without the ability to work effectively with administrators, the community, and the media, in good times and in bad.

interest in an event. Chamberlin (1990) points out that the effective SID is a good writer with sound computer and organizational skills. Davis (1978) puts the word *service* at the top of the list of characteristics that define a good SID (p. 9). His message is to be ready to serve the media on all occasions.

Functions of the SID

The typical sports information director performs both technical and management functions at a college or university. On the technical side, the SID writes news releases and features, prepares brochures and other literature, and coordinates press operations at events. On the management side, the SID takes part in planning and executing the budget, organizing events, and supervising personnel.

The sports information director's primary duties fall into three major categories: dissemination of information, entertainment management, and fiscal management.

Dissemination of information. The SID is primarily responsible for publicizing athletics, maintaining records and statistics, and acting as liaison with area media and other sports information directors. The SID's responsibilities in this regard entail writing, public speaking, and coordinating indirect public relations activities such as overseeing the press box and postgame interview room.

The effective sports information director arranges interviews with players and daily press contacts with the head coaches in a timely and organized manner. The SID should be aware that star athletes who are articulate will demand almost daily media attention. If possible, interviews should be scheduled for coaches' and players' off-hours, such as during lunch breaks or after practices.

Emerging telephone and computer technology in recent years has made it possible for SIDs at major universities to set up sessions with the coach, who will discuss the most recent game and the next one on the schedule. Members of the media can call a "Hotline" number in order to obtain comments and the coach's perspective on the game, either live or on tape. Often these teleconference sessions are archived and made accessible on a school's website.

Because of the profit-driven nature of sport organizations and the media, obtaining publicity for high-profile sports such as football and basketball is relatively easy. Less visible sports demand more work by the SID, often for only minimal results from a public relations perspective.

However, the job demands that the sports information specialist push to "sell" the media on low-profile stories. The SID should report scores, updated standings, and schedules of low-profile sports as regularly and as vigorously as he or she reports those of high-profile sports. The SID should also look for interesting feature stories from the low-profile sports and share them with

> **The Responsibilities of an SID**
>
> - Writing: news releases; features; statistics; radio and TV copy; media guidebooks; game programs; newsletters; promotional materials for individual sports; photography and graphic design; audiovisual and video scripts; and correspondence with the media, the community, and colleagues.
>
> - Production: guidebook and program design and editing, slide/tape and audiovisual production, video and film production, and publications management.
>
> - Public speaking: writing speeches, making speeches, and arranging appearances by coaches and athletes.
>
> - Managing events: press conferences, media days, and other functions aimed at increasing media exposure.
>
> - Media relations: handling inquiries and requests from the media, dealing with negative publicity, and acting as point person in crisis management.

the media. There might be an audience for a story on a 35-year-old cross country runner, a wrestler with one eye, a baseball player with an interesting hobby, a fast-pitch softball player who hurls a no-hitter, or a volleyball player who is invited to the U.S. Olympic Festival.

Although the SID can suggest stories and arrange interviews, no one in the sport organization can control the focus of the story, of course. The best the SID can hope to accomplish is to guide the media toward more positive stories.

Entertainment management. The sports information director is a key figure when an institution is planning an event, whether the activity is a game, fundraiser, or publicity campaign to promote an athlete for league, conference, or national honors. The SID's entertainment-management responsibilities combine technical and management functions. Both come into play in organizing media coverage of games and staging special events such as awards banquets, hall-of-fame recognition, and special public relations campaigns.

The SID is in charge of the press box for football and baseball games, and the press table for basketball, swimming, volleyball, wrestling, hockey, and other sports. He or she is responsible for providing information to the attending media. The pregame list includes information on the event and participants, past records, injuries, notes about the team or school, depth charts, and programs. During the game, the SID must supply statistics at the end of each period or half, a running play-by-play, and other information specific to the sport, such as drive charts on scoring drives for football. At the conclusion of the game, the SID should distribute to the media a full set of statistics, play-by-play, and a box score of the game. In addition, any records or milestones that were achieved during the contest should also be included in the packet. The publicist also may include direct quotations from coaches and key players, gathered by sports information personnel. Many staple all the postgame information together into a packet for each reporter, to aid in composition of the story.

> **The Primary Entertainment Responsibilities of an SID**
>
> - Game management: press-box and press-table organization, mechanical and technical arrangements, postgame group-interview sessions.
>
> - Special events: open houses, awards banquets, fundraising events, conference meetings, and postseason-tournament hosting.
>
> - Publicity campaigns: the making of an All-American or conference player of the year.

The SID is effectively the quarterback in any campaign to promote an athlete for postseason honors such as college football's Heisman Trophy. The campaign starts with the approval and commitment of the head coach and the player. The SID oversees production of a good photograph for 35mm slides, black-and-white action shots and head shots, shots of game action, and a professional portrait. Next comes a compilation of the player's statistics and an in-depth interview with the player. The SID writes a feature on the player for distribution to the media.

During the season, the sports information department provides weekly updates to the media on the player's accomplishments and includes mention of the athlete in every news release about the team. The SID also encourages the print and broadcast media to do stories, and arranges interviews as needed. Sports information personnel may put together a flyer promoting the athlete's candidacy (if the budget allows) and send it to national media, especially media representatives who vote in the Associated Press and coaches college polls each week.

Fiscal management. Sports information directors often play a role in the creation and implementation of the university public relations or athletic budget. The university's public relations office, public information division, or athletic department normally controls the SID's operating budget.

At the collegiate level, an athletics department budget includes operating expenses, salaries of the coaching staff, grants and scholarships for athletes, and recruiting expenses for each sport. Depending on whether a school is at the Division I, II, or III level, the differences in athletics budgets can be staggering. For example, in an academic year, the Division I average for operating expenses is almost four times that of Division II schools.

Institutions generate revenues through a variety of sources: gate receipts, student activity fees, guarantees and options, contributions, distribution of funds from athletic conferences, concessions, and state and federal government support. Even with these sources of revenue, by and large, athletic departments are faced with supporting a majority of nonrevenue or low-profile sports. In fact, generally the only two sports that generate a profit are football and men's basketball. If an institution or conference can attract a sizeable fee for broadcast rights to a high-profile sport like basketball or football, the revenue might be used to fund low-profile sports.

Arranging corporate sponsorship of events and radio and television contracts for games often is not a direct responsibility of the SID, but the sports publicist usually is involved in the process. The SID often is the point person when a college or university arranges for corporate sponsorship of an event such as a holiday basketball tournament. The athletic director typically will negotiate the contract with corporate sponsors. Any information for the media about the deal goes through the sports information director's office.

Tips for Aspiring Sports Information Specialists

1. Learn the philosophy of the athletics program, its missions, its goals, its structure, its personnel and its athletes—past and present.

2. Know as much as possible about the coaches and the athletes; keep a biographical file, statistics, and pictorial data on each. Also, maintain alumni files if space allows.

3. Learn the local media, their missions, their target audiences, their structure, and their personnel.

4. Know your business. The SID must understand what is going on in the athletic world, the entertainment world, and the media in order to guide journalists to write and tell upbeat, positive stories.

5. Define your public relations target market. Know who should receive information about the athletics program to ensure maximum success.

6. Learn the production and printing deadlines of local media, and time announcements to attain maximum benefit. Obviously, broadcast media can "break" a story almost immediately. Not so with the print media, which have strict copy and publication deadlines.

7. Encourage coaches and athletes to grant interviews, to return media telephone requests, and to take an active part in the publicity thrust. Guide those who are ill-prepared or inexperienced so they will present a positive image and reflect the appropriate view of the university.

8. Identify and suggest good feature stories and personality profiles to the media, whether the stories concern a volleyball player, a cross country runner, or the star quarterback.

9. Know what types of information and messages are likely to generate the most media interest. Also, recognize the potential results from an organized public relations program focused on athletics.

10. Exhibit courage in crisis situations. Be tactful and informative in times of coaching changes, protests, boycotts, drug problems, or any other potentially awkward situations.

11. Remember that credibility, integrity, versatility, and service are the characteristics that define successful sports information directors. An outgoing personality is an asset to an SID, but never can substitute for in-depth knowledge of the school's program and consistent and quality information about the program.

JOHN CARROLL UNIVERSITY DEPARTMENT OF ATHLETICS

INFORMATION AS OF FEBRUARY 6, 2007

STAFF BREAKDOWN

22—Full Time

34—Part Time

9—Graduate Assistants

Full-Time Head Coaches and Staff

A. **21 Varsity Sports**
Football
Volleyball
Men's and Women's Cross Country
Men's and Women's Golf
Men's and Women's Soccer
Wrestling
Men's and Women's Basketball
Men's and Women's Indoor Track and Field
Men's and Women's Swimming and Diving
Baseball
Softball
Men's and Women's Outdoor Track and Field
Men's and Women's Tennis

B. **12 Head Coaches**

Tracy Blasius	Cally Plummer
Matt Lenhart	Regis Scafe
Kristie Maravalli	Marc Thibeault
Hector Marinaro	Dr. Bruce Thomas
Mark McClure	Kerry Volkmann
Mike Moran	Gretchen Weitbrecht

C. **6 Administrative Staff**
Ray Bolger
Dwight Hollins
Sandra Howard
Laurie Massa
Jim Pancher
Chris Wenzler

D. **2 Trainers**
Don McPhillips
Julie Prusock

E. **2 Secretaries**
Nancy Coyne
Bea Stofcho

The sports information director often is expected to raise money to offset some costs within the department. Selling advertising for both football and basketball programs and guides generates revenue to print the materials. In fact, successful advertising sales not only can pay the cost of the guides and programs, but also can contribute to the total assets of the budget. On some occasions, the SID can conserve limited budget resources by using in-house printing services, such as desktop publishing programs for newsletters. Utilizing student help and interns is also, of course, a money-saving opportunity for the SID.

Working Relationships with Media

The effective sports information director cultivates an open and honest relationship with members of the press and the community. The relationship is based on trust and mutual respect. The SID understands the push for details on a big story among competitive media and forgives the overzealous reporter who becomes a bit too pushy on occasion. The journalist recognizes the administrative constraints on the SID and accepts limitations placed on release of information, albeit grudgingly.

Both understand the give-and-take nature of the business. The SID provides a little more information on one story and expects the journalist to follow up on a lukewarm story idea in return at some point. As payback for the same deal, the reporter, on the other hand, expects the SID to deliver a useful nugget of information (at the very least) for a major breaking story under deadline and competitive pressures.

Federal and state laws called *Sunshine Laws* require publicly funded institutions to open certain records and meetings to the press and public (see Chapter 13). The laws aim at making the public's business open to public inspection, so police reports, athletics budgets, graduation rates, and other such records are open to the public. However, the law makes exceptions for meetings that deal with sensitive personnel or privacy issues. The arrest report for an athlete would be open to the public. Disciplinary action taken by the coach or university would not, unless the university chose to disclose the information. A federal law called the *Family Education Rights and Privacy Act* requires consent of the student for release of any information except "directory information." Directory information includes the student's name, address, telephone number, date and place of birth, major field of study, activities, dates of attendance, awards received, and the most recent year attended. That means sports information officials can release overall graduation rates and grade point averages, but not individual grades or averages.

In their text on advanced reporting procedures, Schulte and Dufresne say the most successful public relations specialists are "available, knowledgeable and credible" (1994, p. 420). That means they respond promptly to media inquiries and requests. They know the media people who regularly cover their teams, the stories that appeal to them, their space limitations, and especially their deadlines. Successful PR people handle conflict and crises coolly and professionally.

Conflicts with reporters over story content are inevitable. So are public relations crises, such as alleged drug abuse, recruitment violations, and cheating and other academic problems. The way the SID handles these matters is all-important to the institution and to the public relations specialist's credibility. The media are always interested in negative news. Remember, conflict is one of the criteria that elevate the news value of a story.

Most public relations experts recommend dealing with major and minor crises honestly and forthrightly. They suggest announcing information regarding injuries, players dropped from a squad, or other negative issues to all the media as soon as possible. An SID should try to prevent the media from discovering negative news on its own or giving the appearance that the university is trying to hide stories. Developing credibility with all the competing media earns respect and encourages cooperation in difficult times.

An effective working relationship is not built on gifts and favors. Sportswriters generally will not respond favorably to attempts to wine and dine them or shower them with gifts. In fact, the ethics codes recommended by professional journalism organizations and adopted by most media prohibit or limit acceptance of anything of value from a source. The sports information specialist can boost credibility far more easily by showering journalists with information—by distributing facts and features, and plenty of them.

Sports information directors who deal honestly and ethically with the media usually receive the same treatment in return. The SID should never deliberately dodge the difficult request or question, but should instead learn how to handle it. Even if the SID must say, "No comment" sometimes instead of providing information, journalists usually will honor the statement.

Journalists expect sports information specialists to spice up news releases with adjectives and to accentuate the positive concerning athletes and the program or special events. They understand that the job of the SID is promotion, competing for a share of the entertainment spotlight and audience. However, the SID must recognize those times when straightforward facts better serve the media. For example, hype and statements of false hope are inappropriate when an upcoming opponent is far superior. A wiser strategy is simply to present the records and strengths/weaknesses of both teams, filtering in as much positive information as possible about the underdog. Do not neglect the prowess of the opponent, either.

Sports information directors and sports publicists should also avoid overpromoting an athlete. If the player does not live up to the advance hype, the SID's credibility and the school's or team's image may suffer. For example, the Cleveland Cavaliers won only 15 games when they joined the NBA in 1970–1971. The team's publicist actually promoted the strength of opponents and provided only the basic statistics and accomplishments of the Cavs.

Journalists do not expect sports information specialists to penalize them or to "cry the blues" to a sportswriter who authors a negative but truthful story. The late Joe Tom Irwin, longtime SID at Murray State University in Kentucky, did not complain when a columnist critical of the university's handling of the resignation of the head football coach revealed that Irwin took back a news release containing the president's reaction. The president had called to ask Irwin not to release the statement until after the press conference announcing the resignation. The sports information specialist should remember, too, that editorials are just opinions, nothing more.

Although the publicity model of public relations does not demand complete truth, most modern sport organizations adhere to the basic precepts espoused by Lee in his declaration of principles. The Public Relations Society of America adopted standards that call for dealing fairly with clients, employees, and the public; adhering to truth, accuracy, and standards of good taste; and not intentionally communicating false or misleading information. (See page 77 for the ethical code of the College Sports Information Directors of America, or CoSIDA.)

Summary

The public relations director or sports information director is a professional whose primary responsibility is to create a favorable public image of the company or sport organization. For the sports information specialist, the job entails promoting individual stars and specific events in an attempt to boost spectator interest and grab a share of the entertainment dollar. It also involves disseminating information that attracts media coverage and reaches the public via the media.

Because they operate in the center of Wenner's (1989) sports production complex, directly between organizations and the media, sports information specialists serve two masters: the institution and the media. They translate the institution's philosophy and character into story ideas and images that cast the institution in a positive light. They dictate how much information the media receive and for what purpose. They initiate more than half of the news that appears in the print and broadcast media.

However, they also provide information requested by the media and arrange interviews, press conferences, and media kits. The media package the information or translate it for the public, according to their own mission and objectives. Therefore, the sports information specialist exercises limited control over the content of the message the media deliver to their audiences.

Historically, public relations evolved from a business of gimmickry and hype to a multifaceted profession that attempts to serve the best interests of the company and the consumer. Two former journalists played pivotal roles in the evolution. Ivy Ledbetter Lee initiated a shift from hype to accuracy, from gimmickry to honesty. Edward L. Bernays added a scientific research component to the process that led to a two-way information flow, incorporating consumer attitudes and feedback on public-relations decisions. The work of Lee, Bernays, and their followers led to the development of four models of public relations. Sports public relations aligns most closely with a model that emphasizes publicity.

However, the field of public relations is most diverse. Public relations positions range from the recreation director or high school athletics director who provides scores and arranges interviews for the media to public relations departments that oversee a company's advertising, marketing, promotions, publicity, and media relations. The sports information director at a large university typically is involved

CoSIDA Code of Ethics

ETHICS (eth'iks) noun, plural. 1. (construed as singular or plural) A system of moral principles: the ethics of a culture. 2. The rules of conduct recognized in respect to a particular class of human actions or a particular group, culture, etc.; Medical ethics; Christian ethics. 3. Moral principles, as of an individual; his ethics forbade betrayal of a confidence. 4. (usually construed as singular). That branch of philosophy dealing with values relating to human conduct with respect to the rightness and wrongness of certain actions and to the goodness and badness of the motives and ends of such actions.

Random House Dictionary of English Language

FOREWORD

In order for members of College Sports Information Directors of America to enjoy professional status, it is imperative that a viable Code of Ethics be observed. This Code of Ethics must embrace and reflect the high ideals and moral fiber of the educational institution which the Sports Information Director serves.

It is essential that the Sports Information Director conduct and discharge his/her duties and responsibilities with dedication, integrity, sincerity, and respect of his/her constituency (peers) as a representative of an academic institution.

Members who do not wish to meet these basic responsibilities have no place in CoSIDA and such detractors should be referred to the Committee on Ethics for appropriate disciplinary action.

Membership in CoSIDA is a privilege, not a right.

COLLEGE SPORTS INFORMATION DIRECTORS OF AMERICA CODE OF ETHICS

In order for the Sports Information Director to serve his/her institution and the College Sports Information Directors of America most effectively, he/she should observe these basic tenets:

Always be mindful of the fact that he/she represents an institution of higher learning and that exemplary conduct is of paramount importance.

Intercollegiate athletics is an integral part of the total university program, not the denominating force. Promote them accordingly and not at the expense of other areas.

Policies of the institution, its governing board, administration, and athletic hierarchy must be acknowledged and supported whether or not the Sports Information Director agrees with them.

A challenge of controversial policies should be resolved within the appeals framework of the institution. No public forum should be encouraged or developed. Internal problems, such as disagreement over policy, should not be "leaked" or in any other way be exploited.

Loyalty to the athletic administrator, his/her aides, and the coaching staff is imperative. No confidence should ever be violated, regardless of how apparent or insignificant it might appear. Above all, avoid criticism of staff members. Administrators and coaches should be encouraged to answer questions from the media honestly and accurately. In the event they choose to avoid a sensitive question or area for any reason, it is incumbent upon the Sports Information Director to honor the "no comment" by refraining from any subsequent "briefing" session with the media, particularly in an informal atmosphere where misuse of the information could be most damaging to all concerned.

Respect for athletes and their values should be encouraged. The confidence of an athlete must not be violated, particularly as it pertains to information regarding academic, disciplinary, and health information. To release this type of information without the athlete's permission is a violation of the Family Privacy Act of 1974. Also it is highly unethical to falsify weights, heights, and other personal data.

Relations with the media must be established and maintained at a high professional level. Fairness in the distribution of information is paramount, regardless of the size or importance of the publications or station. Student media must be accorded the same privileges and rights of the commercial of non-campus media.

Operation of all facilities in which members of the media may be in attendance should be professional in all aspects. Cheerleading in the press box, for example, is gross and undesirable. Other distractions, such as extraneous describe and unrelated announcements should be discouraged.

Criticism of officials is totally unethical, either before, during, or after a contest.

It is essential that the Sports Information Director be cognizant and observant of all institutional, conference, and national governing body regulations as they pertain to his/her functions within the framework of his/her institution.

It is incumbent upon a Sports Information Director to take immediate and appropriate action when he/she has knowledge of a fellow/sister Information Director who has violated the CoSIDA Code of Ethics, institutional, conference, or national regulations.

Association with professional gamblers should be discouraged.

Endorsement of Products or commodities which reflect a conflict with regular duties is not in the best interests of the institution or the profession.

Lack of cooperation by members of CoSIDA in not responding promptly and accurately to requests is deemed irresponsible, hence unethical.

in publicity, event planning, and financial management. The SID at a smaller institution may handle multiple chores with the help of student volunteers and interns. Regardless of the size of the institution, an effective public relations strategy requires identification of the institution's audiences or publics, assessment of the relationship with each group, development of a policy to improve the relationships, and implementation of that policy. Implementing the strategy is the primary responsibility of the sports information department.

Sports public relations requires strong writing, speaking, and visual skills; effective interpersonal skills; good organizational and problem-solving skills; an even temperament; and a good sense of humor. The profession is very demanding, because the SID must perform a wide range of management and technical duties. The public relations director for a professional sports organization performs many of the same duties but focuses energy on a single sport and team. In high schools and amateur organizations, an athletics director or publicity person generally limits his or her activities to media contacts and publicity.

The most successful sports information specialists are available, knowledgeable, and credible. They respond to media requests quickly. They are knowledgeable about their own organizations, the local media, and the business of public relations. They deal honestly with the media without ducking difficult or sensitive issues. Most adhere to standards of ethical behavior prescribed by professional organizations.

DISCUSSION QUESTIONS

1. What time of day is best to hold a news conference to make a blockbuster announcement, and why?
2. How does a sports information specialist handle the announcement of a negative situation? How does he or she put a positive spin on the situation?

SUGGESTED EXERCISES

1. Establish a promotional program for a major event to be held at your institution.
2. Formulate a one-month work schedule of a sports information director during a typical school year.

Chapter Five

NEWS RELEASES: THE SPORTS JOURNALIST'S LIFELINE

When Cleveland State University announced its new basketball coach in April 1996, the sports information department launched a "fast break" to get the most mileage out of the university's high-profile choice.

Cleveland State hired Rollie Massimino. Massimino had been a college basketball icon since directing an underdog Villanova University team to an upset victory over Georgetown University in the 1985 NCAA Division I championship game. Winning more than 60% of his games, Massimino led Villanova to 15 postseason tournament appearances in 19 years. He left Villanova for the University of Nevada-Las Vegas in 1992, only to be dumped after two years of less-than-spectacular results with the Running Rebels.

Still, Massimino was a catch for Cleveland State, which had competed mostly in the shadows of Division I elite like Villanova and had a hint of scandal hanging over its program. Cleveland State wanted to spread its good news—big news for the university—far and wide.

Chapter 5 examines various types of news releases and their functions. It offers guidelines for writing releases and distributing them to the media. Finally, the chapter looks at common errors that propel releases into the trash instead of into the sports section or the TV script.

The sports information department prepared a nine-page news packet for distribution to the media following the introduction of Massimino at a news conference. The packet included a news release announcing the selection of Massimino, a year-by-year summary of his coaching career, and a sheaf of fact sheets: NBA Players Coached by Massimino, Rollie's Record Year-By-Year, Massimino in Postseason Play, Massimino Home & Away Year-By-Year, and Massimino vs. All-Opponents.

The weight of the information purposely sent a message that Cleveland State had made a big, positive move. The materials mentioned neither Massimino's troubles at Villanova nor the problems that led to the resignation of Cleveland State's previous coach. The focus remained on Massimino's reputation and successes. The packet provided a wealth of details that testified to that success, to make it possible for the media to develop a story on deadline to match the magnitude of the announcement.

Seven years later, in April 2003, Massimino, who had compiled a 90-113 record as the head coach at Cleveland State, was relieved of his duties. It was big news in

CSU _Cleveland State University_

SPORTS INFORMATION

2000 Prospect Avenue • CSU Convocation Center • Cleveland, OH 44115

FOR IMMEDIATE RELEASE
Tuesday, April 30, 1996 • 2:00 p.m.

CONTACT: Rick Love /
Assistant Athletic Director

ROLLIE MASSIMINO NAMED HEAD BASKETBALL COACH AT CLEVELAND STATE UNIVERSITY

CLEVELAND, OH -- Cleveland State University today ended a month long search for a new head men's basketball coach, filling the position with veteran coach, Roland V. Massimino. The announcement was made as Massimino was introduced at a press conference at CSU's Convocation Center.

"It is my distinct pleasure to announce the hiring of Rollie Massimino as the new head coach at Cleveland State University," stated Dr. Claire Van Ummerson, President at Cleveland State. "Coach Massimino brings a wealth of experience, success, and dedication to the student-athlete and the game of basketball. He will be a fine representative of this University on and off the court of play. Both his coaching record and academic record are impeccable over his 23 year coaching career."

Massimino, who guided the Villanova Wildcats to the 1985 NCAA National Championship with a 66-64 win over the Georgetown Hoyas, comes to CSU with 23 years of experience as a college head coach and 21 at the division I level. His 23-year head coaching record is 427-278 (.606). That includes 11 NCAA I Tournament appearances in which he posted a 20-10 mark. Massimino most recently coached at UNLV where he posted a 21-8 mark in '92–93 and a 15-13 mark in '93–94. He has spent the past two years as a radio and television commentator for the Prime Sports Network on college basketball games.

"Coach Massimino is the man to lead the Vikings to a successful future in the Midwestern Collegiate Conference," said Monte Ahuja, Chairman of Cleveland State's Board of Trustees. "He will represent the University in a first-class manner in the Cleveland community. This is a great opportunity for Cleveland State."

Massimino's four-year contract makes him the 12th men's basketball coach in the school's 65-year history of the sport, dating back to Homer E. Woodling who started the program in 1929–30 at Fenn College, predecessor to Cleveland State. "The search committee did a tremendous job of working with a field of outstanding candidates," stated John Konstantinos, Cleveland State's Director of Athletics. "Rollie is a proven winner, a players coach and will become a favorite at the Convocation Center this season."

When Rollie Massimino was hired by Cleveland State, the focus of the news release was on his previous success.

1996 when Massimino was hired with the intent of lifting the fortunes of the Cleveland State basketball program. It didn't work out as planned, and several days after he was "unofficially" fired at CSU, a lesser-known coach named Mike Garland, who was an assistant to Tom Izzo at Michigan State University, was at a press conference announcing his hiring as the seventh head coach at Cleveland State.

Despite hiring a coach not as well known as Massimino, the sports information department still was once again very dutiful in establishing a news conference to introduce Garland to the local media. And as was the case when Massimino was hired, the sports information department also put together a packet for the media detailing Garland's entire coaching history and quotes from the newly hired coach. The information provided in the packet and by Garland at the press conference was enough for the print media to write comprehensive stories on his hire, and gave television and radio stations an opportunity to enhance their coverage of the event.

The packet is a small example of the symbiotic journalistic relationship between sports information specialists and the media. The public relations or sports information director uses the media to reach the public with news about the company or the university. Information supplied by SIDs provides sports journalists with story tips, statistics, background, quotations from players and coaches, photographs, and even prepackaged stories. All may help journalists do their job more quickly and completely.

A steady stream of news releases from sports information directors keeps a professional or college sport organization in the public consciousness. Of course, no sports journalists worth their laptops or microphones would miss the announcement of a new basketball coach, but even the best of journalists at the largest news organizations find it virtually impossible to keep up with all the local athletes who go outside the region to play collegiate and professional sports. In addition, even the best of sports departments cannot stay on top of every local team and athlete at all times. A newspaper or television station's sports coverage is only as good as its poorest beat reporter. Consequently, journalists depend on contacts in the community and sports organizations to inform them of newsworthy items, remind them of upcoming events, and suggest story ideas. Most content analyses indicate that half of the stories in daily newspapers, and even more in smaller papers, contain information from news releases.

The sports organizations and teams that receive the most consistent coverage are the ones that develop an effective working relationship with the local media, the ones that do not sit back and wait for the media to come to them. The organizations that receive the most consistent coverage also are the ones that consistently supply the media with useful information and story ideas about teams and athletes.

The oldest and most common tool utilized by sports information specialists to communicate information to the media is the news release. Consequently, the sports information specialist must be proficient at writing and must learn how to write for the media, that is, the SID must learn how to write a story that mimics the structure and satisfies the news requirements of sports journalism.

Purpose and Function of News Releases

Writing is much like athletics. Some individuals possess innate qualities that facilitate development of the skills required—a creative imagination for writers, for example—but it takes a lot of practice to excel at a craft or a sport. Any good writer will tell you that the secret to success is practice, practice, practice.

An aspiring SID does not have to be "a born writer" with the skills and stature of a Dave Anderson, the Pulitzer Prize-winning sportswriter for the *New York Times.* However, anyone in the business of sports information must learn the fundamentals of good writing and practice them diligently to develop proficiency in the craft. A professional cannot succeed without a thorough understanding of the parts of speech, sentence structure, grammar, spelling, punctuation, and theme development. A knowledge of writing techniques—use of description, direct quotations, analogies, similes, and metaphors—is also helpful.

Although creativity is an asset, writing for the media is more like theme or report writing than creative writing. James Stovall (1994), author of *Writing for the Mass Media,* draws these distinctions between writing for the media and other forms of writing:

Subject matter. Writers for the mass media must take on a wide variety of subjects, including news stories, feature stories, advertisements, letters, editorials, and so on.

Purpose. Writing for the mass media has three major purposes: to inform, entertain, and persuade.

Audience. Mass media writing is often directed to a wide audience, and this fact dictates not only the subject matter but also the way in which something is written.

Circumstances of the writing. Writing for the mass media often takes place in the presence of others who are doing the same thing. The writing is frequently done under deadline pressure, and often several people will have a hand in writing and editing a particular item for the mass media. (p. 8)

A news release is very similar to a news story written by the print or broadcast media. Both may emphasize the *hard news* angle of a story, such as the announcement of the selection of a new coach, a scholarship recipient, or a new facility. Both also may take a *soft news* approach, as in a personality profile of the new coach. In simplest terms, hard news generally centers on issues, events, actions, and their consequences. Soft news usually revolves around people such as athletes and their connection to the event or issue.

The purpose of a news story is significantly different from that of a news release, however. The primary objective of a news story is to inform (i.e., to present information in a fair, objective manner). A secondary function (though no less important) is to entertain, so the sports journalist works hard to inform and entertain an audience. The primary intent of a news release is to persuade (i.e., to present the organization's message or image in the most favorable light). Secondary functions may be to inform, to entertain, and in some cases, to educate. So the SID strives to use information to persuade, to enhance indirectly the image of the college or university in the public eye, rather than simply to inform for information's sake.

In *Becoming a Public Relations Writer,* Ronald D. Smith (1996) says all public relations writing seeks to influence a reader in some way:

> As a writer, you have a particular effect in mind when you write. (If you don't intend to have an effect with your writing, you're wasting your time because you won't produce anything useful.) You present many messages on behalf of your organization, client or cause. Every time you do so, you are trying to add information to what the public knows. Usually you provide this information to affect how the public feels or the way it acts. (p. 7)

Sports information specialists usually structure news releases like news stories, with some modifications, to enhance their publication or broadcast prospects. Hard news stories generally follow a simple but rigid *straight news* format designed to deliver key information quickly, whereas soft news stories may take a variety of creative or *feature* approaches that emphasize the people in the story as much as the information.

The most common structure for hard news is called the *inverted pyramid* because it places the most important information at the top and the least important at the bottom. The lead of the story quickly summarizes the basic news elements: *who, what, when, where, why,* and *how* (known as the *5Ws and H* in journalistic jargon). It emphasizes the most important element of the news and presents the details of the six elements in descending order of importance. The story does not have a conclusion, but ends with the least important detail:

Most Important Information or Element

Quick Summary of 5Ws and H

Most Important Details

Less Important

Least Important

No Conclusion

The information or "news" drives the story in the inverted pyramid. The structure is effective for two reasons. First, it quickly delivers the information readers are most likely to want. Even those who do not read more than a couple of paragraphs will obtain a quick summary of the facts, with emphasis on the most important details. Second, the story is very easy to trim if it is too long to fit the space allotted on a newspaper page or the time allotted on a newscast. The journalist sacrifices only the least important—and least read—details.

- -

HIRAM, OHIO, March 15, 1996 (WHEN) — Andover resident Bill Bates (WHO) earned the first victory (WHAT) of his career for Hiram College in the Terriers 11-5 victory (WHY) versus Rockford College in Fort Meyers, Florida. (WHERE)

Bates, a junior majoring in business management, allowed three runs (HOW) in six innings of work. Bates' victory is the first for Hiram this season.

"Bill has shown steady improvement in his career at Hiram and his performance today shows that he can win at this level," Hiram head coach Howard Jenter said. "Bill worked out of some tough situations and got outs when he needed them."

Hiram also defeated the University of Wisconsin-Stout 6-5 yesterday to raise their record to two wins and three losses. Hiram will play three more games in Fort Myers before returning to Ohio to begin its Ohio Athletic Conference schedule.

- 30 -

- -

The inverted pyramid approach is most appropriate for stories such as announcements, meetings, and breaking news because the reader does not already know most of the basic information. Sports information directors most often use the inverted pyramid approach for game advances, news releases, and announcements. Sports information personnel also use the inverted pyramid leads on stories they submit to the news media immediately following a game.

Journalists use a number of variations on or alternative to the inverted pyramid for soft news stories in which the basic information will not "hook" the reader. For example, the reader already may know the basic details—the 5Ws and H—of last week's football game, so the journalist looks for an entertaining angle to encourage people to read further in the story. The journalist often starts with a literary device that emphasizes the drama, the suspense, the irony, or some unusual or intriguing facet of the topic. The story may open with a narrative lead, a re-creation of

---

• NEWS TERMS •

advance—a story written before an event, such as a preview

alternative structure—any one of several literary formats, including a circle and an hourglass, utilized to organize information in a story

5Ws and H—the six questions (who, what, when, where, why, and how) that all news stories must answer

feature release—a news release that spotlights, or "features," a particular athlete

follow—a story written after an event, such as coverage of a game or an update to an earlier story

game advance—a news release that offers a preview of an upcoming game

header—information at the top of a news release that provides contact information and suggested release time for the story

hometown release—a news release about an athlete that is sent to media in the geographical area in which the athlete lives

inverted pyramid—a story format in which the writer organizes information in descending order of importance

lead—the first sentence or paragraph of a news story

news peg—a phrase or sentence that connects the story to the most important news element or news event

tieback—a phrase or sentence that explains how a story relates to an earlier news event

weekly preview/review—a weekly schedule of all the organization's athletic teams

a key play, an anecdote, a quotation, an ironic twist, a question, or some other common literary technique that engages readers.

The rest of the story also may take a variety of forms, depending on the technique utilized in the beginning. A story that opens with a scene-setter might relate the rest of the action in chronological order. A story that begins with a re-creation of the turning point in a game might move from one key play to another. A story that features the star player might move from one key play by the star to another. Such stories generally require more description and detail than do stories that follow the inverted pyramid format. They also require greater creative writing skill.

No matter what technique the writer uses, stories that follow the alternative structure *do* have several common organizational elements. They use a literary device to establish a theme or focal point, then follow with a *news peg* or *tieback*. A news peg connects the story to the most important news element like the first sentence of a story written in the inverted pyramid style. It also may summarize the 5Ws and H to remind the reader of the basic news details. A *tieback* explains how the story relates to a previous news event (i.e., it ties the opening back to the original news announcement or news event). The body of the story adds details in a logical order and wraps up the story with a conclusion that reinforces the theme. The alternative styles may take more of a circle approach in that they "come full circle," or conclude with the emphasis on the same point as the beginning.

Feature Opening—Theme

News Peg or Tieback

Points in Logical Order

Conclusion—Reinforce Theme

Alternative approaches put greater emphasis on the people and the drama of the event. As a result, they usually contain more description that re-creates the scene or event and more quotations that give voice to the "characters" in the stories. They are most effective for stories about athletes in which most readers already know the basic information or the news details are secondary to the person or theme of the story. Journalists utilize alternative styles most often on personality profiles, human-interest features, and *follow* stories—stories printed a couple of days after an event. Sports information directors use them for feature releases and weekly reviews or previews.

A journalist actually can use either or both approaches to tell the same story. Here's an example of an inverted pyramid lead and an alternative lead and news peg on the same story:

Inverted Pyramid

HIGHLAND HEIGHTS, KY – Northern Kentucky University's Kerry Lewin became the all-time leader in college volleyball with her 2,136th ace in the third set of a 15-11, 15-2, 15-8 victory over

Mount st. Joseph at Regents Hall, surpassing Kim Koehler of Murray State, who accumulated 509 from 1987 to 1990.

The Notre Dame Academy graduate and Engelwood native also had 17 kills in helping NKU extend its school-record winning streak to 21 matches.

Her record-breaking serve came near the end. . . .

Alternative

HIGHLAND HEIGHTS, KY—Kerry Lewin was feeling the pressure.

Family, friends and media from all over Greater Cincinnati had filled Regents Hall to watch the Northern Kentucky University hitter set the all-time collegiate record for service aces.

Now the game against Mount St. Joseph was in the third set and it looked as if the Norse would close out the game still one ace short. But Lewin took a running start, leaped into the air and smashed her patented overhead serve. It dived over the net and the opposition made a feeble lunge at it.

Lewin's teammates piled on top of her.

"I didn't have time to react," she said after the record-setting 2,136th ace of her career. "The gym just exploded and everybody mobbed me."

Broadcast journalists use a modified, and abbreviated, inverted pyramid approach to most news stories. Kohler (1994) says broadcast journalism is "writing for the ear" instead of for the eye (p. 2). Stories for broadcast open with a catchy word, a phrase, or a sentence designed to catch one's attention—to give the ear time to listen for the important element. The rest of the story is written in a conversational style, just as in telling a story, but generally follows the inverted pyramid style.

The TV or radio story emphasizes the same basic news elements as those of a newspaper story. Because of time limitations and the emphasis on immediacy in broadcast journalism, a story may cover only the *who, what, when,* and *where.* The accompanying video in TV news may provide the details in a couple of highlight film clips. In fact, the video, or visual images from the video, serves as the attention grabber.

Radio reports generally cover only the results and, if time permits, a single quotation from the coach or a player who starred in the game. Broadcast news reporters have to write stories to fit a specific time allotment. According to Kohler (1994), most radio stories are 10 to 45 seconds long, 25 to 110 words. Most TV news stories run 15 seconds to 2 minutes, or no more than 300 words. That means broadcast journalists often do not have time for the *why* or the *how* unless those are the most important angles of the story.

Sports information specialists can enhance the possibility that a newspaper, a radio station, or a TV station will use the information in a release by writing in a

News Releases

One type of release is a game advance, which will assist the media in its coverage of the upcoming event.

style similar to news formats. Of equal importance is providing the name and telephone number of a contact person a reporter can call for additional information or clarification.

Editors generally prefer releases on standard, 8 1/2"-by-11", white paper in black ink and a standard typewriter character (or computer font such as Courier), because they are easy to read. Stories on eye-catching colored paper with computer "clip art" incorporated in the text smack of promotion—anathema to objective journalists. Stories on legal-size paper do not fit conveniently into file folders or drawers. Editors also prefer stories that are double-spaced, so they can insert editing notes and symbols between the lines for the data transcriber or reporter who next handles the release. An editor rarely will run a news release without making some changes in style, structure, content, or length for policy or space reasons.

From a structural standpoint, the SID must pay close attention to two primary elements of a release: the *header* and the *story*. The header at the top of the page identifies the college and provides other information useful to a reporter or editor. The story, of course, is the release.

Header

The header on a news release generally includes the following information:

1. College or team's name and address—to identify the sender.

2. Contact person—the SID or the person who wrote the release.

3. Telephone numbers—day, night, and fax, if desired.

4. Release date—a requested publication or broadcast date. "For Immediate Release" means the media are free to use the information whenever they wish. "Embargoed until 7 AM Aug. 18" or "Not for release until 7 AM Aug. 18" indicates a preference that no one print or broadcast the information prior to the specified time. However, the "embargo" is not legally binding on the media. It is only a polite request.

Public relations firms often attempt to embargo or to dictate a release time out of a sense of fairness. They hope to give all a chance to release the information at the same time, to nullify any competitive advantages. However, differences in newscast times and newspaper deadlines make it impossible for all to release the information at the same time. In addition, public relations personnel may send information they plan to reveal at a press conference to the media in advance so the media can gather background and other details. The objective is to give reporters a head start on a story that might be released on their deadline.

Use embargoes carefully. Remember, the media are under no obligation to honor them. Some reporters do not honor them, as a matter of policy. They argue that their job is to disseminate news as soon as they are aware of it. Competitive pressures lead others to break embargoes. They can get the jump on the competition as well as on the story by breaking an embargo before a press conference.

Release

Although a good news release is similar to a news story, it contains additional elements designed to serve the purposes of the sport organization. Two parts of the story are optional:

1. Suggested headline: A newspaper seldom will use a headline suggested by the sender. Reporters do not write the headlines on most dailies. Copy editors write the headlines to fit a given type size and space dictated by page-design considerations. However, the headline may give a reporter or editor a quick idea of the subject matter.

2. Dateline: The dateline identifies the city in which the release originates. It is printed in all-capital letters, followed by a dash (—), at the start of the first sentence. Newspapers traditionally used datelines on stories from cities outside their circulation areas, but the practice is declining. From the perspective of the SID, a dateline quickly gives the media a clue to the proximity of the sender.

The majority of news releases follows the inverted pyramid structure but may add a concluding paragraph that provides direction on how to obtain additional information. The most common structure contains the following components:

1. Lead (5Ws and H)

2. Details

3. Background

4. Sport organization tag

The lead starts with the element most important to the audience, or the readers. For example, a release announcing an award would emphasize the "who."

HIRAM, Ohio—Katherine Blake Mitchell has been awarded an academic scholarship from Hiram College, a private liberal arts institution in Ohio.

The lead also zeroes in on the strongest "news" characteristic. As noted in Chapter 2, editors make content decisions based on criteria that assess the newsworthiness of a story. Although journalism texts offer anywhere from five to eight criteria, most include these six: timeliness, proximity, prominence, impact or consequence, the unusual or odd, and conflict. The sports information specialist can improve a release's publication or broadcast prospects by emphasizing the same elements.

Emphasizing the timeliness would be effective in the lead on a story announcing the selections on an all-star team.

BEREA, Ohio—The 1996 CoSIDA-GTE team announced today included Baldwin-Wallace left fielder Dawn Neighbarger. The career .362 hitter was named to the second team.

The SID most likely will focus on proximity in a hometown release. Note how the SID might change the Dawn Neighbarger release sent to the *Mount Vernon News.*

BEREA, Ohio—Mount Vernon High School graduate Dawn Neighbarger recently completed her third season as a member of the Baldwin-Wallace College softball team. For her efforts both on the softball field and in the classroom, Neighbarger was named as a 1996 second-team CoSIDA-GTE Academic All-American.

Prominence would be significant in a release announcing a speaker or a new employee.

SPRINGFIELD, Ohio—Dr. Carl F. Schraibman, who heads the graduate program in sport administration at Kent State University, has been appointed Director of Athletics and Recreation at Wittenberg University, effective August 15, Provost Sammye Greer announced.

Emphasizing the impact or consequences might be effective in the lead on a story about the upcoming season.

CLEVELAND, Ohio—Cleveland State University's schedule for Rollie Massimino's first season as head coach will include seven teams that made postseason tournaments last year, including the Georgetown Hoyas and the Michigan Wolverines.

"Our fans will enjoy some of the top college basketball teams in the country at our Convocation Center this season," Massimino said.

The odd or unusual might catch editors' and readers' attention in a news feature.

BEREA, Ohio—Staying at home has always been a big thing for recent Baldwin-Wallace graduate and four-year varsity standout Larissa Heynysh. From her first days of playing tennis at age 7 to her present position as an assistant coach at Strongsville High School, Heynysh has always stayed close to home.

Conflict could come into play in a story about resignations, conference alignments, or suspension of players for rules violations.

PROVIDENCE, Rhode Island—The presidents of the remaining schools in the Big East Conference are threatening to sue the University of Miami and Virginia Tech University for breach of contract after both institutions announced they are leaving for the Atlantic Coast Conference next year.

The body of the story should begin with details that elaborate on the basic news elements in descending order of importance. Obviously, the first details should provide amplification of the news element emphasized in the lead. The writer should put times, dates, and other specific information in the body.

A story that leads with the announcement of the selection of a coach, for example, should go on to provide more information on the coach's experience, coaching record, reasons for accepting the job, etc. Background on the circumstances that led to the search for a new coach, on the outgoing coach, and on team record for the season would follow. Newspaper editors who do not want to run the entire story or do not have space for all of it can easily eliminate the background, the information that followers of the team already will know.

An announcement about ticket sales, scheduling, or other matters about which readers might want additional information should close with a paragraph that tells them how to find it quickly.

Times for all CSU basketball games will be announced at a later date. Season tickets, starting at $100 for all 15 home games, are on sale at the CSU Athletic Ticket Office or by calling 216-687-4848.

An alternative lead uses a literary technique to emphasize the theme or news element of a story. It incorporates the peg or tieback that explains the news connection. Here's how Kevin Aprile of the Elyria (Ohio) *Chronicle Telegram* handled an article announcing the selection of Debbie Borsz as head volleyball coach at Cleveland State University (March 11, 1995, p. 3-C):

The former star is now the coach.

Debbie Borsz, a former Cleveland State volleyball star, was recently named the team's coach following a national search. Borsz served as interim coach this past year.

The body of an alternative story is similar to that of an inverted pyramid. However, it flows in a logical order appropriate to the style. Because the emphasis is on people, the story may contain more direct quotation from those included in the story. The writer must be careful to attribute the direct quotation to the speaker. The story may close with a direct quotation, an example, additional details, or a technique that reinforces the theme.

Types of Releases

Different types of releases naturally lend themselves to an inverted pyramid or alternative style. News releases fall into five broad categories.

Game Advance

An advance is a preview of an upcoming game. The story is designed to provide basic details on time and ticket information, as well as a rundown on team records, strengths and weaknesses of the teams, etc.

For the news media, the release provides useful information about the game for readers. From the perspective of the SID, the advance may help to stir interest among readers and to draw a crowd.

A game advance usually is written in the style of a feature story (i.e., an alternative approach). One popular supplement is a *fact box,* which is a format that lists basic facts (similar to the 5Ws) in a brief and punchy writing style. This technique makes it easy to find the primary information. The reporter or editor who receives the advance (fact box) can immediately gather information of importance.

If written in essay or narrative form, the release should take the inverted pyramid form, with the most important information on top and the least important on the bottom. All releases must contain the basic news components. For example, an advance on a football game should include the following:

1. What is the event? (conference game, nonconference)
2. Who is participating? (teams, players, etc.)
3. When will the event take place? (date and time)
4. Where will the event take place? (stadium and address)
5. Why are these teams meeting? (league game, national ranking, or major rivalry)
6. How do they match up? (style of play of both teams, strengths and weaknesses, and assessment by coaches/players)

The story should give information about which radio or television stations, networks, or cable outlets will broadcast the game, and include the time.

Other important details on both teams are injuries, notes, and statistics on key players, coaches' records, team records, and notes and statistics on the rivalry. The advance also may include a brief preview of the style of play of both teams. Further notes about the sender's team and athletes should be included.

The timing of the release of a game advance is most important. It should be in the hands of the media five days in advance of the event.

Hometown Release

A hometown release is a story about a student-athlete that is sent to the media in the player's hometown. Weekly newspapers that do not have the staff or resources to write about stories outside their circulation area often will run a hometown release as submitted.

Hometown releases generally are no more than six or eight paragraphs and follow the inverted pyramid style. They identify the athlete, the sport, and any honors earned. They could also list the student's major field of study and a cumulative grade point average if noteworthy.

A hometown release includes a brief background of the high school the student attended and athletics achievements there. Information about the parents or guardians and other family members also goes into the release. A photograph is included, if possible. Most sports information departments shoot pictures of all the athletes on a team on media day or at the first practice, then keep them on file for use in releases.

Feature Release

A feature release is intended to spotlight a student-athlete. The student does not have to be the most visible or talented athlete on campus. The SID can highlight some unusual or interesting facet of the athlete, such as hobbies or academic activities.

Because the emphasis is on an athlete rather than an event, and the purpose is to entertain as well as to inform, most feature releases use an alternative lead. The first paragraph must "grab" the reader immediately. A feature release should include the basic news details, such as the student's sport and performance. The body might follow the inverted pyramid style, or it might develop an interesting angle. In either case, the presentation should be "bright" and "tight," because the primary purpose is to entertain.

News Release

The basic news release is newsworthy because it provides information that most readers do not yet know. It may announce the hiring of a new coach, the signing of an outstanding high school athlete, the firing of a coach, or the groundbreaking ceremony for a new facility.

The release often supplements information announced at a news conference. The emphasis on timely and new information calls for an inverted pyramid approach and a concise explanation of the details. The release also may include quotations from appropriate coaches or university officials that elaborate on the news or put the significance of the announcement into perspective.

Weekly Review/Preview

The weekly review/preview is a necessary evil for sports information directors. This type of release amounts to a weekly schedule of all the institution's athletic teams. It gives a summary of the records, opponents, and key players.

No other releases call for as much budget scrutiny as do reviews/previews. With distribution and printing costs escalating constantly, the SID can waste a lot of time and resources sending these releases to media people who will not use them. Targeting reviews/previews to specific print and broadcast reporters is most important.

Types of News Releases
Game advance
Hometown release
Feature release
News release
Weekly review/preview

Audience Awareness

Regardless of the type or structure of a news release, it should conform to strict media standards of accuracy, clarity, and brevity.

A media organization's credibility and professional reputation depend to a large extent on the accuracy of news reports. A reporter who consistently submits stories with errors or inaccuracies will not last long with a newspaper, magazine, radio, or TV company. Likewise, a sports information specialist who consistently submits releases with errors will soon find that no one in the media will trust or use any of the information.

Accuracy means the story is correct in every detail. To ensure accuracy, the SID must double-check to make certain that all times, dates, numbers, etc., are correct. The SID should check the spelling of all names, addresses, and titles; he or she should also take care to list the titles of (or to otherwise identify) all people in the story and to attribute all direct quotations and statements that contain opinion.

The writing style should be clear and concise. Remember, both the media and sports information specialists are writing for a mass audience. The reading ability of members of the audience may vary widely; some may not read at more than a sixth- or seventh-grade level. To reach the broadest audience possible, the journalist or SID must write in a simple style that is easy to understand.

Stories with short, simple sentences, shorter and simpler words, and short paragraphs are the easiest to read and understand. Numerous studies have shown a correlation between sentence length and readability. The longer the sentence is, the fewer the people are who can understand it in its entirety. Journalists disagree on the optimum sentence length, but sentences averaging 16–25 words will pass most readability tests. In addition, journalists prefer one- and two-syllable words to longer ones that are more difficult to understand. The SID should avoid the use of jargon or technical terms the reader might not understand. For example, a recruiting story that refers to a "Proposition 48" recruit should briefly explain the term or substitute a phrase that specifies the restrictions on eligibility.

Long paragraphs are a barrier to readability. Readers mentally interpret long paragraphs as dull and tedious, so journalists arbitrarily limit stories to two or three sentences per paragraph.

Print journalists generally use third person and past tense; broadcast journalists favor present tense because of the emphasis on immediacy. The SID should avoid "we" or "you" in most stories.

Courtesy of Dan Mendlik/Cleveland Indians

Determining the sports media outlets in which to send a news release is determined in part by the target audience of that specific release.

The SID should be particularly careful with both opinion that is not attributed and interpretive adjectives. They compromise the objectivity of the story because they suggest bias in favor of one side. It is better to forget the self-serving praise, or what editors call "gush." The SID should avoid the superlatives and interpretive adjectives; for example, "Matt Smith, the best player in the conference, is approaching a school record." Clichés ("a classic game," "a coach on the field") are another thing to be avoided. An editor will purge all of them . . . or pitch the release in the trash.

The SID can make certain a story conforms to news style by stocking the office with reference guides used by the media. Here are some of the most popular:

- *The Associated Press Stylebook and Libel Manual* (New York: Addison-Wesley Publishing Company, Inc.). The stylebook provides guidelines on news style for titles, addresses, numbers, dates, etc. It also includes tips on word usage, grammar, and punctuation. One chapter is devoted exclusively to sports.

- *Broadcast News Writing Stylebook,* Papper (New York: Allyn & Bacon). The guide not only offers tips on style, but also addresses leads, endings, and story forms for both radio and television.

- *The Elements of Style,* Strunk and White (Macmillan). This book has served as the authority on grammar, spelling, style, and usage for years.

Common Errors

1. Lack of newsworthiness. The story fails to emphasize the most important news element or buries it in the middle of the story.

Wrong:

The University of Southern Ohio will play an interesting nonconference basketball schedule next winter with some Division II schools slated to play at Gund Arena.

The Bearcats will play 10 nonconference games and the usual 12 contests in the Mid-Continent Conference.

A new head coach, Adolph Smith, will lead USO into battle when the season begins. Smith was named yesterday as the 43rd head coach at Southern Ohio.

Right:

Veteran Adolph Smith was named yesterday as the 43rd head basketball coach at the University of Southern Ohio.

Smith replaces Bob Elias, who had an 82-205 record in 10 seasons. Elias was released from his contract after the 'Cats posted a 9-18 record this past season.

The Bearcats will play four Division II schools as part of a 10-game nonconference schedule.

2. Lack of objectivity. The story promotes instead of reports. It sounds like a sales pitch for the school instead of an objective news story.

Wrong:

Utah A&M is the third best defensive basketball team in the United States, allowing only 62 points per game.

Unfortunately for the Utes, they are scoring only 53 points and are winless after 16 games. The Fighting Utes are a scrappy, hard-working young squad that tries hard every game, but the breaks have been going against it, especially from the officials.

The Utes never seem to get the calls. Coach John Silver said, "I don't think the officials like us. If they did, we might win some games."

Right:

The Utah A&M Utes are off to their poorest start in basketball in school history.

Opponents are outscoring the Utes by nine points per game. Because of their lack of production, they are still looking for their first victory 16 games into the season.

Poor shooting has hurt the Utes all year. They are hitting only 25% of their floor attempts, while the opposition is making 48% of its attempts.

The Eight Most Common Mistakes in New Releases

1. Lack of newsworthiness.

2. Lack of objectivity.

3. Too many superlatives and interpretive adjectives.

4. Self-serving quotations.

5. Emphasis on the obvious.

6. Lack of a local tie (on out-of-town releases).

7. Unnecessary background.

8. Wordy.

3. Too many superlatives and interpretive adjectives. The story hypes the team or the game.

Wrong:

Sharpshooting off guard Chip Glass has been uncanny this basketball season.

With the touch of a safecracker and the precision of a diamond cutter, he has led Cincinnati Poly to a break-even season, standing at 12-12 at the three-quarter mark of the campaign.

"Chip is only 5-foot-6, but plays as though he stands 6-foot-6," said CinPoly coach Sam Cameron. "He wasn't named to the all-conference team, but he has had a much better season than Curly Grimes of Indiana Tech, who was named to the first honor squad.

"I will take Glass over Grimes every day of the week. You will agree with me when CinPoly meets Indiana Tech tomorrow night at Riverfront Arena. Come see for yourself."

Right:

Arguably the two finest guards in college basketball will face each other tomorrow night at Riverfront Arena when Cincinnati Poly meets Indiana Tech.

CinPoly's Chip Glass will trade shots with All-Conference choice Curly Grimes when the Pollys hope to snap a five-game losing streak.

"It will be interesting to see the guard matchup," said CinPoly coach Sam Cameron. "Each is a skilled player, and they both know how to score lots of points in a basketball game."

4. **Self-serving quotations.** The direct quotations aim at self-promotion instead of at explaining and providing perspective on the subject matter.

Wrong:

"I firmly believe we have the finest college basketball team in all of Division II," said Baltic University coach Kelly Smith.

"We have great shooters, we are quick, and we play tenacious defense. I say we have it all and it's a shame we are only 5-12 this season. We have so many injuries, and they have hurt our chances."

BU will try to snap a nine-game losing streak tonight when the Overseas take on Wall University, which is 19-1.

"We have played a much tougher schedule than Wharton, and we are a better team than the Stockbrokers," added Smith.

Right:

Baltic University will try to snap a nine-game losing streak tonight when the Overseas play host to Wall University.

BU, which is 5-12, has not won since defeating Baker Barber College, 112-111, on Nov. 11.

"Wall is 19-1 and playing very well right now," said BU coach Kelly Smith.

"We have our job cut out for us, and we know it will not be easy, but the Wall players put their shorts on one leg at a time, just like we do."

However, last week, Patricia DeAngelo, BU's 5-foot-4 point guard, sprained an ankle during a collision in practice. She will be out at least one week.

5. Emphasis on the obvious. The story leads with information the reader already knows or with obvious information that does not encourage the reader to go further.

Wrong:

Jane McIntyre, of Hoboken, NJ, plays on the Ashoil University basketball team.

Right:

Jane McIntyre, the only player from Hoboken, NJ, on the Ashoil University women's basketball team, has been the unsung hero for the Eagles this season.

McIntyre leads the Eagles in steals, taking offensive charges, and forcing turnovers and has helped carry Ashoil to a 12-0 record going into conference play.

6. Lack of a local tie (on out-of-town releases). The story does not quickly make clear that some aspect of the story has a local connection (proximity).

Wrong:

Release sent to the *Plain Dealer* in Cleveland.

FORT WORTH, Texas—The Texas Christian women's basketball team will play host tonight to Southern Methodist for the tournament championship of the Southwest Conference.

The Lady Horned Frogs are led by sophomore Becky Lane of Houston, who has averaged 25.4 points per game this season.

Right:

Release sent to the *Plain Dealer* in Cleveland.

FORT WORTH, Texas—Sophomore Becky Lane of Cleveland, Ohio, will lead the Texas Christian Lady Horned Frogs into tonight's Southwest Conference championship women's basketball game against Southern Methodist.

Lane, who attends TCU because her aunt lives in suburban Fort Worth, averaged 25.5 points and 12.7 rebounds per game this season as the Frogs posted a 28-2 record.

7. Unnecessary background. The story contains too much "old news" at the top of the story, obscuring the new or important element.

Wrong:

Jane Schmidt was a high school All-American before she decided to attend Miami University on a basketball scholarship and became the star of last night's playoff game.

Schmidt was a middle school phenomenon before she starred in high school and then played a key role for a team that won the Amateur Athletic Union (AAU) 16–18 title.

In middle school, she averaged 40.4 points per game. Then, in her four years of high school, she averaged 23.8 ppg, and in her four seasons at Miami she has continued her solid offensive play with a 22.1 scoring average.

In her first competitive game as an 11-year-old, she scored 18 points, grabbed 22 rebounds, and still handed out a dozen assists as her team defeated a much older team 76-52.

Schmidt scored 25 points last night as the Lady Hurricanes defeated Georgia 77-71 in the first round of the NCAA tournament.

Right:

Jane Schmidt, who has been one of the nation's top women basketball players for nearly a decade, scored 25 points last night to lead the University of Miami to a 77-71 victory over Georgia in the first round of the NCAA championship tournament.

8. Wordy. Long sentences filled with clauses that cover two or three ideas confuse and lose readers.

Wrong:

Johnny Jones, who is from Paducah, Ky., is one of the finer young golfers in the nation who play on Wednesdays and Fridays during July and August in preparation for the National Junior Golf Championships.

Jones, who is a southpaw, and James Johnson, another teenager, will compete with Bill Brown, who has a very good game, and George Green, a vegetable farmer from Athens, Ga. This group, which has a combined age of 98 years, is, as a group, quick on the draw, and each one, when the climate is right, can putt with the tour professionals.

These young golfers from the Midwest also are very good students, and several of them, when not playing golf, work out in karate classes. This helps them develop the arm strength needed to be good golfers. His long drives are one of the reasons Jones is one of the favorites in the tournament and the person many pros think will win.

Right:

Johnny Jones, a smooth-swinging teenager from Paducah, Ky., is the odds-on favorite to win the National Junior Golf Championships that begin today at FOX Den Country Club.

Distribution of Releases

Two considerations figure into decisions about who should receive a news release: (a) the news organization and (b) the target audience. A news organization's story selection depends on its mission and audience. That is why *USA Today* offers a comprehensive sports section every day, whereas the *Columbus Dispatch* seldom sends sports reporters outside the state. Similarly, a news organization shapes its coverage to meet the interests of its viewers or readers. College athletics are big in the Midwest; pro sports are the draw in New York City. Stories on local athletes are more interesting than information about athletes outside the circulation/coverage area.

A Cleveland, Ohio, sportswriter will have little use for a Texas Christian University football review/preview or a feature release about a women's basketball player at Louisiana State University. Unless the athlete is from Cleveland, or LSU plays an Ohio team, the information in the release likely will offer little or no benefit to the Cleveland media. Sending the release is a waste of the SID's energy and budget.

It is imperative for the sports information specialist to know the sports reporter and the editor or director who supervises sports coverage for each of the local media. It is also important to know the types of sports and the types of stories each uses most frequently. Finally, it is helpful to keep directories in the office that provide names and addresses of sports editors and directors to whom the SID might send hometown releases. Two such directories follow:

- *Editor and Publisher International Yearbook* (New York: Editor and Publisher)

- *Broadcasting/Cablecasting Yearbook* (Washington, DC: Broadcast Publications, Inc.)

The personal contacts and yearbooks make it possible for an SID to keep a mailing list up to date and use it to his or her best advantage. In trimming the list to get the most out of releases, the SID can determine who is sincerely interested in receiving a specific kind of release. Mailing an inquiry card to those receiving the releases may prove beneficial. The SID should ask if the sports department still wants to receive releases, if the address and the name of the media contact person are accurate, and what types of releases they will consider running. Sports journalists usually respond to these cards, because they enable the news organization to weed out information it does not want and ensure it receives information it does want.

The SID should be careful not to overwhelm the local media in the primary target market who regularly cover the school. Too much of a good thing can work against the SID, too. The SID should know when to use the telephone instead of a news release.

Simply put, the SID or public relations director must know the target market and the media market, then use common sense about the distribution of releases. The U.S. Postal Service may serve well for some SIDs, but a fax or computer email message may be just as effective for others, and less expensive as well. Use of fax machines replaced mailings, and use of email has now become the most prevalent method in submitting news releases, particularly in conveying news with a tight time frame.

In every case, the SID should send the release to a specific person. Releases addressed to generic titles like "Sports Editor" are junk mail to journalists. Sending the release to a specific person takes on added importance in fax releases and electronic communication because releases of every type may pour into a common pool.

Timing is another critical factor. If the information arrives too early, it may wind up buried at the bottom of a pile of submissions. If it arrives too late, it is worthless to the media and the sport institution. Vruggink (1985) says timing is everything. A game advance, for example, should be sent on the Sunday prior to the Saturday game, to give the sports journalist as much lead time as possible on story development.

Summary

Sports information specialists and sports journalists enjoy an interdependent relationship. The SID or public relations director is a source of sports information for the media. The media are the channels through which the sport organization or team reaches followers and potential fans. The most common means of communication is the news release, a prepackaged story distributed to the media in hopes they will pass the information on to the public. Because printed releases are the most common form of information distributed by sport organizations, strong writing skills are essential to success for SIDs.

News releases are similar to news stories, although their primary objectives differ. News releases attempt to persuade—to create a favorable image of an athlete, a team, or a sport organization. News stories attempt to inform—to present a balanced view of a topic to readers or viewers. They also entertain. The structure of a news story depends on the information or entertainment value of the story. The inverted pyramid puts emphasis on the information in the story, pushing the most important details to the top. Alternative structures emphasize the human-interest angle or entertainment features. They are used most often when readers already know most of the basic facts or when the news value is minimal.

A sports information specialist can increase the chances that the media will use a news release by writing in a style similar to that of journalists. Game advances, hometown releases, and news releases follow a standard format—lead, details, background, and where to call for more information—built on the inverted pyramid model. Feature releases and weekly reviews/previews often will take an alternative approach. The SID will add information at the top of a release that provides contact information to reporters seeking additional details. The SID can request that the media withhold publication or broadcast of the information until a specified time, but the media are under no legal obligation to honor an embargo.

The most effective releases emphasize the characteristic that makes the story newsworthy, whether it is the announcement of a new coach or the success of an athlete from the media's city. Because the media reach a broad, mass audience, effective releases also are clear and concise. Short sentences, simple language, and short paragraphs are the most readable. Guidebooks such as *The Associated Press Stylebook and Libel Manual* provide direction on how to write according to news style. The most important consideration for every release is accuracy. The SID must check and recheck every name, date, number, and fact to maintain credibility and cooperation among the media.

SIDs maintain up-to-date mailing lists and information on the types of releases specific news organizations use. SIDs also pay close attention to deadlines and the timing of releases. A release that arrives too late is of no value. The SID who knows the target media, the target audience, and news structure can write a release that emphasizes the same elements a sportswriter would emphasize. A well-written release may be utilized by both print and broadcast media in different locales, with little alteration.

DISCUSSION QUESTIONS

1. When making an announcement, plea, or request in the form of a release, how do you persuade your audience to take the action you desire?
2. What are the criteria used to determine what angle will be taken when preparing to write a news release? Create an illustration and discuss it.

SUGGESTED EXERCISES

1. Write four one-page releases (hometown, feature, news, and weekly review/preview).
2. Apply a readability formula to a story you have written and determine the reading level at which you write.

Chapter Six

MANAGED NEWS EVENTS: NEWS CONFERENCES AND MEDIA DAYS

It was a Monday in midsummer in 1996, a rare open date for the Cleveland Indians. Ballplayers put the sport out of their minds for the day. Many of them went off to play golf. In the Indians' headquarters at Jacobs Field, then General Manager John Hart and his staff worked feverishly to make a trade with the New York Mets. Rumors of a trade had circulated for days, but no one expected a blockbuster announcement on an off day.

Around 3 P.M., Indians' officials called popular second baseman Carlos Baerga off the golf course. They told him that he and teammate Alvaro Espinoza had been traded to the Mets for infielders Jose Viscaino and Jeff Kent. Baerga was shocked. Minutes later, Director of Public Relations Bob DiBiasio and Media Director Bart Swain began to make arrangements for a 5 P.M. news conference at Jacobs Field. They had less than two hours to invite the Greater Cleveland media and prepare background information and statistics on the players involved.

> Chapter 6 explores the function, organization, and management of news conferences and media days. It surveys planning, budgeting, and duties the sports information director or public relations officer must perform on the day of the event.

Swain and his assistant, Joel Gunderson, immediately put together biographical sketches of the incoming players and the two Indians headed for the Mets. They also wrote a news release announcing the trade. They distributed the information to reporters after they arrived for the announcement. Hart and former manager Mike Hargrove were on hand at 5 P.M. to meet the media, make the announcement, and answer questions about the controversial trade. By the time the press conference began, Baerga was already on his way to New York.

The trade was the lead story on all local telecasts that evening and the top story in every northern Ohio newspaper the next morning. Talk shows flooded the airways with endless conversation and comments about the wisdom of the trade and the value of the players involved. The news conference made it possible for the media to scramble together well-rounded stories within tight deadline restrictions.

News conferences are one of the most important means through which sport organizations communicate with the media and the public. Managed events, such as news conferences, enable sport organizations to distribute the same information to large groups of reporters at the same time. News conferences also give the media the opportunity to ask questions and to obtain information from key players, coaches, and team or athletics department officials at one location and at one time.

The most common types of managed events are news conferences and media days. Sport organizations set up news conferences to make major announcements (usually positive) such as trades, signings of new players or coaches, changes of ownership, or details on a new facility. They use media days primarily to kick off a new season. Reporters who attend can talk to coaches and players as well as take group and individual pictures for use throughout the season. College conferences also organize media days prior to the start of a season. Each college sends a coach and selected players to a joint media day, giving the media access to representatives of each team. Reporters can gather information, media guides, and pictures they can use in stories throughout the season.

News Conferences

A news conference is an effective tool for making announcements to a large audience at one time. However, the announcement must be worthy of a news conference. In the 1980s, when one of the authors of this text was city editor for a metropolitan daily newspaper, a would-be politician called a news conference at the Northern Kentucky/Greater Cincinnati International Airport to state his opinion on a hot national issue unrelated to the local campaign. Few attended, because the candidate was not well known and his topic was not relevant to the local campaign. In short, the candidate called the news conference hoping to attract attention to his campaign. He failed because his meeting notice, faxed to the media, promised no news—only his opinion on a topic in the news.

Sport organizations must take care to ensure that every news conference delivers information that meets the media's criteria for news: timeliness, proximity, prominence, importance, oddity, and conflict. In short, the announcement should deal with a timely issue concerning the local school or team and must be significant enough to have a major impact on a player, a coach, a team, or the sport organization itself. In other words, the announcement must be important enough to the media to justify rearranging schedules and reassigning reporters.

Helitzer (1992) says a news conference should not be called unless it is absolutely necessary, and consideration of the media comes first. For example, the sports information director or public relations specialist should schedule the news conference early enough to enable TV reporters to prepare their stories for the next telecast and to enable print reporters to make the next deadline.

Although an announcement may force editors to rearrange the daily schedule or change reporters' assignments, a news conference *does* serve the media in an efficient manner. By bringing the principals together in one location, the conference eliminates the need for reporters to track down individuals and make followup calls; that is, it saves time for both reporters and institutional representatives.

On the professional level, most news conferences concern the hiring and/or firing of general managers, managers, and coaches; player trades or signings; injuries and other personnel matters; and ticket, stadium, and franchise issues. Professional sport organizations are more likely than colleges or high schools to schedule news conferences to address negative issues such as the punishment for a player who violates the organization's substance-abuse policy.

NASCAR driver Dale Earnhardt Jr. participates in a news conference at the Chicagoland Speedway.

Colleges and universities typically call news conferences to make announcements in high-profile sports such as football, men's basketball, and women's basketball. They also use conferences in other sports in which their teams are prominent (e.g., Louisiana State University in baseball, University of Houston in golf, and University of Iowa in wrestling). The coaches and programs in these sports are generally high profile. In addition, news conferences may announce the decision by a talented high school athlete to sign a letter of intent to attend the university.

High school administrators seldom arrange a news conference for anything other than the introduction of a new coach or administrator.

Colleges and high schools generally avoid calling attention to negative news, because handling conflict and controversial issues involving players is particularly tricky. In the first place, the Family Educational Rights and Privacy Act prohibits release of information of a personal nature on a college player. (See Chapter 13: Law and Ethics.) Second, it is extremely difficult to manage a negative announcement in such a way that it reinforces the positive image the sport organization wants to foster.

A news conference aims at attracting broad media attention and the bright glare of the public spotlight. The less light the better on negative news, in most cases. Sports information directors typically send out a news release instead of calling a news conference for negative announcements. In the case of a coach's firing, the university or professional team will more often call a news conference to name a successor, thus staging a positive news conference rather than a negative one.

However, a college or a high school may set up a news conference to quell rumors, quash false information, or demonstrate how well it is handling a serious problem. At a news conference in November 1996, Boston College announced the results of an internal investigation into allegations that members of the football team had bet on football games. The gathering enabled Coach Dan Henning to clarify conflicting information reported by the media, to announce the punishment for players who bet on games, and to strongly reiterate the university's opposition to gambling on sports by athletes.

Planning the News Conference

Planning a news conference is a team effort that may involve administrators, coaches, and sports information personnel. The roles and responsibilities vary according to the makeup of the sport organization. A team owner may instruct the public relations director to arrange a news conference when the owner fires a general manager (GM) or manager. The GM may order a news conference to announce a trade. The president of a university or the athletics director may request a news conference to announce the hiring of a coach.

The sports information or public relations director must work with administrators to create a chain of command and a roster of responsibilities for news conferences. The document should spell out the roles and responsibilities of each person in the chain. It should specify who decides when to call a news conference and what information to release, who makes the physical arrangements, who prepares the information released at the meeting, who makes the announcement, and who answers questions.

Typically, sports information personnel begin notifying the media of a news conference three to five hours in advance. The objective is to give reporters sufficient time to make arrangements to attend the meeting, but not enough time to gather enough information to "break" the story before the announcement. In an age of high-intensity investigative reporting by the media, keeping the name of a coach or other major news absolutely secret is almost impossible. In all probability, the media have speculated for days on the most likely candidates for a coaching position, but the sports information or public relations director still should make an attempt to keep the information secret until the formal announcement. Also, the sport organization should go ahead with the news conference—including the news release, biographical information, and statements from university or team personnel—even if members of the media accurately reveal the name of the new coach in advance.

Preparations will not vary significantly from small college to large, or from college to professional organization. What will vary according to the size of the sport organ-

One SID's Preparation for a News Conference

When John Carroll University in suburban Cleveland hired Mike Moran as men's basketball coach in 1992, Sports Information Director Chris Wenzler began making arrangements a day in advance of the news conference on campus. In an interview with Bill Nichols, Wenzler said he followed these steps:

1. Contacted local media immediately, particularly print media reporters.

2. Composed a news release, including comments from both Moran and Tony DeCarlo, John Carroll University's athletic director.

3. Arranged with physical plant personnel to set up a podium, microphone, sound system, and chairs in the atrium, the site of the meeting. He also arranged for the Marriott Hotel to provide beverages.

4. Notified the local bureau of the Associated Press to ensure rapid distribution of the announcement via the wire-service lines.

5. Organized work-study students into teams to post signs with directions to the atrium. The work-study students also assisted during the news conference.

6. Met with athletic department officials who would participate in the news conference. They discussed, among other things, how to handle questions they anticipated. Wenzler, DeCarlo, Moran, and sports information intern Beth Arrowsmith also planned the order of events.

"We figured it was best to have the SID open the festivities with the introduction, listing the order of speakers, followed by the athletic director, who introduced the new head coach," Wenzler recalled. "The coach gave opening comments and then fielded questions from the attending media."

Wenzler set aside time after the formal news conference for Moran to meet with television reporters and print reporters. He provided working space for reporters who wanted to file stories immediately, making certain they had enough space and electrical outlets to use their portable computer terminals.

Following the news conference, Wenzler called area media outlets that did not send reporters, advised them of the announcement, and answered their questions. He also contacted the physical plant office again to make sure someone cleaned up the conference area.

izations will be the number of people available to assist with planning, preparation, and presentation of the news conference, and the number of media representatives who attend.

The team owner, president of the college, general manager, or athletics director—not the sports information director—usually conducts the news conference. At the collegiate level, the president usually issues a statement but does not participate in the news conference unless the announcement deals with a controversial subject, such as NCAA violations.

The athletics director (AD) usually will open a news conference announcing a new coach with comments about the direction in which the university wants to turn the program. The AD may make an oblique reference to the previous coach—"a difference in coaching philosophy"—but generally will avoid rehashing specific reasons for the change in coaches if the previous coach was fired.

If questioned about negative matters, such as an NCAA investigation, the athletics director should answer truthfully. Generally, the media will see through a falsehood or a ruse. Truthfulness speaks to the organization's integrity. Lies come back to haunt.

Here is a list of suggestions for SIDs to follow in organizing effective news conferences regardless of the size of the organization:

1. Make certain the announcement is newsworthy.

2. Inform all members of the media whom you want to attend. The timing of the invitations should allow reporters enough time to arrange schedules, but not enough time to find out and to report the particulars of the announcement.

3. In the case of a "blockbuster" announcement, issue verbal invitations three to five hours in advance of the news conference. Blockbuster announcements would

include the naming of a coach, the completion of a trade, or a decision to build a new stadium.

In the case of a "soft" announcement, such as a groundbreaking ceremony for a new stadium, mail, fax, or email invitations three to five days in advance.

4. Make certain that sufficient parking space is available close to the meeting room.

5. The room for the news conference should be large enough to handle the crowd but small enough to create an atmosphere of intimacy and importance. A handful of reporters in a large room has a hollow feel, perhaps creating an impression that not many reporters showed up or felt the announcement was important enough to attend. The announcement should be made on the organization's own turf—campus, stadium, office, gymnasium, or conference room.

6. The facility should be attractive and functional. Provide an adequate number of chairs and easy access to restrooms and telephones. Also, make certain sufficient working space is available to reporters. You should incorporate the institution's name and logo in the backdrop or place them on the front of the speaker's podium.

   Remember, your job is to put the university in the public eye. One of the simplest and most effective ways to do so is to display the institution's name and logo in such a manner that they appear prominently in photographs or video clips from the news conference.

7. Make the media feel welcome by offering refreshments, such as cookies or donuts along with coffee, tea, and soft drinks. Do *not* serve alcohol. In today's society, news conferences are work sessions, not social get-togethers. Furthermore, most media representatives will not drink alcohol if they are "on the clock" (i.e., working on a story for the next edition or telecast).

   Do not spend more than you can afford on refreshments. If a modest lunch fits into the budget, a meal is more than acceptable to members of the media. Coffee, soft drinks, and pastry generally are sufficient, however.

8. Provide the media copies of the news release. The release should supply all basic information but not all the details.

9. Allow enough time in the schedule for media questions. Do not let the question-answer session run longer than 30 minutes.

News conferences are sometimes called to announce marketing or sponsorship agreements.

10. Supply photographs to the print media if they will enhance coverage. Also, 35 mm color slides often will find their way into the 6 o'clock television news shows. The SID or public relations director should arrange the photographs in advance.

11. Following the news conference, allow 15–30 minutes for additional one-on-one interviews. If you let the questions continue for more than 30 minutes, you infringe on the time available to media representatives to prepare their stories for publication or broadcast.

Media Days

Media days are popular and effective publicity-generating events for Division I universities and for professional teams. In Divisions II and III in most parts of the country, media days usually are limited to college football and/or basketball. Colleges and conferences may organize media days for other sports depending on the visibility of the sport in a particular area.

The sport organization gives the media the red-carpet treatment on these days, so careful planning and attention to detail are essential. Sportswriters are accustomed to being pampered on such occasions. For example, the Division III North Coast Athletic Conference builds two media days a year around the "big ticket" sports of football and basketball. At the time of the conference's inception in 1983, officials of the nine Ohio, Indiana, and Pennsylvania schools involved decided to go with a fall media day in August with emphasis on football and another fall sport; and a winter media day in November focusing on basketball and another winter or spring sport.

The fall, or football, media day is the first opportunity each year for reporters to visit a college campus or professional team's facilities and interact with the athletes in person. In the case of a conference, the fall media day gives journalists a chance to meet new coaches, athletic directors, and sports information directors, too. Of particular importance is luring journalists new to the school or conference beat. There is perhaps no better opportunity to treat the journalist to a taste of the school and to begin to establish a favorable one-on-one relationship.

A poorly organized media day can be a disaster and can result in poor public relations that may take a long time to overcome. Organizations should take full advantage of the tools and people available when bringing media on campus. Asking members of the spirit group or the band to participate in the event is one way to utilize the resources on your campus to the fullest.

For example, Northern Kentucky University used to stage a simple luncheon off campus for boosters prior to the start of the basketball season. Fresh off a runner-up finish in the 1996 NCAA Division II Men's Basketball Tournament, university officials organized a special "preview" for the 1996–97 season. The media/booster event opened with a reception offering refreshments and comments from the coaches. Fifteen-minute intrasquad exhibitions by the men's and women's basketball teams followed. Members of the teams were available to the media for interviews after the scrimmages.

College conferences also arrange media days prior to the start of the football and basketball seasons. Such events typically include a luncheon, comments from the men's and women's coaches for each team, opportunities for interviews with coaches and selected players, and announcement of the results of preseason voting on the top teams and players in the conference.

As in planning for a news conference, preparations for a media day are a team project. The planning must start much further in advance and involve more people, however, because of the multifaceted nature of the program. The media day amounts to multiple announcements and interviews all rolled into one package.

Planning the Media Day

The planning typically starts nine months in advance. As in the case of news conferences, the effective sports information or public relations director must develop an organizational chart that spells out responsibilities for administrators, coaches, and others. The plan should include a budget and a timetable that lists deadlines for completion of specific tasks and dates for particular steps, such as the date for mailing out invitations. Here's a rundown on the most important steps in the process:

1. Choose a date and a starting time.

2. Choose and reserve a place to hold the event.

3. Choose and reserve a caterer if the school or the facility selected does not have one.

4. Determine the schedule of events for the day.

5. Announce the media day and send out invitations, preregistration forms, and maps.

6. Prepare a preregistration list and add names as they come in.

7. Prepare information packets (press kits) for the media and for others who attend.

8. Prepare a biography sheet on the coach(es) who will attend.

9. Notify the caterer of the final count for the meal.

10. Create a checklist of duties to be performed the day of the event.

The most important considerations at the beginning of the planning process are the date, the site, and the facilities. Early to mid-August is the best time to schedule a football media day, to avoid conflicts with other professional sports or other university media days. Mid-November is prime time for a basketball media day. However, the ideal time for the sport is around a month before the first game. SIDs consider practice schedules, other conference and school media days, and coaches' schedules in making the choice. Midmorning is the best time of day for those who have to travel lengthy distances to get to the event. An early afternoon finish gives most a chance to get home by dinner.

The next consideration is the site or city and facilities available. Most colleges stage the media day on campus in order to capitalize on the familiar resources that are readily available to them. The SID must reserve a room in the athletics com-

Planning a Conference Media Day

1. Choose a date and time for media day, keeping in mind
   * The start of the season (preview the season around a month before the first game)
   * The practice schedule of the conference teams and coaches
   * Other conferences' and schools' media days
   * No-news weekdays (keep away from Mondays, Fridays, and weekends)
   * Mid-morning starts are advantageous for those traveling lengthy distances
   * Mid-morning starts allow the event to complete by midday, giving everyone a chance to be home by the ever-so-important dinner time, or for coaches, the ever-so-important practice time

2. Choose and reserve a place to to hold your media day (give a ballpark figure on attendance)
   * Choose a city geographically pleasing to the majority of your media
   * If the conference holds more than one media day (multiple sports), a good idea is to split geographical sites among the two events to please media from other regions
   * Rotate media day by region on a yearly basis
   * Reserve at least six months in advance in a clean, roomy, atmospheric place to hold the actual event
     Examples:
       * A nice restaurant
       * A catered banquet hall
       * A museum's banquet facility
       * A stadium's or arena's banquet facility

3. Choose and reserve a caterer if the facility does not provide it's own—a selective menu and good food is important to all attending
   * Select the menu for for the luncheon, keeping in mind price, while also giving attendees an option
   * Be sure coffee and water can be served from the start of the event and throughout
   * If feasible, have pastry available as people arrive and have a variety of nonalcoholic beverages available throughout the event

4. Determine schedule of events for the day; try to keep events within a three-hour time range
     Example:
       * *Opening Remarks and Welcome*
         A prominent national or local figure as master of ceremonies always is a nice touch and offers more media appeal; information director should be the MC if there is no other master of ceremonies
       * *Coaches Presentations*
         Have each coach present a preview of their upcoming season in a short, three-to-four minute synopsis
       * *Preseason Voting*
         Have the media, sports information directors, and coaches cast their votes, respectively, for the preseason rankings
       * *Lunch*

plex, university center, or other facility well in advance to avoid conflicts with other university functions. Similarly, the SID must arrange for a catering service or for university food services support before they are booked for other events.

Most college conferences rotate media days among cities near member schools or among metropolitan areas with major media outlets. Seven of the schools in the North Coast Athletic Conference (NCAC) are in central and northern Ohio, two in western Pennsylvania, and two in Indiana. The conference typically alternates the fall and winter media days between Cleveland and Columbus each year. Cleveland is attractive because it is close to many of the Ohio schools as well as the Pennsylvania media, it is home to the headquarters of the NCAC, and because the *Plain Dealer* in Cleveland boasts the largest circulation among daily newspapers in Ohio. Columbus is centrally located; more athletics directors and faculty representatives can attend without an overnight stay. In addition, media from Cincinnati, Dayton, and Indianapolis can attend easily.

The NCAC chooses a specific site, designed to send a positive message about the conference and member schools. The conference has staged previous media days at the Stadium Club at old Municipal Stadium in Cleveland, Gund Arena, and the members-only Terrace Club during the first year of operation of the Indians' Jacobs Field.

"This conference of academically highly selective colleges feels that where it hosts a media day makes a statement about itself and its colleges, the priority it places on quality and excellence, and the degree of respect it has for sports journalists," said Brian Sullivan, NCAC director of information.

Other site-related considerations are availability, discounts on room-rate availability (if a hotel is considered), cost and safety of parking, and access to an interstate highway. Also important are services provided—microphones, display signs, and servers. For example, the room for a conference media day should include three large tables near the entrance to the program room, one for a registration table and two for media guides and other handouts.

The sports information or public relations director always should visit a site before making a selection. It is also a good idea to visit the site again when the program is complete to reassess logistical needs, such as the location of the head table and interview areas.

Preparing for Media Day

Once the site has been selected, attention turns to preparing the program, gathering materials to be distributed, inviting school and media people, and coordinating reservations. The well-organized SID will create a timetable and stick to it. Falling behind may mean missing a key deadline.

The actual program, of course, is the showpiece of the day and the key to a successful event. Early in the planning process, the appropriate officials must decide the format. Important considerations include choice of an emcee (if desired) and speakers, as well as decisions on whether to offer a meal; a special feature, such as a golf outing; and other attractions, such as a raffle or a prize giveaway. When the decisions have been made, the SID should prepare a minute-by-minute agenda for the day and send it to all participants. For example, organizers of the NCAC media days limit each coach to five minutes. Most athletics departments and teams try to fit the entire program into three hours or less.

Sports information personnel spend the time between the selection of the site and the date of the event preparing materials to distribute. The primary handouts are the media guide and the press kit. The press kit consists of a folder of information designed specifically for the day. Organizers usually put all the information in a folder with the school or conference logo.

Here is a rundown on what a press kit for a conference media day usually contains:

- A nametag with the person's name and affiliation
- A cover sheet welcoming the person to the event and listing items in the press kit (including the agenda and a person to contact with questions)
- The appropriate media guides. Take extras for conference media days because SIDs like to pick up a handful for use in pregame information kits during the season
- Preseason voting ballots to rank the teams. The ballot for coaches should include one fewer space and instructions not to rank their own teams
- Biography sheets on any players who attend the media day
- Statistics packet with year-end statistics for the team(s) involved. The packet will make it easier to flip from school to school or sport to sport without digging through a media guide
- Composite photo sheet or compact disc (CD) with all coaches and players in attendance
- A logo sheet or CD with camera-ready copies of the team and conference logos
- Composite preseason national polls list, including rankings for any schools in the conference
- All-time conference preseason polls sheet with the rankings year by year as well as the actual year-end standings
- Composite schedule listing a schedule for each team and/or a rundown showing which teams play on each day of the season

The press kit for a media day at a single school should contain everything but the preseason ballot and the all-time conference polls sheet.

The SID should keep a running list of the names of people who preregister. The list provides a working number for giving the caterer a meal count, as well as a checklist of who has not responded to the invitation. It also serves as a guide for spelling names and affiliations for nametags and press kits.

Sports information personnel should prepare all press-kit materials, nametags, and other handouts (including names for door-prize drawings) in advance. There will not be time for a lot of scrambling on a day in which activities are planned to the minute. Last-minute scrambling leads to mistakes and an appearance of poor organization.

The Day of Media Day

The sports information director cannot sit back and relax when the big day arrives. On the contrary, the SID is the air traffic controller who makes sure the event gets off the ground and flies smoothly. The media day team, headed by the SID, makes certain all materials are in place, all participants are briefed, and all activities are finished on time. The SID also is responsible for handling any emergencies or problems that arise involving the media in attendance.

On the media day, the SID generally arrives two hours before the event. The first order of business is to check the facility—a check with personnel in charge of the event if off campus or a visual check if on campus. The SID should make certain the tables are set up properly, the sound system is working, and service providers are familiar with the agenda. For example, the SID should make clear to the caterers when they can start setting up coffee and pastry, serving the meal, or clearing tables.

The sports information team next sets up the room with the appropriate team or conference paraphernalia—banners, pennants, centerpieces, etc. They also can set out nametags at the head table if desired or designate tables for specific schools or media. Attention then turns to registration. The SID's on-site team should set up the registration table in such a way that it facilitates an orderly flow into the program room and discourages bottlenecks (spots where people stop to chat and block hallways).

They also should place media guides on tables just beyond the registration area. It is a good idea to have 5–10 extra guides available for media members who show up without registering. Conference officials recommend bringing an additional 100 guides for distribution among SIDs at conference schools. It is also wise to have available extra press kits, nametags, and other materials.

The SID should leave the registration to student assistants or other department personnel. To get an exact count of participants, the registration team should mark off names on the preregistration list as people arrive.

Five Ingredients Essential to Success of a Media Day

1. Create a checklist of details to make the media day run smoothly. The list should outline all activities for the day, specify who is in charge of each, and identify tasks they must perform. (See the sidebar on page 111)

2. Make the day enjoyable for everyone involved. Schedule a round of golf or other icebreaker as part of the day. Make refreshments available or offer a lunch. Set up a hospitality room for the media and for everyone who takes part in the activities.

3. Provide reporters media guides as well as photographs of standout players. Arrange a separate room for individual player interview, to minimize distractions.

   If the media day is conducted by a conference rather than by an individual school, a standout player who is articulate should accompany the head coach to meet the media. The SID for each school should supply photographs at the event. Prior to the day, the SID should forward to the conference information director head shots of the coach and of a key player who will attend.

4. Provide reporters media packets. A typical media packet will include a conference news release, player and coach photographs, and forms for the coaches' vote for the preseason picks.

5. At a conference media day, conduct a preseason poll by both coaches and media. Preseason predictions make for good news stories. The preseason pick for conference champion always is popular with the media.

Media are assembled together during a press conference by the Cleveland Browns during the NFL's college draft day.

The SID should act as the official greeter. He or she also should remain free to welcome and to brief participants of the program on the agenda, seating arrangements, operation of the microphone, etc. In addition, the responsibility for beginning the program on time falls to the SID. The SID should start the proceedings and push to ensure that all stay on schedule or should make an effort to catch up if they fall behind.

At the end of the activities, the SID should be sure to say good-bye to as many guests as possible. That provides a personal touch to the day and helps media representatives to put a name and face together. A simple gesture, it may pay off the next time the journalist needs to get information about the SID's team or school.

Summary

Managed news events give a sport organization an opportunity to communicate its mission, goals, and philosophy to the public through the media. The packaged events enable the organization to plan and to control the release of information to a much greater extent than in any other form of communication.

The two most common types of managed events are news conferences and media days. A news conference is a meeting called to make an announcement or to release information to representatives of the media. A media day is an event designed to introduce the media to players, coaches, and other athletics personnel. It also may provide a preview of the season, an introduction of players, or a scrimmage that gives the media a chance to see the players in action.

A news conference is an effective tool for distributing the same information to a large group of reporters simultaneously. The news conference serves both the sport organization and the media. Professional and collegiate sport organizations use news conferences primarily to make positive announcements about coaches, players, programs, and facilities. The news conference enables representatives of the sport organization to present information in the most favorable light and ensures that the appropriate people answer questions from the media. The news conference makes it possible for reporters to collect information and conduct interviews quickly on deadline, and it may eliminate the need for followup calls to other people.

A media day is an elaborate news conference with a more social atmosphere. One purpose is to provide information to the media on players, teams, and season prospects. Another is to introduce the media to players and coaches and to create a favorable working relationship. The typical media day includes presentations by coaches, interview opportunities, and a social function. Media packets distributed at the event give reporters a wealth of background information they can filter into stories about the team throughout the season.

News conferences and media days require meticulous planning and teamwork on the part of administrators and sports information personnel. For both types of managed events, the sports information or public relations director should develop an organizational chart and timetable with duties and deadlines for all involved to ensure that tasks are completed on time and that activities run smoothly. Poor organization not only may detract from the event, but also may damage the image of the institution.

DISCUSSION QUESTIONS

1. What would you do differently in setting up a football media day for a Division I-A university or a Division III conference?
2. How do you prepare your subject (e.g., new coach) for a hastily called news conference?

SUGGESTED EXERCISES

1. Set up a news conference whereby students do the role-playing. One student should act the part of the athletics director, another as a coach, and yet another as the sports information director. All others are reporters from different newspapers who write for different audiences.
   a. The athletics director will announce that three starting basketball players on a very good college team have been arrested for alleged drug possession. A news release should accompany the announcement and be distributed to the assembled media.
   b. Allow time for questioning and then, if possible, videotape the news conference and replay it to the students to enable them to critique themselves.
   c. Last, each of the reporters should write a news story applicable to his or her audience: national, regional, or local.
2. Plan a conference football media day, then set up the media day with everything from a rostrum to coffee and cookies.

Chapter Seven

MEDIA BROCHURES: MIRROR IMAGES OF SPORTS PROGRAMS

The NCAA Division I basketball championships are over. The last of the basketball banquets is over, the last of the team and conference awards have been distributed to deserving athletes. After six months and a seemingly endless string of exhibitions, games, and tournaments, the collegiate basketball season is at an end.

It is time for a well-deserved break for the communications staff of the Big Ten Conference, right?

In his book, *Media, Sports and Society,* Wenner identifies these key questions to ask about the process, function, and influence of sport communication:

- What is the nature of the relationship between media organizations and sport organizations?

- What does the sports contest mean to the audience and how do audience members consume it?

- How much power do sports journalists, media, and sport organizations wield in determining how audience members consume and interpret the sport?

Wrong. It is time to begin work on the conference basketball guide for next season. There is no time to waste. The conference media day is only six months away, and a mountain of work lies ahead. Statistics need to be updated. Interviews need to be conducted. Stories need to be written. Pictures need to be shot. Covers need to be designed. Proofs need to be read. Advertisements need to be sold. Printing contracts need to be arranged.

Coordination. Coordination. And more coordination.

By the time Media Day rolls around in October, sports information directors from 11 universities, at least three members of the Big Ten staff, two representatives of a printing company, two representatives of a publishing company, and an art studio will be involved in one or more facets of production of the glossy basketball media guides. Wait too long to start, and everyone will have to swallow the elephant whole.

That's the analogy insiders use to describe the time, energy, and coordination required to plan and deliver eye-catching and effective brochures and media guides. The choice is simple: Take one small bite at a time, or wait until the deadline crunch and eat the elephant all at once.

Planning and Budgeting

The first thing the sports information director must understand is that a media brochure serves different segments of the sport organization and the public in different ways. The coach looks at it from a recruiting angle; admissions passes it out at college nights, and the president of the institution shows it off to the board of trustees (Davis, 1978). Morgan (1985) adds that alumni also are eager for an outstanding media brochure.

Whether a guide is for a professional team or for a Division I, Division II, or Division III team, the required information must be consistent, and it must be put together in a format that will serve all segments of the sport organization and target audiences to the fullest.

Production of a media guide requires a complex team effort by a diverse group of administrators and media specialists. The team usually consists of hired professionals and in-house personnel, including administrators and sports information staff members. In interviews with Bill Nichols, Kevin Ruple, SID at Baldwin-Wallace College in Berea, Ohio; and Merle Levin, former SID at Cleveland State University, recommended tapping into resources outside the athletic department. They suggested recruiting assistance from the university's professional staff, such as graphic designers and artists, and lining up a group of student interns or helpers. They also encouraged SIDs to create a volunteer group made up of professionals from the business world along with alumni who work in related fields. For example, the SID may call on alumni or professionals in the agency business, in printing companies, or in photography studios for assistance. There is more than enough work for everyone, particularly at small colleges.

The sport organization's publication budget will dictate the number and the sophistication of media brochures. The annual publication budget ranged in 1996 from $18,000 at Division III John Carroll University to $23,000 at Division II Northern Kentucky University; and from $50,000 to $100,000, respectively, at Kent State University and the University of Illinois in Division I, according to fig-

Overseeing the production of media guides and game programs is a primary role of a sports information specialist.

ures gathered from the universities' sports information departments. With increased printing costs, those figures have steadily increased and there seems to be no indication that publication budgets will level off in the near future. The sale of advertising can boost the pool of money available for a particular guide and make it possible to produce a higher quality product. The 1994–1995 Mid-American Conference women's basketball media guide contained seven full-page ads, including color ads on the inside of the front cover and on both sides of the back cover.

At most colleges and universities, the top publication priority goes to a magazine-style guide or pocketsize booklet for football and men's and women's basketball, even if the books are black and white. Larger colleges also produce full-color media guides for all prominent sports at their institutions. Smaller colleges may print only a roster sheet for low-profile sports or a one-page guide that folds into a pocketsize pamphlet, if anything.

The number and size of the brochures the sports information office must produce will determine the amount of help needed. At a Division III institution, the sports information director may do everything except the printing. The university's public relations office or printing services may take care of that. A multicolor, multifaceted magazine requires a large team. The sports information director supervises the team. Here is a list of considerations:

Budgeting

The budget generally is determined by university administrators. The SID receives an annual allotment for publications and supplements it through advertising. The SID, in concert with public relations or athletics administrators, decides how to divide the publications budget among various sports.

Advertising

The more advertising the SID can sell for media guides, the more attractive the guide. Consequently, the sports information office may solicit advertising to supplement the budget allotment. The advertising rate depends on the cost of production per page and the number of pages earmarked for advertising. The SID may line up an advertising manager to oversee solicitations; however, sports information personnel or the SID proofs the ads, that is, reads them and notes corrections needed.

Written Content

The sports information or public relations director oversees all the written material in the guide. Sports information personnel will write most of the stories and compile the statistical sections. Sometimes, local sports reporters contribute features on prospects for the season or biographies of the head coach or star player.

Photographs

The sports information or public relations director also arranges for all photographs. The SID selects action pictures from the previous year and arranges for new head shots of coaches, team members, and athletics officials. A staff photographer, a freelancer, or a studio photographer may shoot the pictures. The SID also may hire a professional photographer to shoot a color picture for the cover.

Art and Graphics

The SID arranges for all charts, drawings, and illustrations. The artist may be a volunteer, a member of the art department, an in-house professional, or a hired studio artist.

Page Design

The page design may be created by members of the sports information or public relations staff, personnel in the college's printing services offices, or printing company employees. As in the case of advertisements, the SID or sports information staffers read and mark corrections on proofs of all pages.

Printing

Most colleges contract with professional printing companies for multicolor, magazine-style guides. Local print shops or university printing services often can handle small brochures. The SID or an athletics department administrator negotiates the printing contract or oversees competitive bidding for the contract.

Content Considerations

In planning a media guide, the SID must keep in mind that he or she is serving the media, not the coaching staff, the president and trustees, or boosters and alumni. That means that philosophical conflicts between in-house people and members of the working media over the content of the guide may sometimes arise. The most effective way to resolve such conflicts is to survey the media and find out what they want, then to sell coaches and administrators on the concept.

Remember, the best brochures are media guides—not recruiting guides. The savvy sports information or public relations director turns out attractive media guides that athletics officials can use in recruiting. If you give the coach a guide that puts the institution in a favorable light and makes the job of the media easier, it *will* be good for the coach.

The guide should include every detail about the players, coaches, team, and sport organization that will aid in the coverage of games. Because the media often work under intense deadline pressure, they may need to check a record, a past score, or a player's hometown. The more easily they can find the information in the media guide, the more favorably disposed toward the institution they are likely to be.

Some large guides include such nonessential extras as photographs of the campus, future schedules, past letter winners, past glories (conference finishes and championships), star athletes and record holders, and the radio and television schedule.

Media guides for low-profile sports are less pretentious and less expensive, but they still need the primary content ingredients essential to the media—roster, schedule, last year, season's prospects, quick facts, and short biographies and pro-

Mandatory Content Items for a Functional Media Guide

- Alphabetical roster: a line about each player including name, height, weight, position, age, class, experience, hometown, and high school.

- Schedule: a list with each opponent, date, place, starting time, and, if available, television information for each game.

- School records: a statistical rundown on the season-by-season records of the team, dating back to the first year of the program.

- Last year's results: a capsule of each game in the previous season, including both individual and team statistics.

- History: a history of each series with each opponent on the schedule.

- Season prospects: a brief overview of the previous season and a general preview of the upcoming season. The overview should include comments from the head coach and perhaps from competitors.

- Quick fact: an informational listing about the institution, which should include the location of the institution, founding data, enrollment, denomination (if affiliated), the stadium or arena and its capacity, and key personnel. Begin with the president and work down to the secretaries. Include important telephone numbers and best times to reach coaches.

- Table of contents: a complete listing of contents of the guide from the front to the back of the publication.

- Pronunciation guide: the name of each of the athletes, spelled phonetically to assist those in broadcast media.

- Biographies of coaches: a relatively complete minibiography of the head coach, including an up-to-date coaching record. Short biographies (one or two paragraphs) on assistant coaches, athletic trainers, strength trainers, and other key support personnel are helpful, but not vital. Photographs of the coaching staff help dress up a media guide and create a favorable impression.

- Profiles of players: a brief profile of each player, including a photograph and statistics for each season the athlete has performed for the institution. Due to the nature of sports, player profiles have a short lifespan; however, the media frequently use them for reference.

- Stadium or arena layout: information about the stadium/arena. A diagram and information are interesting, if not essential, and may help to set apart the guide from those of competitors.

- Media information: a section that explains how members of the media obtain credentials, the procedures to be followed by broadcast media, parking information, working media room facilities, and interview procedures.

files of the coaches (if possible). Normally, these guides are one-color and four or eight pages. The sport organization generally prints fewer copies of these than of football or men's and women's basketball guides.

The Production Process

The sports information director serves as the quarterback in the production process, motivating the team and carrying out the game plan. That means the SID is the "coalition builder" who makes certain that secretaries, advertising salespeople, writers, photographers, designers, typesetters, and proofreaders all feel like an integral part of the team. The biggest challenge often is not motivating the role-players, but working with the coaches. The SID must make sure coaches realize that the media production team is a group of colleagues working toward the same goals as the coaching staff.

The sports information director absolutely must create a production schedule with realistic deadlines. Meeting deadlines is essential to success. Missing a deadline for a story throws off the design timetable, the printing schedule, and the delivery date; therefore, it is vital to create a schedule of activities, to distribute copies to all members of the team, and to enforce deadlines.

Veteran sports information directors recommend dividing the workload into a series of doable tasks. Here is a typical timetable for a football media guide:

- Begin the day after the football banquet (late November or early December, unless the team qualifies for a bowl game). You can begin to gather and update information, even if some of it may change between the end of one season and the start of the next:

  – Compile a list of letter winners and returning players

  – Update the school history

  – Update seasonal and team records

  – Update directories

- Update coaches' biographies

- Get an outlook for next season from the head coach

Some information may change before the print date. Coaches, sports information personnel, and athletics officials may leave at the end of the academic year, but it is easier to make a few adjustments in June when the university issues personnel contracts than to start from scratch a month from the printing deadline.

- Create a budget for the media guide as soon as publication budget numbers for the next academic year are available. If final figures will not be available until May or June, develop a working budget based on the current year and any projections available for the coming year.

- Determine what you will charge for advertisements—full page, half page, and quarter page—as part of the budget process. Look for other opportunities to gain funds, such as sharing some expenses with the athletics department. Set the budget early and live within the budget—no last-minute switches from color to black and white to offset unexpected expenses or overly ambitious estimates.

  Use students as ad solicitors. Most ads are repeat business (i.e., companies that advertise every year). You may come out ahead if you offer students a commission of up to 5% of the total for a repeat ad and 10% of a new ad.

- Decide on the size of the media guide as part of the budget process. Sports information directors generally decide the size, the amount of color, etc., with the approval of their immediate superiors (college public relations directors or athletics directors). The size, use of color, and number of pages all figure into the expense of the guide.

  The 4"-by-9" guide once was very popular because it fit into coat pockets and was less expensive to mail. Now, the most widely used size is 8 1/2"-by-11", which fits neatly into a file drawer or briefcase.

- Decide upon the art and photography needed as early as possible. Make the appropriate arrangements with the staff photographer, volunteer, or freelance professional. Make certain all art and photographs are in hand by the end of March.

- Take all content information, including art and graphics, to the designers in April. Set an April deadline regardless of whether the design is produced by the sports information staff, the university public relations department, or outside volunteers.

- Meet with the coach in April to gain approval on the preliminary design.

- Assemble all information in May.

- Take all final drafts of content to the designer in June.

- Meet with the coach and administrators in June, when production nears completion. You can get final approval of the design. You can make any changes in players, coaches, or personnel at that time.

- Take the guide to the printer in early July. Printing contracts generally call for the completion of the job within two or three weeks.

- Make certain you print enough guides for the media who regularly cover the organization or team, for Media Day, for distribution to recruits, for athletics department personnel, and for visiting media at each game. You should print a few extras to keep on hand for unexpected requests and for the department's archives.

Professional leagues often dictate a standard size for guides. On the collegiate level, many conferences adopt a standard format on a league-wide scale. The NCAA also puts limitations on brochures. For example, the NCAA now prohibits color on the inside pages. However, there are subtle changes in style almost yearly, according to new rules set down by the NCAA.

The NCAA prohibits publication of advertisements designed to attract recruits to the program, and publication of a separate guide or brochure to give to prospective recruits is illegal.

Media guides are a source of pride and competition among sports information directors across the country. The College Sports Information Directors of America (CoSIDA) sponsors a national competition each year and often the competition in the publishing business rivals that on the athletics fields. The CoSIDA competition includes judging in approximately 40 categories ranging from posters to football guides.

Summary

Media guides serve a number of constituencies within the university—the coaching staff, the administration, and alumni—in different ways. All are secondary to the media from the standpoint of the sports information director. For the SID, the media guide is a tool that facilitates coverage by the media and enhances the image of the university.

Production of the most lavish media guides, those for football and basketball, requires coordination of a large team of specialists over a period of up to six months. To be effective, the sports information director must control the production process instead of being controlled by it. The SID must start the planning process and line up assistance well in advance. The most important considerations in the process are the establishment of a budget and the creation of a deadline schedule.

Professional sport organizations always sell advertising to offset printing costs. Colleges and universities may boost funds by selling advertising or sharing expenses with the athletics department. Professional teams also sell media guides. Colleges and universities typically give them away.

After a budget is determined, the sports information or public relations director decides on the format and content based on possible uses within target markets—media, university personnel, and alumni. The SID then creates a production schedule and coordinates the work of advertising salespeople, writers, photographers, artists, designers, and printers.

Media guides can be of any size and any style. What is important is to make the most attractive and most functional guide possible. The more functional the guide, the more favorable the impression among members of the working media who need to find specific information on deadline will have of the sport organization.

Winning awards for the design of a media guide is a plus for a sports information director. It also is ego fulfilling, but remember, if the book does not contain all the information the media need, the award-winning artistry means very little. A well-organized and useful media guide will not win any games, but a poor one may do irreparable harm to the image of the institution.

DISCUSSION QUESTIONS

1. How would you structure a football media guide to be effective in recruiting student-athletes and still be used as a reference source for the media?
2. What are the differences in media guides on collegiate and professional levels of sports?

SUGGESTED EXERCISES

1. Create a media guide for a less visible sport, such as golf, tennis, swimming, cross-country, or gymnastics. Make this guide a foldout, using no more than four pages. Include all the proper components, including art, which can take the form of sketches (even stick figures).
2. Establish a budget for a Division I-A football media guide and then cost out the production. Call a Division I-A school. List all costs. (Contact an SID at a Division I-A institution.)

Chapter Eight

INTERVIEWS: FROM PERSONAL TO PACK JOURNALISM

The "Star of the Game" interview is a staple of radio and television broadcasts of Major League Baseball games.

Professional basketball and football broadcasters frequently grab coaches at half-time for a quick assessment of the game and catch players at courtside or on the sidelines for postgame comments. National Football League, National Basketball Association, and Women's National Basketball Association teams also arrange postgame interview sessions for all media representatives.

College athletics officials often set aside a room for impromptu question-answer sessions with players and coaches after games. They also open their locker rooms to the media for one-on-one interviews. In fact, the National Collegiate Athletic Association requires teams to send a coach (preferably the head coach) and 2–3 players to an interview room after basketball tournament games and to open their locker rooms to reporters for individual interviews after an appropriate "cooling off" period, usually 10 minutes.

Chapter 8 examines the nature of the working relationship between sports journalists and sport organizations at its most personal level—the interview. The text explores the interaction from the standpoint of both the media and the sport organization, including the interview's effect on the public's perception of each participant. It also addresses the role of the sports information or public relations director in suggesting interviews, arranging interviews, and facilitating positive interactions between journalists and representatives of the school or team.

This policy exists because television's influence on sports coverage since World War II has made the interview an integral part of sports journalism, that is, a communication tool to show the human side of the statistics and highlights. Interviews with players, coaches, and athletics administrators give sports reporters insight into the "how" and the "why" of a game's outcome. Interviews give players public exposure—celebrity in some instances, scorn in others. Interviews also give fans an "up-close-and-personal" look at the stars of the game, as ABC-TV Sports programmers used to say.

The interview has also become a key component of the working relationship between the media and sport organizations. The journalist depends on information from players, coaches, and team officials to produce a knowledgeable game preview or an in-depth account of a contest. The sport organization attempts to use the pregame report and game coverage, with comments from representatives of the team, to project its image and philosophy in the most favorable light.

Prior to the emergence of television in the mid-20th century, sports reporters did not depend heavily on player interviews for story material. They often maintained chummy, off-field relationships with players that provided the grist for news stories and columns, but the personal interview was confined to features or personality profiles. Reporters relied primarily on their own observations and rich, narrative prose to re-create a "picture" of a game. They often wrote a game story without ever going to the locker room or talking to players and coaches. Radio announcers, as noted in earlier chapters, did not even *go* to the games in many cases. They orally re-created the drama based on play-by-play they picked up off the Western Union tickers in the station.

Television put the game on the stage and gave viewers at home front-row seats to the action. The live pictures changed forever the nature of sports coverage. With the drama of the game already played out on the television screen, radio and television journalists turned to the "actors" in search of something new to offer audiences. Both radio and television reporters began to crowd into locker rooms to get postgame comments from players to supplement what happened with how and why. Such interviews quickly evolved into a staple of all the media and an integral part of all types of sports-related stories—news reports and postgame "Star of the Game" shows in the broadcast media; and game stories, features, and columns in the print media. Often, at the conclusion of a news conference, journalists will strive for at least a few moments of one-on-one with the subject in the never-ending quest for an exclusive. In addition, the 1970s phenomenon of talk radio has changed the interview process even more. Not only do talk-show hosts interview the celebrity guests, but the callers do so as well. It makes for a very good entertainment mix.

Although the media today rely heavily on pregame and postgame interviews, not all journalists seek the same information from an interview. Barone and Switzer (1995) contend in *Interviewing Art and Skill* that the needs of journalistic audiences vary according to medium:

Interviews with coaches or players can range from one-on-one personal meetings to "pack" interviews.

> Newspaper and magazine audiences expect articles that convey answers to the standard questions of who, what, where and when. Viewers of television news shows, on the other hand, expect brief capsule summaries of stories with pithy "sound bites," five- to ten-second edited quotes, that capture a response to a situation. Radio listeners have a different set of needs; they want to hear voices that convey information with sufficient intensity and brevity to hold their attention despite the lack of face-to-face contact. (p. 146)

Demand for interviews also forever changed the working relationships among journalists, athletes, and sports information professionals. Athletes are no longer just buddies who provide information anonymously; now, they are expected to provide information openly, to talk publicly when they are at the lowest depths of disappointment or at the highest peaks of success. The media scrutiny often can strain the relationship between athletes and reporters.

Demand for interviews changed the relationship between journalists and sports information and public relations directors as well. No longer are SIDs simply information and service providers, people who supply statistics, game notes, and workspace. Now they are intermediaries as well. Members of the media expect SIDs to provide access to players and coaches for interviews, to set up one-on-one interviews and postgame news conferences, and even to collect postgame comments from coaches and players for "pool" use, that is, for use by all the media in attendance.

Members of the media also expect sports information personnel to intervene when athletes balk at interviews and to arbitrate when tempers flare in emotional situations. Athletes sometimes ask SIDs and public relations directors to shield them from probing reporters, to answer questions from the media, and to bar particularly "negative" reporters from the locker room. The expectations of both reporters and athletes put sports information personnel squarely in the eye of the "interview hurricane."

| A Two-Way Relationship | The sports interview is a question-answer strategy employed by members of the media to gather information to present to an audience, thereby to provide insights into an athletics contest or contestant. It is an interactive technique used by journalists to answer the basic news questions, particularly how and why, that are essential to construction or presentation of the sports story. |

What journalists, athletes, and sports information professionals all must understand from the outset is that an interview is a complex and imperfect process of communication. In the simplest context, it is a dialogue between two people. In the most complex analysis, it is an intense minirelationship between two people that is subject to all the pitfalls and influences of interpersonal communication, both verbal and nonverbal. Words, gestures, and facial expressions send messages that constantly influence the responses of both or all parties to the interview. The relationship may change from congenial to contentious in an instant of misinterpretation. Consider the difference in how a football player might interpret the reporter's intent simply because of the phrasing and emphasis on words:

Example 1

A. *How could you* drop that quick slant pass that *bounced* off your chest on fourth-and-goal at the two on the last play of the game?

B. Explain what happened on that incomplete pass on fourth-and-goal at the two on the last play of the game.

Example 2

A. How does it feel to *drop* a pass that would have given your team a trip to a bowl for the first time in 10 years?

B. What went through your mind when your opponent took over on downs?

Both questions in each example ask for the same information. However, the first question in each example may *sound* like an accusation to a player feeling ashamed and embarrassed over his role in a defeat. The second question, in each case, is far less personal and far more palatable in a sensitive situation. The second question, of course, would be the question that most journalists would ask had they the time to carefully plan out questions, but time is not a luxury the journalist enjoys in a postgame interview. The journalist must compose questions on the run, in immediate response to answers to a previous question; for this reason a postgame interview demands the most sophisticated interpersonal skills in one of the least controlled and least conducive communication environments.

What is important to keep in mind is that an interview is an interchange of information between journalists and athletes. It is as critical to the image of the athlete and the sport organization as is the game itself, because the performance in the interview setting may reinforce or repudiate the message the team or organization intends to deliver to its audience. Stewart and Cash (1994) characterize an interview as an exchange of information between two parties. Each has something to gain and each must participate in order for it to be successful. The gain for the journalist is a stronger story of greater interest to readers or viewers. The gain for the athlete and sport organization is reinforcement of the team's goals, philosophy, and image.

Communication scholars offer somewhat different definitions of an interview (for examples, see Barone & Switzer, 1995; Sayer & Hoen, 1994; Stewart & Cash, 1994). The definitions generally include several common characteristics:

Interviews with coaches help the media supplement coverage by detailing the how and why of specific sporting events.

1. An interview is an interchange of information between two or more parties. In the sports setting, it may involve an interaction between two parties, such as in a one-on-one interview for a player profile. It also may involve multiple parties, as in postgame news conferences and impromptu interviews with reporters crowded around a player in the locker room.

Stewart and Cash (1994) contend that an interview is an "exchange of behavior" as well as information (p. 3); the parties to the interview exchange both verbal and nonverbal messages. During the interview, they may share roles, attitudes, and feelings. Such sharing is particularly important to a sports interview. Al McGuire, who turned to television broadcasting after coaching Marquette University to a national men's basketball championship, once said the rollercoaster fortunes of sports make coaches feel big enough to soar with the eagles one day and low enough to play handball against a curb another day. Journalists ask athletes to share those feelings with thousands (sometimes millions) of eavesdroppers (an audience), at the peak of the emotion.

2. An interview has a specific purpose or goal. Remember, the primary purpose of a newspaper story, a radio interview, or a television broadcast is to inform and/or entertain. If stories or broadcasts consistently inform and entertain, they draw a large audience and enhance the media company's revenue prospects, so the goal of the journalist is to gather material from coaches and athletes that informs and entertains. An interview with a coach or athlete provides description, explanation, and opinion that inform readers. It also provides entertaining examples, anecdotes, and comments from the participants.

Who can forget the sentiment Lou Gehrig expressed in his farewell speech at Yankee Stadium: "Today, I consider myself the luckiest man on the face of the earth"? How much more entertaining is the local report of a junior college basketball rout when the star player says, "I went through their defense like a fat rat in a Swiss cheese factory"?

Coaches and athletes also may go into an interview with a goal in mind. They may *want* to explain a key play, a critical call, a development that went unnoticed by reporters and cameras. The interview gives them an opportunity to be understood, to put their performance in the most favorable light, and to demonstrate their character to fans who are readers and viewers. In the broader perspective, interviews afford the sport organization an opportunity to reinforce positive images of the team's strength and character. Interviews give them a chance to put their own spin on the story, rather than leaving it up to the interpretation of the journalist.

3. The parties in an interview exchange information by asking and answering questions. Note that *both parties* exchange information by asking and answering questions.

Contrary to the popular misconception, an interview is not an interrogation in which reporters heap blame on the poor wide receiver who dropped the pass that extinguished the team's last chance of winning. Questions that start out "How do you feel? . . ." or "How could you drop that pass? . . ." or "Don't you think? . . ." may sound like accusations because they are poorly worded, but remember, the motive of the reporter is not to humiliate or embarrass the player. The goal is to obtain information that explains the play. When an interviewee balks, something still happens. If the interviewer persists, the player can come off looking like either a victim or an uncooperative "loser."

The athlete can address any concern about the motive behind a question by asking a question: "Why do you want to know that?" or "Why are you asking me?" A successful interview includes questions by both parties that attempt to clear up any confusion or mixed messages resulting from inconsistent or contradictory verbal and nonverbal signals. Too often, one of the parties makes assumptions about the meaning of a question or answer on the basis of the other's expression, tone of voice, or reaction. An interview relationship can quickly deteriorate because of false assumptions or incorrect interpretations of verbal or nonverbal cues.

Note the difference in these exchanges that involve questions and answers by both parties:

Example 1

Receiver: . . . . I took a step to the outside, then cut sharply across the middle. The play fake took the middle linebacker out of the way. He crashed the line expecting a run. The pass was on target, but I took my eye off it for a minute.

Reporter: . . . . Afraid you were going to take a hit from that free safety?

Receiver: . . . . You think I'm afraid to take my shots across the middle?

Reporter: . . . . No, I was just asking what caused you to take your eye off the ball.

Receiver: . . . . OK. I was trying to see if my feet were gonna come down in the end zone or I had to fight past the safety.

Example 2

Reporter: . . . . How come you dropped that pass on fourth-and-goal at the two?

Receiver: . . . . (*sarcastically*) I dropped it on purpose so all you @#$%*! reporters would have someone to blame. You never come around here when we're winning. You only come around when you're looking for something negative or sensational to sell newspapers.

Reporter: . . . . Why did that question upset you?

Receiver: . . . . How would *you* feel if this happened to you?

Reporter: . . . . I'm not trying to blame you or embarrass you. I'm just trying to explain to readers what happened on the play, to help them understand what went wrong.

In the first example, the reporter incorrectly assumed the player took his eye off the ball to look at the safety. From the wording of the question, the player incorrectly assumed the reporter was questioning his courage. By asking a question, the receiver cleared up the misinterpretations by both parties. Had not the receiver asked the clarifying question, the interview relationship might have soured. By asking the clarifying question, he not only cleared up the confusion and cleared away the simmering hostility but also enabled the reporter to restate the question and to get a fuller explanation.

In the second example, the reporter probably suspected that the receiver responded angrily out of embarrassment and frustration. By asking the followup question, the reporter confirmed it. The reporter knew the player's response was not a personal attack and promptly made clear to the athlete the question was not one, either. The reporter's response to the receiver's answer attempted to mute the personal side and focus on the goal of the question. In other words, it tactfully offered the player an opportunity to shift the blame, to shoulder the blame, or to otherwise enlighten readers or viewers—to share information.

Both examples provide insight into the common characteristics of an interview. The brief exchange of questions and answers by *both* parties ultimately cleared up misinterpretations, repaired rifts in the relationship before they destroyed the interview, and helped both participants achieve their goals. The reporter got better information. The athlete got understanding and the opportunity to present himself and his performance in a clearer light.

The examples also illustrate that members of the media and sport organizations have a mutual interest in a positive outcome. The broadcast interview—and the print interview, to a less direct extent—sends a message about the media and the teams to the public, even if it is not purposeful. The confrontational reporter who asks inane questions in front of a television camera influences public perceptions of the character of the newspaper, magazine, radio station, television station, or cable channel the reporter represents. The player or coach who is surly, uncooperative, and noncommunicative even in victory encourages a negative reaction in the public mind.

Most sports journalists understand that their stories are no better than their ability to get athletes or athletics officials to talk and to keep them talking. They realize that if they consistently and deliberately bait or provoke interviewees, they risk losing access to the sources of information essential to success in the highly competitive media environment. They still *will* ask the tough question of the basketball player who misses the game-winning free throw, but they will do so with a measure of tact and compassion.

Most sport organizations understand that the conduct of the parties in an interview, particularly a broadcast interview, can say as much about the team as its performance on the field. The sports information director can facilitate a positive interaction by helping athletes, coaches, and administrators understand the role of the media. Members of the sport organization often believe the media—particularly local newspapers, radio stations, and TV outlets—should help promote the institution. They see the role of the media as community service and the institution as a member of the community that journalists *should* promote. What athletes and coaches must realize is that the job of the media is to inform about, explain, and examine the institutions within the community. The sport organization must understand that questions are the tools journalists use to probe for explanation and response to complaints or criticism from the public—not to promote accusations or to generate conflict. Members of the sport organization also must recognize that reporters seek reaction to an official's call, a pivotal play, or to the outcome of the game in order to add the participants' point of view to the report—not just the reporter's. They should know that reporters ask the tough questions the fans want to ask but do not have opportunity to ask except on talk radio. If athletes, coaches, and administrators do not understand these roles, the SID can aid the institution by educating them and training them in how to deal with the media.

Structure of an Interview

The best interviews are purposeful and planned, even if the interview consists of a couple of quick questions about a key play under the pressure of deadline. Even then, the reporter usually has jotted down a couple of questions in the margin of notes as the game has progressed.

Most print and broadcast journalists try to find out as much as possible about the subject and the interviewees in advance. The homework makes for a more well-informed list of questions and generally elicits more specific and thorough answers. A high school athlete who has little or no experience dealing with the media is a tough interview, but a journalist who learns about the athlete's interests and hobbies in advance might be able to find common ground that puts the athlete at ease. Perhaps both admire the same professional players or enjoy the same hobbies. The journalist can put the high school athlete at ease, perhaps, by talking about their hobbies before starting the interview.

The planning begins with background research well before the interview; the focus of the research is dictated by the type and purpose of the interview. For example, the preparation for an interview with a new coach would focus on learning as much as possible about the person—personal background, coaching record, coaching philosophy, family, hobbies, and other interests. The preparation for coverage of a game would focus on the records of both teams, the strengths and weaknesses of each, the key players for each, and any positive or negative factors related to the game. For example, a losing coach's job might be on the line, or a player or team might be on the verge of setting a record.

Preparation generally centers on two broad areas: the person and the topic. The degree of emphasis on each depends on the type and purpose of the story. Here is a rundown on the primary types of journalistic stories and the kinds of interviews involved:

News Story

The news story includes all types of hard or breaking news, from the release of the team's schedule to announcement of plans to build a new baseball field. The purpose of the story is to inform, that is, to tell the reader or viewer who, what, when, where, why, and how. The background preparation focuses on the topic and on all people involved. The reporter interviews all those affected by the story for explanation, insight, and reaction.

Feature Story

The feature story includes all types of soft news, from a human interest story about players' work at a soup kitchen during Thanksgiving to a story about a milestone achievement such as the volleyball star's NCAA record-setting service ace. The primary purpose of the story is to explain and entertain, to give readers and viewers a behind-the-scenes or below-the-surface look at the sport organization and its representatives. The reporter's preparation centers on the people involved and how they relate to the topic, so the reporter will interview all the principal people involved, with emphasis on the whys and the hows.

Personality Profile

The personality profile is an in-depth look at a player, coach, or other person in the sport organization. The primary purpose is to inform, to give readers and viewers a broad portrait of the individual. The emphasis is heavily weighted toward background on the subject of the profile. The reporter interviews the subject, teammates or coworkers, coaches, athletics officials, friends, and family about the subject's background, family, personal interests, hobbies, and athletics career.

Sports Column

The sports column is a personal commentary written at regular intervals by a designated member of the staff. Consequently, the column is more subjective than any other story type. The purpose and the focus of the background preparation vary according to the columnist's topic of the day. It may be similar to a news story on one day, a feature on another, and a personality profile on a third. Most often, it offers the writer's opinions of a player, a game, the organization, the team's performance, business matters, or community issues related to the team. That means the purpose often is to persuade. As a result, the reporter interviews players, coaches, officials within the organization, outside athletics experts, fans, and others to seek support for or confirmation of the point the column is trying to make.

Notes Column

The notes column is a collection of small items about the sport organization. The tidbits may range from personal notes about off-field activities such as a professional player's cameo appearance in a movie to game- and team-related information such as a coach's comment on the status of an injured player. Some notes attempt to inform; others, simply to entertain. Often, they are a collection of brief items picked up during interviews for other stories, information that does not warrant a story on its own. Reporters generally collect the notes while talking to coaches, players, and teams officials before or after games.

Enterprise Story

The enterprise story is an in-depth examination of a topic or issue. The story may be explanatory, such as a look into the feasibility of launching a football program at a university with a Division II basketball program. It also may be investigative, looking at such problems and solutions as the low graduation rate for athletes in a particular sport at the local university and the university's attempt to raise that rate. The purpose is to explain, with heavy emphasis on the how and the why.

Enterprise reporting requires considerable background reporting on the issue as well as on the people involved. In fact, the reporter often conducts a number of preliminary interviews during the preparation stage to confirm or correct assumptions (or accusations). The initial interviews often dictate the focal point of the inquiry. The preinterviews also may scuttle the story, if the information does not confirm suspicions or support accusations. The reporter usually conducts multiple interviews with those who have a connection to the issue, those whom the issue affects. Interviews for enterprise stories usually are more like interrogations than are the other types of interviews, because the purpose of the story is to identify the causes of problems and to suggest solutions.

**Types of Stories:
Topic and Purpose**

News story

Feature story

Personality profile

Sports column

Notes column

Enterprise story

Pregame story
(or "Advance")

Postgame story
(or "Game story")

News conference

Pregame Story or "Advance"

The pregame story is an advance on an upcoming game. The purpose is to give readers and viewers information about the game. The story will explore strengths and weaknesses of each team, key players, and possible game strategies. The background preparation will entail perusal of player/team statistics, team rosters, and injury reports, as well as interviews with coaches and/or players about opponents, strategy, etc.

Postgame Story or "Game Story"

The postgame story is the coverage story, the story about the game. The purpose is to inform, to explain to readers what happened and why. Prior to the game, the reporter examines the same information used in a pregame story. The most significant preparation consists of notes and questions scribbled on play-by-play sheets as the game develops and postgame statistics distributed by the sports information or public relations staff. After the game, the reporter interviews coaches and players to get descriptions of key plays, viewpoints on critical game developments, and reactions to the results. A secondary purpose is to entertain, to re-create the game for fans and followers who did not witness it.

News Conference

The news conference is a group interview arranged by sport organizations to give all reporters a chance to question the appropriate players, coaches, or athletics officials for a news story, a pregame story, or a postgame story at the same time. Reporters call the news conference *pack journalism* because they are herded together in a pack for a group interview.

The news conference is arguably the most difficult type of interview situation for both journalists and members of sport organizations. The reason is threefold. First, the print, radio, and television media serve different audiences, as noted, so their goals may be different. Second, every reporter in the room may want to explore a different aspect of the game or its ramifications, depending on the type of story, the angle (focus) the reporter is pursuing, and the media organization's audience. For example, a reporter for a small weekly might ask a question about the player from back home, even if the player did not figure prominently in the outcome. As a result, a news conference is a jumble of random questions from different reporters, with little continuity or congruity. Third, both journalists and organizations of the press conference usually have little time to prepare for an intense interaction in a highly charged situation. The fly-by-the-seat-of-your-pants nature of preparation and the timing of the interviews (at an emotional high or low for the interviewees) are less than ideal for development of a positive interview climate. In fact, the setting increases the barriers to an effective interview and inhibits the kind of interaction that eliminates those barriers.

An effective interview demands preparation on the part of both parties involved. The athlete, coach, or athletics official can better anticipate and answer questions by knowing the type and purpose of the story for which the reporter is gathering information. The SID and other members of the athletics organization should ask about the purpose when a journalist requests an interview. Good reporters will not hesitate to explain the nature and the purpose of the interview; they understand that they will get better answers if the subject(s) has (have) time to gather information and to prepare. Most use "ambush" interviews—the equivalent of a surprise attack—only as a last resort or when necessary to assess the subject's reaction to revealing information in an enterprise story.

It generally is to the reporter's advantage to explain the purpose of the interview. Which of these examples do you think will create the best interview climate?

Example 1

Reporter:. . . . . I'm calling to set up an interview with the football coach.

SID:. . . . . What do you want to talk to him about?

Reporter:. . . . . I just want to talk to him about the season.

SID:. . . . . Is this a pregame story for Saturday's game?

Reporter:. . . . . I'll talk to him about that when I get there.

SID:. . . . . It will help him prepare if I can at least give him an idea of the purpose of the interview.

Reporter:. . . . . Well, I'm going to write the story with or without his cooperation.

Example 2

Reporter:. . . . . I'm calling to set up an interview with the football coach.

SID:. . . . . What do you want to talk to him about?

Reporter:. . . . . I'm writing a story about the six-game losing streak and its impact on the team.

SID:. . . . . What is the story going to say?

Reporter:. . . . . I can't answer that until I have finished my interviews.

SID:. . . . . Is it about all the rumors that he's being forced to resign? I can tell you there is nothing to that.

Reporter: . . . . Yeah, I have to ask him about that. But I don't know how much of the story that will be.

SID:. . . . . You don't think he'll really talk to you about that, do you? What can he say that won't just add credence to the rumors?

Example 3

Reporter:. . . . . I'm calling to set up an interview with the football coach.

SID:. . . . . What do you want to talk to him about?

Reporter:. . . . . I'm writing a story about the six-game losing streak and its impact on the team.

SID:. . . . . You mean about the rumors that he's under pressure to resign?

Reporter:. . . . . I don't know how big a part of the story that might be—if any—until I talk to everyone. It's important to get his perspective before I write the story. He's the expert in this situation. He's the one who knows if there is any substance to the rumors.

The first two examples do not lay the foundation for a good interview. The first heightens suspicion about the reporter's motives and creates an atmosphere of mistrust. The coach might adopt a defensive attitude at the outset of the interview. The hostility not only might influence the question-answer exchange negatively, but it also might send the wrong message about the coach's concern. It might reinforce the idea that the coach is under extreme pressure and reacting accordingly. The second example might suggest to the reporter that the coach is trying to dodge the issue or that the sport organization is not going to cooperate if the story includes undesirable information.

The third scenario promotes a climate of trust and cooperation. The SID asks about the purpose of the interview and tactfully probes for details on the focal point of the interview. The reporter makes clear the interview will address the sensitive issues but that the reporter will approach them with an open mind. Both the SID and the journalist recognize that each is probing subtly for more information to clarify assumptions about the intentions of the other. The responses of both attempt to send a positive message: "I'm cooperating . . ." on the one hand; "I'm not drawing any conclusions yet . . ." on the other.

Although the first example mimics a stereotype, the third more closely mirrors reality. The most effective interviews for all parties arise from a foundation of trust.

The Interviewer

A controlled interview consists of an opening, a body, and a closing. Control is limited, however. When journalists enter into an interview relationship, they are expected to go into the situation with no particular preconceived ideas other than a few "icebreaking" questions or comments.

The primary objective of the opening is to create rapport and to put the interviewee at ease. Print reporters often begin an interview with light and sometimes

Reporters should do their homework prior to conducting interviews in order to create a more well-informed list of questions, especially when dealing with high school or collegiate athletes who may not be accustomed to speaking with the media.

meaningless questions to "open up" the subject; they also might chat casually with the interviewee about common interests to close the "differences" between them. Likewise, the broadcast reporter or announcer will chat with players prior to warmups or during the setup by the videographer in an attempt to create rapport and encourage trust. The objective is to promote a positive image—to make clear that the journalist is a storyteller, not an FBI interrogator. The more honest and compassionate the image, the more likely the interviewee is to cooperate and to share information on the most sensitive questions.

The skilled journalist will explain the purpose of the interview before beginning the more meaningful questions—to reinforce the positive climate and allay concerns about an ambush. In fact, a good reporter will make the interview a simple, straightforward dialogue—an exchange of information for an inquiry into the topic. Trying to strengthen the foundation of trust, the reporter will work from the questions most easily answered to the most sensitive and difficult. The hope is that the interviewee will be less reluctant to answer the sensitive questions if the reporter demonstrates that the interview is not an attack or an interrogation.

Reporters generally jot down a few questions or topics to discuss. However, many prefer to go with the flow after the preliminary questions, encouraging the subject to speak freely and provide additional information. Followup questions are important for a good story. Reporters will have more information than they can use. They will sift out the information most pertinent to the story.

Radio and television interviews are somewhat different if they are live. Nothing the interviewee says can be retracted or changed. There is no eraser on the live radio or TV interview. The reporter must plan questions carefully or risk looking foolish. However, taped interviews can be edited and fit comfortably into a format of the reporter's choice.

Skilled reporters will ask a lot of *open-ended questions*. Open-ended questions are questions that give interviewees an opportunity to elaborate on the response, to say what they want to say in the manner in which they want to say it. In that respect, open-ended questions are easier to answer and less threatening. They encourage interviewees to explain how or why or give an example. *Closed-ended questions* ask for specific answers or a yes/no response and make it difficult for interviewees to evade an answer. Good reporters often move from open-ended questions to closed-ended questions and vice versa as the situation or need to pin down the interviewee dictates. Consider the following interview excerpt:

Reporter:. . . . . Have you heard the rumors that your job is on the line in the season finale this Saturday?

Coach: . . . . . . Yes. I've heard about a dozen different versions, including the ones I have read in the papers or seen on TV.

Reporter:. . . . . What have you heard?

Coach: . . . . . . Well, I don't want to give any credence to any of the rumors by repeating them.

Reporter:. . . . . Why do you think they are so widespread?

Coach: . . . . . . I think most of them are just speculation, the kind of rumors that always come up when you're having a losing season.

Reporter:. . . . . Has anyone suggested that you might be fired?

Coach: . . . . . . Dozens of callers on those radio call-in shows have suggested I *should* be fired.

Reporter:. . . . . I mean, anyone in a position to influence your job? The president? The athletics director? Influential boosters?

Coach: . . . . . . No one has told me directly that my job is on the line.

Reporter:. . . . . Has anyone suggested it to you indirectly?

Coach: . . . . . . No.

Reporter:. . . . . The president of the university told me she plans to reevaluate your position at the end of the season. Has she told you that?

Coach: . . . . . . Yes.

Reporter:. . . . . Tell me about that. What did she tell you?

Coach: . . . . . . She just told me we'd get together at the end of the season and reevaluate the football program.

Reporter:. . . . . What prompted that conversation?

Coach: . . . . . . She was just talking to me about the game in my office after the loss last Saturday.

Reporter:. . . . . Does she usually talk to you in your office after games?

Coach: . . . . . . Sure. She's a big fan. She often comes into my office after a game to rehash it.

Reporter:. . . . . Does she often talk about your future during those meetings?

Coach: . . . . . . Not really.

Reporter:. . . . . How did it come up in the conversation this time?

Coach: . . . . . . As I recall, we were talking about the people booing as the players left the field and all the nasty comments on the call-in shows. She asked me how I thought we should respond to them.

Reporter:. . . . . And?

Coach: . . . . . . And I asked her how *she* thought we should respond. She said the university could not ignore their feelings. I asked if that meant my job was in jeopardy. She said we'd wait until the end of the season to evaluate everything.

Reporter:. . . . . What did you think when she said that?

Coach: . . . . . . I expected it. The administration reevaluates every athletics position at the end of the season.

Reporter:. . . . . So it didn't worry you?

Coach: . . . . . . I didn't say that.

Reporter:. . . . . What *would* you say?

Coach: . . . . . . I would say I can't really worry about things I can't control. I can only worry about the things I can control—preparation for this week's game.

Reporter:. . . . . Have you put the president's comments out of your mind, then?

Coach: . . . . . . I wouldn't exactly say that.

Reporter:. . . . . How would you describe how it has affected you?

Coach: . . . . . . It's a concern . . . in the back of my mind.

Reporter:. . . . . Have you had that much concern any time previously in your career here?

Coach: . . . . . . No.

Did the reporter learn for sure whether the coach's job is on the line? No. Did the reporter learn anything of value? Yes, considerable insight into the coach's tenuous status. The reporter learned the president is concerned about the reaction of fans to the lengthy losing streak. The reporter also learned the coach is more worried than ever about his future, based on the president's comments.

Note that the reporter did not jump right into the tough question: "Is your job on the line?" That might have put the coach on the defensive immediately, and the coach might have dismissed the subject with a prompt, "No." The reporter asked a series of 18 questions that eased the coach from discussion of the rumors into consideration of his job status.

Note that the reporter used open-ended questions to get the coach to talk and to reveal a little information. Then the reporter followed with closed-ended questions to pin down specifics. The coach did not want to lie, so he tried to evade some questions, but the reporter came back with closed-ended questions that dug into the coach's vague responses and led him to elaborate on his answers. In short, the reporter skillfully, politely, and effectively used questions to gather pieces of information that ultimately provided considerable insight into the coach's status.

Obviously, such a line of questioning is most effective in a one-on-one scenario. It is also most effective if the coach knows the purpose of the interview in advance. He expects questions about his job status, so he is not surprised or alarmed when the reporter asks them. He has had time to consider what he wants to say and how he will say it, so he answers some questions with confidence because he anticipates them: "The administration evaluates every athletics position at the end of the season."

The reporter pushes gently for more information with open-ended questions that give the coach a little room to wiggle, to put the situation in the perspective *he* chooses. The reporter also presses a little harder with closed-ended questions, leaving less room to wiggle. That is not to suggest that the reporter tricks the coach into revealing more information than he intended. However, it is fair to say that the reporter encourages the coach to confide more than he initially intended by creating a comfort zone that inspires trust.

In news conferences and postgame locker-room interviews, such ideal one-on-one exchanges are seldom possible. After the game, the door to the dressing room is usually open whether a team wins or loses. The room might fill with parents and friends as well as reporters. The interview occurs while the player is dressing and other people are talking on all sides. The setting clearly is not as comfortable as the cozy intimacy of the coach's office.

In addition, print and broadcast journalists on a deadline must pursue a more direct line of questioning. They do not have the time or opportunity to ask 18 consecutive questions to get a small amount of information. Expediency is key. A reporter on a deadline, in all probability, will need just a few comments—description, explanation, or reaction—to tie into the play-by-play and statistics. In fact, it is common in deadline situations for reporters to share quotes or to exchange them (if they are not direct competitors). Sometimes, the SID or public information director will assign a pool reporter or student volunteer who gets quotes for everyone. Sports information personnel will make copies of quotations for everyone in the press box.

For example, the public relations staff at Churchill Downs sends reporters to the jockeys' quarters after the Kentucky Derby to gather comments from the riders. Media relations personnel also bring the winning owner(s), trainer, and jockey to the press box for news conferences. While the news conferences are underway, the Churchill Downs staff will print copies of the other jockeys' and trainers' quotations for all to use.

Journalists call such interviews "meat and potato" interviews, conducted exclusively when reporters are backed up against strict deadlines. The questions aim at the substance—the meat and potatoes of the story—rather than the subtleties.

Honesty in reporting is a must. A good reporter must have three important characteristics: writing skills, editing and/or speaking skills, and integrity. A reporter without integrity will not last long in the media community.

To help ensure both integrity and accuracy, some print reporters carry a small tape recorder and microcassettes. Taping an interview enables the reporter to review anything the interviewee said and pick up voice inflections. The reporter can better assess whether the interviewee is happy, sad, excited, disgusted, etc. The tape also gives the reporter an exact record of what the person said, to ensure accuracy in using direct quotations. Furthermore, the tape can definitively settle disputes about the accuracy or context of a quotation or comment that appears in print if a source complains later.

The downside of the tape recorder is that the reporter has to transcribe the spoken words—a cumbersome task, especially in a noisy press box or media room. In addition, the recorder or tape may fail. The reporter who depends entirely on a tape, only to discover it will not function properly on playback, is doomed.

The reporter who jots down information in a notebook can quickly find specific information and also can mark key information in the margin during an interview to make it easier to find. However, keeping up with a person who talks rapidly is difficult. If the interviewee speaks too quickly or the reporter cannot understand every word, the reporter cannot be sure all the words are correct and cannot use the information in a direct quotation. Furthermore, it is difficult to listen to both the interviewee and formulate follow-up questions while trying to scribble down quotes.

Often reporters will use the tape recording as a supplement to note taking. The reporter uses the tape to double-check information and the exact wording of direct quotations, along with other information.

The Interviewee

Just as members of sport organizations judge journalists on their interview postures, reporters evaluate athletes, coaches, and administrators on their cooperation and responses to questions. Every journalist who ever faced a deadline rankles at the coach who says, "I can't comment until I see the film." The reporter on deadline cannot wait for the film review. Journalists also cringe at stock answers

Sports information specialists are typically in charge of coordinating postgame interviews with coaches and players.

from coaches and athletes, such as "It was a team victory" or "I feel good about the way I played." They offer little that tells the audience members anything they do not already know.

Remember, journalists are seeking explanation of who, what, when, where, why, and how. Although the unskilled may ask, "How do you feel?" what they really want to know is "What happened?" Representatives of sport organizations can present themselves in a more favorable light by learning the kind of information journalists seek for specific kinds of stories and providing it. For example, members of sport organizations will serve themselves and their organizations well in postgame interviews by describing the key play, explaining why it worked or why it did not. Journalists are only as good as the information they gather, so the interviewee who provides that information actually helps the journalist to present a better story, and journalists appreciate it. That is why they seem to interview the same people repeatedly in game stories. They go immediately to the players or coaches most likely to give them "meat and potatoes" on deadline.

Journalists and readers/viewers also judge athletes and coaches (managers) on their actions in high-pressure situations, such as a particularly difficult defeat. Athletes who falter in crucial game situations are not expected to be enthusiastic about counting how they failed. Cognizant of verbal abuse and physical encounters that occasionally occur, journalists are not particularly excited about interviewing them in such situations, either. All who watched the 1994 World Series broadcast will remember when Atlanta Braves outfielder Deion Sanders dumped water on Tim McCarver in the locker room after a game because of critical remarks on air by the former Major Leaguer-turned-broadcaster. Athletes and athletics officials must remember the reporter is simply doing a job. It may be painful for the interviewees, but it also can be painful for the interrogator. It is not fun to interview athletes when they talk about their failures. Success is easy to talk about, but failure is a different matter.

The effective interviewee also does a little preparation work before an interview. The interviewee should learn as much as possible about the journalist's interviewing style, the target audience of the media organization, and the subject. The interviewee can see and feel a reporter's style of interviewing, but the interviewee who does not know the reporter may mistake an aggressive style for harsh criticism or hostility. Likewise, interviewees who do not know the media organization and its audience might not understand why a reporter is questioning them when they played little, or not at all, in the big game.

The interviewee should listen carefully to each question then take a moment to formulate a response before answering. An insightful answer, a well-considered answer, is far more important than a quick answer, particularly in broadcast interviews. The interviewee can rephrase an answer or ask a print reporter to cross out a mistake or a poorly worded response. No second chance is possible in a broadcast interview, and the repercussions of an ill-conceived response can be devastating. The late Al Campanis, vice president for player personnel for the Los Angeles Dodgers, used a racial stereotype in response to a question from Ted Koppel of ABC-TV, on opening day of the 1987 baseball season, about the lack of African-Americans in managerial and front-office positions in Major League Baseball. The next day, the Dodgers dismissed Campanis, who had been with them since 1943 in positions ranging from player to vice president. The interview also prompted an avalanche of commentary in the media condemning Campanis' comments.

When an interview is live on radio or TV, the subject must be conscious that what is said cannot be taken back. Therefore, it is all the more important to listen to the question carefully and to consider the implications—and possible misinterpretations—of the response.

Interviewees also should make certain they understand the question and the intent of the question before answering. If unsure of the focus of the question, they should ask the reporter to rephrase it. If unsure of the reporter's motive, they should ask the purpose. Remember, asking questions is one way the interviewee can verify that the reporter is sticking to the stated purpose and clarify conflicting verbal and nonverbal messages. Asking questions keeps the lines of communication open and mends tears in the relationship before the damage is irreparable.

Reporters do not like evasive answers. Evasive replies damage the relationship and hurt the interviewee's image. The interviewee should answer all questions honestly, forthrightly, and clearly. He or she should avoid rambling. A short answer is best for radio and TV interviews; long answers will end up on the editing floor because of the time limitations. However, the interviewee should elaborate if necessary to ensure the reporter understands. Interviewees should not allow interviewers to interpret what they mean, but should be succinct and direct.

An interviewee should refrain from simply nodding to signify a yes or no answer. Elaboration is the substance of interviews—the direct quotation for the print reporter and the sound bite for the broadcast journalist. In a very real sense, the interviewee is the expert on the topic under discussion. Former National Basketball Association coach Bill Fitch once said there are no dumb questions, only dumb answers. Often a skilled interviewer will ask what appears to be a meaningless or dumb question when in reality the purpose is to establish a frame of reference to set up very important questions to follow, such as the first question in the interview example with the football coach earlier in this chapter. Obviously, the coach had heard the rumors that his job was on the line. The reporter knew that and used the question to introduce the topic in a nonthreatening manner.

Integrity is as important to the interviewee as it is to the interviewer. If an interviewee cannot comment on a question, he or she should say so and explain why. Reporters respect a "No comment" if they understand why the interviewee cannot answer. For example, most reporters will drop the line of questioning if a football player says, "Coach told us not to talk to anyone about why those players were suspended for the game." Many journalists will push a little harder to get the interviewee to disclose more information but will not be surprised or upset if the interviewee sticks to the "No comment." An interviewee who does not know the answer to a question should say so and should not fake it. Experienced reporters can see through a lie, and the interviewee compromises his or her trustworthiness.

Controlling one's temper also is important. Temper tantrums directed at the media will brand the interviewee as a sorehead and a poor loser. Complaints about minor mistakes and critical comments are best ignored. Complaints to journalists that direct quotations are "out of context" are common. Most of the complaints lack merit. Some are meant to deflect criticism from the interviewee to the journalist. What the person often means is, "Gee, I wouldn't have said it that way if I had known how people would react." However, if the inaccurate quotation or context puts one in an unfavorable light unfairly, the speaker has a right to complain. Anyone who believes he or she has been quoted "out of context" should make certain of being correct in that assessment before complaining.

If the comment reflects negatively on character or reputation, the interviewee should broach the subject with the reporter to ask for a correction or a clarification. If the reporter refuses, the interviewee should ask the coach or SID to raise the issue with the appropriate editor or station manager.

A beat reporter who covers a team on a regular basis often will write a story with comments critical of an athlete or a coach. The reporter, particularly the columnist, reports the critical information because it is essential to the reporting process, not because he or she enjoys it. Other journalists call reporters who write only the positive side of the sport organization *homers* because they "root, root, root for the home team." *Homers* lose the respect and following of the audience (fans) because they do not provide an honest and well-rounded account of events. Fans want the reporter to be on their side when they criticize the team, or at least to address their complaints.

After reporting something critical, most reporters will make themselves available to the athlete or other team representative soon after the publication or broadcast. That gives the athlete or coach the opportunity to confront the reporter and complain. If the athlete refuses to communicate or the journalist refuses to answer the complaint personally, a rift in the relationship is possible. A rift that goes unaddressed eventually damages the relationship and creates a barrier in future interviews.

Depending on the type and purpose of an interview, the sports information or public relations director may be the intermediary, the interview coach, the interviewer, the news conference director, and the arbiter of interview disputes.

Here is a brief look at the SID's multiple roles:

Intermediary

Journalists generally work closely with sports information and public relations directors in arranging interviews at the collegiate and professional levels. At the high school level, they will go through the coach or athletics director. At the collegiate level, the first contact is with the SID, in the interest of professional courtesy as well as convenience. The SID usually will know the class schedule, practice times, and hours at which players and coaches are available for interviews. SIDs can make contact and set up the interview much more quickly than the journalist can. At the professional level, journalists usually make first contact with the public relations department; however, beat reporters often have the home telephone numbers of players and coaches and call them directly.

The SID may help to arrange one-on-one interviews with players, coaches, and athletics officials for all types of stories. The sports information staff also may set up conference calls, which enable a group of reporters to interview a coach or player by telephone at the same time.

The SID's Multiple Roles
Intermediary
Interview coach
Interviewer
News conference director
Arbiter

Interview Coach

The SID can enhance the prospects of a positive outcome by helping both the journalist and the representative of the sport organization to prepare. A member of the SID staff can provide the journalist with background information on the interviewee and the subject as well as arrange the interview.

The staff member can prep the interviewee on the journalist's style, the media organization and its audience, and the purpose of the interview. The sports information person also can brief the interviewee on topics likely to arise and can offer advice on how to handle sensitive subjects. Some colleges and professional sport organizations provide training sessions on interviewing to new players and other members of the organization. More often, sports information personnel work with individuals on an informal basis on interview strengths and weaknesses.

Interviewer

Sports information personnel assume the role of journalists for all types of news releases: game advances, hometown releases, feature releases, and weekly reviews/previews. They also may interview coaches and athletes for media brochures and other publications.

The SID will seek some of the same types of information as the journalist, but the purpose and interview relationship will differ somewhat. The primary purpose of news releases is to present a positive image of the sport organization to the public, so the SID will emphasize the positive aspects of the athletes, coaches, and sport organization and may even include self-serving quotations that praise the organization. In addition, the interviewer for the sport organization is a "friend of the court" in the interview relationship. The information specialist may help the interviewee phrase an answer better or may suggest the most appropriate type of response—anything short of putting words in the mouth of the interviewee.

News Conference Director

The sports information or public relations staff generally is responsible for setting up news conferences and postgame group interviews. Sports information personnel may be responsible for everything from the logistics to the conduct of the news conference. The SID may even serve as the moderator during the question-answer session.

Arbiter

Journalists typically direct complaints about interviewees to the sports information or public relations director first. Complaints range from cancelled interviews to lack of cooperation to verbal and physical confrontations. If the problem does not improve, the journalist may take the complaint higher in the chain of command.

Players, coaches, and athletics officials should raise complaints about the media through sports information personnel first, also. Complaints may range from misquotes to critical comments, to confrontations. The SID has the closest working relationship with the members of the media; therefore, the SID is in the best position to mediate, and the odds of a favorable response from journalists are higher if the SID intervenes. In the case of serious, ongoing problems, the athletics director, university president, general manager, or team owner may request a meeting with executives of the media organization.

The SID often plays the role of peacemaker in disputes. The SID attempts to get each side to understand the other's concerns and to soothe hurt feelings on both sides. In short, the sports information director attempts to repair the tears in the relationship before they grow into holes that cannot be stitched back together. Not every relationship can be repaired, of course. That is why some professional athletes refuse to talk to the media or why they snub reporters whom they believe treated them unfairly or unprofessionally.

The percentage of time a sports information professional spends in each interview-related role depends to a large degree on the sport organization. At the Division III level, journalists seldom interview athletes prior to contests. Most of the interviews take place after the games. At football and basketball games of little or no significance in the conference standings, writers and broadcast reporters either see the head coaches on the playing field/floor or in the home team's coaching office. They also catch up with players on the field/floor or in the locker rooms. The SID, a student assistant, or a graduate assistant will alert the athlete of an interview request and make sure the player hooks up with the proper reporter.

In games of greater significance, the SID coordinates the postgame interviews. The SID secures a room to conduct a postgame news conference. This room must have enough seating and microphones to enable all the media to hear the intervie-wees. The SID begins and closes the news conference and coordinates the order in which questions are asked. While the news conference is taking place, SID assistants will put together a postgame statistical package with all the team and individual stats, along with play-by-play and quotations gathered by a pool reporter, to aid the print reporters who were unable to attend the postgame news conference because of tight deadlines (see Chapter 9).

When John Carroll University and national Division III power Mount Union College played an important football game, the sports information director followed these steps to set up the postgame news conference:

1. The SID received permission from the Physical Education Department to use a classroom in the department.

2. The SID obtained a banner from the Alumni Office to display behind the podium in the designated classroom, so the name and logo of the university would appear prominently in any photographs or video clips of the interviews (see Chapter 6).

3. The SID stocked the room with a coffeemaker and necessary supplies, as well as cold beverages and snacks. The staff set up enough chairs to accommodate all who requested press credentials.

4. Late in the game, the SID informed the media in the press box of the news conference location. Also, the media were surveyed about which players they wanted to interview in addition to the two head coaches.

5. Sports information workers distributed a complete set of statistics to media representatives just prior to the news conference.

6. Sports information assistants rounded up the coaches and players and brought them to the news conference.

7. Mount Union won the game; therefore, the order of participants was the John Carroll coach and selected players, followed to the podium by the Mount Union coach and his players.

8. The SID conducted the news conference, introducing the coaches and players.

9. The SID left time after the formal news conference for the media to interview coaches on a one-on-one basis.

In Division I, the procedure is similar but on a much larger scale. Coaches and players address reporters in a room designed for news conferences in the stadium or arena. The SID moderates the news conference, and assistants puts together the stats package and distribute copies to the media sometime during the news conference. In football, many writers work in the press box or at the press table. However, the sports information staff provides an accessible pressroom with enough outlets and telephones to serve the working media.

Some players refuse to talk to the media. Larry Bird refused to talk to the media during his final season at Indiana State University. He later said he chose not to talk to reporters so that they would talk to his teammates and give them their fair share of the credit for ISU's success.

After the press conference, reporters also go to the locker room to talk to players not summoned to the podium. There, reporters may also encounter parents, friends, and boosters. Marion West (1985) recommends delaying the invasion of parents and relatives until the media have had a 15-minute head start. The postgame locker room is open to *all* reporters.

The operating procedures in professional sports are much the same as in high-profile, Division I collegiate sports. In the National Football League, locker rooms are open to the media until 45 minutes prior to kickoff. Reporters try to get pregame comments and interesting sidebar information for notes columns, which they complete after the postgame interviews.

This same pattern takes place in the National Basketball Association and in Major League Baseball. The public relations director makes sure the media meet the NBA coach after a 10-minute cooling-off period. Then, as a rule, the reporters are free to go into the locker room and talk to athletes of their choice. However, there often is an interview room in which to talk to the players, and the reporters never go into the dressing areas of the locker room. The public relations director helps there, serving as the moderator for the postgame news conference. Meanwhile, assistants put together the stats package, which is distributed to the media in the media room. These packages will include quotations obtained by a pool reporter.

In Major League Baseball, the media relations person goes to the locker room before the conclusion of the game and greets reporters upon their arrival. That person assists in obtaining players, which often is difficult. The trainer's room is off limits to reporters, and players often will hide there, especially if they do not want to talk to the media.

Summary

Interviews provide the foundation for much of sports reporting today. Both print and broadcast reporters use interviews with athletes, coaches, and athletics officials to add the personal side of the story to the action on the field of play. Reporters use material gathered in interviews for description, explanation, and elaboration of what happened, why, and how. They also use direct quotations from the characters in the sports drama to present insights into the action, much as a novelist uses dialogue to put scenes into their proper perspective.

Interviews are one of the linchpins in the working relationship between media and sport organizations. The journalist depends on contact with members of the sport organization for the raw materials of story composition. The more information a reporter acquires from the participants in the contest, the more thorough and entertaining the story. Sport organizations depend on stories by journalists, in part, to present the organization's philosophy and image to the public. That philosophy comes indirectly through the comments and reactions of members of the organization in the printed word and broadcast sound bites.

The sports interview is a complex mini-relationship between a journalist and an athlete, coach, athletics executive, or team owner. The relationship is different in every meeting, depending on the purpose and circumstances of the interview, even if the journalist has interviewed the athlete many times previously. The interview itself is an information-gathering strategy designed to elicit insights that expand on a news story, a sports personality, or an athletics contest. It always involves an interchange of information through questions and answers between two or more parties, one or all of whom have goals they want to achieve. The goals of the journalist and the goals of the interviewee may not be congruous.

The goal of the journalist varies according to the type of story—news story, feature story, personality profile, opinion column, notes column, investigative story, pregame story, or postgame story. So does the preparation. Journalists use information gathered on both the subject and the people involved to prepare questions and topic areas to explore. The purpose of the story dictates whether the emphasis of the background preparation centers more on the people or on the topic or issue.

The most effective interviews include a semistructured opening, a body, and a close. The opening is designed to establish rapport, generate trust, and encourage the interviewee to speak freely. The body consists of questions and answers. Many reporters plan the first few questions and go with the flow of the interview thereafter. Skilled interviewers start with the easiest and least sensitive questions and work up to the more difficult or threatening ones. The close is intended to wrap up any loose ends and to conclude the interview relationship on a positive note.

Interviews conducted on deadline, such as postgame interviews, are the least structured because of the time constraints. Gathering information quickly with two or three key questions is paramount; concern about the relationship and the rapport is secondary. The postgame news conference is even less structured, because the questioning is open to everyone. Several different reporters may ask unrelated questions, because the goal of each is different.

Members of the sport organization can present their best faces to the public by preparing in much the same manner as journalists do. Interviewees can project a far more positive image if they have learned as much as possible about the interviewer and the media organization, the purpose of the interview, and the subject matter. The athlete or coach also can positively affect the interview by offering description, explanation, and elaboration instead of simply nodding yes or no or giving one-word responses. The interviewee should listen to questions intently and take a moment to consider the ramifications of the response before answering, particularly in live broadcast interviews. Such care can eliminate hasty responses that may embarrass the interviewee and the organization. Because an interview is a two-way relationship, the interviewee can ask questions, too. The interviewee should clarify any vague questions and ask for an explanation of the purpose of questions that appear designed to trap or embarrass.

Integrity is the key to a trusting relationship among all parties. Everyone must interact honestly to maintain an effective working relationship. Ethical reporters do not attempt to mislead interviewees or to unfairly portray them in stories. Members of sport organizations who present the most positive images are those who cooperate in interviews, do not lie to the media, and do not take out their frustrations on interviewers. Both journalists and athletes should address complaints immediately and resolve differences before they fester and irreparably damage the relationship.

The sports information or public relations director plays a variety of roles in connection with interviews. The SID may act as an intermediary, arranging interviews for journalists with players, coaches, or other representatives of the organization. The information specialist may serve as an interview coach, offering direction on how to handle an interview. The SID also conducts interviews for news releases and arranges postgame news conferences. Perhaps the most important role is that of peacemaker. The SID or media relations director is in the best position to mediate disputes and soothe emotions because of the close contact with all parties.

Members of sport organizations must remember that the media have a job to do, and that they often must do it in emotionally charged and time-precious situations. Sports organizations that make the interaction easier find most often that the interview is a positive experience.

DISCUSSION QUESTIONS

1. Explain fully the differences between a feature story and a personality profile.
2. Give a thorough explanation of open- and closed-ended questions, and funnel and inverted-funnel interview approaches.

SUGGESTED EXERCISES

1. One student should interview an athlete, preferably one with a unique story. Then, with a 15-minute deadline, that student should write a short news story using quotes from the interview. This should be done in a one-on-one situation. Roles should be reversed so that the other student asks the questions and writes a news story.
2. Make a list of appropriate questions for interviewing an athlete who played an important role in a basketball game just completed.
3. Gather a list of 20 ideas that would make a good sports column, and support your reasoning.

Chapter Nine

GAME MANAGEMENT: PRESS-BOX AND PRESS-TABLE OPERATIONS

It's the first conference basketball game of the season, and what a matchup!

The home team is 10-0 and ranked number 2 in the nation—its first time ever in the *Associated Press* Top Ten. The visiting team, 6-0 behind the best defense in the league, is rated number 18.

The gym is overflowing with reporters attracted by the matchup of unbeaten conference powers and by a game of national significance in a December filled with top-rated teams beating lesser opponents. In fact, the demand for credentials more than doubled any previous request. The sports information director even squeezed in a TV production company that put together a regional broadcast package at the last minute, thanks to fan interest in the game.

What a game!

The visitors outscore the home team 18-2 in the first 10 minutes of the second half to erase a 13-point deficit and go on top 47-44. The visitors build the lead to six points before the star for the home team pours in seven points in a flurry that ties the score 59-59 and prompts a timeout with 2:51 remaining. Athletics administrators for the two Division I schools could not have written a better script for this big moment in the media spotlight.

> Chapter 9 examines the role of the sports information or public relations staff in press-box and press-table operations. The chapter outlines steps the staff must take before, during, and after the game to ensure a smooth and effective working relationship.

As the cheerleaders exhort the home crowd to its feet, however, a radio announcer waves frantically for attention. He wants to know the career high for the star, who already has 30 points. Unfortunately, the SID is tied up with a student assistant, who is keeping the running play-by-play and missed a basket somewhere.

A frantic TV production assistant intercepts the SID en route with the stats to the radio table. An exuberant fan kicked loose a cord taped to the floor, and the electrical hookup went on the fritz. The SID asks the public address announcer to solicit an engineer from the crowd, but no one appears, and the TV crew has to work the last critical minutes one camera short. After the game, a reporter from a large daily newspaper confronts the SID. The reporter is up against her deadline, and no one told her she could not send a story via computer modem from the telephone at her seat. She hastily dictates a story over the telephone and storms out with a promise to write the president about "this bush-league operation." Her parting words: "I'd forgotten why we don't usually cover this podunk school. But I won't forget again."

What a disaster!

The team won—barely—in a regionally televised game. The university lost—perhaps big time. The TV production company, irritated over the technical problems, may not return; neither may the radio station and the big-city reporter visiting for the first time. They all left unhappy because circumstances beyond their control made it impossible for them to do their best work. They may blame the SID for the lack of control, and the university for a lack of class. Perhaps they will return if the team remains unbeaten, and the sports information staff will get a chance to mend the working relationship. If they do not, perhaps the damage to the university's reputation will be permanent.

This example illustrates one of the critical roles the sports information or media relations department plays in promoting a sport organization's image. The department's actions under pressure say as much about the quality of the organization's management and operation as does the performance of its teams. Poor planning and execution can be as damaging to media relations as to team won-lost records.

A Place to Work

The responsibility for running a clean and efficient media work area belongs to the sports information or media relations staff. The staff is responsible for everything from issuing credentials to keeping accurate, detailed records of developments in the game. The demands from the media may vary from high school to college to professional teams. They also may differ for high-profile and low-profile sports, but what does not change are the criteria that define a successful operation—professional courtesy and effective service.

Courtesy is both an attitude and a guiding principle for working with the media. It is an attitude in that the SID or media relations director must maintain composure and treat the media with respect even when the media are making outlandish demands or complaining about problems of their own making. Courtesy is a guiding principle in that it must underlie the approach the staff takes to serving the media. The staff must respond promptly and efficiently to fill requests and to solve problems, whether the problem is a missing meal or a malfunctioning camera.

Courtesy, however, is fool's gold if not backed up with effective service. The press table is the "office" for the working media. To be of real service, the sports information staff must efficiently provide the materials and assistance the media need to perform their jobs. Good intentions and "I'm sorry" mean nothing to the football announcer who just stumbled through player identifications for four quarters because no pronunciation guide was available. What makes a difference is anticipating every problem that might arise and resolving it quickly. Dale Gallagher, former sports information director at Kent State University, sums up the challenge simply: "The SID needs to remember to anticipate problems and requests ahead of time, keep a cool head, and improvise until solutions are found."

Sports reporters rely on the media relations staff to prepare a clean and efficient work area such as the one in the Cleveland Indians' press box.

When the games begin, the SID or public relations director is the managing partner in the working relationship between media and sport organizations. The press table or press box is the work area. "Work area" is the operative phrase. The space reserved for the media at athletics events is a work area, not a social club or party room. Press boxes are not places for VIPs and friends of the university to watch the contests and enjoy free food and drink. That is not to say the press box should be off limits to everyone but the working media; it is to say that the sports information staff should restrict access and eliminate any activity that is not work related.

The press box can double as a mini-dining room for the working media, and no one will complain if university administrators and special guests share the refreshments. However, the SID should seat them away from the areas in which the media will be working during the game. After the game, staff members should ask outsiders to leave, because the press box, press table, or media room immediately turns into a very busy and hectic place—like a subway station when the train arrives. Everyone scrambles to get to work quickly. Providing workspace for the media is much the same as arranging office space where lawyers, accountants, and brokers can work without interruption and interference (Manasseh, 1985).

At no time is the partnership between journalists and sports information personnel under greater pressure and strain than at game time. The sports information staff often must cater to the needs of a large group of media with diverse interests. Broadcast journalists must deliver their stories live. Many print reporters must file stories within 20 to 30 minutes after completion of the game. All must work quickly in a setting with little margin of error and few advantages of the home office. In fact, journalists are simply tethered to the home office by telephone or electrical lines, and they cannot stay late to finish the job. Finishing the job before the deadline takes precedence over social graces and professional amenities. Any self-respecting reporter will trade two hot dogs for a wall plug and a telephone any time. The tools of the trade can make or break a reporter covering an event on deadline.

To illustrate, speed is paramount for wire-service reporters at National Football League, Major League Baseball, and National Basketball Association games. Reporters are graded on quality, brevity, and speed in filing stories. The *Associated Press* (*AP*) rates correspondents against those from other wire services. If one *AP* reporter writes a more concise and higher quality story than a wire competitor does but takes a few seconds longer, the *AP* reporter may be penalized. The *AP* reporter that is consistently slower than the competition may even be fired, because a wire service's most important selling points are quality of writing and speed of delivery. A newspaper is most likely to subscribe to the service that delivers fastest and thereby helps the newspaper meet deadlines more easily.

Three Stages of Operation

The degree of difficulty in providing work space and coverage support for the media directly correlates to the level of competition, the amount of work space available, and the number of media to serve. The job is much easier for a high school or Division III game, in most cases, because fewer media attend. Little assistance or space is needed. In fact, at many high school football games, reporters prefer to walk the sidelines and soak up the atmosphere rather than to sit in a small, cramped press box. Difficulty arises if media interest exceeds space. For example, many high school gymnasiums do not have a press box or a press table—just a table for the timekeeper and official scorers between the two team benches. Finding a place to put a table or a workbench for a half dozen reporters during an important rivalry or conference basketball game can prove challenging, particularly if a stage is on one side and the walls are three feet from the baselines. Likewise, many older gymnasiums lack adequate electrical and telephone wiring to accommodate a large number of radio or print reporters filing stories via computer/telephone hookups.

The technical and space limitations are not as critical at the other collegiate and professional levels, but the demand for space and the load on the electrical system may be far greater. The facilities at many Division II schools are closer to those at high schools than to those at Division I colleges; even football and basketball games typically do not draw more than three or four reporters. However, requests for working press credentials may double or triple if the team climbs into the national rankings and plays an important game with postseason playoff implications. In such cases, the sports information staff must limit press credentials, find a way to put additional tables on the floor, or convert a section of seats from fan use to media work area.

Space is seldom a problem at the Division I or professional levels. The challenge in high-profile collegiate or professional sports is accommodating large numbers of journalists of all kinds—print, radio, and television. Consider the difficulty in serving the media efficiently if the hundreds of journalists covering the Super Bowl requested assistance at the same time. The sports information or media relations director must create a contingency plan for every potential problem and co-ordinate a staff of assistants large enough to handle more problems than appear conceivable at any given time.

It should be clear that the key to effective service is planning—anticipating problems and preparing contingency plans to address them. Consequently, successful sports information and media relations directors divide preparations for press-box operations into three phrases: (a) *pregame*, (b) *game-time*, and (c) *postgame*. Pregame preparation focuses on logistics: providing adequate workspace and working materials to accommodate the needs of all media representatives who attend. Game-time planning concentrates on organization and service—organizing a staff large enough and flexible enough to handle specific responsibilities and to respond to unexpected problems quickly. The SID must arrange for spotters and stats crews, as well as *runners* who act as utility infielders, performing whatever chore is needed. Postgame preparation emphasizes express service—supplying postgame statistics, escorting coaches and players to the news conference, and dealing with individual journalists' problems quickly.

Effective planning starts with organization. Developing pregame organizational charts, media credentials lists, seating charts, and press-box checklists that cover everything from working materials to individual staff responsibilities can head off a lot of problems. Gallagher, at Kent State University, created a sports information game-management form that addresses four areas: pregame preparation, staff, media, and postgame. The pregame section covers credentials, workspace, and working materials. A separate checklist identifies materials needed, down to such minute details as the number of binoculars, reams of paper, and telephones to make available in the working press area. Gallagher's staff section deals with recruitment, training, and management of game workers. The media section covers service concerns during the game. The postgame section explains staff responsibilities in arranging interviews and providing game information such as statistics and coaches' quotations.

Gallagher recommends reviewing the previous year's procedures for each sport prior to the first game. Staff members can then evaluate, revise, and add new ideas. She also encourages training and practice for staff members for all game responsibilities well ahead of the first game, and a walk-through in the press areas the day before each game. That's also the time to test all equipment, replenish supplies, and counsel staff on arrival time and dress code (if any). A dress code is optional, but all sports information personnel should be clean and neatly dressed. Remember, both appearance and performance should reflect the image the university intends to project.

Managing the Media

One simple rule ranks above all others: The SID or media relations director should *never* fill a specific job in the press-row or press-box operations. The person at the top of the organizational chart must act as coordinator in the pregame planning, and as comptroller once the game begins. The SID must remain free of specific duties, to be able to roam among the media, answer questions, and field requests. The SID also must avoid getting tied down in one chore, in order to be in position to improvise when an emergency arises. The SID must know whom to grab and where to send them on an errand, whom to consult on a question about statistics, and whom to call or page to handle an electrical or personal emergency.

During pregame preparations, the SID or media relations director serves as the liaison with radio and TV media as well as the contact person for the print media. The print and radio media require little assistance prior to the game. At most, print media reporters may need to check on telephone and electrical service for hookup of a portable computer. Radio stations usually make their own arrangements for broadcast lines, but they often will expect the sports information office to provide two or three additional telephones.

On the other hand, television production crews usually demand substantial technical assistance and support. In fact, the complexity of TV production greatly multiplies the pregame preparation of the sports information department and the number of people utilized in press-box operations during the game. The SID must provide information well in advance on parking locations for broadcast trucks, setup times and arrangements, and security measures to protect all equipment. The SID can avoid problems by involving the facility manager and the electrician in discussions of the best place to set up cameras and other equipment, power-up time (when the TV crew can connect and turn on lines), and other technical questions. An electrician should be on hand on game day to assist with the power-up and emergencies.

The producer usually will arrive a day or two before the game and will check out camera locations and lighting, and perhaps pre-event accommodations for announcers.

Game Management Concerns

The major areas of concern in pregame preparation, game management, and postgame service are credentials, work space, work crews, working materials, and food.

Credentials

The sports information staff should develop a written policy for working press credentials. The SID can avoid confusion and mute complaints by including in the media guide the policy and procedures for arranging credentials.

The policy should address eligibility for credentials, limits per media or other organization, and arrangements for travel companions. The eligibility requirements should specify what types of publications or broadcast media are not eligible for credentials. For example, a university might choose to exclude gambling publications; Internet-based publications; free publications, such as advertising tabloids; and publications that do not regularly cover sports events. The policy should explain how the university will handle requests from scouts (i.e., general admission, VIP, or working press credentials). It also should explain accommodations (credentials or tickets?) available for spouses, if any. Most college and professional organizations do *not* give working press credentials or seats in the working press area to spouses, though some do provide guest tickets and special seating sections.

The credentials policy should spell out differences in press passes for reporters, photographers, announcers, videographers, and other broadcast personnel, as well as the limit for each media organization. The SID may set limits on the number of reporters and photographers from a single media organization based on the print or broadcast company's size, coverage area/audience, and proximity to the school or city. For example, Churchill Downs in Louisville will issue far more photography passes for the Kentucky Derby to the Louisville *Courier-Journal*, the largest newspaper in the state, than to the Paducah *Sun*, a 30,000-circulation daily in far Western Kentucky.

Newspapers and magazines typically send a beat reporter and a photographer to a college or professional game. They also may want to send a columnist or general assignment reporter and a second photographer to games between rivals and games with postseason playoff impact. A radio station usually will send a two- or three-man crew—a play-by-play announcer and color man, and sometimes an engineer/technician that take care of the equipment. However, a television production crew may need 8–10 press passes—2 for talent (announcers), 1 for a statistician, 1 each for a director and a producer, 2–3 for videographers (camera people), and perhaps a couple for technicians in the truck (who might need to come and go in the stadium/arena).

The credentials policy should specify the work areas to which each person with credentials has access. The *press pass* or working credential issued to each person should provide direction—by written or color code—that aids university officials monitoring access. For example, a football pass might enable reporters to walk around freely in the press area, in the locker rooms, and on the sidelines for a football game. Colleges and professional teams often issue armbands to photographers that define access to the field, the court, and/or the locker rooms. The passes and armbands might limit access strictly to the field or only to the press box.

The SID is in charge of issuing the credentials and keeping a running count to avoid overbooking the work space and must realize that establishing a cutoff point and sticking to it is more important than trying to accommodate everyone who wants a credential. The cutoff policy can create conflicts with a journalist denied a credential, but the media organizations at the bottom of the priority order are the least important to the school or team. Assigning a reporter to a seat behind a pole or crowding everyone to squeeze in a few more journalists may cause greater relationship problems with those media organizations that regularly cover the team. It is better to deny access to low-priority journalists at the outset than to provide substandard work space and assistance to all. Media organizations recognize that space is limited, particularly for high-profile events, and accept decisions of the host organization when those decisions are backed up by printed policy.

The SID should assign a staff member to prepare the credentials, each of which should include the name of the individual and the organization represented.

Work Space

The three primary workplace concerns of both print and broadcast media are space, electrical outlets, and telephones.

As a general rule of thumb, the sports information staff should provide a working space at least 24 inches wide for every person assigned to a spot in a football press box. That is the absolute minimum for a print reporter with a portable computer, a radio announcer with a control panel, or a television announcer with a video monitor. These dimensions can easily be applied to basketball and other indoor sports, as well as track and baseball.

The SID should try to arrange the seating so that everyone has as good a view of the playing field or court as possible. The press box high above the field is best for softball, soccer, baseball, and football because it provides a view of the entire field as a play unfolds. Seating at courtside is preferable for basketball, volleyball, wrestling, gymnastics, and individual sports because of the close, physical nature of the action. The standard setup for basketball is a row, or rows, of tables along the sidelines. For a major game, a playoff, an all-star game, or simply a contest between rivals, it is common to add tables on each baseline or to convert the first few rows of seats down one sideline to a press row. The conversion will require adding a workbench to provide a 24-inch space so journalists won't have to work in their laps.

The SID should post copies of the seating chart at entrances to the press box or at the ends of tables on press row to help all reporters find their seats. Sports information personnel should place name tags at each seat to further eliminate confusion.

Electrical outlets should be strategically placed to provide an outlet for every individual workstation. Also, the sports information office should make certain that sufficient telephone lines are available, whether the telephones are ordered by the journalists or by the SID. If the university cannot put an electrical outlet or a telephone at each workstation, the sports information staff should set up a separate room close to press row—or the baseball field, soccer field, or tennis court—where reporters can go after the game to compose and file stories. If the number of outlets in the press box or the arena is limited, first priority should go to beat reporters who cover the university or the team and media organizations within the immediate geographical area. Pregame media kits should provide instructions on how to dial for outside access.

If possible, the university should provide a darkroom for photographers to develop and transmit photographs. This is common practice at stadiums for professional teams and major colleges, although the majority of major media outlets now utilize digital photography, thus eliminating the need for a darkroom.

Gallagher of Kent State says, "Putting everyone in the right place is like a jigsaw puzzle."

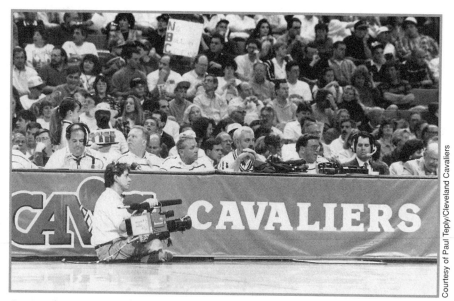

Seating for sports reporters should be arranged so that the media has a clear view of the playing field or court.

Game officials—timers, scorekeepers, and public-address announcers—must be in the center of the field or court. The next best spots should go to statisticians, because they must be able to see the action well to provide accurate information. Helitzer (1992) puts seniority at the top of the list and importance second when it comes to seating the media. Beat reporters and other regulars usually sit in the same locations each week, and the SID fills in the rest of the seating chart based on other requests. Gallagher suggests putting the visiting SID near a telephone and near the visiting media from that university's home base.

Press-Box Team

The press-box team at the high school and collegiate levels typically consists of a collection of sports information department personnel, adult volunteers, and student assistants. The SID assigns the most important jobs to members of the staff, then fills in with dependable volunteers. In the professional ranks, members of the statistical crews are paid employees of the home team.

The number of volunteers needed depends on the nature of the sport and the number of media who request credentials, particularly radio and TV media. High-profile team sports, such as football and basketball, require large statistical crews and several runners to distribute information. A two- or three-person crew and a runner or two generally will suffice for low-profile and individual sports with fewer statistical categories. The primary personnel needs for serving the media are as follows:

- Sports information director: The sports information director serves as the comptroller and troubleshooter. As noted earlier, the SID should act as overseer and manager rather than performing a specific job.

- Statistical crew: The most important permanent unit of the press-row team is the statistical crew, which may consist of as many as 10–12 people for football. Remember, journalists' hunger for information is greater than their hunger for food. The statistical crew often is comprised of students under a *work-study* program, a financial-aid program that pays them for work on campus, under the direction of a full-time staff member. The stats crew for football should consist of one play-by-play typist, a spotter for defense, a spotter for offense, and a spotting coordinator. The spotters advise the typist on the name of the ball carrier, the tackler(s), yardage gained or lost, and down and distance to go for a first down.

The SID may supplement the basic crew with specialists who keep *drive* and *tackle charts*, information that aids in identifying the star performers as well as the statistical differences in the game. A drive chart is a schematic drawing of a football field that shows the starting point and progress on each play of a drive. A tackle chart is a compilation of the number of tackles, sacks, fumble recoveries, and interceptions by each player on the defense.

A basketball crew consists of a play-by-play typist; a spotter who records points and fouls for players for each team; a spotter who tracks rebounds, turnovers, and assists; and a spotting coordinator.

Press Box Seating Chart

Baldwin-Wallace vs. John Carroll University

First Floor

* 826-2429 The George Finnie Booth The George and Nita Finnie Family	* 826-2451 Dave Van Slyke Play-by-Play Typist SID Caller	Geoff Henson Official Statistics	Jim Ressler Official Statistics	Neil Beswick Defensive Stats	Donnie Palm Opponent Spotter	Dr. Lou Barone P.A. Announcer	John Tudhope B-W Spotter	Bobby Brown OAC Officials Observer	Eddie Dwyer OAC	Gerry Henson Elyria Chronicle-Telegram The Plain Dealer	WUJC RADIO	826-2450 WUJC RADIO	Baldwin-Wallace WBWC Radio Jason Tirotta Rob Wylduga * 826-2453 * 826-2428

* -- denote working phone outlets for MEDIA and emergencies ONLY.

Downstairs: Upper Level

Aaron Chimenti Concessions/ Runner	Scott Runyan Scoring Summary	Brad Kuhbander Promotions	Ryan Rhea Phones/ Other Game Scores	* 826-2449 Chris Johnson The B-W Exponent	Jeff Miller Visiting SID from Oberlin College	Scott Volpe ~~Brian Murphy~~ Lake County News-Herald	Chris Wenzler JCU SID	JCU Sports Information Staff	Tim Gleason OAC Commissioner	Open

Second Floor

Upstairs

* 826-2452 WHK RADIO B-W and JCU Adam Mendoza Dom DiPasqua	Baldwin-Wallace College Coaches	Camera Bay Used For Team & Television Stations	John Carroll University Coaches	The Seitz and Len Thasho Timers Booth

- Duplication specialist: The duplication specialist makes the predetermined number of copies of statistical information, ranging from quickie stats at halftime to books of final statistics. The copy machine utilized should be capable of producing a minimum of 40 pages per minute.

- Runners: Runners distribute duplicated materials and other information to everyone seated in the press box. Football runners pass out "quickie" stats (summaries) after each quarter of a football game, halftime statistics, and final statistical packages. The same holds true for basketball, but on the collegiate level, quickie stats are provided at halftime.

- Pool reporter: The SID may assign one assistant to each locker room to gather quotations from players and coaches to distribute to the media. Either the play-by-play typist or one of the SID assistants can type the quotations and deliver them to the duplication specialist.

- Telephone person: The telephone person calls the *Associated Press* and other media outlets with updates on scores as requested. The telephone person also calls the newspapers and broadcast outlets on a predetermined list with scores, statistics, and highlights after the game. The assistants who gather quotations can double as telephone specialists.

    The telephone person also can gather scores from other league games during the contest and pass them on to the public address announcer and broadcast media.

- News conference aids: The SID may assign an assistant to bring players and coaches from each team to the designated room for the news conference. The SID may rely on assistants or volunteers who perform other duties during the game, as long as the duties are completed by game's end.

- Media spotters and runners: A radio station sometimes will request a spotter, especially for football, although such a request is rare. Television production crews frequently will request a couple of runners—a statistician and someone to manage the cords for videographers who move about the court or sidelines.

The SID should ask about personnel needs when radio or television media request credentials. It also is a wise policy to keep a volunteer or two on standby if media interest is high, to handle any last-minute requests. Merle Levin, a former SID at Cleveland State University, says student volunteers are acceptable if they are "absolutely dependable." A dependable pool may be found in the university's communication, journalism, and/or electronic media departments. Many of those may be knowledgeable about the media's needs as a result of course work and previous field experience.

- Hospitality and concessions: The SID should assign a volunteer or two to assist with food and other amenities. The volunteer can advise food service personnel of supplies running low, spills, etc. In many cases, the caterer or university food-service people will take care of this responsibility.

While budget and the pool of volunteers available may limit personnel resources, the SID should keep in mind that efficiency is inseparable from the size of the press-box staff. Mistakes are more likely to happen if people are assigned multiple duties, particularly if the timing for different responsibilities is tight. Service is more likely to falter if flexibility is limited by insufficient personnel at the site. Gallagher always keeps one extra person in the press box, a backup to assign to needs that arise.

The SID also should bear in mind that efficiency is inseparable from preparation. The SID should train statisticians ahead of time, even if that involves practice with videotapes. Sports information personnel should schedule volunteers well in advance and call to confirm their participation a couple of days in advance of the game. A walk-through and check of equipment is also good practice.

Remember, a satisfied reporter is likely to speak highly of the accommodations. Word of mouth inside media circles spreads like a wildfire. Good news can spread as quickly as bad news.

Working Materials

Print and radio journalists generally are self-sufficient during the game if provided adequate pregame information. The television crew may need more assistance, particularly prior to the game. The SID may need to arrange an on-site walk-through for production people unfamiliar with the facility, review team information with announcers, meet with graphic coordinators, and set up pregame interviews. The sports information department also may be asked to supply videotaped highlights from previous games, institutional promotions, etc., for use during halftime, time-outs, and other breaks. In fact, the SID should offer to provide such promotional material if the production crew does not request it—it's a fair tradeoff.

"For one thing, almost every televised event will have room during the telecast to show a one-minute spot providing information on the school itself," Levin says.

```
Official Basketball Box Score -- GAME TOTALS -- FINAL STATISTICS
Illinois vs Ohio State
03/06/05 12:00 p.m. at Value City Arena; Columbus, Ohio
-------------------------------------------------------------------------------
VISITORS: Illinois 29-1, 15-1
                        TOT-FG   3-PT         REBOUNDS
## Player Name          FG-FGA FG-FGA FT-FTA OF DE TOT PF  TP  A TO BLK S MIN
40 Augustine, James.... f  4-11  0-0   1-3    3  5  8   3   9  0  2  0  0  21
43 Powell, Jr., Roger.. f  4-10  0-2   4-5    6  5 11   2  12  1  2  0  0  34
04 Head, Luther........ g  3-9   3-6   3-3    0  7  7   1  12  6  3  0  1  38
05 Williams, Deron..... g  1-7   0-4   0-0    1  5  6   3   2  3  0  1  1  33
11 Brown, Dee.......... g  3-11  2-6   5-8    0  0  0   4  13  4  0  0  0  38
33 McBride, Rich.......    0-0   0-0   0-0    1  0  1   2   0  0  0  0  0   6
41 Carter, Warren......    2-2   0-0   0-0    1  0  1   0   4  0  0  0  0   8
45 Smith, Nick.........    2-2   0-0   0-0    0  0  0   1   4  0  0  0  0   6
50 Ingram, Jack........    4-8   0-1   0-0    0  1  1   1   8  0  1  0  3  16
   TEAM................                       1  1  2               1
   Totals.............     23-60 5-19 13-19  13 24 37  17  64 14  9  1  5 200

TOTAL FG% 1st Half: 14-33 42.4%   2nd Half:  9-27 33.3%   Game: 38.3%   DEADB
3-Pt. FG% 1st Half:  3-12 25.0%   2nd Half:  2-7  28.6%   Game: 26.3%   REBS
F Throw % 1st Half:  7-11 63.6%   2nd Half:  6-8  75.0%   Game: 68.4%   2,1

-------------------------------------------------------------------------------
HOME TEAM: Ohio State 19-11, 8-8
                        TOT-FG   3-PT         REBOUNDS
## Player Name          FG-FGA FG-FGA FT-FTA OF DE TOT PF  TP  A TO BLK S MIN
00 Sullinger, J.J...... f  1-3   0-0   0-0    0  5  5   3   2  1  1  0  1  21
03 Harris, Ivan........ f  0-0   0-0   0-0    0  0  0   1   0  0  0  0  0   5
34 Dials, Terence......  c  8-13  0-0   5-7    5  3  8   1  21  3  1  1  1  39
14 Butler, Jamar....... g  0-2   0-1   0-0    0  2  2   1   0  0  2  0  0  17
23 Foster, Je'Kel...... g  3-8   2-5   2-3    0  2  2   1  10  2  1  1  1  33
02 Fuss-Cheatham, Brand    2-4   0-1   1-2    0  2  2   2   5  2  0  0  0  23
10 Stockman, Tony......    1-6   0-4   0-0    1  3  4   1   2  3  1  0  0  26
40 Sylvester, Matt.....    8-17  2-5   7-9    0  5  5   4  25  3  2  1  0  34
54 Marinchick, Matt....    0-0   0-0   0-0    0  0  0   0   0  0  0  0  0   2
   TEAM................                       1  2  3
   Totals.............     23-53 4-16 15-21   7 24 31  14  65 14  8  3  3 200

TOTAL FG% 1st Half:  9-22 40.9%   2nd Half: 14-31 45.2%   Game: 43.4%   DEADB
3-Pt. FG% 1st Half:  1-7  14.3%   2nd Half:  3-9  33.3%   Game: 25.0%   REBS
F Throw % 1st Half:  8-13 61.5%   2nd Half:  7-8  87.5%   Game: 71.4%   4,4

-------------------------------------------------------------------------------
Officials: Ed Hightower, Ted Hillary and Rick Hartzell
Technical fouls: Illinois-None. Ohio State-None.
Attendance: 19200
Score by Periods          1st  2nd   Total
Illinois..................  38   26  -   64
Ohio State................  27   38  -   65
ID-287171
```

"They will want a tape in advance and you should have one or more in readiness for them when they arrive. Check in advance to see what their requirements are, then do what you need to do to come up with tape. Bottom line—treat the radio and TV crews well and they will respond in kind."

The primary materials the sports information staff should supply include the following:

- Press Packet—The sports information staff should put a packet of pregame information at every seat on press row at least one-half hour before the game begins. Also, the seat should be marked with a sticker with the reporter's name and media organization name.

At the minimum, the packet should include rosters for each team, a flip card with a numerical roster, and a depth chart (usually two deep—starter and first substitute) for both offense and defense. Another common item is a page of notes pertaining to the game, which would include lineup changes, an injury report, statistics, records, and possible records that could be set in this contest. Often, a note provided by the SID will serve as just the right clause in a sentence of a story. Details can create a positive press-box experience, and a lack of them can confound it.

If budget and time permit, the SID should put all the materials into a heavy folder (with school or team logo on the outside). This allows reporters to keep all the pertinent information together.

The Baldwin-Wallace staff put 10 different items in a manila envelope at each seat in the football press box for an Ohio Athletic Conference match with Otterbein College of Westerville, Ohio, in 1996. The game was of special significance in that it was the 18th annual Lee Tressel Shrine Classic Game. Proceeds from the game went to the Al Koran Temple, Shriners Children's Burn Fund.

Items included in this press packet were as follows:

- an agenda of activities, from a luncheon at 11:30 a.m. to the Shrine parade and ceremony at the stadium, from 12:45 P.M. to 1 P.M. to the kickoff at 1:30 P.M. to the halftime tribute to Tressel to the postgame presentation of awards to the Shrine Players of the Game

- a three-page list of Baldwin-Wallace notes, with information on the series, last week's game for each team, Baldwin-Wallace highlights and statistics, records in jeopardy, an injury report, and contact numbers for SID Kevin Ruple and football coach Bob Packard

- numerical rosters, one team on each side of a one-page sheet

- one-page sheet (both sides) of season-to-date Baldwin-Wallace football statistics

- one-page sheet (both sides) of season-to-date Otterbein football statistics

- a flipchart with a two-deep diagram of numbers/players at each position when Baldwin-Wallace had the ball on offense on one sheet, and a similar diagram on the flip side when Otterbein had the ball

- a scoring summary and final statistics from the 1995 game between the two teams

- a scoring summary and final statistics from the previous week's game for each team

- a Baldwin-Wallace program for the game and an Otterbein media guide

- a three-page OAC release on the players of the week and conference football statistics

An agenda or timetable is particularly useful to broadcast media. The more details provided, the better. The electronic media broadcasting the game live can better coordinate commercials, film clips, etc., with a timetable that includes the national anthem, announcement of starting lineups, actual tip-off time, length of halftime, and length and number of scheduled timeouts. The Baldwin-Wallace agenda included a time breakdown for segments of the 20-minute halftime tribute to Tressel.

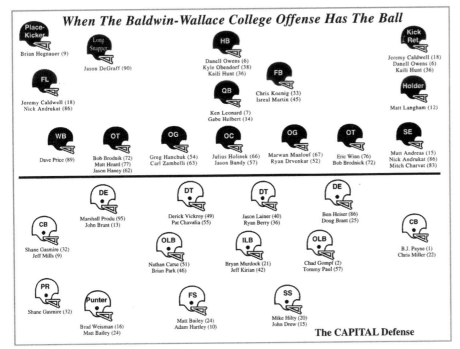

When The Baldwin-Wallace College Offense Has The Ball

- Quickie stats—A runner should provide statistical updates to the broadcast media during timeouts or other breaks. The updates can include statistical leaders, team yardage totals, shooting percentages (basketball), etc. (i.e., running totals as the game unfolds). Radio stations should be the first to receive the information, because immediacy is everything to the radio announcer.

- Score updates—At the major college and professional levels, a public-address announcer usually advises the crowd of key game developments. The SID or media relations director usually passes on scores from other schools or teams, records, the extent of any injuries, and other interesting and important bits of information.

- Halftime statistics—A runner should compile a complete rundown on scoring plays, individual statistics, and team totals. Most colleges and professional teams supply the numbers on standardized forms that are easy to read.

- Halftime interviews—The broadcast media may want help in arranging a couple of quick halftime interviews. Likely candidates for interviews are former athletics greats from the participating schools, sports dignitaries in the crowd, athletics directors, and conference commissioners. Levin says presidents rank just above SIDs and coaches of other sports in terms of media interest. He advises against professors and fundraisers "unless they have a darned interesting message." Remember, the broadcast media are looking for information, not self-promotion or thinly disguised advertising. The TV team may request a quick comment or two from each coach at halftime.

- Final statistics—The final statistical package is an expansion of the halftime package—a compilation of all pertinent individual and team statistics. The sports information staff may supplement the package with pool quotations from coaches/players and with updated season statistics. (Team statistics can be tabulated quickly if computerized.)

The final statistical packages for Division I football games typically consist of seven items:

- A scoring summary.

- Team statistics, including first downs, net yards rushing, net yards passing, total yards, etc.

- Individual statistics, including rushing, passing, pass receiving, punting, field goals, and returns.

- Individual defensive statistics, including tackles (assisted, unassisted, and tackles for losses), quarterback sacks, fumble recoveries, fumbles forced, pass interceptions, passes broken up, and blocks.

- A drive chart showing the starting field position and time, and end result of the drive for each team.

- A participation chart showing each player that performed during the contest.

- A play-by-play rundown from coin toss to final play.

```
                          Scoring Summary (Final)
              Clarion University (2-3,0-2) vs. Edinboro University (4-1,2-0)
Date: Oct 01, 2005   Site: Edinboro, Pa          Stadium: Sox Harrison Stadium
Attendance: 4822


Score by Quarters     1   2   3   4    Score
-----------------    --  --  --  --    -----
Clarion University..  0   0   0   0  -   0
Edinboro University.  7  16  14   7  -  44


Scoring Summary:
1st 00:00 EDIN - Kyle Witucki 14 yd pass from Justin Bouch (Kody Robertson kick)
                            13 plays, 80 yards, TOP 6:22, CLAR 0 - EDIN 7
2nd 09:00 EDIN - Kelvin Collins 1 yd run (Kody Robertson kick blockd)
                            4 plays, 11 yards, TOP 1:20, CLAR 0 - EDIN 13
    02:11 EDIN - Jeff Dinger 7 yd pass from Josh Hinkle (Kody Robertson kick)
                            9 plays, 54 yards, TOP 5:04, CLAR 0 - EDIN 20
    00:23 EDIN - Kody Robertson 20 yd field goal
                            8 plays, 53 yards, TOP 1:10, CLAR 0 - EDIN 23
3rd 14:20 EDIN - Jordan Bobitski 12 yd pass from Justin Bouch (Kody Robertson kick)
                            4 plays, 80 yards, TOP 0:40, CLAR 0 - EDIN 30
    04:22 EDIN - Ryan Valasek 43 yd pass from Justin Bouch (Kody Robertson kick)
                            6 plays, 80 yards, TOP 2:58, CLAR 0 - EDIN 37
4th 04:30 EDIN - Joe Gable 5 yd pass from Josh Hinkle (Kody Robertson kick)
                            12 plays, 85 yards, TOP 6:17, CLAR 0 - EDIN 44


Kickoff time: 2:00pm    End of Game: 4:50pm    Total elapsed time: 2:50
Officials: Referee: Richard Stanley; Umpire: Tim Linnartz;
Linesman: Chris ROss; Line judge: John Pujia; Back judge: Frank Usseglio;
Field judge: Tim Kerwin; Side judge: J. Czajkowski; Scorer: Bob Shreve;
Temperature: 68 deg    Wind: 5-10 SE    Weather: Sunny

Edinboro has season-high 561 yards and is 2-0 in PSAC West
for first time since 1996 ... Edinboro is ranked 21st in
AFCA ... Clarion had initial first down at 4:07 of 3rd qtr..
Clarion's -8 yards rushing 8th-lowest figure by Edinboro.
```

```
                            Drive Chart (Final)
                   Drive Started          Drive Ended          Consumed
Team    Qtr Spot Time  Obtained     Spot Time  How Lost      Pl-Yds   TOP
------------------------------------------------------------------------------
CLAR    1st C23  11:51 Missed FG     C25  09:20 Punt          3-2    02:31
CLAR    1st C26  08:21 Punt          C27  06:22 Punt          3-1    01:59
CLAR    2nd C24  15:00 Kickoff       C25  13:10 Punt          3-1    01:50
CLAR    2nd C03  11:45 Punt          C11  10:20 Fumble        3-8    01:25
CLAR    2nd C32  09:00 Kickoff       C29  07:15 Punt          3--3   01:45
CLAR    2nd C29  02:11 Kickoff       C25  01:25 Punt          3--4   00:46
CLAR    2nd C34  00:23 Kickoff       C34  00:15 Fumble        0-0    00:08
CLAR    2nd C30  00:00 Missed FG     C30  15:00 End of half   0-0    00:00
CLAR    3rd C39  14:20 Kickoff       C15  11:47 Punt          3--24  02:33
CLAR    3rd C32  09:09 Downs         C40  07:20 Punt          3-8    01:49
CLAR    3rd C26  04:22 Kickoff       C38  02:10 Punt          4-12   02:12
CLAR    4th C12  14:40 Punt          C44  10:47 Punt          8-32   03:53
CLAR    4th C31  04:30 Kickoff       C36  02:30 Punt          3-5    02:00

EDIN    1st E20  15:00 Kickoff       C23  11:51 Missed FG     7-57   03:09
EDIN    1st E33  09:20 Punt          E37  08:21 Punt          3-4    00:59
EDIN    1st E20  06:22 Punt          C00  00:00 *TOUCHDOWN    13-80  06:22#
EDIN    2nd C46  13:10 Punt          C46  11:45 Punt          3-0    01:25
EDIN    2nd C11  10:20 Fumble        C00  09:00 *TOUCHDOWN    4-11   01:20#
EDIN    2nd E46  07:15 Punt          C00  02:11 *TOUCHDOWN    9-54   05:04#
EDIN    2nd E44  01:25 Punt          C03  00:15 *FIELD GOAL   8-53   01:10#
EDIN    2nd C34  00:15 Fumble        C30  00:00 Missed FG     1-4    00:15#
EDIN    3rd E20  15:00 Kickoff       C00  14:20 *TOUCHDOWN    4-80   00:40#
EDIN    3rd C49  11:47 Punt          C32  09:09 Downs         5-17   02:38
EDIN    3rd E20  07:20 Punt          C00  04:22 *TOUCHDOWN    6-80   02:58
EDIN    3rd E34  02:10 Punt          C39  14:40 Punt          5-27   02:30
EDIN    4th E15  10:47 Punt          C00  04:30 *TOUCHDOWN    12-85  06:17#
EDIN    4th E24  02:30 Punt          E37  00:00 End of half   5-13   02:30


CLAR                     1st   2nd   3rd   4th    1st   2nd
                         Qtr   Qtr   Qtr   Qtr    Half  Half  Total
--------------------------------------------------------------------
Time of possession      04:30 05:46 06:34 05:53  10:16 12:27 22:43
3rd Down Conversions    0/2   0/4   0/3   1/3    0/6   1/6   1/12
Avg Field Position      C24   C22   C32   C21    C22   C28   C25
4th Down Conversions    0/0   0/0   0/0   0/0    0/0   0/0   0/0


EDIN                     1st   2nd   3rd   4th    1st   2nd
                         Qtr   Qtr   Qtr   Qtr    Half  Half  Total
--------------------------------------------------------------------
Time of possession      10:30 09:14 08:26 09:07  19:44 17:33 37:17
3rd Down Conversions    3/6   3/5   0/1   0/4    6/11  0/5   6/16
Avg Field Position      E24   C41   E31   E19    E46   E27   E38
4th Down Conversions    1/1   0/0   0/1   2/2    1/1   2/3   3/4
```

- News conference (optional)—The SID should coordinate the postgame news conference and arrange for press-box staffers to bring the coaches promptly. Some follow a win/lose order to give the losing team a chance to compose itself. Others prefer a visiting/home order to give the visitors a chance to get on the road sooner. The order may be affected by commitments to specific broadcast media; for example, a coach may insist on conducting a postgame interview for the hometown station first.

Members of the sports information staff should make themselves available to help individual members of the media as needed in completing and filing stories. Someone should stay until the last media representative leaves. One of the authors of this text, slowed and frustrated by a balky computer, found himself locked inside Churchill Downs one Derby night. He had to search out maintenance personnel in order to get out.

```
                              Individual Statistics (Final)
Clarion University                        Edinboro University

Rushing         No Gain Loss  Net TD Lg  Avg   Rushing          No Gain Loss  Net TD Lg  Avg
-------------------------------------------   --------------------------------------------------
Tyrone Buckner   6   19    0   19  0  4  3.2   Ulysee Davis     22  155    8  147  0 46  6.7
Josh Province    4    9    1    8  0  4  2.0   Kelvin Collins   10   67    0   67  1 16  6.7
Tony Easterling  1    5    0    5  0  5  5.0   DeMark.Robinson  11   47    3   44  0 16  4.0
David Murzynski  6    5    9   -4  0  3 -0.7   Justin Bouch      4   13    0   13  0  4  3.2
Vincent Kirk     1    0    5   -5  0  0 -5.0   Josh Hinkle       4   12    3    9  0  9  2.2
Matt Foradora    1    0    6   -6  0  0 -6.0   Deonte Peters     1    4    0    4  0  4  4.0
Brandon Dando    9   12   37  -25  0  9 -2.8   TEAM              1    0    1   -1  0  0 -1.0
Totals...       28   50   58   -8  0  9 -0.3   Totals...        53  298   15  283  1 46  5.3

Passing        Att-Cmp-Int Yds TD Long Sack    Passing        Att-Cmp-Int Yds TD Long Sack
-------------------------------------------   --------------------------------------------------
Brandon Dando    9-4-0    40   0   15    5     Justin Bouch     22-8-0   188   3   43    0
Matt Foradora    2-1-0     6   0    6    1     Josh Hinkle       7-7-0    90   2   23    0
Totals...       11-5-0    46   0   15    6     Totals...        29-15-0  278   5   43    0

Receiving       No.  Yds   TD Long           Receiving       No.  Yds   TD Long
-------------------------------------         --------------------------------------
Tony Easterling  2   21    0   15            Ryan Valasek     3   84    1   43
Michael Byrd     2   19    0    8            Aaron Fetty      3   54    0   23
Jewell Stephens  1    6    0    6            Jeff Dinger      2   46    1   39
Totals...        5   46    0   15            Kyle Witucki     2   32    1   18
                                             Nate Eimer       2   20    0   16
                                             C.J. Trivisonno  1   25    0   25
                                             Jordan Bobitski  1   12    1   12
                                             Joe Gable        1    5    1    5
                                             Totals...       15  278    5   43

Punting        No.  Yds   Avg Long In20      Punting        No.  Yds   Avg Long In20
-------------------------------------------   --------------------------------------------
Nicholas Perla  10  438  43.8  73    1       Kody Robertson   3  108  36.0  43     2
Totals...       10  438  43.8  73    1       Totals...        3  108  36.0  43     2

                Punts   Kickoffs  Intercept                  Punts   Kickoffs  Intercept
All Returns   No.Yds.Lg No.Yds.Lg No.Yds.Lg  All Returns   No.Yds.Lg No.Yds.Lg No.Yds.Lg
-------------------------------------------   --------------------------------------------------
Corey Giles    0  0  0  1  3  3  0  0  0      Jordan Bobitski 1  0  0  0  0  0  0  0  0
Dane Williams  0  0  0  2 35 18  0  0  0      Rod. Stevenson  1 12 12  0  0  0  0  0  0
Dwaon Woodard  0  0  0  3 35 15  0  0  0      Deonte Peters   2 31 22  0  0  0  0  0  0
Totals...      0  0  0  6 73 18  0  0  0      Totals...       4 43 22  0  0  0  0  0  0

Field goal attempts                           Field goal attempts
-------------------------------------         --------------------------------------
                                              Kody Robertson 1st 11:51  40 yds - Missed
                                              Kody Robertson 2nd 00:23  20 yds - Good
                                              Kody Robertson 2nd 00:00  48 yds - Missed

FUMBLES: Clarion University-Corey Giles 1-1; Michael Byrd 1-0; Vincent Kirk 1-0; Tyrone Buckner
Edinboro University-Josh Hinkle 1-0.
```

```
                           Play-by-Play Summary (3rd quarter)

C 1-10 C30    Start of 3rd quarter, clock 15:00, CLAR ball on CLAR35.

              Kyle Snoke kickoff 65 yards to the EDIN0, touchback.
   E 1-10 E20    EDINBORO UNIVERSITY drive start at 15:00 (3rd).
   E 1-10 E20    Justin Bouch pass complete to Ryan Valasek for 28 yards to the EDIN48, 1ST DOWN EDIN (James Charles).
   E 1-10 E48    Ulysee Davis rush for 1 yard to the EDIN49 (Jordan Hicks).
   E 2-9 E49     Justin Bouch pass complete to Jeff Dinger for 39 yards to the CLAR12, 1ST DOWN EDIN (Elijah Evans).
   E 1-10 C12    Justin Bouch pass complete to Jordan Bobitski for 12 yards to the CLAR0, 1ST DOWN EDIN, TOUCHDOWN, clock
                 14:20.
                 Kody Robertson kick attempt failed, PENALTY CLAR offside 2 yards to the CLAR1, NO PLAY.
                 Kody Robertson kick attempt good.

              ================================================
              CLARION UNIVERSITY 0, EDINBORO UNIVERSITY 30
              ================================================

-------------- 4 plays, 80 yards, TOP 00:40 ---------------

              Chris Avery kickoff 41 yards to the CLAR24, Dwaon Woodard return 15 yards to the CLAR39 (Pat Aretz;Jim
              Soltis).
C 1-10 C39    CLARION UNIVERSITY drive start at 14:20 (3rd).
C 1-10 C39    Brandon Dando sacked for loss of 9 yards to the CLAR30 (Chris Amico).
C 2-19 C30    David Murzynski rush for loss of 1 yard to the CLAR29 (Ben Stroup;Greg MacAnn).
C 3-20 C29    Brandon Dando sacked for loss of 14 yards to the CLAR15 (Greg MacAnn;Ben Stroup).
C 4-34 C15    Nicholas Perla punt 46 yards to the EDIN39, Rod. Stevenson return 12 yards to the CLAR49 (Matt Morris).
-------------- 3 plays, minus 24 yards, TOP 02:33 ---------------

   E 1-10 C49    EDINBORO UNIVERSITY drive start at 11:47 (3rd).
   E 1-10 C49    DeMark.Robinson rush for 10 yards to the CLAR39, 1ST DOWN EDIN (Quintyn Brazil).
   E 1-10 C39    PENALTY CLAR offside 5 yards to the CLAR34.
   E 1-5 C34     DeMark.Robinson rush for 4 yards to the CLAR30 (Matt Niedbala;Kevin Rigby).
   E 2-1 C30     Justin Bouch pass incomplete to Jeff Dinger.
   E 3-1 C30     DeMark.Robinson rush for loss of 2 yards to the CLAR32 (Matt Morris).
   E 4-3 C32     Justin Bouch pass incomplete to Jeff Dinger, dropped pass.
-------------- 5 plays, 17 yards, TOP 02:38 ---------------

C 1-10 C32    CLARION UNIVERSITY drive start at 09:09 (3rd).
C 1-10 C32    Josh Province rush for 2 yards to the CLAR34 (Ben Stroup;Chris Amico).
C 2-8 C34     Brandon Dando pass incomplete to Josh Province, dropped pass.
C 3-8 C34     Brandon Dando pass complete to Tony Easterling for 6 yards to the CLAR40 (Chris Avery;Damion Malott).
C 4-2 C40     Nicholas Perla punt 60 yards to the EDIN0, touchback.
-------------- 3 plays, 8 yards, TOP 01:49 ---------------

   E 1-10 E20    EDINBORO UNIVERSITY drive start at 07:20 (3rd).
   E 1-10 E20    Kelvin Collins rush for 6 yards to the EDIN26 (Jordan Hicks).
   E 2-4 E26     Kelvin Collins rush for 10 yards to the EDIN36, 1ST DOWN EDIN (Deonte Cooley;Jordan Hicks).
   E 1-10 E36    Kelvin Collins rush for 7 yards to the EDIN43 (Brock Luke;Dwaon Woodard).
   E 2-3 E43     Kelvin Collins rush for 9 yards to the CLAR48, 1ST DOWN EDIN (Joshua Best).
   E 1-10 C48    Justin Bouch pass incomplete.
   E 2-10 C48    PENALTY CLAR offside 5 yards to the CLAR43.
   E 2-5 C43     Justin Bouch pass complete to Ryan Valasek for 43 yards to the CLAR0, 1ST DOWN EDIN, TOUCHDOWN, clock 04:22
                 Kody Robertson kick attempt good.

              ================================================
              CLARION UNIVERSITY 0, EDINBORO UNIVERSITY 37
              ================================================

-------------- 6 plays, 80 yards, TOP 02:58 ---------------

              Chris Avery kickoff 39 yards to the CLAR26, downed.
C 1-10 C26    CLARION UNIVERSITY drive start at 04:22 (3rd).
C 1-10 C26    Brandon Dando pass complete to Michael Byrd to the CLAR34, fumble forced by Hardin Moss, fumble by Michael Byrd
              recovered by CLAR Zack Snyder at CLAR40, 1ST DOWN CLAR.
C 1-10 C40    Brandon Dando rush for 3 yards to the CLAR43 (James English).
C 2-7 C43     Brandon Dando sacked for loss of 5 yards to the CLAR38 (Hardin Moss).
C 3-12 C38    Brandon Dando pass incomplete to Michael Byrd.
C 4-12 C38    Nicholas Perla punt 50 yards to the EDIN12, Deonte Peters return 22 yards to the EDIN34 (Matt Morris;Jordan
              Hicks).
-------------- 4 plays, 12 yards, TOP 02:12 ---------------

   E 1-10 E34    EDINBORO UNIVERSITY drive start at 02:10 (3rd).
   E 1-10 E34    Ulysee Davis rush for 6 yards to the EDIN40 (Joshua Best).
   E 2-4 E40     Ulysee Davis rush for 15 yards to the CLAR45, 1ST DOWN EDIN (Zach Gourley).
   E 1-10 C45    Ulysee Davis rush for 4 yards to the CLAR41 (Jordan Hicks;Matt Ritter).
   E 2-6 C41     Ulysee Davis rush for 2 yards to the CLAR39 (Matt Niedbala;Matt Ritter).

              =============END OF 3rd QUARTER============
              CLARION UNIVERSITY 0, EDINBORO UNIVERSITY 37
              ================================================
```

Food

Budgets and sport organization policies dictate the menus, if any, in the press areas of both football and basketball games. Professional football, baseball, and basketball teams often treat the media to sit-down dinners before games, and snacks at halftime. High-profile Division I schools often do so as well.

Small schools can provide niceties, too, without stretching budgets. Small colleges typically offer coffee, soda, and donuts in working media areas. Others, with a bit more money to spend, add hot dogs, pizza, or submarine sandwiches to the pregame fare.

The budget should be the guiding factor in formulating the menu. Remember, the press area is a workplace, first and foremost—not a restaurant. The SID should *never* exceed the budget simply to impress the media. Reporters are more impressed with courtesy and service.

The *NCAA Public Relations and Promotion Manual* lists these MUSTS, DO'S, and DON'TS regarding press boxes:

Do's and Don'ts

Musts

- Must have adequate space for working media.

- Must be functional before making it fancy.

- Must be heated in cold climate.

- Must keep nonworkers out of working area.

- Must have adequate area for service and statistical crews and equipment.

- Must have an electrical outlet at every seat.

- Must have adequate space for home and visiting coaches' phone booths.

- Must have adequate space behind writers for traffic.

Do's

- Do have food service available.

- Do have adequate toilet facilities for men and women.

- Do have water fountains.

- Do have pay telephones available for emergencies.

- Do have adequate storage space for stats crew materials.

- Do have easy access to field and dressing rooms.

- Do have adequate communications between stats crew and working media.

- Do have adequate lighting, power, and telephone cables and outlets.

- Do install a bank of telephones throughout the working media area to assist writers filing a story.

- Do have specially designed television booth and camera spaces.

- Do have conduit of sufficient size to handle television cable.

- Do have an elevator.

Don'ts

- Don't have poles, pillars, posts, or lattice-work windows that obstruct view.

- Don't have so many entrances to the press box that policing is a problem.

- Don't mix scouts and other necessary fringe workers with working media.

- Don't lead VIPs and other nonworkers in working press area.

- Don't put food bar in main stream of press-box traffic.

- DON'T CHEER—THERE IS NO CHEERING IN THE PRESS BOX.

Summary

Game time is the sports information or media relations staff's time upon the stage. That's when the sport organization's staff demonstrates its efficiency in serving the media under the most challenging conditions. The smoother and stronger the performance on press row, the more likely the media are to leave with a positive impression of the sports information staff and of the sport organization.

An effective operation is built on two primary criteria: courtesy and service. Courtesy encompasses the attitude the staff exhibits in assisting the media. Service involves the manner in which the staff goes about the job. The SID or media relations department will get high marks from the media if they respond to requests pleasantly and promptly. They also will enhance their image by anticipating problems and resolving them quickly, and by providing complete information quickly.

The press box or press table is the office away from home for the media. They expect a businesslike performance from the SID, who acts as the office manager. They expect the sports information staff to provide adequate work space, working materials, and support in completing their jobs. Amenities such as meals are extras, not essentials.

Press-box management demands preparations at three levels: pregame, game time and postgame. Pregame preparations deal primarily with logistics, such as credentials, seating assignments, electrical outlets, and telephone lines. Game time management deals with organizing, training, and supervising staff and volunteers who provide game information, assist broadcast media, and perform other necessary chores. Postgame responsibilities center on churning out game information, arranging and conducting interviews, and troubleshooting problems.

The SID acts as the traffic director as well as the office manager. How well the team manages the workplace at game time plays a more pivotal role in the image of the department than does any other activity. Efficient compilation of final statistics and coordination of the news conference are the ultimate measure of the press-box operation. The quicker and more accurate the delivery system on deadline, the better the reputation of the sports information office. A fast and efficient operation can do wonders for one's working relationships.

DISCUSSION QUESTIONS

1. What information would you include in your press-box policy when setting up for a football game?
2. What material would you include when making up a media packet for a football game?

SUGGESTED EXERCISES

1. Assign class members to the jobs in a press box/press table, including that of public-address announcer.
2. Have the class take over the press box at a junior varsity football game and/or a women's varsity basketball game.
3. Have each student perform his or her duty, then have each write a 200-word paper describing the job and how it relates to all the other jobs in the press box. In other words, the students should write how their particular spokes fit into the wheel.
4. For the reporters, hold a postgame news conference with coaches and athletes and have reporters write the appropriate news story or column.

Chapter Ten

SPECIAL EVENTS: FROM AWARDS BANQUETS TO NATIONAL TOURNAMENTS

The National Collegiate Athletic Association Division III Wrestling Championship at John Carroll University in Ohio lasted one week. The planning took more than a year. Full-scale preparations began 11 months before the event, and the wrap-up continued a week past the end of competition.

By July 1, 1996, a Media Center Checklist was available for the 1997 U.S. Open scheduled at Congressional Country Club near Washington, D. C., Craig Smith, manager of media relations for the United States Golf Association, prepared the document, called an *administrative summary*. The 12-page summary included organizational guidelines for seven sections of the media center, ranging from the USGA office trailer to the photo lounge for photographers to the interview room for all working media. The guidelines identified major needs and responsibilities, such as setup of the stage and power sources in the interview area. The checklist broke down every major area into minute details, such as padding for carpeting and covering for tables throughout the media work sites.

> Chapter 10 outlines types of special events the sports information specialist may be called upon to plan and supervise. The chapter focuses primarily on the role of the sports information director, public relations director, or media relations manager in staging special activities ranging from awards ceremonies to national tournaments.

Preparations for the National Collegiate Athletic Association Division I Men's Basketball Final Four in Indianapolis in 2000 actually began seven years in advance. The city of Indianapolis, Butler University, and the Midwestern Collegiate Conference (MCC) developed a 45-minute presentation to the NCAA Division I Men's Basketball Committee in 1993. The committee recommended Indianapolis for the site of the tournament in 2000, based on the presentation. A 15-member "local organizing committee" planned to begin preparations for the tournament itself about two years in advance, according to the committee's timetable; that gave Butler, MCC, and Indianapolis officials about a year to catch their breath after staging the 1997 Division I Men's Division I Basketball Tournament.

Staging a special event as large as a national championship is a time-consuming and challenging undertaking. It demands involvement of a large number of people and often involves team or athletics officials from more than one sport organization, business people in the community, and citizen volunteers. It requires a diverse range of skills and responsibilities—from planning to promotion to publicity to media operations. Organizers generally call on sports information specialists to provide the leadership and direction in those areas.

The term *special event* in this chapter encompasses in-house promotions tied to scheduled games or sport seasons as well as one-time events in which the host team/institute may or may not participate. Both are promotional, designed to enhance the image of the sport organization and/or to increase revenues. Olson, Hirsch, Breitenbach, and Saunders (1987) say special events can help develop a positive public image for an athletics department by cultivating the media to show the positive contributions that athletics make. (Although news conferences and media days fall within the broad definition of special events, they are treated separately in Chapter 6 because the emphasis of each is on its usefulness in delivering news, rather than on its promotional values.)

At the amateur level, an in-house special event might be a country-club tennis tournament or a YMCA swim meet. On the collegiate level, activities ranging from the Shrine Day/Lee Tressel Tribute in connection with a Baldwin-Wallace football game (see Chapter 9) to the end-of-season awards banquets fall into the category. Promotions associated with invitational tournaments, playoff, or bowl games for which a team qualifies, and key conference games or big games between rivals, such as the Crosstown Shootout each year between the men's Division I basketball teams in Cincinnati (University of Cincinnati and Xavier University) or the Old Oaken Bucket football battle between Indiana University and Purdue University, are further examples of special events. On the professional level, in-house events include preseason promotional "caravans" or visits to selected cities by the manager or coach and several players; opening day activities at Major League Baseball games, including parades; and game-to-game promotions, such as Fan Appreciation Day.

Special amateur events run the gamut from charity fundraisers to city championships to national tournament qualifiers such as area and regional Amateur Softball Association eliminations. In some cases, cities and local sports associations vie to host events, as with the national figure skating and gymnastics championships. Colleges and cities collaborate on bids to host preliminary and championship rounds of NCAA regional or championship tournaments and meets in swimming, wrestling, track, gymnastics, golf, and tennis. At the professional level, special events embrace everything from all-star games to sites for professional tour events or league championships, such as the Super Bowl.

The common denominator among special events is promotion. The objective of an in-house promotion or a single, special event is to advance the financial goals of the sports organization and/or sponsors. An in-house promotion for a game may aim at generating media interest in a team or sport in hopes that increased publicity may result in additional ticket sales. The city of Evansville, Indiana, and the University of Evansville presented a bid to host a preliminary round of the NCAA Men's Division I tournament in 1983 to gain exposure for the university's basketball program, which had jumped from Division II to Division I just four years earlier.

Major one-time events, such as the U.S. Figure Skating Championships, are intended to attract regional or national media exposure, to draw spectators/visitors from a larger audience base, and to generate substantial revenues for the host sports organizations (amateur or professional) and the community. A study conducted by Larry S. Davidson and Bruce L. Jaffee of the Department of Business Economics and Public Policy at Indiana University found that the 1991 NCAA Men's Division I Final Four in Indianapolis brought an estimated $23 million into the city. The revenue represented a total economic impact of $46 million when reinvested in the local economy, according to the news release announcing the selection of Indianapolis as host for the 2000 NCAA Men's Division I Final Four.

A USGA handout (USGA Championship Programs, 1996) lists six reasons to host a championship event:

1. Recognition for golf course and club

2. Alignment with the USGA, including other championship opportunities and course maintenance support

3. Course layout recommendations

4. Increased membership

5. A proud membership

6. Profit

Although boosting attendance and revenue at sports-related events may not be the direct responsibility of the SID or the team public relations director, the marketing function and public relations thrust often mesh in staging special events. As in many other aspects of the business of sports, marketing and promotions specialists may lead the way in identifying target audiences and determining the best ways to reach them. Wang and Irwin (1993) studied sponsorships and the economic impact to be gained not only by the institution but also by the surrounding community. They concluded that potential markets must be analyzed and goals established to create a basis for evaluating efforts. Sports information or media relations personnel play roles in achieving such goals, both through pre-event publicity, such as news releases, and through media management during and after the event.

The marketing and public relations functions vary according to the type of event. The university development or professional marketing departments play the larger role in events with heavy emphasis on identifying audiences, conducting advertising campaigns, and selling tickets and sponsorships. Promotions and marketing people generally handle direct mail, telemarketing, personal contact, group ticket discounts, game-day promotions, and paid advertising or sponsorships. For example, a university promotions specialist or athletics director would most often negotiate the sponsorship of an invitational tournament and halftime giveaways/contests by local businesses. Those assigned promotional duties also would oversee individual game promotions. For example, they would take care of a promotion that promised free admission to a college women's basketball game to youngsters wearing T-shirts from the university-held sports camp the previous summer.

The sports information or public relations departments play the larger role in events with heavy emphasis on generating publicity and assisting the media in information delivery. The emphasis on media management is why the sports information department takes the lead in news conferences and media days. The objective of each is not to sell tickets, but to deliver information through the media that will heighten interest and indirectly boost ticket sales. Likewise, the sports information office will play a significant role in the awards banquet, postseason playoff events, and all-star games.

Promotional Activities

Directed primarily by marketing personnel—opening day activities, such as parades; single-game promotions; ticket discount promotions; advertising campaigns (including posters, flyers, billboards, etc.); tournament sponsorships; halftime giveaways and contests.

Informational Activities

Directed primarily by sports information personnel—news conferences, media days, news releases on promotional activities, awards banquets, postseason playoffs, all-star games, programs for special events, tournament press operations, tournament all-star teams, and awards.

In most major special events, the marketing and information departments coordinate activities. For example, promotional personnel most likely would arrange

Courtesy of U.S. Navy

Public appearances and autograph signings, such as the one pictured above by Bo Jackson, are examples of special promotional events that require the organization and direction of a sports information specialist.

the program for a special ceremony at halftime of the football game. They would be responsible for all arrangements, including advertising and ticket promotions. The SID would handle pre-event publicity announcing the event, the program, and special attractions. On game day, the promotional department would direct the ceremony. The sports information office would provide a schedule of activities to the assembled media and perhaps send a write-up on the ceremony to media representatives who did not intend.

In multifaceted events, such as a USGA tournament or an NCAA championship event, both marketing and sports information people play integral roles in planning and preparations. Named to the 15-member Local Organizing Committee for the NCAA Final Four in Indianapolis in 2000 were the athletics director at Butler University, the sports director of the Indiana Convention Center and RCA Dome, two national sales managers for the Indianapolis Convention and Visitors Association (ICVA), and the director of publications for the ICVA. The marketing people at the tourist promotional association, and sports information people affiliated with Butler, the MCC, and the ICVA were incorporated in the promotional and informational structure. They coordinated efforts in planning, promotion, publicity, and media operations.

Planning the Event

When an amateur organization, an institution, or a team decides to stage a special event, everyone must get involved: coaches, athletics directors/general managers, business managers, marketing/promotions directors, advertising managers, sports information directors, and even the athletes. Successful events are the result of well-coordinated efforts by specialists in a variety of fields. Each specialist contributes expertise in one area of a multifaceted plan. Like spokes in a wheel, all spin off a hub of common objectives and establish timetables that complement and supplement the work of others. If one spoke breaks, the wheel does not turn as smoothly. For example, a ticket discount is doomed to failure without advertising and publicity at the appropriate time prior to the start of ticket sales. Word-of-mouth publicity alone simply will not do the job unless the special event is as small as a marble match or a turtle race. Likewise, a ton of advertising and publicity is worthless if the discount is not worthwhile to ticket-buyers or the date conflicts with another major audience draw.

The planning process for a special event is similar to the preparations for media brochures or media days, but it is far more extensive. It calls into play all the skills and functions of the sports information specialist—for example, news releases, managed news events, media brochures, interviews, and press-row operations. Planning news releases, news conferences, and other pre-event publicity is part of the job, but the SID may have to think in multiples, scheduling releases and news conferences over a one- or two-year period to maintain public interest and to coincide with the start of ticket sales, selection of teams, etc. Preparing media brochures is essential, but the workload may increase tenfold for a national event that will draw hundreds of media representatives. Setting up media operations follows the same procedure, but the complexity of the puzzle may jump from that of a 50-piece jigsaw to that of a 1,000-piece challenge. Similarly, the space, equipment, and interview room demands increase a hundredfold. The checklist for the 1997 U.S. Open called for 550 armbands (two categories) and more than 3,000 media badges (five categories and access levels).

Julie Dalpaiz, the sports information director when John Carroll University played host to the NCAA Division III wrestling championships, kept a diary that described responsibilities before, during, and after the event. She concluded that the tournament was "a nice place to visit, but I wouldn't want to live there." Dalpaiz wrote,

> Hosting a national championship can be a lot of fun. It is definitely a lot of work and not something you want to do on an annual basis. Be prepared for it to throw a wrench into your regular SID work. Try to get as much of both your regular work and your event work done in advance. That will make things easier as the tournament approaches.

Being prepared for such a special event and being as organized as possible will make the event that much simpler. You may actually have a minute or two to enjoy and watch the event. However, no matter how well-prepared you are, there are always going to be last-minute occurrences that you cannot possibly foresee (last-minute media calls for credentials, participants who lose passes, computer foul-ups). Don't let them get the best of you or upset you. Handle them as quickly, efficiently and as best you can. If you let them bother you, you will be irate the whole weekend.

Do *your* job. Do what *you* are supposed to do and are prepared for. Delegate to your staff when necessary. If the tournament is well organized, everyone on the committee will have been delegated duties and know what he/she is supposed to do. Help out where needed (if you have time), but don't try to do everyone else's job. It will only drive you crazy.

Planning for a special event is a multifaceted process. The primary planning concerns, in order of importance, are as follows:

1. Scope and size of the event

2. Budget

3. Planning committees

4. Operations manual

5. Timetable of duties and activities

The first considerations are the scope and size of the event. They will dictate the budget, the number and nature of planning committees needed, and the timetable for performing duties. The second consideration is the budget. The budget will have a bearing on everything from advertising efforts to promotional activities to paid staff to media operations. If existing budget resources *may* limit the scope and size of the event, organizers should create a fundraising or sponsorship committee to come up with additional financial resources. The event itself should dictate the budget in this case, not vice versa. If the event is billed as a special attraction, the final product cannot be sophomoric if it is to send a positive message. It must be *special*. Organizers should consider the financial obligations *before* deciding to host an event, not afterwards.

Creating planning committees and assigning responsibilities follow development of the budget. The budget will identify the paid staff members. Organizers then can determine the number of volunteers needed. The organizers or executive committee will delegate responsibilities to each committee. Individual committees will decide how much volunteer help they will need and how they will fulfill their assigned responsibilities. Each will come up with an organizational chart, complete with group and individual assignments and responsibilities.

Once the budget, organizational structure, and human resources are in place, the real work of planning can begin. All planners must become "detail conscious." Lack of attention to details can destroy an event. Paying close attention to details can make that same event very successful by anticipating and preparing for snafus that might occur. The most effective way to organize the details is an *operations manual*. Organizers put information on the budget, organizational structure, and timetables in a single document or package available to all key personnel. The 12-page administrative summary prepared by Craig Smith of the USGA for the 1997 U.S. Open addressed such minute details as the time to begin cleanup every night, the size of a plywood sheet for mounting a key rack for the registration area, and lighting in the parking area for the media. However, that is only one part of the operational materials available to planners. The USGA also provides a publicity handbook that offers suggestions on promotions, media days, and programs; and a one-page, general media relations project list with duties to perform before, during, and after the championship.

Preparing a timetable for completion of duties and activities is an effective way to organize details, in three respects. First, it can serve as a logistical tool, identifying needs and the timelines to fulfill them. The local organizing committee for the 1997 NCAA Division I Men's Basketball Final Four in Indianapolis created a timeline for sending equipment to the RCA Dome. The timeline staggered the equipment shipments over a three-month period and specified quantity, shipping date, and receipt deadline for 13 items ranging from basketballs to wire bottle-holders.

Second, a timetable can double as a calendar of activities that ensures that organizers keep the event in the public eye in the months and days leading up to the event. Marketing personnel and sports information staff can time advertising efforts, promotional gimmicks, news conferences, and news releases to appear at regular intervals. The calendar of activities also provides a checklist or deadlines that aid organizers, planners, and volunteers in time management.

Third, a timetable facilitates the coordination of the work of all committees. Putting together the timeline requires adjustments within committees, to mesh their efforts with the overall plan. Development of the timetable helps the promotional unit and sports information personnel to coordinate advertising and news releases in particular.

Circumstances and the size of the event determine the appropriate startup date for the planning process. Organizers may have little time to prepare for events dictated by team performance, such as postseason playoff games. Northern Kentucky University had only one week to find an arena (the gym on campus was too small) and prepare for the first round of the Division II men's basketball tournament in 1995, because the Norse did not clinch a share of the Great Lakes Valley Conference tournament and a chance to host the tournament until the final weekend of the regular season. However, NKU athletics officials had done some advance planning, such as checking on the availability of Riverfront Coliseum in Cincinnati, in the event they qualified. A committee was in place and ready to act the moment the NCAA selected NKU as the host team. Sports information personnel can do much of the planning in advance with the assistance of the NCAA and timetables utilized by colleagues for such events. If the event is sponsored by the NCAA, for example, the first places to turn for financial assistance are local franchise dealers of NCAA corporate partners.

For multiday events such as the NCAA Final Four and the USGA championship, veteran sports information directors and media relations executives recommend lead time of at least one year for organizers. A good starting point is the tournament itself, a year or a couple of years in advance; that gives planners a chance to observe the work of other committees to pick up hints, generate ideas, and note the kinds of problems that arise. Some organizers divide the planning process into long-term and short-term timetables or "before, during, and after" guidelines. The local organizing committee in Indianapolis for the NCAA Final Four broke down a single timeline by year, month, and day for a two-year-period. The calendar for the first year specified tasks to be fulfilled by the first day of selected months, in most cases. The timetable for the year preceding the event followed a first-day deadline for the first six months, then dates within each month as the event drew nearer. The work agenda for public relations directors for the National Football League Pro Bowl included a detailed rundown on duties to be performed daily for two weeks prior to the game.

Dalpaiz, the SID at John Carroll University, set up a timeline for the Division III wrestling tournament that moved from monthly to weekly to daily as the event drew closer. The plan carried through the week following the event. Although the details will vary according to the event, her guidelines are applicable to most major special events:

One Year in Advance

- If you know you are going to host an event the following year, try to attend the year before so you can observe and learn from another host's successes and failures.

- When you receive confirmation of your selection as host, send out a press release and call the newspapers, radio, and television outlets on your media list.

- Correspond with ESPN and other TV venues to let them know you are the host, and invite them to cover the event.

Eleven Months in Advance

- Hold first meeting with tournament director and other tournament committee members. Specific duties are detailed.

- Make a list of everything you will need to do for the tournament and dates of when items need to be completed. Refer to the list weekly (daily as the event approaches), and check things off as you accomplish them.

- Decide where the pressroom will be and what amenities it will have. Make arrangements to have necessary phone lines installed in the pressroom if they are not already there.

Eight Months to Four Months in Advance

- Bearing in mind the budget with which you have to work, solicit quotations for printing of program.

- Set price schedule for program advertising, and make preliminary list of advertisers to solicit.

- Contact photographers to cover event.

- Plug tournament into as many other university athletics publications and programs throughout the year as possible.

- Plug tournament news in local media whenever opportunity arises.

- Order media/coaches' favors.

Three Months in Advance

- Begin solicitation for program ads.

- Solicit all people (students and adult volunteers) whom you need to help you do your job during the tournament.

- Talk with NCAA representative handling your event to see what regulations, advice, or help is available. Clarify any questions you have about tournament operations.

Eight Weeks in Advance

- Assign feature story for program.

- Design program and begin formatting text.

- Order all needed supplies for event, including photocopy paper and laminating supplies for media credentials.

- Send letters to mayor and university president that request welcoming letters for program.

- Design and order tickets.

- Order all photos needed for program.

- Check with source of photocopy machine to be used weekend of tournament on availability and working order.

- Arrange for program and bracket-sheet sellers.

- Arrange to have one or two people available through the tournament to staff "hotline" phones, where people can call through the tournament for results. (The best way to make arrangements is through one of your secretarial offices.) Although this may appear unnecessary for a Division III event, you should prepare for it. Family, friends, fans, and participating schools will find a way to call, even if you do not have someone set up to field calls.

Six Weeks in Advance

- Design and format media credentials, coaches' passes, participant passes, workers' passes, and parking passes. Take them to the printer.

- Design and order invitations for pretournament dinner.

- Continue formatting program.

- Send letters to guests presenting awards during tournament to verify their appearance.

- Send NCAA-prepared radio and TV promos to local media, and ask them to use the promos as public service announcements as often as possible.

- Order signs needed for weekend (e.g., press room, hospitality room, coat check, programs) from university print shop.

- Typeset and take to printers the promotional flyers to be distributed on campus.

Four Weeks in Advance

- Send out second press release on tournament to all media on your mailing list as well as to all participant schools and their media who will participate in the tournament.

- Send media credential request form to all potential media who will cover event.

- Begin making participant and worker passes.

- Edit all copy for program and continue formatting.

- Send copy of program cover to NCAA for approval.

- Begin media list and passes; add names and prepare credentials as requests come in. Send out credentials and parking passes as requests come in and time permits.

- Give security director your list of concerns and where you will personally need security for the weekend (e.g., entrance to press and media rooms). Discuss the situation with the director. Show the person the pass structure and what passes allow which people access to what locations.

- Book coaches and other athletics department personnel on local radio and TV stations where possible to generate tournament publicity.

- Talk to local media to see what they will write or broadcast and what information you need to supply for their previews.

Two Weeks in Advance

- Take final, camera-ready copy for program to printer, except for 10 pages that you cannot complete until the week before the event.

- Format five cover pages for the five different bracket sheets that will be used.

- Continue preparing credentials.

- Reconfirm dates and times with photographers; go over final details of the type pictures you want them to take. Mail their credentials.

- Reconfirm copy-machine status and make plans for a backup system.

- Enter generic bracket-sheet form into computer.

- Place ads in local media (newspapers, radio, TV).

- Put up posters about tournament throughout your campus and immediate campus area.

One Week in Advance

- Forward copy of pretournament press release to BW Sportswire for immediate release.

- Format final pages of program and take to printer.

- Write script for announcer for tournament.

- Prepare media call list with names and numbers to call, including time to call and information each outlet will need.

- Prepare welcome letter for media packets.

- Finish all credentials.

- Prepare and copy MVP wrestler and coach of the year ballots, as well as finalist information sheets.

- Check with wire services (and any other key media that have not responded to credential request) to see what information they will need and when.

- Go to bank and secure all needed change for program and bracket-sheet sales throughout the tournament.

- Begin to distribute credentials to all tournament workers.

- Confirm times, dates, and schedules with program and bracket-sheet sellers.

Three Days in Advance

- Help prepare competition packets. Make sure correct coach and participant credentials go into each packet.

- Make sure all phones are labeled with their correct number and are working properly; set up press room. Make sure directions on how to use the phones are posted nearby. Make sure working tables are set up and electric bars (if needed) are in room. Other things to consider for pressroom are a coatrack and refreshments (if room is not near hospitality room).

- Post all signs throughout the gymnasium.

- Put together media packets with everything except program and bracket sheets (credential, souvenir, schedule, welcome letter, and any other tournament promotional materials).

Two Days in Advance

- Pick up programs from printer. Insert them in media and participant packets.

- After seeding meeting, type names on bracket sheets.

- Greet local media, sports information directors, and others who arrive early. Familiarize them with the facility and its amenities (e.g., press room, hospitality room).

One Day in Advance

- Make amendments to bracket sheets and make copies for coaches and for sale as soon as brackets are finalized.

- Hand out remaining credentials to all tournament workers.

- Take coaches' copies of bracket sheet to pretournament dinner and distribute.

- Attend dinner and socialize. Answer any questions anyone may have about the tournament.

Tournament: Days 1 and 2

- Leave all unmailed media credentials and other tickets at will-call window as early as possible.

- Hand out money and programs/bracket sheets to sellers. Instruct them on prices, etc. Check with them throughout the day to collect and put aside excess money and to see if they need more change.

- Keep extra copies of programs and bracket sheets at head table.

- Prepare computer setup at head table for updating bracket sheets as matches end. Update bracket sheet as soon as possible after results are submitted. Copy and distribute immediately.

- Give script to announcer and be sure he or she is familiar with what he or she needs to announce and when.

- Keep a copy of bracket sheets and results with you at all times. You will receive a steady stream of questions about them.

- Be sure results are placed in pressroom as soon as possible after they are finalized. Make sure whoever handles your results phones gets updated results periodically.

- Act as troubleshooter. Keep yourself available to answer any questions and help at any part of the tournament where an emergency may arise.

- At the end of the day, collect all extra programs, leftover bracket sheets and money from sellers. Double-check with sellers about time to start work the next day. Phone or fax all results to media on the call list as soon as final results become available. Be aware of the media's deadlines and call sooner if you have to. Be sure all final results are posted and available in pressroom.

- Supervise the photographers.

- (Day 2 only) Hand out finalist information sheets immediately after the semi-final matches. Be sure you get the information sheets back before the sheets leave the gym. Type biographies for finalist introductions that night.

Post-Tournament: *That Night*

- Prepare final results packet. Copy and distribute to coaches and media as soon as results become final.

- Collect final money and extra program and bracket sheets from sellers.

- Be aware of their deadlines, and phone or fax all results to media on list.

- Prepare short post-tournament release and fax to media not in attendance, if time permits.

Post-Tournament: *The Day After*

- Fax post-tournament release and results to BW Sportswire for distribution.

- Fax post-tournament release and results to anyone else (e.g., magazines, NCAA) who has requested information but is not on an immediate deadline.

Post-Tournament: *The Week After*

- Dismantle pressroom and any other facilities set up especially for the tournament. Return all borrowed equipment and take down all signs. Help return your facility to normal.

- Mail copy of final results to head coach and SID of every school that had a participant in the tournament. If you have extra programs, send a copy with results as well.

- Tally and account for program and bracket-sheet income. Deposit money in tournament account. Give detailed report of program sales and advertising income to tournament director to reconcile with NCAA budget.

- Make sure commission checks are cut for advertisement solicitors.

The Weekend After

- Sleep, sleep, sleep. You will need it.

Promotion and Publicity

Effective planning and preparation may ensure that a special event runs smoothly, but they will not guarantee a large audience. Promotion and publicity are the keys to building excitement for a special event and boosting spectator and media participation. Promotional activities should be structured much like a seven-course dinner: They should start with appetizers and work up to a sumptuous main course. In short, each activity should create a hunger for more that entices the media and fans to attend.

The promotional activities and publicity plan should be established early in the planning process. They should be incorporated into the operations manual and/or timetable, and they should be structured in such a way that they periodically remind the public of the upcoming event, its significance, and its entertainment value.

Publicity serves a dual purpose. First, it provides both the public and the media with information about the special event. The nature or significance of the event alone may be sufficient to attract spectator and media interest. Second, publicity complements promotional activities. It calls attention to activities and entertaining aspects of the event. In that respect, the objective of the publicity is to drum up fan and media support.

Promotion aims at selling tickets. Although promotional activities may incorporate publicity and information materials, the primary objective is to persuade people to attend the event.

Key Components of a Publicity Plan
Media list
Announcements
Timed releases
Interviews
Media Day
Dinner
Press packet and program

Publicity

One way or another, organizers should work to maintain a steady stream of publicity about the event. News releases, features, and news conferences should build until the final advances are written and broadcast on the day of the event. The *USGA Publicity Handbook*, for example, includes sections on media lists, who the media are, promotional and informational tools, tips on newsy angles for releases, guidelines for a media day, USGA news-release schedule, media relations on site, and the championship program guidelines.

Here are the key components of a typical publicity plan:

Media List

Sports information directors use their working media list for local special events, such as awards banquets or game promotions. They expand the list to include the appropriate media in geographical areas for regional or national events. Sponsoring organizations such as the NCAA, USGA, LPGA, and NFL provide hosts with media lists and telephone numbers.

Announcements

The SID should send out an announcement for any special event when plans are finalized. Organizers sent out a release on the selection of Indianapolis as the site of the Final Four in 2000 in July 1993, as soon as the NCAA Men's Basketball Committee made its choice.

If time allows, sports information specialists also should call a news conference to announce the event. They should invite both print and broadcast media members who are involved and potentially interested in the event. The news conference should be timed to get maximum coverage. Mid-afternoon of a *slow news day* is ideal. A slow news day is a day, typically early in the week, when the calendar of scheduled news events is smaller, that is, a day with a light activity schedule and/or little breaking news. The announcement will make both the 6 P.M. and 11 P.M. television newscasts, and will give reporters for morning newspapers plenty of time to prepare their stories.

Although most of the attention focuses on television and major print media, the SID should not neglect weekly and school newspapers. They too are very important because they may reach audiences (potential ticket buyers) not served by the larger media.

Sports information directors do not always send out releases or call news conferences for annual events or game promotions. They may send out a release covering all the promotions for a sport or team for a year; they may distribute a release with a list on a monthly or weekly basis, or they may include information about the special promotion in game advances or notes releases.

However, any one-time or special event, such as a playoff game or a tournament, should receive special treatment, that is, an announcement and a press conference, if possible.

Timed Releases

The publicity plan should include a schedule for releases to selected media. The releases must be newsworthy to be effective. The *USGA Publicity Handbook* says simply, "If you don't have news, don't fake it." Reporters recognize promotion disguised as news and trash it. Furthermore, the fakery may damage the reputation of the organization and douse the interest of some media.

That is not to say sports information personnel should avoid sending releases on promotional activities, such as ticket sales and event-related contests; however, stories about promotional activities should focus on the news elements of the activity, not the promotional come-on. A release on ticket sales should emphasize the essential information, that is, ticket prices, limits, sales points, and business hours. A release on a contest or giveaway should center on information useful to readers, listeners, or viewers who might want to participate: eligibility, rules, time, and place.

The most effective timed releases are those that relate to details of the event or information about the event. Timed releases include stories about the teams involved, features on the athletes competing, and announcements about the program speakers. Stories on teams and players always should include photographs. Every release should include the pertinent facts of the event: date, time, and location, along with ticket price and location of purchase.

Interviews

If possible, periodically arrange telephone interviews with top competing athletes for the local media. Such interviews are most popular among the media and most effective for the host organization in the month prior to the event.

The *USGA Publicity Handbook* contends that radio and television do not generate as much advance publicity as do the print media. However, the handbook suggests trying to interest radio and TV stations in conducting live reports and/or phone interviews during the championship week. TV stations sometimes will air a remote broadcast during a tournament.

Media Day

A media day prior to the event can generate a load of publicity. The sports information or public relations director can draw a good audience by including participants in the event on the program. Setting up a round of golf, a go-kart race, or other activity involving participants may lead to photographs or video on the local TV news as well.

Dinner

Sport organizations often schedule a welcome ceremony, including a dinner, the night before a major special event, such as a tournament. The dinner provides an opportunity to meet and to orient the media and the participants; it also may generate additional media coverage on the opening day of the event.

Organizers should establish a menu equal to the status of the event itself. In the case of a professional championship game, a full sit-down meal is in order. If it is a small college basketball tournament, pizza is satisfactory.

When hosting a large-scale tournament, sports information specialists plan various details from as far out as a year in advance. Trophy presentations, such as the one shown here involving John Wooden and the Purdue men's basketball team, are typically planned closer to the date of the tournament.

Press Packet and Program

Depending on the time they are distributed, press kits and programs may not produce much pre-event publicity. However, they provide useful information for advance stories immediately preceding the event, and they unquestionably help reporters prepare accurate and thorough stories once the event begins.

The number and scope of publicity efforts should correspond to the stature of the event as well. A single release may be sufficient for an awards banquet or a game promotion. A full-scale campaign may be more appropriate for an event with nationwide interest.

The two-week agenda for the public relations directors at the Pro Bowl included a number of publicity-related activities, as well as promotional and media service duties. The public relations directors arrived on Sunday, two weeks prior to the all-star game. Publicity activities included the following:

Monday

- Call all media in Honolulu regarding Thursday luncheon or news conference. (Note: The plan recommended setting up a telephone news conference on Thursday with a player at the Super Bowl site or a breakfast on Friday with a player and/or coach already in Hawaii for the Pro Bowl.)

Tuesday

- Make roster additions, including 43rd player selected by coach. Prepare bio sheets on the players as well as new bio sheets on substitutions due to injuries.

- Prepare special notes and news release for two teams.

Wednesday

- Finalize special notes and news release for two teams.

- Compile press kits (recommend 14-inch folder with NFL logo). Include all bios, statistics, notes, rosters and changes to rosters, Pro Bowl program (if available), press information sheet, itinerary, and player arrival information, including Super Bowl flight.

Thursday

- Prepare all materials for today's luncheon or news conference. Items needed: game credentials, game booklets, gifts, hats, pennants, Pro Bowl and Super Bowl programs, press kits, photos, and clippings from all NFL clubs.

- Advise media of next week's schedule, including hospital visit (by players). Coordinate media coverage.

- TVs may ask you to go on camera to answer questions. Provide 5- to 10-minute talk on game and other pertinent information.

- Visit offices of any key media people who were not at luncheon.

Friday

- Visit newspapers and wire services to deliver photos or any news you can dig up. Make phone calls and send emails to some media with any notes.

- Prepare special packet for *USA Today* with ideas for charts, stories, photos.

- Prepare game packets to deliver to major media on check-in at hotels.

Sunday

- Super Bowl party. Coordinate media efforts if there are any roster changes or other information following the Super Bowl.

Monday

- Deliver press books, credentials, and notes to newspapers, wire services, and TV stations.

- Phone work.

- Make corrections to flip card. Prepare pronunciation guide.

Tuesday

- Conduct interviews in locker room today before photos:
  9:00 a.m.—All players on one team lined up for team picture.
  9:30 a.m.—All players on other team lined up for team picture.

Thursday

- NFL Charities/NFLPA Golf Tournament after practice.

- Teams make annual hospital visit. Be sure to arrange proper media coverage.

- Try to arrange a media dinner for local media and some mainland media.

Friday

- Arrange radio interviews for pregame show.

- Call papers if Saturday practice routine has changed.

Saturday

- Final chance for credential additions and creating master list.

Sunday

- Game day. All responsibilities for public relations directors on game assignment sheet.

Promotional Activities

The sports information or public relations staff's involvement in promotional activities will depend on the size of the sport organization. Athletics officials may have to take care of both publicity and promotion for high schools and amateur organizations. Sports information personnel may have to assume some promotional duties at the collegiate level. As noted in her diary, Dalpaiz had to handle some of the work on posters, flyers, tickets, and program sales for the NCAA Division III wrestling championships. At the Division I and professional levels, separate departments generally take care of most promotional responsibilities. The USGA suggests involving club members and the community in the promotion for championship events.

Most of the promotional activities involving SIDs and public relations directors are informational, not marketing oriented. The SID seldom will be involved in advertising and ticket sales, unless the advertising is for the program prepared by the sports information staff. However, sports information personnel may be called on to help with posters, flyers, and other printed materials.

Common Promotional Activities:

• posters	• prize giveaways	• banners
• flyers	• event T-shirts	• billboards
• placemats	• bumper stickers	• portable signs
• grocery stuffers	• free merchandise	• proclamations
• direct mailings	• complimentary tickets	• PA announcements at other events
• public service announcements	• speakers at civic clubs	

Major special events generally are an easy sell. Promoting annual events and games is far more challenging, particularly for low-profile sports and losing teams. Obviously, a team in competition for a championship year after year or a team in a city with no other major sports should draw good crowds. The real challenge in marketing is to attract large crowds for less well-known products.

Marketing a losing team takes work and plenty of it. Promoting a losing professional team is often more difficult than promoting a noncompetitive team at the collegiate level. At the collegiate level, a pool of loyal students and graduates will attend regardless of the team's record; however, their interest will also increase dramatically as the victories increase. Game giveaways and other promotions also may fuel interest.

At the Division III collegiate level, the most important "sell" is on campus even if the tickets are free. Although the major purpose of attendance is to generate revenues, the sports information and marketing people can push other attractions, such as school spirit and support.

The following are general suggestions that relate to increasing attendance at games as well as at special events:

1. Establish a budget for promoting attendance, and set realistic goals for the budget. If goals are met, the budget for the next season may be increased.

2. Make ticket buying easy. Set up a number of ticket outlets with clear information about when, where, and how to secure tickets. This is important not only for professional teams but also for amateur contests.

3. Work with local banks, department stores, or other businesses to help in promotion and ticket sales.

4. Keep a mailing list of potential ticket buyers. Included on this list should be graduates, new students, area businesses, and past ticket holders.

5. Keep the people on the mailing list informed regarding schedules, ticket prices, season-ticket availability, special ticket packages, and special events such as Community Day or Homecoming.

6. Do not overlook less visible or nonrevenue sports on the collegiate level. Any publicity and promotion may bring a few more people into the stands.

7. Utilize students in promotional activities at the collegiate level; the results can be most worthwhile.

8. Design publications that are not only valuable to the media but also act as promotional literature that will help boost attendance in recruitment of athletes.

9. In addition to media guides, flyers and posters should be designed to increase attention and attendance.

10. Contacts with the media should include invitations to promotions and special events. Unexpected positive publicity can result from bonds forged among the media, graduates, and coaches at a golf outing or other activity in connection with a special event.

Media Operations

Considerations in planning for media coverage of a special event are identical to the pregame, game management, and postgame preparations for a press-box operation. The planning process must address credentials, work space, work crews, working materials, and food.

The differences between planning for a game and planning for a special event are a matter of degree—primarily, differences in logistics and in numbers of media to serve. The needs for an annual event, such as an awards banquet, are fewer because most information distributed to the media can be prepared in advance. The setup for a game promotion or postseason playoff match is virtually identical because it is linked closely to the game and the playing field or court. The details and duties for a major event expand a hundredfold, in some cases, because far more members of the media attend, and the event may last more than one day.

The size and nature of the event determine the planning needs for media management. A simple checklist that addresses tickets, seating, meals, information sheet, and individual reporters' needs (e.g., telephone, power source) may suffice for an annual event such as an awards banquet. A game promotion may require minor tinkering in the standard setup and operation of press row. For example, the SID may have to include an agenda for a halftime ceremony in the press packet, or distribute and tabulate ballots for an all-tournament team. However, preparations for a major event, such as the NCAA Final Four or a national championship, demand substantial expansion of the plan and elaboration of details. The media management plan for the Pro Bowl provides a day-by-day assignment list for public relations directors at the site for the two weeks prior to the game. The USGA operations materials assess needs and responsibilities for the host course/club a year prior to the U.S. Open. They also include a checklist on how to set up a media center successfully (see sidebar).

After promotion begins, the sports information or public relations director should establish a plan for estimating media attendance and issuing credentials. The first step is creation of a priority plan (with information on pass limits and guest accommodations) and a system for ordering credentials. Next, the SID must design credentials for the working press area, for locker rooms, and for field or courtside access (usually for photographers).

The estimate of the number of people likely to attend will help in assessing workspace and other logistical needs. The best way to estimate the number of media likely to attend is to add the number on the organization or institution's local media list to the total media attendance at the previous year's event. Simple mathematical ratios will enable organizers to calculate the need for telephones, electrical outlets, mechanical equipment, and supplies. Similarly, the estimated media attendance will provide a working number from which to figure the amount of work space required, the daily amount of food, the number of copies of materials to distribute, and the size of the sports information team needed. An additional consideration for a national event is a hotline to provide information to people who call in for results, as noted in Dalpaiz's plan for the NCAA Division III wrestling championships.

Still another option is an on-line website. The host committee can create a link on the school or sport organization's existing site or develop a new site for the event. Today, the vast majority of professional sport organizations maintain their own websites. So do virtually all colleges and universities. As the popularity of on-line communication continues to grow, colleges and universities are teaching faculty and students how to create web pages. Numerous self-help guides are available at bookstores and on the Internet, and academic computing departments at area colleges can provide direction and assistance on where to start. Students who want to go into sports information or sport management should learn how to create a web page as part of their undergraduate studies.

The press-row or press-box setup and seating should follow the same priorities established for the regular season by the host school. However, the hosts may have to devise additional seating for the media if existing facilities are inadequate. They also may have to create separate areas for different functions. Perhaps the most important consideration is the postgame interview room, particularly if the event attracts national TV coverage. The chosen site must be large enough to provide seating for all members of the media and room for lots of television cameras, radio microphones, and other electronic equipment.

USGA Media Center Checklist

The Media Center Checklist for the U.S. Open divided media operations into seven sections:

- USGA Office Trailer: adjacent to Media Center

- USGA Registration Area: for USGA staff and volunteers

- Photo Lounge: for media photographers

- Dining Area: for members of the media and staff only

- Media Area: for working print and radio media

- Interview Room: for all working media

- 18th Green Quotes Trailer Area: for USGA staff and select media only

HOW TO SUCCESSFULLY ESTABLISH A USGA MEDIA CENTER

Media Center Checklist

___ **Location and size of the Media Center**

The number of media expected will help determine the size of the room.

- More often than not, the office area is where a half-dozen people can work comfortably. Preferably on the ground level or the first floor of the clubhouse within walking distance to the course and the public scoreboard and separate from USGA office area.

___ **Equipment required in the Media Center**

The number of media expected will help determine the amount of equipment required for the Media Center. Here we have listed the essentials. If your championship attracts a larger media contingent, think more. And remember, the USGA Media Relations staff is always available to review your specific needs.

- Several 8-foot work tables (other than round tables) and comfortable chairs.

- Good lighting. Both general overhead lighting and several desk lamps (if possible).

- HP Laser Jet Computer Printer. A power cord strip to handle all of the electric plugs.

- Minimum office supplies.

- Three dedicated outside phone lines placed adjacent to a work table area (not across the room). Two lines will be used for telephones and one will be issued for the fax machine.

    Avoiding the "9". Please make all phone lines direct.

- Two telephones.

- One fax machine (plain paper).

    Numbers should be available at least three weeks in advance of championship dates. These are available from the phone company.

- Copier and ample supply of paper.

Please provide phone numbers for service technicians for the telephones, fax machines and copier (including weekend service phone numbers).

- Beverage service throughout the day.

___ **Registration**

- Credentials pickup and information handout area.

- Biographical Information Sheets.

___ **Match Play Draw Sheet**

- Finding a printer to work on short run, short notice.

- Getting the match play information.

___ **Signage (on grounds and on roads)**

___ **Volunteers**

- At least one club volunteer is required to work with media services area for the entire championship.

___ **Hotel Accommodation for Media**

- Hotel rooms should be blocked for media at certain events (USGA Communications Department will have the approximate number to reserve).

___ **Carts for the USGA Media Staff**

- *Carts are not to be driven by the media, but the media may be escorted to a specific location for drop-off.*

___ **Security**

- Please provide us with any keys, if necessary.

___ **Etc. for the Media**

- Parking.
- Eating arrangements.
- Media Gift or Merchandise Discount in Pro Shop.

___ **Extra, Extra**

- Bulletin board in the locker room and possibly in the clubhouse to display newspaper articles.

The USGA media center checklist (see previous page) for the U.S. Open divided responsibilities into two categories, one for the USGA operations department in conjunction with the host club and the other for the USGA communications department staff. Note that the operations department and the host club are assigned logistical and equipment duties, that is, the setup of the media center. The responsibilities for the communications department (sports information specialists) involve operation of the center and service to the media; that is, credentials, media day, media kits, press packets, seating chart, interviews, and work materials.

1. Areas of responsibility for USGA operations department and host club:

- Cart allocation: for media center staff during championship week

- Clean-up: cleaning times and garbage pickup instructions

- Course map and guide: for media use and reproduction

- 18th green exclusive area for media: access and security

- 18th green quotes trailer: equipment and materials for general and restricted area interviews

- 18th green general media interview area: roped off area for general media "hometown" interviews

- Corral at 18th greenside: space and security for area on each side of fairway for media to observe players as they finish

- Electrical power: rundown on lines and other equipment needed for media tent and dining areas, including registration area, scoreboard, and interview area

- Equipment and supplies: office equipment, electrical supplies, mechanical equipment and other materials for USGA registration area, media work area, photography lounge, interview area and dining room

- ESPN preview show: staging area for nightly wrap-up shows, location of production truck, and construction of set

- Food service/catering: serving times, daily head count, cost of food and drink, catering service

- Local TV compound: NBC compound and areas for local TV vans and equipment

- Media mailing list: for invitations, credential applications, and information on the championship

- Media parking: parking passes, parking areas and shuttle service

- Media shuttle to parking areas: operating schedule and signage for parking

- Media shuttle to hotel: schedules, drop-off, and pickup points.

- Media relations office trailer: equipment needs

- Photo darkroom trailers: trailer designations for specific media (such as the *Associated Press*), and equipment and supplies

- Photo lockers: for storage of equipment by photographers

- Programs/pairing sheets: numbers needed at media center each day

- Radio booths: number of partitions and power supply needs

- Scoreboards: types needed and scoring style (red for under par, black for par, etc.)

- Security: daytime, nighttime, last day, and 18th green restricted media area

- Signage: for all working areas

- Telephone directory: help phone numbers for copiers, security, and management

- Telephones: applications for media and needs for registration area, back of media area, media trailer, interview area, 18th green quotes trailer, and darkroom trailers

- Volunteers: shifts and volunteers needed to answer phones, run copiers, and serve as runners for U.S. Championship Golf Network

2. Areas of responsibility for the USGA communications department:

- Armbands: access codes, number needed for general media and number needed for NBC-TV (approximately 150 people)

- A.S.A.P. reporting: instructions on planned interviews, phone line at reporting table, and printer

- Badges: quantities needed and breakdown by media group (working media, photo, NBC, media guests, and media staff

- Credentials: application and issue of credentials

- Gate passes: passes to be exchanged for credentials at media center

- Hotel: media headquarters and reservation information (including telephone numbers and contact person)

- Hotel hospitality room: hours of operation, equipment, and food and beverage information

- Media day: tentatively set for a Monday in May; financial responsibilities for airfare, hotel, program, and golf-cart fees; and format (midmorning news conference, brunch, and round of golf for media suggested by USGA)

- Media gift: none

- Media kit: prepared at USGA Far Hills, NJ, office

- Media outing: for Wednesday, the day prior to start of the tournament

- Media packets during championship: printing and delivery.

- Media registration: start time for registration

- Media seating: seating chart

- Newspapers: daily delivery of newspapers to media center and players' lounge

- Paper for copiers: supplier and amount

- Prechampionship interviews: distribution of interview schedule for Tuesday and Wednesday

- Score pads for interview room: number of pads needed (1,000)

- Scrip: packets to cover USGA work volunteer staff for lunch (if needed)

If the planning is thorough and the size of the support staff is sufficient, management of the media during the event should almost take care of itself. The sports information or media relations director will be free to troubleshoot, to answer questions, and to act as cordial host.

Summary

Sports information and public relations directors may be called on to assist with a variety of special events, by choice or by circumstance. Special events may be as simple as a club tennis tournament or as complex as the U.S. Open. They include in-house promotions designed to boost interest and attendance for a specific game or team as well as invitational tournaments, postseason playoffs, and championship events intended to put the sport organization into the national spotlight. The sport organization may serve as host for national events, even though the team or institution may be participating.

Successfully staging a special event, whether a midday luncheon or a four-day tournament, requires extensive planning and organization. Obviously, the more complex the event and the larger the media draw, the more planning is needed. The planning process begins as much as two years in advance for such events at the NCAA Division I men's Basketball Final Four. Participation by specialists in several departments of the sport organization or institution is essential to success. In addition, local businesses and associations often lend their support and expertise to the planning and preparation for national tournaments and championships.

The purpose of all special events is to increase exposure of the sport organization and boost ticket sales or other revenues. In some cases, financial objectives are uppermost. In others, such as hosting a national tournament, the financial rewards are indirectly related to spectator interest and media attention to the event; however, the financial gains for the institution and community can be substantial in national events.

Planning and staging a special event rely heavily on the skills of marketing and sports information specialists. Marketing or development department personnel play important roles in identifying target audiences, devising advertising campaigns, and selling corporate sponsorships and spectator tickets. Sports information specialists handle publicity, including news releases on promotional activities, and oversee media management from the planning stages through the coverage of the event. Effective coordination of promotional activities and publicity is integral to the success of a major special event.

The primary responsibilities of sports information personnel are planning, publicity, and media management. Consequently, a special event on the magnitude of a national championship calls into play all the skills, resources, and functions of the sports information or media relations department. The SID and staff must write a variety of news releases about the event and promotional activities; schedule and supervise news conferences and media days; develop programs, brochures, press kits, and other media materials; arrange and supervise pre-event and postgame interviews; and organize and manage a press row or a media center, depending on the size of the event.

The planning process should address five major concerns: size and scope of the event, budget, planning committees, operations manual or checklist, and timetables for activities. The publicity involves a series of releases, news conferences, and interviews that keep the event in the public spotlight and build interest as the event nears. Media management entails preparation of credentials and materials for the media prior to the event and supervision of media operations during the event. Publicity and media management duties intensify as the event nears. Public relations directors in the NFL actually arrive at the site of the Pro Bowl two weeks in advance to begin media operations. The director of media operations provides each person with a daily rundown on duties and responsibilities as well as specific game-day assignments.

A national tournament or championship event is the most challenging assignment a sports information or public relations director will face, because of the complexity and size of the event. To be successful, the preparation must be equal to the event. Lack of attention to details can undermine media management before the event even begins; detail-oriented planning can enhance the odds of a sellout crowd and smooth media operations.

DISCUSSION QUESTIONS

1. What duties must be performed by an SID and his or her staff in preparing for an important basketball game against a fierce rival—a game that will have more fan and media interest than a regular season contest against a much lesser rival?
2. When planning for a major golf event, which media should receive a full set of credentials and why? Explain who would be refused and why.

SUGGESTED EXERCISES

1. Determine the proper budget to stage a golf tournament on the LPGA Tour.
2. Use a period of one month to plan all the publicity for a four-team, Division I women's basketball tournament. Handle all the publicity and all the detailed chores to make the event a success. Make a timeline for releases.

Chapter Eleven

THE PUBLICITY CAMPAIGN: THE MAKING OF AN ALL-AMERICAN

The star center on the women's basketball team set the school record for rebounds as a junior. Barring injury or catastrophe, she will eclipse the conference mark early in her senior season. The national collegiate record for Division III also appears within reach. If she maintains the same rebound average as last year, she will pass the current record-holder in the next-to-last game of the regular season.

A couple of regional sports publications have mentioned her name among possible All-America candidates. However, media exposure of her record performance as a junior was minimal. The college is in a rural area, and no metropolitan dailies or local TV stations report regularly on the team. Furthermore, the women's team never has qualified for the national tournament and has seldom won more games than it lost in a season. Prospects for a winning record in the upcoming season do not look good either, because the star center is the only returning starter.

Chapter 11 looks at publicity campaigns designed to promote an individual athlete, coach, or team for postseason recognition; it also explores development of objectives, media targets, and campaign strategies. It examines campaign techniques, particularly ways to incorporate the promotion into news releases, notes, and statistical packages without engaging in outright hype. It explains how to use videotapes and game highlights to advantage in the electronic media. The chapter closes with a discussion of dangers and ethical considerations.

Students, fans, coaches, and college administrators believe she deserves to be rated among the nation's top players, but none of them gets to vote for the all-star teams. Coaches' associations pick a couple of all-star teams, but the media choose the most publicized and most prestigious All-America teams. Odds are that not many reporters *or* coaches outside the region will hear about the local star before the end of the season.

What a shame, in the view of fans. What an injustice, in their estimation. What an opportunity, in the creative mind of a sports information director.

The SID huddles with the coach and the player to develop a strategy to increase the star rebounder's national visibility. They come up with a nickname, "The Sweeper." The nickname creates an image of a player "sweeping" rebounds off the backboard. It also offers a lyrical alliteration with the player's last name when spoken, a catchy "sound bite" for the electronic media: "Leeper the Sweeper."

The SID prepares a packet for distribution to selected media (and voters) with photographs, biographical information, a feature story, a statistical history, and rebound comparisons (including her current standing on the all-time list). The sports information staff devises a publicity strategy, with news releases timed to coincide with rebounding milestones and important games. They create "Countdown" and "Rebound Watch" features (with logos) for insertion in game advances and notes columns. Perhaps a newspaper will print an updated chart with each game story, or a TV producer will flash the graphic on the screen with the results of each game.

The SID puts together a videotape of highlights, including clips of the celebration when the athlete set the school record and a series of "sweeping" rebounds. He even creates miniature brooms (sweepers) with the athlete's picture and pertinent statistical information for distribution to media, fans, students, and graduates. All the efforts are calculated to thrust the rebounder into the national spotlight and keep her there as she closes in on the record. The SID hopes the flood of information will find its way into a *Sports Illustrated* "Faces in the Crowd" at least, a full feature at most. Maybe a clip from the videotape will wind up in a segment of highlights or star players on ESPN. Even the smallest mention will improve the odds in favor of the athlete's selection for All-America honors. Who knows? If the publicity campaign catches the media's eye and the public fancy, "The Sweeper" could be a household name by selection time.

Sound more like promotion than sports information? It is, in some respects. It also is a standard method of publicizing a star in the entertainment industry, and sport *is* entertainment. Although such scripted promotion still evokes criticism from some media and sport organizations, publicity campaigns designed to bring recognition to a school or an athlete are common practice.

A Worthy Candidate

Most of the approaches to delivering mediated information to the public discussed in earlier chapters follow the traditional news model. Strategies for "The Making of an All-American" borrow heavily from the principles of advertising and promotional public relations. The intent is not simply to present information through the media in a manner reflective of the sport organization's goals, philosophy, and character. The unapologetic purpose is to persuade and influence, to "sell" the excellence of the athlete, coach, or team to the media and through the media via selective distribution of information. In the case of an outstanding athlete, the objective of a publicity campaign is to persuade the media and coaches who vote to put the player's name on their All-America ballots.

Of course, the media recognize the promotional nature of publicity campaigns. However, they generally will not trash the information outright unless it is purposely misleading (deceptive), overblown to the point of blatant hype, or overwritten with an excess of puffery. They often sift through the information looking for evidence that the athlete, coach, or team is worthy of attention. They make their judgments based on the criteria of news: timeliness, proximity, prominence, impact or importance, rarity or uniqueness, and conflict. To be effective, a publicity campaign must start with a worthy candidate and emphasize one or more of the elements of news. In the case of the star rebounder detailed in the beginning of this chapter, the campaign will most likely be effective if it revolves around her pursuit of the national record (impact/importance and rare/unusual).

Wilcox, Ault, and Agee (1992) say campaigns that promote a person are successful for a variety of psychological reasons, including "hero worship" and "a sense of belonging" (p. 521). They note that people who lead routine lives look for heroes to emulate. Sports provide heroes of sorts, and sports journalists build them through emphasis on their athletics achievements. Just look at the media attention and fan adulation generated almost instantly by the performance of Kerri Strug in the 1996 Summer Olympics in Atlanta. How often did the public see pictures or video clips of her vault on an injured ankle that helped the United States team win a gold medal in gymnastics? The sense of belonging helps to generate support for athletes and teams. One can't walk through a mall in Kentucky during basketball season without seeing someone wearing a hat, jacket, sweatshirt, or T-shirt with a University of Kentucky Wildcats emblem. Kentuckians' association with UK basketball is well documented but not limited to the commonwealth of Kentucky. Nor is the sense of belonging divorced from sports publicity.

> Emphasis on individual stardom in college football and basketball is heavy because stars sell tickets, and college football is big-dollar business. Star-studded winning teams fill the seats, earn money and public attention from postseason games, and encourage graduates to make contributions. Thus the campaigns by sports practitioners to get college players named to All-American teams are intense, often employing attention-getting techniques that have little direct bearing on the games themselves. (Wilcox et al., 1992, p. 530)

The goal of a publicity campaign, then, must be to project the athlete or team as an athletics hero and generate a sense of belonging that extends beyond the natural cocoon of the community. That means the campaign *must* be grounded on athletics excellence—uncommon excellence. Ethically, it also *should* be grounded on personal integrity and character traits worthy of emulation. It would be naive to suggest that all highly publicized athletes are model citizens; in fact, whether character should be a factor in selection of all-stars is an ongoing ethical issue in sports conversation, print editorials, TV commentaries, and talk radio. Look no further than the on-going debate of whether or not Major League Baseball's all-time hits leader, Pete Rose, should be allowed in the sport's Hall of Fame after admitting to gambling on baseball and serving a lifetime ban from the sport. However, sports organizations in general and schools in particular run great risk in promoting an athlete with legal problems, personal difficulties, or major character weaknesses. Once publicists succeed in boosting an athlete into the public spotlight, they find it most difficult to hide any information from the media. A publicity campaign subjects every aspect of an athlete's life to intense media scrutiny. If that close inspection reveals unsavory information or false images, the campaign may well backfire. The fallout can range from temporary embarrassment to major damage to the institution's reputation.

In short, the sports information or public relations director should consider both the candidate's athletics performance and his or her personal behavior. The campaign has a greater chance of succeeding and less chance of backfiring if the athlete's integrity is on the same level as his or her performance. The publicity campaign also has a greater chance of success if it promotes an athlete or team in a high-profile sport. If the object is to achieve high visibility, the potential gains are minimal if the media pay little attention to the sport anyway. For this reason, football and basketball players most often are the focus of publicity efforts on a college or high school campus. An SID often will focus on an outstanding athlete from one or both of these sports. The SID may achieve success in promoting an athlete in another sport if the campaign identifies and motivates a receptive media audience. For example, a campaign promoting a volleyball player should aim at media in cities with all-star voters and consistent volleyball coverage as well as at the local media.

In publicizing an athlete, school officials should never go overboard on a player they know, in their hearts, is not worthy. Be sure the player is really as good as the coach, the SID, and others believe the individual to be. Remember, the reputations of all involved are on the line. Making a decision on the worthiness of a candidate is not as easy as it appears to be. Publicity campaign preparations must begin well before the start of the season for the sport in which the athlete participates. The push must start in late spring for athletes in fall sports such as football, in summer for winter sports, and in fall for spring sports. The SID must organize the campaign and prepare the avalanche of information well before the particular season is underway; consequently, the SID must evaluate candidates well before the season begins. Is the junior who blossomed in postseason play at the end of last year a one-shot wonder or a superstar in waiting? Will the rebounding star perform as well with a new supporting cast? How can one know?

Ask the coach. The first step in developing a publicity campaign for a worthy athlete is to meet with the appropriate coaches. Cooperation and participation by the player's coaches are essential. The head coach must agree to a huge publicity campaign.

Making a name for himself in the community may have assisted former University of Pittsburgh wide receiver Larry Fitzgerald in earning All-America honors and the 2003 Biletnikoff Award, given annually to the nation's best collegiate wide receiver.

Before requesting approval, the SID should carefully explain the pluses and minuses to the coaching staff. The pluses are obvious: recognition for a deserving athlete; increased media exposure for the team, coaches, and university; and enhanced reputations for the player, team, coaches, and university.

However, a publicity campaign also can be disruptive. Special treatment for an individual may conflict with the coach's team concept, and it may foster jealousies among teammates. A publicity campaign may create additional time demands on the head coach and the athlete. Both will have to work with the SID on publicity materials. If the campaign is successful, they also will have to set aside additional time for personal interviews and media appearances. In addition, the heavy media scrutiny may increase the stress on the athlete, and the time demands and pressure may negatively affect the player's athletic performance, academic work, and personal relationships. The SID should solicit the coach's opinion as to whether the athlete can handle the pressure of the media and the fans along with the pressure to perform in every game. The SID might also talk with teammates, family members, and teachers about the athlete's personality, temperament, and reaction to stress.

If the coach supports the proposal for a publicity campaign, the SID should meet with the athlete in the presence of the coach. Again, the SID should carefully go over the pluses and minuses. The explanation should put particular emphasis on the three Ds: demands, demeanor, and dangers. The SID should fully explain the implications of publicity/media demands on the athlete's time, temperament, and personal privacy. The publicist should orient the athlete regarding the demeanor expected of an all-star athlete. The discussion should cover personal integrity, relationship with the media, and interaction with fans. It should be made clear that the campaign will put the player into the public spotlight on and off the playing field or court. The athlete should also be made aware of the intrusion, likely in every aspect of personal life, and receive direction on how the university expects the athlete to behave. The athlete should be provided suggestions on how to handle media scrutiny, probing interviews, pushy reporters, and critical comments. Finally, the SID should alert the athlete to the dangers of dishonesty, a lack of cooperation with the media, and personal indiscretions. By the end of the conversation, the athlete should be well informed and forewarned of all that may come once the campaign begins. If the athlete is not fully comfortable and cooperative, the plan should be dropped. Pressing the idea will not serve the athlete or the university well.

If the athlete is amenable to a campaign, the SID should next conduct an in-depth personal interview to find out as much as possible about the athlete's personal background, likes and dislikes, hobbies and other interests, church and community activities, goals and dreams, and attitudes and beliefs about athletics, education, and other pertinent subjects. The interview will serve two purposes. First, it will give the SID a fuller portrait of the athlete and insight into personal strengths and weaknesses that may affect the campaign. The interview also may forge a strong personal relationship between the athlete and the SID—important during those trying times when the pressure becomes unbearable for both the athlete and the SID. Second, and equally important, the interview may generate a lot of ideas for story angles to develop or to suggest to the media during the publicity campaign.

Once all involved parties commit to undertaking a campaign, they should sit down together and develop a campaign plan. The plan should be divided into two phases, one for activities prior to the season and another for activities during the season.

Prior to the Season

Sports information directors generally enjoy developing a publicity campaign because they can turn their creative instincts loose—at least in the planning stages. The SID is the artistic creator in the formation of the campaign, leading the way in developing objectives, identifying target audiences, and devising strategies to reach them.

A brainstorming session with the coach and the athlete may help to generate ideas. SIDs should keep in mind that professionals recommend no barriers for brainstorming sessions. Each participant can throw out any idea, no matter how ridiculous or unfeasible the idea might sound. Furthermore, no one can reject or make judgments about an idea until it is discussed fully. A lot of solid ideas may bubble to the surface as participants stir a seemingly useless suggestion around in their collective intellects.

The primary objectives of a publicity campaign are obvious. The ultimate goal is to gain postseason recognition for the athlete (preferably All-America honors). Secondary objectives may include such goals as improved professional prospects for the athlete, additional media exposure for the team and university, a broader fan base, increased ticket sales, additional financial contributions to the sport or the athletics program, and an improved public image for the university. The campaign plan should list objectives and ways to achieve them, much as in the "strategic planning" process popular in business and higher-education administration. The plan also should identify the target audience. Will the information be sent to media, coaches, businesses, or all of these? If so, which media, which coaches, which businesses? Just those who vote on specific all-star teams, the media in major metropolitan areas, the coaches with influence at other institutions? The plan should consider which audiences and/or markets will be most helpful in achieving campaign objectives. The SID should create a corresponding mailing list. Of course, the SID should include all names on the standard media list. It also does not pay to ignore loyal supporters.

The campaign strategy should be customized to suit the specific athlete, sport, and objectives. According to Smith (1996), the most effective advertising campaigns put heavy emphasis on two broad areas—the visual messages and the textual messages. The visual messages come from pictures, artwork, graphics, and headlines. The textual messages are incorporated in the written materials. Smith says, "Think artwork. Think words. And try to think of these at the same time" (p. 231).

The words and pictures should complement each other, that is, send the same message. They also should be consistent. Every component of the campaign should send the same message. The "Sweeper" nickname and miniature broom handouts in the hypothetical campaign in the introduction to this chapter are examples of complementary messages. Both the artwork and the name (text) suggest an athlete who sweeps the boards clean of rebounds. All other written and pictorial aspects of the campaign should send the same message: This is an athlete who dominates at her position by "sweeping" the rebounds against all opponents.

Simply put, the message should loudly declare that the athlete is the best in the country in some respect. A simple message is best. Experts recommend focusing on a single element that best illustrates the message; in the case of athletics, the element might be a statistic, a record, an unparalleled single-game performance, or a scoring streak. "Find one unique statistic and milk it," says Helitzer (1992). This can be fun while looking for unique numbers. The rebounder's pursuit of the national record might work marvelously because the importance or singular accomplishment increases with each game. Each game also provides a timely element (news criterion) to encourage the media to revisit the story.

Once the campaign strategy has been formulated, the SID develops a budget to cover the extra printed materials, photography, artwork, videotape, and postage. The budget will dictate the size of media kits, the number of mailings, and so on.

The next chore is preparation of a photo file, a video file, and an information file for use during the campaign. A photo session with a professional should be arranged. The photographer can set up head- and posed-action shots of the athlete. Also, the photographer can take some candid shots of the athlete, possibly during a practice session. The SID can supplement the file with action photographs from the previous season or from a scrimmage and can convert some of the photographs into color slides to send to local television stations to be kept on file for spot use during the season or when the athlete receives awards. Posed, as well as informal, shots of good quality in black and white are acceptable and used often by the print media. The photos may be used by publications ranging from very large newspapers to some very small periodicals. Every photograph should be of high quality, because the quality reflects on the athlete, the campaign, and the university. If the message cries excellence, the quality of the photographs should shout it as well.

After building an ample supply of still photographs and slides, the SID should gather video footage featuring the athlete in "positive" game situations. The footage should emphasize the athlete's best plays, particularly those that demonstrate the athlete's particular strengths or skills—shooting, rebounding, running, passing, serving, spiking, and so on. The SID can send the video segments to TV stations that may use clips in preseason previews or a couple of frames for background during reports of game results.

The SID should complete the bulk of the printed materials prior to the season. Anything that can be done in advance lightens the extra burden the campaign will create when the season begins. The SID should write an introductory news release, prepare a biographical sheet, compile statistical charts and comparisons, and compose hometown and news features for inclusion in media kits and for distribution to journalists who request information during the season. Any area of excellence can be supported with selective use of statistics. How the athlete's ranking, scoring, yardage, and other averages stack up nationally, in the conference, and on the career school charts always provides evidence of excellence. The SID can devise new stats to fit a story idea. Statistics are very good supportive material.

The preseason preparations aim at planting the seed—planting an image—in the minds of the media and the public. The primary publicity tool used by sports information and public relations directors is a *media kit*. The kit contains information and artwork designed to trumpet the visual and textual message of the campaign. Sports publicists also use a number of other visual and textual devices—as part of a media kit or separately—to reinforce the message.

The media kit typically will include a packet of information and artwork that emphasizes the *selling point*, the single element that best illustrates the athlete's excellence. The kit will include some combination of these items:

- News release: A story introducing the athlete, built around a news angle. For example, the release on the rebounding star would focus on her pursuit of the national record and her prospects for eclipsing it by season's end (maintain current average).

- Suggested stories: A list of story ideas/angles for the journalist who receives the kit. Make it easy for the journalist to pursue a story.

- Biographical summary: An information sheet similar to a resume.

- Reprints: Copies of newspaper or magazine articles that extol the excellence of the athlete.

- Quotations: A list of quotations drawn from what opponents (players and coaches), scouts, and analysts have said about the athlete.

- Fact sheet: Quick facts on the athlete, team, conference, and school. The fact sheet should include telephone and fax numbers as well as the name of a contact person in the SID office.

- Statistics: One or more statistical lists with individual statistics and rankings (career, school, conference, nation).

- Head shot: A professional, portrait-style photograph.

- Action shots: A couple of posed or candid shots of the athlete in practice or competition (competition is preferred).

- Bumper sticker or magnet A bumper sticker or magnet with the athlete's name, the school's name, and a clever catchphrase.

- Poster: A glossy poster of the athlete in action.

The SID may prepare different versions of the packet for different audiences. For example, the SID may choose not to include the bumper sticker and poster in packets sent to the media. Journalists are not likely to display the bumper sticker or poster, although they might pass them on to a child or fan. The SID definitely would include such items in mailings to graduates, boosters, advertisers, and so on.

The SID would send the media kit to both print and broadcast journalists on the campaign mailing list. The mailing to broadcast journalists also should include the highlights video put together by the sports information staff.

Mailers

Mailers are a form of publicity by which the university can promote an athlete through a vehicle that is, in effect, an advertisement. The mailer should model the format of advertising on high-quality paper and could take the form of a pamphlet or brochure.

For a mailer to be effective, it must catch the eye and command attention. The bumper sticker, nickname gimmick, and poster might be used individually or collectively in a mailer. Sending out mailers is expensive, and the money should be spent wisely. Mailers are used only where the budget allows and should be low on the publicity priority list.

The SID should send mailers only to members of the media who vote for All-America teams. Anything else wastes time and effort. Coaches vote in one major poll, so the SID could conceivably mail them to coaches, too. It is difficult to judge the value of mailers, which often makes the decision to use them difficult.

Media Guide

The All-America candidate should receive special attention in the media guide. The SID can supplement promotion of the star by putting a color photograph on the cover and a summary of the athlete's biography inside. However, the biography should be more comprehensive than the brief sketches of other players. In other words, the guide should feature the star in as many ways as possible. The SID might also include key information—reprints, statistics, photographs—in media packets for games that draw a large contingent of media who do not regularly cover the team.

The University of Memphis created a website in honor of running back DeAngelo Williams in an attempt to garner him consideration for the 2005 Heisman Trophy. Williams placed seventh in the final voting breakdown.

Magazines

The SID should cultivate preseason magazines by sending quality color art and pitching story ideas to editors.

Websites

A popular approach recently has been the creation of a website specifically about the athlete being promoted. The website is usually created by the SID and is hosted by the school's official athletics webpage, which will include a link to the promotional player page. Using a clever URL, such as "JohnDoe4Heisman.com" will make it easier for visitors to remember the web address of the page. On the webpage created by the SID, much of the material contained in the media kit should also be incorporated, including statistics, biographical information, and photography and video archives.

During the Season

The SID changes gears once the season gets underway. Before the season, the SID exercises creative "genius." During the season, the creator switches to the role of organizer.

The SID should set up guidelines to help the star athlete manage time and should prepare a weekly schedule that includes time blocks for practice, games, class, study, and leisure or recreation. Time blocks for interviews should come either early in the week (football) or on a couple of days when the practice schedule is lighter. Group interviews or a block of three or four interviews, depending on their length, is recommended. The SID can control the schedule and length of interviews; for example, he or she could set up a two-hour block for the media on Monday and schedule interviews at 1 P.M., 1:30 P.M., 2 P.M., and 2:30 P.M. The SID should schedule the interviews for the athlete, work out a time limit with each reporter, and enforce the time limit of the interview.

The SID must be sensitive to the needs of the athlete and help him or her to control nonteam and nonclass commitments. Under no circumstances should a college SID give members of the media the telephone number or room number of the athlete. Reporters, trained to dig out information, may well obtain the numbers by other means; however, the SID should encourage athletes not to grant impromptu interviews to reporters who call their room or intercept them on campus after class or practice. The athlete should receive coaching on how to politely refer the reporter to the SID to schedule an interview. Ethical journalists will not take the delay as a rebuff—they understand that university officials attempt to guard the athlete's time and privacy—but the aggressive reporter will make contact with the athlete merely to attempt to breach the defense.

Sports information personnel should take care to keep interviews to a minimum close to game day—the further from game day the better, in fact. Disruptions in normal game preparations can affect an athlete's mental preparation for the game. Coaches, SIDs, and the media should respect and honor requests for privacy on game day. If a particular writer wants an in-depth interview, the SID should set it up at the convenience of both parties, but well in advance of the next game.

The SID may be able to head off conflicts with the media by advising them of the interview schedule, time limits, and other restrictions. Normally, reporters will abide by these guidelines. The SID also may help the athlete present a positive image with a little coaching on interview posture. The SID should encourage the star to be enthusiastic, prompt, and cooperative with the media. It is amazing how often the more congenial and cooperative the athlete is, the more positive the story turns out to be. The great athletes seem to be the most cooperative with the media. Chris Evert, Carol Heiss, Michael Jordan, Jack Nicklaus, and Arnold Palmer set standards of decorum with the media that others should follow. It is very easy to be pleasant.

Telephone interviews are not out of the question. They may be necessary for out-of-town journalists. Keep in mind that lack of face-to-face contact makes it more difficult to create a positive interview relationship, because the two parties cannot read one another's nonverbal cues. Setting up telephone interviews is difficult, too, if the athlete is not available during the reporter's work schedule. For example, early afternoon for a reporter on the West Coast is 1 P.M.; that is 4 P.M., and in conflict with practice, for the athlete on the East Coast. In every case, the SID still should set up the interview rather than giving the reporter the athlete's number.

The SID can set up a time when the athlete can take a call in the athletic or sports information office, or can take a number and let the athlete call the reporter. SIDs should use the telephone only when an in-person interview is impossible or when the reporter insists.

The SID or a designated representative should act as a watchdog on the athlete's time in postgame interviews. Some reporters may ask a lot of questions unrelated to the game in an attempt to squeeze a feature or column out of the postgame interview. If a reporter or two conduct lengthy postgame interviews, the athlete may not even have dressed an hour after everyone else has showered and gone home. The coach or SID should cut off postgame interviews after an appropriate amount of time.

In addition to being a media manager and time organizer, the SID continues to serve as a publicity mill during the season. The SID can recycle the printed materials, photographs, and artwork in a variety of ways as the season unfolds. As noted earlier, the SID can add selected items to press packets distributed at games attended by reporters who normally do not cover the team. He or she can also put together individual packets for journalists or others who call to inquire about the athlete.

The publicity campaign strategy can include a schedule of timed releases to media on the original mailing list. The SID can send out features on different angles at prearranged intervals. Sports information personnel also can time releases to coincide with achievements during the season. For example, a new release would be timely when the athlete sets a personal, school, or conference record.

The SID also can keep the story alive and fresh with updates like the "Countdown" or "Rebound Watch" that chronicle the pursuit of a record. Such simple tools are easy to update and do not take up a lot of space in a newspaper. In addition, the SID should include the star's name in each weekly news release and notes handout on press row before games. An SID can never mention the star to the media too often.

The electronic media are another consideration. The SID can send copies of the videotape highlights to stations or networks that inquire about the athlete; if the SID has time, it is a good idea to edit the videotape periodically to add highlights from the current season. After a game, the SID also can submit video or highlight clips to local TV stations. The clips often will be used on the early news shows the following day. Program directors for such shows often welcome "action art." Television networks may pick up some of the highlights from their local affiliates. The SID also can incorporate recent game footage in 3- to 5-minute video feature stories submitted to the major television networks in conjunction with the campaign plan.

Ethical Considerations

The SID who undertakes a publicity campaign functions in a foggy area between sports information and *press agentry*. Press agentry is a term applied to publicists in the early days of public relations who promoted a client with all kinds of gimmicks and tricks. Some of the techniques were intentionally misleading. Others attracted attention because they were so outrageous. The publicists would promote their clients by any means possible. The SID can avoid straying into foggy areas by measuring every aspect of the publicity campaign and every action in carrying it out by two standards: honesty and information value.

First, no one associated with the campaign can engage in any deceit or appearance of deceit (such as misleading information). The SID cannot hope to hide negative information about the athlete's past or performance. The SID must not distort any information or statistics. Using statistics selectively to support a point is acceptable; juggling or adjusting statistics to fit the point is not. For example, a statistician yearns to "help" an athlete achieve a record, so he or she gives the center credit for a rebound for every touch of a ball that comes off the backboard, even though a teammate may corral it. Judgment call or well-intentioned manipulation? It will be deemed a deception if the totals differ markedly from the statistics kept by the opponent, and word will spread quickly that someone is "cooking the numbers" if it happens in more than one game. Such accusations will undermine the publicity campaign, taint any record the athlete sets, and damage the reputation of the team and the university.

Second, the SID should consider the information value of all materials prepared for the publicity campaign. Certainly, the objective is to "sell" the athlete, but the techniques employed must use legitimate information to do so. The SID may borrow from advertising, using bumper stickers, posters, nickname gimmicks, or giveaways. However, such tools should be clearly identifiable as such and openly distributed as such—that is the honesty in the promotion. Furthermore, all printed materials, photographs, and videotapes should revolve around a core of information consistent with the criteria of news. The media are more likely to use the information if it has news content and are less likely to brand the SID as a huckster or a shill. The SID should not stage a news conference just to gather a media crowd for the athlete; he or she must have real news information to deliver, or the pseudoevent will cross the boundary into misleading manipulation.

> ### Ten Simple Rules to Keep "The Making of an All-American" on an Ethical Track
>
> 1. Pick a worthy candidate. Never promote an athlete you do not believe is deserving of recognition (athletically or personally).
>
> 2. Seek approval of the coach and the athlete before launching any campaign. Explain the demands and dangers in detail to each before seeking approval. Drop the idea if either has misgivings.
>
> 3. Orient the athlete on what to expect during the campaign. The athlete's athletic and academic standings are at stake.
>
> 4. Help the athlete set up a schedule that comfortably absorbs the additional time demands. Make an effort to control media contact and to coach the athlete on handling reporters.
>
> 5. Remember that you put the athlete in this high-pressure situation. You have a responsibility to help the athlete get through it with as little stress as possible. You are the pressure-release valve.
>
> 6. Borrow techniques from advertising for publicity materials, but do not go overboard. Creative presentation is OK. Exaggeration, flattery, and puffery are not.
>
> 7. Clearly identify elements such as bumper stickers and posters as advertising. Use them as such, not as information.
>
> 8. Selective use of statistics is OK. Distorting or doctoring statistics is not.
>
> 9. Treat the media with courtesy and respect.
>
> 10. Never tell a lie. No breach of honesty is acceptable.

Summary

Publicity campaigns to promote an athlete or a team are an acceptable form of sports information. They differ from most other types of sports information in that they are promotional in nature—that is, they directly aim to persuade and influence. The primary objective is to gain recognition for deserving athletes, coaches, and teams.

Although it means more work, publicizing an outstanding athlete is enjoyable for a sports information director because it affords greater opportunity for creativity. The publicity also gives the SID a chance to create and direct a campaign that can increase media interest and public support measurably if it is successful.

The first step in "The Making of an All-American" is identifying a worthy candidate. The primary criteria for "worthiness" are athletic excellence well above the norm and integrity on a par with common values of American society. After identifying a candidate, the SID discusses the proposal with the coach and the athlete. The discussion addresses the three Ds—demands, demeanor, and dangers—as well as the attendant benefits.

If all parties are comfortable, they formulate a publicity campaign. They define objectives, identify target audiences, and devise strategies. The SID puts together a budget to cover additional printed materials, photographs, and videotape to be used in the campaign; he or she also develops a schedule for release of materials.

From the standpoint of the SID, the campaign is divided into two phases—prior to the season and during the season. Prior to the season, the SID prepares the materials to be utilized in the campaign. All the materials aim at sending consistent visual and textual messages about the athlete. Successful campaigns identify a focal point, such as pursuit of a record, and emphasize it in every facet of the campaign.

The SID compiles a file of stories, statistics, photographs, and videotape for distribution to targeted media, fans, graduates, and businesses prior to the season. The media kits may include news releases, biographical sheets, feature articles, statistical data, portraits, action pictures, and other standard informational tools. They also may include advertising pieces, such as bumper stickers and posters. The SID may customize the kits for different audiences, including the items most appropriate for a particular audience.

During the season, the SID periodically sends additional information to the media on the mailing list. The SID may send out updated videotapes and game highlights to television stations and networks. The primary objective is to mention the athlete as often as possible, using as many fresh approaches as possible. The SID also serves as an appointment secretary and mentor of sorts for the athlete, helping the athlete develop a schedule, arrange interviews, and manage time and media pressures.

The SID must bear in mind that a publicity campaign is a hybrid variety of communication, a mix of sports information and advertising. Although creative expression is applauded, deceit and hyperbole are condemned. Sports information specialists can stay on track by measuring every activity against the standards of honesty and informational value. When in doubt, SIDs should think information first, advertising or promotion second.

Publicizing a star is fun, because it gets the creative juices flowing, but the SID should be aware that pitfalls abound. A publicity campaign is like Pandora's box.

Once the lid is opened, the SID cannot simply snap it shut if all does not go according to plan. When the SID exposes an athlete and the university to intense public attention, he or she must be willing to accept everything that such scrutiny exposes. The campaign can be very embarrassing if it exposes negative information. However, the results can be most gratifying when they are positive—when they help to produce an All-American.

DISCUSSION QUESTIONS

1. As a small-college conference commissioner, how would you handle a situation in which the basketball coach at a particular school refuses to nominate any of her players for a Player of the Week award?
2. What is the game plan for an SID when it is decided to push a star football player for the Heisman Trophy?

SUGGESTED EXERCISES

1. Make a mailer, featuring your star athlete. Include a photo (or sketch), statistics, and concise reasons why this person should win the award.
2. Find out the *Associated Press*'s criteria in selecting its All-America football team. Also, who does the voting?

Chapter Twelve

PUBLIC RELATIONS DILEMMAS: UNDER THE MEDIA MICROSCOPE

The telephone awakens you at 11:30 P.M. A beat reporter for the daily newspaper in town launches into an angry tirade the minute you answer. He wants to know how a TV reporter found out about an investigation into transfer credits of two volleyball players. He questions your long-standing friendship with the TV reporter, implying you "gave your buddy the break" on the story. Now he wants fair treatment: He wants you to divulge details not reported on TV.

What Do You Say?

As soon as you put down the telephone, it rings again. This time the president of the university is on the line, and he is upset. He wants to know the identity of "a source close to the athletic program" who revealed the investigation to the TV reporter. He wonders about your personal relationship with the reporter, too. He reminds you that everyone agreed at a meeting earlier in the afternoon to keep the "potential problem" quiet until the completion of the investigation, and he wants to know how you are going to muzzle the media, to quiet rumors and speculation.

What Do You Do?

When you arrive at the office the next morning, the volleyball coach ambushes you. She is livid. She mentions the TV report and slams the morning newspaper down on your desk. A story disclosing the investigation and raising questions about the number of junior-college transfers on the team runs across the top of the sports section under a big headline. The coach wants to know why *you* cannot get so much as a blurb of positive information about the volleyball team in the newspaper, but a reporter can totally discredit the program at the first hint of negative news. She rails about misleading implications in the article. She vows to confront the reporter and demand a "correction" and an apology from the editor; moreover, she wants to know what you are going to do about the injustice. After all, it is your job to deal with the media and to repair the damage, isn't it?

How Do You Deal with the Situation?

All good sports information and public relations directors will tell you that you should have planned—well before the problem arose—what you would say, what you would do, and how you would deal with a crisis. In today's society, athletes, coaches, and teams perform under a media microscope. The spotlight is constantly on, and it often gets very hot under the lights very quickly. Trouble does arise occasionally, even in the best of sport organizations. High school and college athletes behave immaturely at times, no matter how hard everyone in the institution tries to guide them properly. Coaches and boosters cross the boundaries of NCAA rules, sometimes intentionally and sometimes inadvertently. Some professional athletes believe they are immune to the law, because they have been pampered and protected. Others succumb to temptations such as drugs, gambling, and domestic violence.

When trouble arises, the spotlight shines brightly on the sport organization as well as on the athlete. Revelations about NCAA or NFL investigations, disclosures about athletes' indiscretions, and speculation about business matters (e.g., the firing of a coach) can evolve into crises that damage the public image of the organization and its relationship with the media if the matter is not handled quickly and efficiently. The responsibility for effectively filtering the light of media scrutiny and for effecting favorable public reaction rests heavily on the SID's or the public relations director's shoulders. The media expect assistance, or at least cooperation, in gathering information quickly. Team owners and athletics administrators demand limits on information released and control of the content; consequently, sports information specialists often find themselves in the middle of a conflict between school administrators who do not want to say anything and aggressive journalists who dig out details of the story on their own.

If managed poorly, even the most minor problems, such as suspensions for curfew violations, can damage a university's reputation. Chapter 12 discusses common public relations dilemmas and crisis management. The chapter will explain how to foster a climate of cooperation in crisis situations, how to develop a crisis management plan, and how to deal with specific public relations problems.

The first section emphasizes the importance of developing a climate of cooperation, exploring the principles that provide the foundation for a working relationship with the media—a relationship that presents the sport organization in a positive light, even in times of crisis. The second section teaches students how to recognize warning signals and to involve athletes, coaches, administrators, general managers, and owners in crisis management. It discusses how to gather facts and to plot a course of action based on a written crisis-management plan. The plan emphasizes strategies that help sport organizations take control of crises, rather than being controlled by developments. The final section of the chapter provides direction on effective and appropriate responses to common public relations problems experienced by sport organizations. The difficulties range from negative publicity to criticism of the sport organization to lack of coverage of low-profile sports. The final section provides guidelines on what to do and what not to do in dealing with the media.

A person who cannot cope with the heat in the middle of a flash fire (or does not want to deal with it) should not pursue a career in sports information. Crisis situations are challenging, frustrating, and stressful—they are the public arena in which SIDs prove their mettle and earn their pay. If they do not act quickly and decisively, the reputations of athletes, coaches, teams, and owners/administrators may be hurt. If SIDs do not respond tactfully and aggressively, the relationship between the media and the sport organization may deteriorate. If they do not serve both sides effectively, they may find themselves looking for another job.

A Climate of Cooperation

Sports public relations is challenging, exciting, and rewarding when the work involves interviewing athletes, writing features, creating media guides, managing media days, running press-box operations, and directing publicity campaigns. Working with the media, outstanding athletes, and witty coaches during good times and winning seasons is a lot of fun. Unfortunately, the business of sports information is not always about distributing positive information and promoting cordial relationships. Sometimes it requires dealing with negative news, losing seasons, and strained relationships.

The relationship between the media and sport organizations is always a push-and-pull association, because their objectives differ. Although both are in the information business, the media present a selective version of information, interpretation, and entertainment, according to Coakley (1986). In the case of sports journalism, those who control the media not only select which sports and which events will be covered, but they also decide what will be emphasized in that coverage. The emphasis may be positive or negative.

The sport organization presents a selective version of information, also—a version that promotes the organization's philosophy and goals. The emphasis always is positive, or as positive as circumstances permit. The sport organization attempts to push the selection of events and the emphasis in coverage in the direction it favors. Push comes to shove when the media's selection and coverage emphases are unfavorable or unfair.

The challenge for the sports information specialist is far broader than simply controlling negative news that reflects unfavorably on the sport organization. The media's coverage selections, particularly as they relate to women's sports and men's low-profile sports, also create a challenging issue for the SID. Shove comes to confrontation most often on issues of commission, rather than those of omission. The primary flashpoints are events or issues that generate information that appears to contradict the image the sport organization intends to present to the public. However, any threat to the organization's public image represents a potential public relations crisis, and lack of media coverage of men's low-profile sports and women's sports creates an incomplete portrait of the sport organization. Its omission may even suggest the organization is not as committed to those sports as owners or administrators claim.

A crisis for a sport organization is any event, incident, or issue that falls outside the realm of everyday management activities and poses a threat to the reputation of the organization. Crises can strike at any time—crises such as the arrest of an athlete, the dismissal of a coach, or an upset loss in a key game. Crises also can develop slowly over a period of time; for example, frequent criticism of a coach by a disgruntled reporter. Crises also can grow out of long-standing issues, such as lack of coverage of men's low-profile sports and women's sports.

Each type of crisis may demand a different type of response from sports information directors, athletics administrators, or team officials. However, three general truths apply to every crisis:

1. The battle for public support during the crisis is usually won or lost in the first 24 hours.

2. The sport organization probably will lose the battle of public perception if representatives of the organization fail to develop specific procedures for early and regular communication with the public during the crisis.

3. The more complex the crisis procedures, the less likely they are to succeed.

The timeframe is critical. First impressions are most difficult to erase, so the sport organization must develop a course of action and implement it quickly. The athletics director, general manager, sports information director, or public relations director will serve as head of the emergency response team that implements the procedures. Even if the SID or public relations director does not lead the team, he or she will be called upon to guide a critical part of the procedure—the part that decides the battle of public opinion.

The SID must balance the objectives of the organization and the needs of the media in implementing crisis-management procedures; in so doing, he or she must serve two bosses, each of whom is operating on a different schedule. The decision-making cycle generally moves slowly in the world of academia; administrators appoint committees to study an issue, to gather data to formulate options, to analyze and test options, and to choose a course of action. The process can take months.

In the realm of the media, the decision-making cycle moves at whirlwind speed and at deadline intervals—for example, 24 hours between daily newspaper editions; 4–5 hours between morning, noon, evening, and late-night newscasts; 30 minutes between radio newscasts; and 30 minutes between updates on all-news radio and TV channels. Because of the intense competition among the media, reporters, editors, and producers must decide quickly whether a snippet of information is news, how much information they can gather before the next deadline, and what element to emphasize in their presentation of the story.

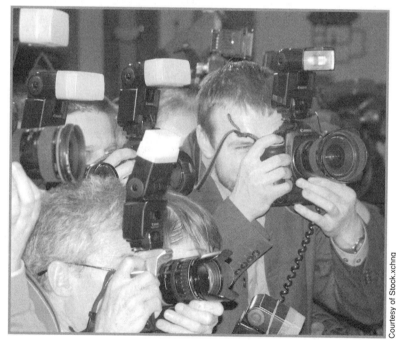

It is important to remember that the objective of the media is not to analyze the facts and draw conclusions. The role of the media is to present information to the public—to present *all the facts that are known at the time of publication or broadcast.* Therefore, the media first will churn out facts about the arrest of an athlete on sexual assault charges—whether or not the athlete is guilty. They will interview people on all sides of the story rather than attempting to decide if people on one side do not want to talk and will report the side

When a crisis occurs within a sport organization, if the media relations staff has already developed a climate of cooperation with local media, often negative publicity can be kept to a minimum.

they have now and continue to try to get the other side for the next news cycle. As a result, the facts of a story may unfold over the course of several news cycles. Reporters usually will not hold a report in order to wait until the story runs its course (judgment on guilt or innocence) unless they are assured no competitor will get the information. A reporter might be persuaded to hold a story on an internal investigation by the athletics director, but no amount of cajoling, stonewalling, or withholding comment will stop a story that comes from a police blotter or from any other record open to public inspection.

Sports information personnel, school administrators, and team executives must understand that the decision-making models they typically follow move much too slowly to keep up with fast-breaking stories and even faster breaking rumors. Whether the crisis is a legitimate story or an unfounded rumor, for example, of an NCAA investigation of an athletics department, news travels swiftly in the community. The media assuredly *will* report legitimate news, and the private lives of public figures such as athletes and celebrities fit the media/public criteria of news in the 1990s. The media also will address rumors if they find some factual basis to support those rumors. Sport organization personnel cannot prevent publication or broadcast of a story simply by refusing to talk about it.

Once one accepts the premise that the media dictate the selection and emphasis of news, it is easy to understand why a climate of cooperation is the best response to public relations crises. Sport organization personnel who provide prompt and direct answers to questions stand a far better chance of forestalling rumors than do those who stonewall. Sport organization officials who avoid the media or offer "no comment" run the risk of fueling suspicions, turning a tidbit of fact into a tidal wave of rumor and speculation.

The starting point for effective crisis management is a relationship with the media that is built on a foundation of cooperation. Charges against a school athletics program, whether they are true or false, should be answered as soon as possible to protect the integrity of the athletics department or the institution. When trouble strikes, coaches, athletics directors, college presidents, and members of the board of trustees may find themselves swept into a controversy. They must realize that expediency in responding to the charges is the best course of action. The longer charges go unanswered, the larger the problem of combating negative perceptions.

An effective climate of cooperation can be built on three simple principles: honesty, availability, and fair play. Strict adherence to these principles by all representatives of the sport organization will enhance the relationship with the media and will put the organization in a positive position from a public relations point of view. In the world of sport, the cooperation must come not only from the SID or the public relations staff, but also from all coaches, athletes, athletics directors, college administrators, and support staff. If all are honest, open, and fair, the media are far more likely to give the organization the benefit of the doubt when facts are in dispute; they are more likely to emphasize the positives, from the institution's perspective. For example, a story about suspension of athletes for team rules violations might focus more on the forthright manner in which the coach and the university dealt with a disciplinary problem than on the violations themselves.

> **Three Guiding Principles**
>
> 1. Deal honestly with the media.
>
> 2. Be available.
>
> 3. Treat all members fairly and cordially.

Three Guiding Principles

Principle No. 1: Deal honestly with the media.

Less than complete honesty will return to haunt those who are not straightforward. Mistrust will feed suspicion and give credence to rumors of wrongdoing or deceit. Honesty is especially important when dealing with sensitive or negative situations. Keith (1985) compares an SID to a successful team possessing speed and quickness; such attributes are assets when dealing with the media in a stressful situation.

An honest approach does not require sports information or other representatives of the institution to tell the media everything they know about a given situation. The institution definitely should exercise some control over the release of information; after all, the objective of the sport organization is to influence public opinion favorably through the selective release of information. However, honesty demands that the sport organization avoid deception in the posture it takes when responding to questions or requests for information. If an SID is forbidden to comment regarding a question or situation because of university policy, he or she should say so. If he or she cannot comment because of the sensitive nature of the issue, he or she should say so. The SID should give a reason for his or her refusal to comment, in every case. Honest, hard-working members of the media will accept a "no comment" without rancor or suspicion if the SID explains why. Reporters will work around "no comment" responses and search for other sources or documents to complete the factual puzzle.

The SID should establish specific ground rules for release of information in the course of casual conversation or discussion of an issue and should make clear to all reporters the organization's policies on off-the-record comments and anonymous sources. Sometimes, an SID or a representative of an organization may need to provide some background information or an explanation to clarify the response to an inquiry. The background or explanation may give the reporter some facts the organization is not ready to announce or disclose. *Before* discussing the information, the SID must make it clear to the reporter that such information is off the record. *Off-the-record* is a journalistic handshake—an agreement prohibiting the reporter from using the information in any way in pursuit of the story. The reporter who accepts comments off the record agrees not to use the information in the story; he or she also pledges not to use the information as a tip, repeating it to other sources in an attempt to confirm and use it.

Some organizations attempt to control public reaction by releasing selected information through anonymous sources. Perhaps someone in the organization feels compelled to reveal certain facts but worries about how the public will view the disclosure if the source were revealed. The person may agree to reveal the information provided the journalist attributes it in a manner that shields the name of the source, for instance as "a source close to the athletics department." The technique is common practice in Washington political circles, where "an anonymous source" leaks selective information to test public reaction. If the public reacts negatively, no harm is done if the source is anonymous. A member of a sport organization under public assault for firing a coach with a losing record might attempt to douse the negative response by anonymously disclosing private factors (such as a drinking problem) that contributed to the dismissal.

Neither off-the-record remarks nor anonymous attribution is recommended. Both practices raise ethical questions. Although off-the-record comments are acceptable, representatives of sport organizations must remember that they cannot control information once it is disclosed. The organization risks revealing information unintentionally or prematurely through off-the-record statements. The sport organization should not stake its integrity and reputation on the honesty of anyone else, including that of journalists. If a journalist violates the agreement, the sport organization should complain about the breach of ethics and trust to the appropriate editor or station executive. Honesty is a two-way street, essential to a positive working relationship on both sides. If the reporter violates the agreement, however, the damage is already done.

Ethics policies for journalistic associations and trade organizations discourage the use of anonymous sources. From the standpoint of the reporter, such sources compromise the credibility of the story somewhat. How can readers or viewers evaluate the accuracy and validity of the information if they do not know the source of the information? Identification of sources helps readers and viewers draw conclusions about conflicting information. Certainly, there is a difference between charges of recruiting violations from a player who quit the team and those from a private detective hired to investigate allegations. Journalistic organizations also recommend against the use of unnamed sources because anonymity provides a shield of protection. It is far easier for a source to make wild and exaggerated accusations under the cover of anonymity than to risk the exposure of identity and accountability. Anonymity gives the source an opportunity to distort or lie about the facts and to leave the reporter to take the fall if the information is incorrect. From the standpoint of the sport organization, a source's attempt to hide behind anonymity raises questions about motives and public posture. From the standpoint of both journalists and representatives of sport organizations, anonymity is, by nature, deceptive—a bruise on the apple of complete honesty.

Principle No. 2: Be available.

The sport organization does not have an opportunity to influence the facts or the focal point of a story if no one talks to the media. Instead of avoiding contact in times of crisis, the designated representatives of the institution or organization should make themselves readily available. The best approach is to remain in the office as much as possible when a crisis arises. If no one can be available to meet with a reporter or to speak on the telephone, a representative should get back to the reporter as soon as possible. A message should be recorded on an answering machine stating the times when someone will be available to answer questions or supply information. The representative should be sure to return all telephone calls. Also, he or she should show up for interviews on time and answer all questions as thoroughly as possible without compromising the organization's crisis management objectives.

Administrators, athletics directors, coaches, and sports information specialists should collaborate on a crisis management policy. The plan should outline steps to follow when a crisis occurs and should spell out the responsibilities of all who make contact with the media. In fact, the plan should specify which members of the organization can speak to the media under which circumstances and any restrictions on what they can say. It should establish a chain of command that details the role of each member in addressing the crisis and should offer guidelines on availability to the media. The plan also should provide direction on the judicious use of "no comment" and tactful responses to typical probing questions. Finally, the crisis management plan should thoroughly explain procedures to follow immediately after the story breaks—news release, news conference, interviews, and so on.

The SID must remember that the decisive battles in the war of public opinion occur in the first 24 hours. The best way to win the battle is to present the positive aspects to the public before the negatives stack up into an insurmountable barrier. A prompt response usually is received favorably by both the public and the media, even if the news is negative; additionally a prompt response suggests the organization is well organized and accountable, rather than being caught off guard or ducking responsibility.

Officials in the organization must decide quickly whether to answer or to quell rumors. A prompt response may limit speculation and exaggeration. If one journalist runs wild with a story without knowing all the facts, the institution and involved individuals may be hurt even if 99 responsible reporters ignore it. Careers may be ruined and reputations damaged beyond repair if a reporter reveals the name of a player under investigation for gambling on sports events. The SID who is available can at least say to the reporter, "You are off base on that story, because that player is *not* under any investigation."

Dispelling misinformation is an important reason for sport organizations to respond promptly to accusations of wrongdoing. If a university with an athletics program is under investigation, the SID should urge the administration to report exactly what happened as soon as the inquiry is made public. In the case of an NCAA investigation, the SID should release the facts as soon as they are known rather than sitting on the story and letting competing media dispense partial and piecemeal information. They should be given a full story from the outset. When a crisis erupts, many sport organizations quickly issue a news release spelling out the facts. Whether the athletics program is guilty or innocent, the SID should present his or her version of the facts to the media and, by extension, to the public. Administrators in the forefront of the investigation should make themselves available to the media. In a situation involving serious charges of wrongdoing, many people in the school's hierarchy must be informed before news releases can be written and disseminated to the media. In fact, for a story as potentially damaging as one dealing with NCAA penalties for rules violations, a news conference should be scheduled as soon as possible after the story breaks.

Every member of the media will want an exclusive interview with everyone involved, of course. Setting up exclusive interviews for a large number of journalists is impossible. A news conference both appeases competing reporters and creates an atmosphere of cooperation that may help to place the stories written and broadcast in a brighter light. If administrators and sports information directors are not available, the opposite is likely to occur. The media will begin to ask about accountability and to question the motives behind the secrecy. The silent organization sets itself up for a public flogging in the media. The same rules apply to revelations about individuals, including criminal activity, alcohol or drug abuse, and in-school disciplinary actions. The federal Family Educational Rights and Privacy Act prohibits disclosure by high schools and colleges of names and other information about students in trouble (see Chapter 13), but institutions can discuss rules and penalties; that gives the SID some control, though not much, over information disclosed. The media can still get the names from police reports or other public documents in some cases, but addressing the issue, even with limited information, is far better than sitting on the story.

Principle No. 3: Treat all members fairly and cordially.

Competition within the media always is intense. It is even more cutthroat when the print media compete against equally aggressive broadcast journalists. An exclusive or "scoop" on an important story, such as an NCAA investigation, is the ultimate badge of achievement for a reporter. It is not surprising, then, that an inexperienced, overeager, or unscrupulous reporter occasionally blows a story out of proportion in an attempt to get a scoop.

According to Chamberlin (1990), it is imperative that the SID establish a strong working relationship with the media. Positive attitudes are essential in this communication; the SID must accept the failings of inexperienced and overeager reporters and not shut those reporters out. Sports information personnel must not allow minor mistakes, disagreements about story emphasis, and criticism about athletics programs to damage the working relationship. They also must take care not to get caught in the crossfire of competing media, favoring reporters they trust and ignoring journalists most likely to focus on the negative aspects of a story.

Sports information personnel must treat all media fairly in times of crisis, when the competition among them is most fierce. First, SIDs must be sure to send news releases to all the media at the same time. Second, they must schedule news conferences at times that are as advantageous, from a deadline standpoint, to as many journalists as possible. Deadline differences necessarily create some inequities, but reporters cannot legitimately complain if the sport organization gives all members of the media the information at the same time. Third, SIDs must not give one reporter any piece of information that they do not give to all the others. Any slight—real or imagined—threatens the SID's working relationship with all the media. Despite their competitive nature, the media are a close-knit community. A slight to one is a slight to all. A tidbit of information disclosed to one creates suspicion among all others.

Additionally, the SID must remain impervious to the negative publicity (as long as it is fair) during a crisis and avoid complaining about minor problems. Words look worse in print than they sound when spoken. The temptation is to complain about being misquoted or having comments reported out of context by the media if an administrator criticizes something you said. The temptation is to blame the media if the words do not come out exactly as the SID intended. During contentious public relations crises, the SID is wise not to accuse reporters of misquoting or of taking information out of context unless he or she can verify it. Good reporters write what is actually said, not what they think someone meant or what someone should have said. By whining, the SID suggests he or she really is mad about the content of the story, and his or her complaints are just a way to dismiss the facts in the story. On the other hand, the SID must demand corrections for misquotes or mistakes that he or she can verify or confirm.

Negative news does not necessarily reflect poorly on the sports information specialist or organization. Likewise, harsh criticism of athletes, coaches, or organization policy is not an indictment of everyone in the organization. The SID must be careful not to overreact to stories with a negative slant, particularly to stories prepared by newspaper columnists, radio and TV announcers/analysts, and talk-show hosts. Part of the job of the columnist, commentator, or talk-show "expert" is to second-guess the institution or organization. These analysts attempt to represent the sentiments of the reading or listening public. When a member of the media levels criticism at an institution, at an event, or at individuals, it usually is intended as honest, constructive criticism. Granted, a few reporters and talk-show hosts are controversial for controversy's sake, but honest journalists abide by an unwritten rule of fair play. When they skewer a team, a coach, or players, they give the subjects of their criticism an opportunity to state a position or to take a written or verbal counterpunch at the journalist. If critics remain aloof from their subjects, professional relationships can deteriorate beyond repair.

In any event, the SID should never get into a battle with a journalist in the media. A minor story could turn into a major story if public complaints are made about the coverage. Political promoters caution against fighting with someone who buys ink by the barrel. In other words, the journalist always has the last word. Furthermore, crisis management and the reputation of the institution may suffer if the working relationship deteriorates into a public squabble in the media.

> **A Climate of Cooperation**
>
> The first line of defense in a crisis is a climate of cooperation. Here are a few guidelines to consider in coping with crises:
>
> 1. Do not underestimate the value of daily communication. Foster a positive working relationship through periodic contact with media representatives year-round, not just in times of crisis.
>
> 2. Get to know the strengths and weaknesses of reporters. Some are better at digging out information. Some are more likely to favor the organization's side or to tell the story thoroughly. Consequently, some actually may help in a crisis situation.
>
> 3. Getting people to listen after the fact is difficult. You must catch their attention early.
>
> 4. Rumors usually are worse than reality. Tackle each issue head on, tracking down the *facts*.
>
> 5. The entire organization—not just the public relations department—must be ready for a crisis.
>
> 6. All constituencies are equal. Keep all fully informed from the beginning of the crisis.
>
> 7. A good lawyer can be the best ally of a public relations operation in a crisis. A lawyer who understands both the legal system and the court of public opinion can provide sound advice.

Crisis Management

Crisis management is not easy. Trouble can strike when least expected and twist in unforeseen directions. Each twist may bring a new topic of inquiry, another round of media scrutiny, and renewed public concern—particularly if resolution of the issue comes slowly. It is not uncommon for the media to draw conclusions as incriminating facts come to light, even if all the facts are not yet known. Investigations by the NCAA, conferences, or university officials usually drag on for a long time, from several months to a couple of years. During the process, representatives of the sport organization may feel as if they are running from one brushfire to another to stem the spread of negative speculation. If investigators ultimately uncover wrongdoing and a penalty is forthcoming, no magic formula or crisis contingency plan can prevent damage to the institution's reputation.

However, effective institutional response and crisis management may blunt the impact of negative information. If a sport organization allows the media to exercise complete control over the release of the information, the winds of public opinion may fan the brushfires into a firestorm that permanently damages the institution. If the organization openly acknowledges the problem and resolves it professionally—in the public's estimation—the damage may be temporary. In fact, effective crisis management and controlled release of information by sports information or public relations directors may restore public confidence. The public ultimately will judge the organization on how well its response matches its philosophy and standards; that is, public opinion will hinge on how well the organization "practices what it preaches."

Although negative publicity may be unpleasant, it seldom is fatal if handled effectively. A series of articles in the Lexington *Herald Leader* in 1985 led to an NCAA investigation of the University of Kentucky men's basketball program. The newspaper won a Pulitzer Prize for its disclosure of cash payments by boosters to recruits and players; the university was penalized and placed on probation by the NCAA. UK administrators brought in a new athletics director, C. M. Newton, and a new basketball coach, Rick Pitino, with impeccable credentials, to bolster their publicly stated intent to restore the reputation of the program. By the time the Wildcats won the national championship in 1996, the damning negative publicity was little more than an afterthought—a couple of paragraphs in a featured column or tournament notes story. Even those stories that recalled the NCAA penalties focused more on the positive comeback than on the fall of one of the elite college basketball programs of all-time.

Of course, crisis prevention is the panacea for public relations dilemmas, that is, SIDs must try to stop problems before they start. Crisis management limits the damage, at best. Crisis prevention can head off dilemmas, and it is the responsibility of everyone in the sport organization. Team owners or school administrators set the standards for the organization and hire people to maintain them. General managers, athletics directors, and coaches implement the standards. They select the players and provide whatever indoctrination is necessary regarding the team or university's philosophy. GMs, coaches, and players also establish and enforce the rules of decorum, discipline, and punishment that maintain the standards. Sports information directors can offer direction on the most effective ways to communicate the standards to the public through word and action.

The sports information or public relations director also can help by setting up a system to monitor what is happening on campus. The staff can be trained to listen for signs of trouble when they interact with students, faculty, athletes, and other constituencies. If a player mentions a "big hit" on the professional football games over the weekend, perhaps it is a warning signal that someone is gambling on the NFL. The SID also can cultivate internal sources by informing everyone from the university president to physical plant technicians that the sports information staff wants to know what is going on, including rumors, in the interest of crisis prevention. The SID should make it clear that he or she will not disclose the names of people who provide information. Additionally, the SID should put his or her name on every campus mailing list. There is no telling when a clue to a problem may surface in the personals in the campus newspaper: "To the minister of defense. I enjoyed the curfew conspiracy in Florida (a tournament site) immensely. Let's do it again. Signed, Your No. 1 yell leader."

No number of internal watchdogs can spot every danger signal; however, sport organization officials can anticipate common problems and be on the alert for warning signs. The staff can study Internet message boards for anything that might suggest impending trouble. They also can read trade journals, NCAA literature, and sports magazines to keep up with the kinds of problems popping up on other campuses. Of course, not every danger sign points to an impending crisis. A missed practice and one-game suspension are hardly an impending crisis; if the SID makes too much of it the media will suspect there is more to the story than the sport organization is revealing.

It's better to start a crisis management plan early rather than late. The gestation period is unpredictable. A day? A week? A month? The speed at which the crisis grows depends on the nature of the situation and the enterprise of the media. The safest approach is to implement the organization's crisis management plan when two or more warning signs appear. It is better to start too early than to start too late.

That strategy applies to the crisis management plan, as well. Representatives of the team or university should establish or review procedures prior to the start of each season or school year. The emergency plan should outline a proactive course of action for dealing with the dilemma and the media for specific problem situations (e.g., dismissal of a coach, criminal charges against an athlete or a coach, or an investigation by a governing body such as the NCAA). The document should identify the primary spokesperson for the sport organization for each or all type of problem. The objective of any plan should be twofold:

> **Clues to a Budding Crisis**
>
> - The campus and public rumor mills are hyperactive.
>
> - The news media are showing interest in the story, or in the rumors.
>
> - Customers, business associates, and friends are inquiring about the situation.
>
> - Murphy's Law seems to be at work (if anything can go wrong, it will go wrong).
>
> - The situation requires action on several fronts at the same time.

1. To quickly and accurately communicate information that will assist in managing the crisis, saving lives, or protecting property.

2. To stabilize the damage to the institution's reputation until the crisis subsides.

Most public relations scholars recommend an open communication policy with the media and all audiences and constituencies in times of crisis. Wilcox, Ault, and Agee (1992) identify three common approaches to crisis management in *Public Relations: Strategies and Tactics:* stonewalling, denying the problem, and refusing to talk to the media; information management, releasing partial and misleading information while concealing damaging facts; and open communication, providing the media with all the facts as well as background information to put the facts in the proper context (pp. 346–347). Stonewalling may foster an image of arrogance and lack of concern for the public, and information management may smell of "cover-up" when concealed facts appear, the authors say. They cite Johnson & Johnson's handling of the Tylenol cyanide deaths in 1982 as a case study in effective corporate crisis management. Someone replaced the medication in Tylenol capsules with poison and put the boxes back on store shelves. Following an emergency plan and corporate principles, company public relations officials quickly gathered as much information as possible and set up a phone bank to answer media questions. Company officials cooperated fully with the media, consumers (toll-free number to provide information and to give out capsules in new, tamper-resistant packages), and investigators. The company unveiled the new packaging with a 30-minute videoconference and followed up with an intensive advertising campaign. Tylenol eventually recaptured most of the market share it had lost (Wilcox et al., 1992).

A sport organization that follows the open communication model will keep the media fully informed at each stage of a criminal case, an NCAA investigation, or the search for a new coach. The organization will not sit on any information unless that information would be detrimental to the investigation or the search.

Development of a crisis management plan should begin with interviews of executives and an examination of the organization's philosophy or mission statement. The planning process should include consideration of potential threats, communication channels, notification procedures, and the chain of command. Once the plan has been completed, the principals involved should conduct a dress rehearsal to determine what works and what needs revision.

Creating a Crisis Management Plan

Research

This should include interviews with the president, the provost, deans, and other appropriate administrators for information on the university's mission, philosophy, and standards. It should also include review of all documents related to ethical policies and legal regulations—student and staff codes of rights and responsibilities, NCAA regulations, Family Educational Rights and Privacy Act, and so on. A code of conduct typically spells out prohibited conduct on campus, an alcoholic beverage policy, and a sexual harassment policy. It also includes regulations related to disciplinary action and appeals. For a professional team, research entails interviews with the president, the chief operating officer, the general manager, and directors of key functional areas. The document examination encompasses league regulations as well as team policies and philosophy.

Assessment

This involves brief situation analysis and an evaluation of common crisis situations. The situations may differ among amateur organizations, high school and college athletics departments, and professional teams.

Communication Channels

It is important to outline all types of communication channels—news releases, news conferences, phone banks, and so on—to be utilized for each type of potential threat. The outline should specify roles for the president, general manager or athletics director, coaches, athletes, sports information personnel, and anyone else in the organization or institution that will have contact with the media.

Courtesy of JimVarhegyi/U.S. Air Force

The public's eyes are constantly on high-profile athletes, so it is important for sports information specialists to have already developed a strategy of how to handle any publicity problems that may arise.

Notification Procedures

This is a procedure to be followed for notification of each member of the crisis management team when an emergency arises.

Communication Control Center

This is the central location for preparation and release of all information to the media. The location also may serve as the strategy room for meetings of the crisis team as needed.

Crisis Kit

This packet lists all items needed to be set up in a communication center quickly. One list would include telephones, copy machines, materials, and other logistical needs. The packet should also contain a media relations checklist with guidelines for dealing with the media in the first hours of the crisis.

Policies and Procedures

This requires a synopsis of key policies, regulations, and positions on issues, drawn from the document research. Copies of all documents reviewed during the preliminary research should be kept in a designated location listed in the crisis kit.

Appendices

Appendices include lists of addresses and telephone numbers of executives, managers, employees, media contacts, and others needed for consultation or for distribution of information.

Rough Draft

A rough draft incorporates the areas mentioned above. One person should prepare the draft; all others on the crisis response team should review it. Include the president, team owner, and board of directors or trustees if they are not assigned duties in the plan.

Final Draft

This is a revision based on input from all who have reviewed the plan. Following approval of the final draft, the SID should send copies to all members of the team and to other appropriate members of the sport organization.

Dress Rehearsal

The dress rehearsal is a test of the plan. The SID should conduct hypothetical exercises or a dress rehearsal to troubleshoot the plan of action, noting the strengths and weaknesses and adapting as needed.

Tough Public Relations Problems

Public relations problems fall into two broad categories: emergency situations and

Media Relations Checklist

1. Prepare a one-page guide outlining steps to take in the first few hours of an emergency situation.

2. Choose an institutional or team spokesperson and a backup. The designated person should release all key information to the media. To ensure a consistent response, no one else should talk to the media without approval.

3. Think about more than the obvious implications of the problem. Come up with 10 questions the media are most likely to ask and prepare answers for them. Also, consider tangential areas into which the media may probe.

4. Deal with the crisis head-on. Do not hide from the media. Face the media quickly and openly.

5. Gather the facts before the meeting. Assign people to gather information on specific aspects of the situation. They should report to the SID or the designated spokesperson from the scene, from the hospital, from the police station, or from any other point the crisis touches.

6. Respond to every media question. Return every media telephone call within 10 minutes, if possible. Return calls in this order: radio, TV, newspapers.

7. Never lie—not so much as "a little white lie." Once you lie to one reporter, you leave a permanent crack in your credibility.

8. Do not babble. Review what you want to say in advance and make sure it conforms to the team philosophy or university mission statement. Say exactly what you mean, and mean exactly what you say. Do not leave your comments open to interpretation.

9. Never volunteer negative information.

10. Avoid off-the-record comments. Stick to the facts. Do not speculate in response to hypothetical questions. In short, do not tell the media anything you do not want to see in print or to hear on radio or television. Even off-the-record comments can be repeated. If you do not want to see it in print, do not say it. You can gain the confidence of both athletes and media by avoiding cat-and-mouse games about what is OK to use and what cannot be repeated.

ongoing issues. Emergencies are unexpected threats to the image and reputation of individuals or organizations. These generally concern actions or events arising from the behavior of members of the organization, as in the dismissal of a coach. Ongoing issues relate most often to policies and procedures that affect the working relationship between the organization and the media. Common issues range from coverage selections by the media to dressing-room policies of the sport organization.

Emergency Situations

These are situations involving the behavior of members of the organization with the potential to generate negative news. Common stories include the firing of a coach or manager, the release or trade of an athlete, player indiscretions, tragedies (e.g., death of an athlete), internal investigations and disciplinary action against members of the organization, criminal charges against members of the organization, and investigation of individuals or of the organization by regulatory bodies.

Ongoing Issues

These issues involve policies and procedures that damage the working relationship between sport organizations and the media or that distort the image and reputation of either party. Common issues include coverage of amateur sports, coverage of men's low-profile collegiate sports, coverage of women's sports, refusal of athletes to speak to the media, and verbal or physical abuse of reporters by players or coaches.

A well-designed and well-rehearsed crisis management plan can help a sport organization take charge of the story in emergency situations. With a plan in place, members of the organization can take a proactive approach to dissemination of information. Development of the plan will provide a blueprint for handling the media, training for all institutional officials, and guidelines on how to answer certain questions. The organization and preparation will help members of the sport organization gather facts quickly, recognize and define the problem in their own terms, and come forward with information promptly.

The primary component of the crisis management plan for the sports information or public relations director is the checklist for dealing with the media (see sidebar).

The list enables the organization to update the media quickly and to advise them of actions being taken to resolve the issue.

Most ongoing issues deal with problems that have simmered for years with occasional movement in positive or negative directions. Although such issues may be as critical to the image of the sport organization or to the working relationship with the media in the long term, dealing with them lacks the communication dynamics of an emergency situation. Because such issues seldom affect sports events per se, they are of less immediate interest to the public as a whole; consequently, a crisis management plan and quick-response procedures are of little value in dealing with them.

Ongoing issues demand a well-organized plan designed to create immediacy in the minds of the public and interest on the part of the media. Of course, immediacy in the mind of the audience will help generate interest on the part of the media. At any rate, a plan of attack on ongoing issues requires a combination of marketing and publicity strategies, much like a campaign for "The Making of an All-American." Like the publicity campaign, management of ongoing issues is both purposeful and planned. It may include advertising elements, marketing promotions, publicity releases or activities, and meetings with individual members of the media. Unlike crisis management, in which the SID responds to the media, management of ongoing issues requires the SID to take the institution's message to the public and to the media. The sports information director must prod and persuade in order to generate movement on ongoing issues such as gender equity in coverage decisions.

The SID bears a responsibility to attack ongoing issues as vigorously as he or she attacks emergency situations and should deliberately prepare strategies for resolving the problem, including techniques to be utilized and a timeline for implementation. Sports information personnel can adapt and adjust as circumstances dictate. They also should involve members of the organization at all levels. For example, they can enlist the development office or marketing department in promotional activities. They can stage events on campus that call attention to a particular team, such as a women's basketball clinic. They can include members of the sport organization in the plan, perhaps by setting up a speaker's bureau that sends coaches into the community to sell their sports.

Coverage of women's sports and low-profile men's sports is among the most important ongoing issues at the amateur, high school, and collegiate levels. For women's sports, the SID should collaborate with administrators and athletics officials on a plan to "sell" events and teams to the public and the media. Before preparing the plan, organizational officials should analyze the current differences in attendance, coverage policies of various media organizations, and emphasis on women's sports by the institution. Planners can use the information to devise "selling points" and strategies.

For example, one of the most important barometers is the relationship between spectator interest and media coverage. Mary Jo Kane, professor of sport sociology and director of the Center for Research on Girls and Women in Sport at the University of Minnesota, says the reasons the media most often cite for inequitable

What Not to Do

As an SID, there are 10 critical errors you can make that may have a far-reaching impact. *Do not, under any circumstances*

1. Divide the media into groups—that is, opponents and proponents, essential and nonessential, large and small. Pigeonholing suggests unequal treatment.

2. Put up roadblocks. Dealing only with selected media members, withholding information, or refusing to discuss an issue makes it more difficult for all concerned to do their jobs.

3. Ignore phone calls or return them the next day. Failure to return a telephone call promptly gives the impression you do not think the caller is important.

4. Scream about negative information in a story. You cannot expect the news media to ignore negative aspects of a story.

5. Talk down to reporters. Do not tell reporters, "There is no story here." Do not lecture reporters on their thirst for negative news and tendency to sensationalize stories or to blow them out of proportion. They've heard it already . . . often.

6. Insist that reporters clear all information with the organization before using it. They will ignore you. "No prior restraint" is one of the legal principles in a journalist's creed.

7. Promise exclusives to several reporters. Giving information to one reporter that you do not give to all others assuredly will damage your reputation. Giving the same information to all and calling it "exclusive" will have the same effect.

8. Torpedo the energetic reporter. Do not badmouth the reporter who breaks a new angle on the story in front of other members of the media. Reporters prize enterprise, even from a competing journalist.

9. Threaten to pull advertising. If you threaten to pull advertising over a story, not only do you compromise your integrity, but you also increase the odds the journalist will run the story, too.

10. Violate any of the these rules. You may gain a temporary ally or two if you favor certain members of the media or criticize competitors, but you ultimately create more enemies.

coverage are lack of participation by women in sports and lack of public interest (Huggins, Oct. 21, 1996, p. 10). An SID may be able to use actual participation and attendance data to dispel such myths. The SID could gather information on the number of female athletes at local high schools, in local amateur leagues, and on intramural and varsity teams at the university. All those players represent potential readers/viewers with parents, family members, and friends who also are potential readers. The SID also could gather attendance figures for schools and events where attendance and public interest are high. ESPN televised the championship game of the Puerto Rico Invitational between the University of Cincinnati and Southwest Missouri University on New Year's Day in 1997; only a couple hundred spectators attended. On the other hand, tickets for the NCAA Division I Women's Basketball Final Four typically sell out shortly after they are made available to the general public. The attendance figures and ticket sales offer strong counterpoints to typical media excuses citing lack of interest.

Promoting women's sports is akin to promoting a new product, because of its limited public exposure to date. The SID must develop ways to make the public and the media aware of the quality of the product. The sport organization can use the same publicity tools for all sports: news releases, hometown features, pregame advances, and so on; however, the SID may have to push to persuade some media to use the information about women's teams. Such pushes should coincide with big games or promotions with the maximum selling points, such as the Hometown Shootout between the women's basketball teams at University of Cincinnati and Xavier or a match between a local team and the conference leader. SIDs should prepare features on selected athletes and pitch the stories to specific reporters during breaks in the sports schedule, when the newspaper is looking for a story to fill space or a TV anchor needs to fill time. Sports journalists often struggle to come up with stories to fill issues bloated with advertising in the days surrounding holidays or school exams.

The media also can emphasize events. Many schools package men's and women's basketball games in part to introduce potential fans to the latter. The University of Kentucky put together a 10-year basketball deal with Riverfront Coliseum in Cincinnati in 1995–1996 that alternates a junior-varsity/women's doubleheader one year with a women's/men's doubleheader the next. To be eligible for tickets to the high-profile men's game every other year, patrons had to purchase tickets to the junior-varsity/women's doubleheader.

The SID should do everything possible to encourage and help the media publicize men's low-profile and women's sports. Calling the media with game reports and statistics is a good strategy; it is hard to turn down a story that is already prepared. At the very least, it may get a paragraph in a roundup in a newspaper or a spot on the list of sports scores displayed on the TV screen during a newscast. The SID can pitch features on athletes' standout-out performances and records to selected reporters and media organizations. The sports information department also can pass along conference standings and individual statistics. The most effective sales techniques are one-on-one. Pitching stories and statistics to selected media members is more effective than blanketing the media at large. It also is less expensive, and it helps the SID identify and cultivate journalists who show some interest. When targeting media, SIDs must remember this old public relations adage: "If you throw enough features on a wall, some of them are sure to stick."

Whereas publicity efforts depend on the media, advertising and promotional activities may take the pitch directly to the public. An SID may plan a schedule of public service announcements for radio to coincide with key games or events. The sport organization also may place a small ad in a local newspaper or on a local cable channel to call attention to a game, the pursuit of a record, or a promotional activity. Game promotions may have a multiplying effect. Let us say an SID gives free tickets to a high school team and an amateur team for each game. The freebies increase the size of the audience. The spectators also may bring along parents and chaperones. Some may pay to come back for other games. In-house promotions that bring students to the gym or the field also boost attendance. A competition of some kind, between Greek organizations or residence halls, might be tied to a game promotion. As attendance and fan interest increase, so may media interest. In any case, more people are exposed to the product and to the organization's selling points.

Sports information directors can utilize similar tactics for low-profile sports, as can amateur league officials, community recreation directors, and club managers. Amateur sports organizations should put public relations strategies right next to fundraising on their lists of responsibilities. Directors or managers should establish communication with the local media, assigning a staff member or volunteer to deliver announcements to the local media about grand openings, facility expansions, special events and tournaments, new equipment, and programs. They can designate someone to call in results of meets and other competitions, as well as team standings. Additionally, they can pitch features about outstanding athletes, accomplishments, and so on to targeted media. If budget permits, the SID may create a newsletter for members and send a copy to the media to remind them of the facility, programs, and participants.

Advertising and ticket promotions are advisable only if the organization has a healthy budget. Amateur organizations and recreation programs should concentrate on the local press, even if it is merely a weekly or a free "shopper." A major daily in a metropolitan area is unlikely to report on amateur events unless they have regional or national significance.

In making a pitch to the media, the SID must be careful not to confuse advertising and publicity. Asking for "free advertising" or "free publicity" or "free" anything is never appropriate. The media separate advertising and editorial departments. All publicity is free. All advertising is paid. Although an SID may mean publicity when he or she says "advertising," the word itself is a turnoff to a reporter or sports director. Advertising and promotion should clearly be identified as such.

A media party often is an effective promotional tool when a club or recreation center opens. The opening should be special and should include community leaders from service, political, corporate, and media industries on the invitation list. Television anchors, sports anchors, feature editors, and program directors should be invited. The SID should also invite sports reporters, feature writers, columnists, editors, and any beat reporters with a related specialty—for instance, health and fitness, nutrition, or medicine. The grand opening might start with a news conference for distribution of media kits, introduction of principals in the club or center, and media questions and answers. The SID should decide in advance how long the news conference will last and observe the time limitations. A menu of refreshments is appropriate, but do not let the food and drink overshadow the business nature of the event.

Whether the dilemma is an emergency situation or an ongoing issue, representatives of sport organizations should avoid actions that intentionally or unintentionally strain the working relationship with the media. They should guard against procedures or comments that belittle members of the media, give one member of the media an advantage over another, or impede composition or presentation of a story.

Summary

Working with the media during crisis situations and ongoing public relations problems is the most challenging, stressful, and joyless part of the job of sports information. The sports information specialist's job shifts from publicizing positive news to combating negative information or rumors. The working relationship with the media may change temporarily from that of a partnership to that of a protagonist or antagonist. A misstep or false step may do far more harm; it may hurt an individual, a group of people, or the organization itself. However, the SID's performance in the midst of a public relations dilemma may do more to enhance the image of the organization than a ton of publicity brochures and media days.

Any event, issue, or incident that poses a threat to the reputation of the sport organization represents a potential crisis. A crisis may arise quickly as a result of the behavior or activities of members of the sport organization. A dilemma may develop slowly in connection with an unresolved issue related to coverage decisions, working relationships, or organizational policies.

Regardless of the origin or nature of the crisis, the sport organization should quickly respond to inquiries and implement procedures planned in advance. The quicker the response, the better, because the battle for public opinion usually is decided within the first 24 hours. The simpler the emergency plan, the better, because response time is critical. The sports information or public information director may have to convince superiors of the need for expediency, because the decision-making process moves at a much slower, more measured speed in upper-level management. In the news media, decision making operates on a deadline cycle, which may be as little as 30 minutes. To deliver its side of a story to the public, a sport organization must be prepared to move at the same speed. Because of deadline demands and competition among the media, a journalist seldom will wait until the sport organization is ready to print or broadcast the story.

An SID or public relations director can project a positive image and reinforce the organization's reputation by maintaining a climate of cooperation in all situations. The foundation for a positive atmosphere, even in times of turmoil, rests on three principles: honesty, availability, and fair play. To be effective, representatives of the sport organization must be open and honest, must make themselves available to the media, and must treat all journalists fairly and respectfully. They must attempt to answer all questions honestly, without relying on crutches such as anonymity and off-the-record comments. They must give information to all the media at the same time through news releases and news conferences. They must return telephone calls promptly, within 10 minutes if possible. They do not complain about the negative elements of stories in the media.

A crisis can arise at any time, and some negative news is inevitable. A crisis seldom is fatal, however, particularly if the sport organization takes control of the story. To put themselves in position to take charge of the situation, members of the sport organization can monitor warning signs of trouble. They can watch Internet message boards, campus publications, and trade literature for hints of danger. They also can pay attention to what faculty, staff, students, athletes, and fans are saying. Excessive rumors, heightened media interest, and unusual inquiries from customers, boosters, and other supporters are among the signals that a crisis is imminent.

To respond quickly in a crisis, members of the sport organization should prepare a crisis management plan. The plan should reflect the philosophy, standards, and ideals of the organization. The primary objectives should be to accurately communicate information to the media and public that will assist in managing the crisis and to stabilize damage to the institution's reputation until the crisis subsides.

The sports information expert and school administrators or team officials should work together to develop the plan. Scholars recommend a plan that emphasizes open communication. The plan should address potential threats, notification procedures (for members of the organization), communication channels, procedures to follow, and media and institutional contact lists. The procedures should specify the responsibilities of everyone on the crisis management team, particularly those of the individual designated as primary spokesperson. What others are permitted to say to the media, if anything, also should be defined.

A crisis management plan is most effective for dealing with emergency situations that involve behavior or actions detrimental to the image of the organization, as in the firing of a coach or an NCAA investigation. Such plans are of little value in handling ongoing issues related to the working relationship with the media, such as coverage choices and access to athletes. The media come to the sport organization in times of crisis. The sport organization must go to the media to address ongoing issues. Such issues lack the obvious expediency and public interest intrinsic to emergency situations. As in crisis management, however, the most effective strategy for dealing with issues is a predesigned plan. The plan may incorporate both publicity and advertising strategies.

Among the most important ongoing issues for amateur organizations, high schools, and colleges are those that relate to coverage of men's low-profile sports and women's sports. Given the dearth of coverage prior to the 1990s, sports information professionals must sell women's sports as they might sell a new product. They must make the public and the media aware of the quality of the product to generate interest; that means the SID and other individuals must devise "selling points" and incorporate them in publicity, promotions, and personal pitches to reporters, editors, and station managers. The SID may use publicity tools such as news releases, hometown features, and game advances; however, he or she must follow up with telephone calls and gentle persuasion to encourage publication or broadcast of the stories. The SID should also make the job easier for the media by providing game reports and statistical information.

The SID may coordinate publicity efforts with advertising and promotional activities. The sport organization can prepare public address announcements for radio and buy advertising in newspapers and on cable TV to promote games and special events. Organization officials also can market game promotions to build audiences, to increase fan support, and to increase media attention.

Amateur organizations, community recreation departments, and private clubs can use similar tactics to sell their programs to the media. In addition, they also can stage media parties and circulate newsletters to attract media interest.

In every type of crisis, honesty and open communication are the best policy. The organization's response to an investigation, player discipline, or contract negotiation may reinforce the image the organization intends to project. The positives may outweigh the negatives in the media and public reaction. The same is true regarding athletes who are in trouble, whether the problem is crime, drugs, alcohol, or discipline. Open communication and early intervention give the SID and the sport organization some control over the flow and focus of information—perhaps not much, but some. Perhaps enough to be pivotal in the battle of public opinion. Unquestionably, the sport organization stands a better chance of winning the battle by employing a proactive plan rather than by sitting on information and conceding control to print and broadcast journalists.

DISCUSSION QUESTIONS

1. How does an SID develop a climate of continued cooperation with the local media?
2. Explain in detail how an SID is able to work effectively with his or her two bosses—the institution and the media—in a time of crisis.

SUGGESTED EXERCISES

1. Role playing—have students match up in pairs wherein one student acts as a sports information director and deals directly with the coach on a delicate subject of your choosing. Examples might include illegal recruiting, gambling on sports, or drug charges against an athlete.

   The reporter should then interrogate and write a story.
2. Have students write news releases announcing that an institution has been accused of cheating in regards to athletics recruitment. They should use the three principles of crisis management.

Chapter Thirteen

LAW AND ETHICS: PLAYING BY THE RULES

An assistant men's basketball coach at the University of Kentucky sued the Lexington *Herald-Leader* for libel in connection with a 1985 series of stories that alleged recruiting violations. The series reported that players were receiving cash payments from boosters and implied that the assistant coach was involved. The assistant coach denied any knowledge of or involvement in payments to players and contended that the articles defamed his character.

A lower-court jury ruled in favor of the Lexington *Herald-Leader*, although the newspaper acknowledged some errors in the story. The jury decided the assistant coach was a public figure, because of the high visibility of the UK men's basketball program. As a public figure, he had to prove actual malice, that is, that the *Herald-Leader* knew the accusation was false or did not vigorously attempt to find out whether it was false. The jury ruled that the coach had failed to prove active malice.

Chapter 13 provides a primer on law and ethics for the aspiring professional. The section on law outlines federal statutes, state laws, rules of regulatory agencies, and institutional policies that affect access to information. It also examines civil remedies for libel, invasion of privacy, and copyright infringement.

The section on ethics explores the foundations for the major ethical concepts espoused by journalists in the United States and surveys broadly accepted professional values, the viewpoints of journalists, a model for decision making, and codes of conduct prescribed by professional associations.

The assistant coach appealed, and the appellate court threw out the judgment, saying that the jury had erred in categorizing the coach as a public figure. The high court ordered a new trial based on the coach's standing as a private individual. Attorneys for the *Herald-Leader* then settled out of court, saying the change in status weakened the newspaper's case significantly. In many cases, a private figure has only to prove negligence, that is, that damaging errors occurred through carelessness.

John McSherry, a National League umpire, collapsed and died during the season opener at Cincinnati in April 1996. One of the metropolitan daily newspapers in Cincinnati published a picture of McSherry as he turned to walk away from the plate. The other ran a closeup of McSherry's face as he lay on the artificial turf, face down. *Sports Illustrated* ran an identical picture. The four television stations showed different clips from a sequence in which McSherry walked away from the plate and collapsed. One showed him walking away, and another showed him falling to the turf. Media critics questioned the ethics of those who ran pictures or videotape of McSherry's face, complaining the shots were insensitive and unnecessary and that, as such, they crossed the boundaries of ethical journalism, good taste, and common sense.

These two examples illustrate the complexity and ambiguity of the legal and ethical issues sports information specialists and sports journalists encounter. The law forces release of information in some instances and prohibits disclosure in others. It also applies differently to private individuals than to public figures, private schools than to public ones. Ethical principles are equally ambiguous, because no universal set of guidelines exists. Journalists evaluate their actions based on longstanding religious or moral standards, professional codes of ethics, and personal conscience. No uniformity exists, because journalists apply different morally defensible principles. Journalists in different media also handle some ethical questions differently because of the unique nature of their medium. For example, a photograph in a newspaper or magazine may have more impact than a film clip on television because the newspaper image is permanent and lasting, while the television picture is temporary and fleeting.

Despite the complexities of legal and ethical issues, sports information personnel and sports journalists must make decisions quickly.

Legal Matters

Why does an aspiring professional in sports information or sport management need a primer on law?

Don't colleges and universities assign NCAA "compliance" responsibilities to athletics administrators?

Don't sport organizations hire lawyers to provide advice and oversight on legal matters?

Don't sports information specialists prepare print and broadcast materials that enhance the images of the organization and its athletes, rather than damaging them?

It is true that colleges and universities generally assign compliance responsibilities to athletics administrators. The compliance officer is charged with ensuring that all activities related to the athletics department conform to NCAA regulations. The officer's primary focus is on the behavior of coaches, athletes, and administrators, but NCAA regulations also include restrictions on such sports information-related activities as use of color in media guides, publication of recruiting brochures, performance of athletes in broadcast promotions, and release of information on recruiting prospects.

Yes, sport organizations hire lawyers to provide advice and oversight on the sensitive issues, such as the release of information on disciplinary and legal action involving members of the sport organization, but lawyers do not work on the same cycles as the media do, and legal guidance may not be readily available. A lawyer may not be available for a quick consultation regarding a dispute between the athletics department and media organizations over access to information about a rapidly growing public relations crisis.

Yes, sports information personnel emphasize the positive, and they do not knowingly invade the privacy of members of the team or institution or produce materials that damage character or reputation; however, federal statutes, state laws, and institutional policies restrict release of certain details and force disclosure of other information. Furthermore, some statutes impose penalties for failure to act within a specified time period.

Consequently, for the sports information specialist there is no substitute for a basic understanding of media law, particularly in an age in which the peccadilloes and personal failings of members of sport organizations attract as much public interest as do the athletes' performances on the field; particularly in an industry in which organizational reputation and public support are inseparable; particularly in a profession in which a person's right to privacy and the public's right to know are often in conflict; and particularly in a work environment that often demands decisions at a moment's notice amid a maelstrom of media pressure and fragments of information, rumor, and innuendo.

The sports information specialist must act quickly and capably when a player is suspended and rumors of drug use swirl around the team. At the least, a primer on media law and institutional regulations provides a foundation from which the SID can act confidently and forthrightly from the outset of a crisis—rather than timidly and apologetically, while waiting for legal counsel. Such a delay, in itself, might suggest to the public a lack of competence or an attempt to stall and conceal vital information.

Accurately conveying a coach's words to the public is vital in establishing a foundation of honesty, which tops the list of ethical guidelines for members of the media.

Whether the perception is logical or not, members of sport organizations are increasingly regarded as public figures under the law. The round-the-clock weight of media coverage, the demand for public money (through taxation, student fees, and donations) for athletics facilities and programs, and the dominance of sports stars in product endorsements and fundraising campaigns put athletes in the public eye. The distinction between public figure and private individual is a pivotal factor in applications of the law. Decisions by the U.S. Supreme Court have given the press great latitude and strong protection in reporting information on the public's business such as, for example, expenditures on athletics at public colleges and universities. In a landmark decision in a 1964 libel case, *New York Times v. Sullivan*, the U.S. Supreme Court effectively gave the press some leeway to err in reporting on public issues and public figures. The decision, written by Justice William J. Brennan, warned against shackling the press and inhibiting public/press scrutiny of public issues and agencies. Justice Brennan favored giving the press a margin of error of sorts, "to assure unfettered interchange of ideas for the bringing about of political and social changes desired by the people" (quoted in Mencher, 1991, p. 653). The

Times decision and subsequent U.S. Supreme Court decisions made it more difficult for a public figure to recover damages for defamation of character than it was for a private individual, by creating a more rigorous standard of proof.

The public-private distinction also affects access to information. Both federal statutes and state laws open a wide variety of records and meetings to public and press scrutiny. The Freedom of Information Act, adopted in 1966, gives the public the right to inspect thousands of federal documents. State "sunshine" laws—laws that open government records and meetings to the light of public examination—make available everything from athletics department expenditures to arrest reports at public institutions. On the other hand, federal legislation designed to protect the privacy of individuals limits access to some records. The Family Educational Rights and Privacy Act (FERPA) restricts the release of certain personal information about students, such as grades. State privacy laws likewise prohibit the publication of certain types of potentially embarrassing personal information. Regulatory agencies such as the NCAA also impose restrictions. In addition, sport organizations themselves develop individual policies that prohibit the release of some records within federal, state, and regulatory agency boundaries.

Because of differences in application of the law to public and private matters, the law can prove slippery and treacherous for the sports information specialist. The law may force the release of information in some cases but restrict it in others. The law may relate differently to professional teams (private businesses) than to public schools. The law may apply differently to private colleges than to public universities. The law may affect the sport organization and the media differently. The law may vary from state to state. An organizational policy may vary from team to team or university to university. Regardless of the situation, a misstep can be costly for a sport *or* media organization. Release of personal data about students by a sports information director can jeopardize federal funding, and publication or broadcast of false and damaging information by sports information personnel or members of the media can provide the basis for a libel lawsuit that can cost the organization millions of dollars.

Laws and regulations that most affect the work of the sports information professional fall into two broad categories: access to information, and publication or broadcast of information. The first category comprises state and federal laws, regulatory agency rules, and organizational/institutional policies that require or prohibit disclosure of information to the public, including the press. It is important to note that the press do not enjoy special privileges under state and federal law; they are simply members of the public. The laws are applicable to all members of the public: press, students, parents, boosters, and other interested citizens. The second category encompasses legal actions or civil torts that enable individuals or corporations to recover damages resulting from printed or broadcast materials that impugn one's reputation, invade one's privacy, or steal one's ideas or work. Such actions give a citizen or corporation legal recourse against abuses by the press, by other institutions, or by other citizens. However, they *do not* give a citizen, a university, a professional team, or any organization a means to prevent publication or broadcast. They only provide for postpublication or postbroadcast recompense.

The First Amendment guarantee of freedom of the press prohibits the government from censoring or blocking publication or broadcast of information. The U.S. Supreme Court has ruled that the government cannot exercise "prior restraint" unless the information would somehow jeopardize national security. The courts have not clearly defined what types of information would jeopardize national security, but it is unlikely that publication of sports information of any kind would qualify. On the other hand, federal and legislative bodies have enacted measures designed to protect individual privacy. Although the laws do not restrict publication or broadcast of information, they make accessing such information more difficult for the media. In some cases, federal and state legislation also provide penalties (or legal recourse) for publication of specific kinds of personal information.

The First Amendment guarantee of freedom of the press and laws protecting individual rights sometimes come into conflict. The sports information professional may get caught in the middle of such conflicts. On the one hand, a sports information director might be forced by law to disclose information that reflects negatively on the character of a coach. On the other hand, the sports information director must try to protect the reputation of the organization by muting the fallout as much as possible. Attempts to protect the organization's image might extend to legal action against an overzealous or disreputable journalist or media organization that oversteps the boundaries.

Access to Information

Federal and state laws, the rules of regulatory agencies, and institutional policies may both aid and hamper attempts by sport organizations to control information in crisis situations. For example, the Family Educational Rights and Privacy Act blocks the release of information about disciplinary action taken against a student-athlete. However, state open-records laws might force disclosure of the arrest report if campus police charged a student-athlete with a crime. Likewise, laws on access may prove ally or enemy to the journalist preparing an in-depth, factual account of an incident.

The Freedom of Information Act (FOIA), state open-record and open-meeting laws, and NCAA regulations require the release of some information. Open-meeting and open-record laws also permit closure of records and meetings in special circumstances. Regulatory agencies and institutional policies sometimes put additional restrictions on the release of information.

Generally speaking, laws of access have greater impact on sports information professionals than on sports journalists. They do not prevent publication or broadcast of protected information, if a journalist can find access to it. The following is a rundown on the most common types of laws, regulations, and institutional policies relating to access to information:

Freedom of Information Act

The federal Freedom of Information Act, adopted in 1966, provided greater access to government files. The intent of the law was to open the public's business to public scrutiny. The act effectively enables the public and the media to oversee the actions of agencies in the executive branch of the federal government, including military departments, government corporations, and independent regulatory agencies such as the Food and Drug Administration.

The FOIA requires agencies of the federal government to make available copies of official records at "a reasonable cost" upon request. Although the act covers virtually all executive bodies, it exempts nine types of records. Among the exemptions are classified or confidential records related to national security; agency personnel rules and practices; trade secrets gathered by federal agencies; memoranda exchanged during the decision-making process; personnel files protected by privacy laws; and files of law-enforcement agencies that might compromise an investigation, reveal an informant, or jeopardize someone's right to a fair trial or right to privacy.

Government agencies are required to respond to an FOIA request within 10 working days, although a backlog of requests and processing time often extends the time period. The agency can black out or delete portions of files that are protected (such as personal medical data) before turning over the records. Anyone whose request is denied can file a lawsuit challenging the decision.

The FOIA is of little practical value to journalists covering sports, and sports information professionals are not likely to have to deal with an FOIA request. Professional teams are private organizations, not subject to much control or regulation by federal agencies. Most public high schools and colleges are supported by state funds, not federal funds. They may receive some federal funds through research grants and financial aid programs. Other than in the examination of sports-oriented research or the investigation of financial aid allotments to athletes, the FOIA provides little help to the sports journalist.

Schulte and Dufresne (1994) say journalists do not file FOIA requests as often as "commercial users, public-interest groups, scholars and prisoners" (p. 425). The primary reason is time. Long delays in obtaining information are anathema to the journalist working on a rapidly breaking story on deadline.

Government in Sunshine Act

Enacted in 1976, this federal law requires some federal agencies to conduct open meetings. The agency still can close a meeting, however, for many of the same reasons it can close records. The act covers the Federal Communications Commission, so journalists can attend meetings relating to broadcast station licenses and regulations affecting broadcast contracts with professional and college teams, but the government open-meetings law has little bearing on sport organizations and provides little help for journalists seeking secret information.

Privacy Act of 1974

This federal legislation prohibits disclosure of personal data by governmental agencies. The act provides protection to the individual on two fronts. First, it allows individuals to examine government records related to themselves and to make corrections. Second, it prohibits federal agencies from releasing personal information. A person can sue federal officials who release protected information for damages, attorney's fees, and court costs (Overbeck & Pullen, 1991). As in the case of the FOIA and the Government in Sunshine Act, the law has little effect on the work of sports journalists and sports information professionals.

Family Educational Rights and Privacy Act (FERPA)

An amendment to the 1974 Elementary and Secondary Education Act, an aid-to-education measure, FERPA has had perhaps greater impact on the work of journalists and sports information directors than any other piece of federal legislation. The legislation, often referred to as the Buckley Amendment because U.S. Senator James Buckley of New York pushed for its passage, restricts access to student records.

The Buckley Amendment (1974) requires permission of students (over 18) or their parents (if students are under 18) before a school can release records containing any personal data other than "directory" information to any outside party. The legislation also enables students and parents to examine their own records and to request that even directory information be withheld. Directory information includes the student's name, address, telephone number, email address, date and place of birth, major field of study, participation in university activities (such as clubs and extracurricular activities), dates of attendance, and awards received.

The law would permit a high school athletics director or a college SID to confirm a student's participation on a team and give out the student's height and weight. It would prohibit the release of information about academic difficulties, medical/mental problems, or internal disciplinary action without the student's approval. It also would prohibit the release of test scores, aptitude tests, and transcripts of grades.

Courtesy of Dan Mendlik/Cleveland Indians

It is important for those in the sports media to understand the various laws in place with regard to access of information.

Failure to comply with the law could jeopardize federal funding. The law states that federal funding can be denied to schools with policies that permit release of such information or schools that consistently reveal such information. It does not prescribe specific penalties for one-time or occasional violations.

The Buckley Amendment places limitations on school officials, not journalists, because it is a component of an education measure. The law does not limit other parties. Journalists may print, without fear of penalty, any information that does not violate state privacy laws. Even a campus newspaper, or a radio or television station at a public college can print grades, disciplinary action, or other such personal information without fear of penalties, under the Buckley Amendment. Censorship is a violation of students' rights at public colleges and universities because such institutions are an extension of the government, and the First Amendment prohibits

Congress from making laws that interfere with freedom of expression. Administrators at private colleges and high schools can regulate school media because they are not bound by the constraints placed on government entities.

School officials can use FERPA to withhold personal information, particularly negative information. However, they cannot keep crime reports covered by open-records laws secret under the Buckley Amendment. The Student Press Law Center, which monitors regulations affecting student media, says that no court rulings have supported such protection of crime records (1990). Furthermore, a federal judge ruled in favor of a student editor, Traci Bauer, who challenged Southwest Missouri University officials who cited the amendment in refusing to release crime records (Overbeck & Pullen, 1991).

Still, release of information at educational institutions is a very sensitive area as a result of the Buckley Amendment. Personnel on the public relations staff, in the SID's office, or in other departments that disseminate information about students to the media must be careful to explain the potential ramifications and to obtain complete approval before writing media guides, news releases, or promotional materials. The law does not forbid an institution to request such information from the student-athlete and to indicate the consequences for the participant. However, schools cannot deny the right to participate in intercollegiate athletics to a student who does not sign the approval form.

Sunshine laws

All 50 states in the United States have open-records and open-meetings laws. Similar to FOIA and the Sunshine Act, they give the public access to records and meetings of state and local governmental agencies, boards, and commissions of all kinds. They also limit access to information covered in state privacy laws and permit closed or "executive" sessions on sensitive or private issues. For example, many open-records and open-meetings acts exempt investigative records of law-enforcement agencies and juvenile courts. The laws vary considerably from state to state. They cover a broad range of records and meetings in some states and allow few exemptions. They open a few specific records and meetings in others and sanction broad exemptions. Copies of the laws can be opened from the office of the attorney general in each state.

To cite an example, Kentucky's open-records and open-meetings acts provide insight into the kinds of information and meetings such laws may cover. Kentucky gives any person the right to inspect all records of public agencies, unless those records fall under an exemption (Bensenhaver, 1996). Books, papers, maps, photographs, cards, tapes, CDs, disks, recordings, and other documentary materials all are classified as public records. Exemptions include records containing personal information that would constitute an invasion of privacy; confidential records connected to loan applications, regulation of a business, or review of a license; records relating to the prospective location of a business or industry; real estate appraisals, engineering, or feasibility estimates and evaluations of property until the property has been acquired; test questions, scoring keys, and data used in administering licensing, employment, or academic exams before they are administered; records of law enforcement agencies, if disclosure would hinder an investigation; and preliminary drafts, notes, and correspondence used in formation of policy.

Most of the exemptions protect records during the decision-making process only. For example, arrest reports are open. Other documents filed in connection with the investigation of a crime are not open until the case is completed. The law would protect records of negotiations on a sports broadcast deal at a university but would open the contract to public inspection after it is signed. The law also would prohibit disclosure of résumés of candidates for coaching positions or discussions of the purchase of property for a stadium until a coach is named or a site purchased. However, none of the exceptions would at any time enable the athletics department to withhold records related to the athletics budget.

Subject to the open-records law are every state and local government officer, department, and legislative board; every county and city governing body, school district board, special district board, and municipal corporation; every state or local government created by state or local statute, executive order, ordinance, resolution, or other legislative act; and any group that receives 25% of its funds from state or local authority (Bensenhaver, 1996). All state-funded elementary and secondary schools, colleges, and universities in the commonwealth receive at least that much. Public agencies, including educational institutions, must respond to a request—by citing an exception or granting access to the records—within three working days. Anyone who is denied access can appeal to the state attorney general or file a lawsuit challenging the decision. If the public agency loses, the agency must pay all the person's legal costs. The court also may award the person as much as $25 per day for each day that access to the records was denied (Bensenhaver, 1996).

The state open-meetings law is similar. The law permits any person to attend meetings of public agencies at which public business is discussed or action is taken. The agency can go into a closed session if officials explain the general nature of the topic to be discussed and cite a specific exemption from the law. Among the exemptions are deliberations of the state parole board; deliberations on the sale or acquisition of property if publicity would affect the value of the property; discussions of pending litigation; grand or petit jury sessions; collective bargaining sessions; hearings that might lead to the appointment, dismissal, or discipline of an employee, member, or student; and discussions between an agency and a business that might jeopardize a deal.

Among those subject to the law are school district boards, the policy-making board of educational institutions and boards, commissions, committees, and advisory councils. An athletics department would be excluded. However, any action that required approval of the Board of Regents would be covered, meaning that the athletics department can interview candidates for coaching positions in private. All the same, the meeting at which the Board of Regents votes to hire a candidate must be open to the public.

Meetings or hearings on internal disciplinary action are protected in Kentucky. Of course, journalists may still press for information on why an athlete does not dress for a game, but athletics officials do not have to state a reason. If they choose to reveal that an athlete has been suspended for disciplinary reasons, they do not have to explain the reasons. If a student accuses an employee of sexual harassment, the athletics department and board of regents can discuss the threat of litigation in private. If the board takes action, the complaint must be revealed. If the student files a lawsuit, the document is a public record, open to press scrutiny. Any agency that violates the open-meetings law is subject to penalties, including costs and attorneys' fees and a fine of $100 for each violation.

Open-records and open-meetings laws are a rich source of information for journalists daily. Although these laws vary considerably from state to state, most exclude records and meetings that would jeopardize a decision-making process or invade individual privacy. They typically prohibit release of information from medical files, tax records, and other documents that might reveal embarrassing details about an individual's personal habits, health, or financial status. On the other hand, most limit the closing of crime records, court records, and judicial proceedings based on the concept that such business should be conducted openly to assure the public that justice is served. Most also provide penalties for agencies or officials who attempt to keep files or meetings secret.

The open-records and open-meetings laws affect only public institutions. They do not cover private businesses, such as professional teams or private schools. That is why professional teams are not required to disclose financial statements, and private institutions can conduct all meetings in private. Private business meetings and private business records seldom are open to the public. Because private business owners spend their own and/or their investors' money (not public dollars), the law recognizes that their business generally is none of the public's business. A limited amount of financial information may be available through records of the federal Securities and Exchange Commission if the business sells stock, but little else is open to the public.

Privacy laws

Many states also have privacy laws on the books. These laws specify types of information protected by statute—primarily information that might embarrass someone, put an individual at risk of harm, or damage an individual's business. State privacy laws typically recognize a right to privacy and define it in terms similar to actions that constitute invasion of privacy in civil law (see next section).

Regulatory agencies

Professional leagues, conference offices, and other groups with which sport organizations affiliate sometimes establish policies that force or restrict access to information about the group or individual members. For example, a league may restrict release of information about drug test results until team or league officials take action.

The major governing bodies for collegiate sports—the National Collegiate Athletic Association, the National Association of Intercollegiate Athletics, and the National Junior College Athletic Association—also make some effort to control the release of information. The National Collegiate Athletic Association prohibits school officials from talking about a potential recruit until the athlete signs a letter of intent, nor can the coach pose with the recruit for a photograph of the signing. On the other hand, the NCAA requires member institutions to reveal collective grade point averages and graduation rates. NCAA schools also must release comparisons on participation, scholarships and financial grants, budget allotments, and expenditures for male and female athletes.

Institutional policies

Individual sport organizations may add restrictions on access to those imposed by law or regulatory policy. Private colleges *can* adopt a totally closed policy if they so choose; they also can muzzle the campus media because the First Amendment prohibits the government—not private businesses—from imposing restraints.

Both public and private high school administrators can censor their newspapers, radio stations, and TV stations as a result of the U.S. Supreme Court decision in *Hazelwood School District v. Kuhlmeier* in 1988. The high court upheld the principal of Hazelwood East High School in Missouri, who had censored two articles. Justice Byron White said in the majority opinion that high school educators could exercise editorial control over school-sponsored activities "so long as their actions are reasonably related to legitimate pedagogical concerns" (Overbeck & Pullen, 1991).

Public schools also may develop policies that incorporate the dictates of the Family Educational Rights and Privacy Act. The Northern Kentucky University Student Handbook combines restrictions from the Buckley Amendment and state confidentiality statutes. The handbook explains categories of officials to whom records may be released and the circumstances under which such disclosures can occur. The policy statement also specifies procedures for granting permission for release, changes in incorrect information, and appeals to the NKU Educational Rights and Privacy Hearing Committee.

The sports information professional should gather and keep on file copies of all documents related to access. As noted, state open-meetings and open-records laws, the rules of regulatory bodies, and institutional policies may vary widely. When an SID or public relations director takes a new job, one of the first priorities should be to get a copy of the sunshine laws from the state statutes (available in any library), a guidebook from the league or sanctioning body, and a policy statement or handbook from the sport organization.

| **Publication and Broadcast** | The First Amendment guarantee of freedom of the press comes with certain limitations. It does not give the press the right to lie about someone, to publicize every detail of a person's life, or to use someone's likeness or work without permission. Private citizens, and public figures in some cases, can file civil lawsuits if the media damage their reputations or publicly embarrass them by revealing personal information. |

Civil redress is possible only after the fact. Whereas some of the laws, regulations, and policies addressed in the previous section attempt to prevent publication or broadcast by closing records, civil actions cannot be pursued before an offense occurs. Once the material is printed or broadcast, however, a person or business may file a lawsuit.

Civil law deals with conflicts between individuals rather than with violations of statutes or ordinances. A judge or jury decides whose rights prevail in a given case. Different juries might rule for different parties in similar cases. In addition, the law evolves case by case—as each case compares with similar cases in the past—and patterns may change as the makeup of courts changes—therefore, generalizing about legal remedies against the media difficult, but it is safe to say that a student, an athlete, a citizen, or a business can recover damages for publication or broadcast of information that is defamatory, embarrassing, or pirated (copyright violation) under certain conditions.

The primary legal actions that affect the work of sports information specialists and sports journalists are libel and slander, invasion of privacy, and copyright infringement. Libel and slander deal with untrue statements that damage an individual's reputation. Invasion of privacy involves an individual's right to be left alone. Copyright infringement relates to ownership of pictures, film, music, or printed matter. Libel/slander and invasion of privacy are of much greater importance to journalists than to sports information professionals, because the emphasis of the latter is on maintaining a positive image. Sport's information professionals are not likely to disclose sensitive personal information about members of the organization or to make derogatory remarks about them. Copyright laws are of equal concern to all who use materials gathered from other sources from time to time.

Libel and slander

Libel and slander are legal terms for what is commonly called "defamation of character." Information in a story may defame someone if it is untrue and damages the person's reputation or business.

Technically, libel is a method of defamation through print, writing, pictures, or signs. Slander is the speaking of base and defamatory words tending to prejudice in the reputation(s) for another person or persons (Wong, 1991): defamatory statements, pictures, or signs use language or symbols that accuse people of wrongdoing, disparage their social habits or business practices, or suggest they are incompetent or mentally ill.

In practical application, libel and slander both are methods of defamation—the former in print, writing, pictures, or signs; the latter in oral expression or transitory gesture. Bailey and Matthews (1989) point out that "oral, temporary defamation is slander; written, relatively permanent defamation is libel." Bruce Sanford, a partner with Baker & Hostetler in Washington, DC, and author of media law books, incorporates both in his definition of libel: "A libel is a false statement printed or broadcast about a person which tends to bring that person into public hatred, contempt or ridicule or to injure him in his business or occupation" (p. 6).

Libel and slander generally are state issues, not constitutional concerns. Laws vary from state to state but generally incorporate two common principles. First, to be libelous, the information must be false. In most states, information is not considered libelous if it is true. Although truth is not an absolute defense, a plaintiff will find it difficult to win a libel case if the thrust of the information (the damaging details) is true. Second, the information must be damaging. If the information is false but not damaging—a misidentified player in a game, for example—no libel occurs.

Individuals and corporations can sue for damages to their reputation or business operations. They may sue anyone who contributes to the libel, including the publisher and the radio station or television station owner. The burden of proof falls on the plaintiff, the person who files the lawsuit. What a plaintiff must prove in court to win the lawsuit varies from state to state. A plaintiff may have to prove some combination of the following elements:

- Publication: the libelous statement was communicated to others.

- Identification: people recognized the plaintiff, even if the person was not named.

- Defamation: the statement damaged the person's reputation.

- Fault: there was careless handling of the facts, either through negligence or actual malice, by the defendant(s).

- Falsity: the statement in some part represented matters of public concern.

- Damages: there was actual injury in the form of out-of-pocket losses, impairment of reputation, humiliation, or mental anguish.

The element of fault relates to the status of the individual, as defined by law. As noted earlier, the *New York Times v. Sullivan* (1964) case and subsequent U.S. Supreme Court rulings created different standards for private individuals and public officials or public figures. The Sullivan decision held that public officials and public figures must prove "actual malice," that is, something more than a simple mistake resulting in a false statement. Contrary to what the phrase might suggest, "actual malice" does not involve ill will or intent to harm. Fedler (1996) says actual malice can occur when the defendant

- knew the facts would raise questions about truth,

- refused to examine information that would determine the truth or falsity of the charge,

- relied on an unbelievable source,

- published an improbable story without investigation, or

- simply fabricated the story.

In most states, a private individual need only prove *negligence*, that the defendant did not take the steps a reasonable person would take to determine the truth or falsity of the information. However, some states require the plaintiff to prove actual malice to recover *punitive damages*, that is, damages for mental anguish.

Supreme Court decisions also created distinctions between private individuals, public figures, and public officials. *Public officials* include elected officials, political candidates, police officers, judges, and others who "have substantial responsibility for governmental affairs," according to Sanford (1984, p. 11). Only those with "substantial influence" qualify, not every government employee. Although part of the funding for an athletics director's salary might come from state (government) funds, the athletics director would not necessarily be considered a public official. It would depend on the amount of influence the official wields within the university.

The U.S. Supreme Court defined the standard of proof for private individuals in *Gertz v. Welch* in 1974. In ruling that a Chicago lawyer was a private individual "who had achieved no general fame or notoriety," the court said he need prove only that the story was false and defamatory as a result of carelessness by the writer. Mencher (2000) concludes that the decision returned emphasis to "the plaintiff's status rather than the subject matter."

Mencher translates the legal language in *New York Times v. Sullivan* and subsequent U.S. Supreme Court rulings into the following categories of public people who must prove actual malice:

> Public Officials: Government employees who have responsibility for government activities—elected officials, candidates for political office, appointed officials such as judges, police officers, and some others engaged in the criminal justice system. The Supreme Court has said that not all public employees are public officials.

> Public Figures: People who have considerable power and influence and those who have "voluntarily thrust" themselves into public controversy. Newspaper columnists, television personalities, and some celebrities who seek to influence the public are included. But not all prominent people are included. (2000, p. 655)

The celebrity and visibility of TV actors, movie stars, and sports figures often put them in the category of pervasive power and influence. Social and political activists, people who take public stands on controversial issues, fit into the second category. Neither category is well defined, which leaves it to judges or jurors to determine whether a plaintiff is a private individual or a public figure. Sanford cites instances in which a football coach and a sportswriter were adjudged to be public figures and a case in which a harness-racing driver was ruled a nonpublic figure. As noted earlier, the distinction can make a difference in the decision, as in the Lexington *Herald Leader* case. The most significant battle in court, in some instances, is over the private/public status of the plaintiff.

Printing or broadcasting a correction will not get the offender off the hook in most states. A retraction will limit the amount of damages in most to *actual damages*, that is, monetary loss.

The primary defenses against libel are truth, fair comment, and qualified privilege. The courts have held that citizens are entitled to make "fair comment and criticism" of public officials. Middleton and Chamberlin (1991) say criticism must relate "to matters of widespread public interest" (p. 167) to be protected by the common law privilege of fair comment. In other words, citizens can offer opinions on an official's performance—that is a foundation of democratic government. However, the protection does not give citizens license to engage in character assassination or to distort facts to support the opinion. The comment and criticism must focus on public performance or activities in office, not personal matters. To call a coach a lousy strategist would constitute fair comment and criticism; to call a coach a drunk would not, even if that conclusion was expressed as opinion by the writer or commentator.

A decision in a sports case eliminated blanket protection for stories clearly identified as opinion, such as in a sports column. Mike Milkovich, a wrestling coach at Maple Heights High School in suburban Cleveland, sued Ted Diadun and the Willoughby *News Herald* over a sports column in which Diadun opined that Milkovich lied at a hearing over suspension of a wrestler. Lawyers for the defendants argued that the comments were clearly the opinion of the sportswriter. The court ruled in favor of Milkovich, saying that the statement implied a fact, that is, people could interpret the opinion as a statement of fact (Sanford, 1990). In other words, readers of the column might believe that Milkovich had indeed told a lie.

Reporters enjoy qualified privilege or absolute protection against lawsuits when reporting on judicial proceedings, legislative sessions, and official documents. The protection covers virtually all levels of government. A journalist can report the accusations in a lawsuit without fear of a libel suit because a lawsuit (a legal action) is a public record.

Publishers and broadcasters obviously do not relish the prospect of a libel lawsuit. They provide journalists with handbooks that summarize the law, and conduct seminars to update them on recent cases. Rarely does a journalist purposely damage someone's reputation and fabricate facts to do so. The duty of reporting the news to the public carries with it an obligation not to interfere with the rights of others. Libelous statements occur most often because of carelessness, sloppiness, or haste on deadline. The journalist may get false information from a normally reliable source, fail to check out data supplied by a source, or offer opinion not easily discernible from the facts. Libel suits often result from direct quotations, statements made by sources in stories. The journalist and the media organization are responsible for *all* statements, no matter who makes them; that responsibility places a heavy burden on broadcast journalists, particularly during live interviews. Talk-show hosts often use a delay mechanism, which enables them to bleep or block out comments before they go over the airways. Still, the host must be able to recognize libelous statements and act quickly.

Journalists and sports information personnel should double-check all statements that might damage someone's reputation. If the SID is in doubt about the truth of the statements, he or she should leave them out. It is also important to be careful with use of some words. Some words are libelous per se—libelous on their face, such as thief, adulterer, crook, drug addict, drunk, liar, or swindler, if false. University officials must be careful of what they say about players or coaches dismissed from a team if the dismissal involved allegations of wrongdoing but no conviction on charges.

Invasion of Privacy Laws

Whereas libel laws protect an individual's right to a good reputation, invasion-of-privacy laws protect one's right to be left alone. Invasion-of-privacy torts only apply to private individuals and personal matters. Public officials effectively give up most privacy rights when they step into the public spotlight. Public matters, such as those covered by open-records legislation, also are excluded. Invasion of privacy applies only to those people and those subjects that are of none of the public's business.

Invasion-of-privacy lawsuits against the media are relatively new. The U.S. Constitution does not guarantee a right to privacy. However, states began adopting privacy laws in the early 1900s after Samuel D. Warren and Louis D. Brandeis argued for a right to privacy in common law or statutory law in an article in the *Harvard Law Review* in 1890. They were concerned that members of the press were trampling on individual rights. In 1960, legal scholar William Prosser set forth four categories of privacy, which form the foundation for invasion-of-privacy lawsuits. A discussion of these can be found on pages 144–145 of Overbeck & Pullen (1991).

1. Intrusion: This constitutes invading someone's personal property or private space. Journalists must have permission to go onto someone's private property; otherwise, they may be intruding. They also may intrude if they take pictures of people in private places, and they may intrude into someone's personal space if they constantly follow that to take pictures of his or her every move. The restrictions generally do not apply to public places or public events. For example, taking a picture of the victim of an accident is not intrusion because it occurs before the public eye. Taking a picture of an athlete during a game would not constitute invasion of privacy. Shooting a picture of the athlete in a sauna at home might.

2. Disclosure of private matters: The courts have ruled that the information must be "highly offensive to reasonable people," not just embarrassing, to constitute an invasion of privacy. Private matters subject to litigation might include physical health, mental health, sexual habits, idiosyncrasies, and business affairs. The facts must be private to qualify.

3. False light: An individual is cast in a false light if the journalist distorts the facts or puts the person in an unreal situation that creates a false impression. A journalist might run the risk of portraying an athlete in a false light in a fictionalized account of a true story. A sports information director or sports photographer might put an athlete in a false light by using a picture from one event to illustrate a point in another story; for example, running a picture of an athlete talking to someone in a dark alley in connection with a story about shady practices of sports agents might cast the athlete in a false light.

4. Appropriation: No one can use the name, picture or likeness of another person for personal gain without permission. The most common type of appropriation is use of a celebrity's picture on T-shirts, calendars, or other commercial products. A photographer who shoots news pictures of star athletes cannot sell copies, make picture books, or otherwise use the pictures for commercial gain.

Similarly, publicists cannot use pictures of athletes for calendars, promotions, or advertisements without permission of the student and the NCAA.

Statutes in every state protect against appropriation. However, state laws differ on how many of the other three privacy categories they recognize. The primary defenses are newsworthiness and consent. Newsworthiness corresponds to public interest; in other words, the matter is not private because it is of public interest. However, persuading a jury that publication of salacious details of an athlete's private life is of public interest could be risky. Consent is the best defense against invasion of privacy, particularly appropriation. It is virtually impossible for a plaintiff to win an invasion-of-privacy lawsuit if he or she has a signed a consent form.

Sports information professionals can guard against invasion-of-privacy complaints by asking members of the sport organization to sign consent forms or releases as noted earlier in the chapter. Such forms should specify how information and pictures may be used. The sports journalist also can avoid invasion-of-privacy complaints by securing written consent for the use of private information and pictures outside normal sports reporting activities.

Federal Communications Commission rules

Broadcasters have to obey some rules that their counterparts in the print media do not, because the Federal Communications Commission licenses and regulates radio and television stations. The FCC can revoke a station's license if it does not follow the rules.

Because radio and TV are easily accessible to children, the FCC can act against indecent content. The FCC can fine a station or revoke the license if disc jockeys, announcers, or talk-show hosts use indecent language.

Television stations have become even more aware of the FCC's rules after the organization severely punished CBS after the network aired on live national television the infamous "wardrobe malfunction" during the Super Bowl XXXVIII halftime show February 1, 2004, involving singers Janet Jackson and Justin Timberlake. Viacom, which owned CBS at the time, received a record fine of more than $500,000 by the FCC and the ripple effect has led to tighter control of live television broadcasts.

Copyright

This provides legal protection for copyright. Every person has a right to control the use and sale of materials he or she creates. The individual has a right to sell them, rent them, or give them away, but copyright gives the owner the right to make that choice.

The federal copyright act, enacted in 1976 and revised in 1978, protects literary works, musical works, dramatic works, photographs, paintings, sculptures, recordings, movies, and radio and TV broadcasts. Sports information personnel and newspapers can copyright their work. However, no one can copyright the news. All a newspaper can copyright is the account of the news—for example, the story and the pictures.

The copyright effectively gives an individual property rights over particular material. The copyright holder holds exclusive rights to make a profit from the work. The owner may sell the work, rent it, or charge a fee for its use. For example, anyone can produce a copyrighted play, use a musical composition, or reproduce a book by paying a *royalty fee*. Failure to pay the fee, or infringement on copyright, can result in civil litigation and a demand for some payment for damages, such as the amount of money collected from illegal use of the material.

Both sports information specialists and journalists must pay attention to copyrights when gathering information from other sources for stories or publications. The federal copyright act does permit "fair use" of a limited amount of copyrighted material. The Fair Use Doctrine allows the copying of a small portion of copyrighted information for educational, research, reportorial, and artistic-criticism purposes, but guidelines on how much of a document can be copied are ambiguous. Therefore, the best course of action is to seek permission of the copyright owner for use of any materials. The print journalist and the sports information director should attain permission for the use of information, cartoons, sketches, photographs, or other materials drawn from magazines or other publications. The broadcast journalist and the SID must get permission or pay royalties for the use of musical recordings, clips from TV broadcasts, and so on, for music or film incorporated in a production.

Trademark

Like a copyright, a trademark is a property rights construction. A trademark is a name, logo, or phrase used to identify a business or its product. The federal Lanham Trademark Act (July 5, 1946) gives exclusive rights to the name, logo, or phrase to the business that registers it. Ronald B. Smith (1996) compares trademarks to cattle brands in that they identify the owner—in this case, the owner of the product. Consequently, the trademark law does not attempt to limit use of the information, as copyright laws do; rather, trademark law ensures that the product will be identified with the proper owner.

For example, Styrofoam® is the trademark for a specific brand of plastic foam materials. It is not the generic name for all such plastic cups, plates, and so on. If journalists and the general public begin to label all such products as Styrofoam®, the manufacturer will lose its identity; additionally, other companies that make similar products may profit from the identification with Styrofoam®. Anyone can use the Styrofoam® trademark name without permission. However, journalists and sports information specialists should take care that the plastic materials thus designated are indeed made by Styrofoam®. The news media generally are protected in reporting names and in using logos with stories about teams, as long as they use the trademark designation (®). Sports information directors can prevent pirating of promotional materials by registering a trademark. Professional conferences, amateur leagues, collegiate conferences, and individual schools frequently register their names and logos for advertising and promotional purposes. Using the trademark of another entity can result in a civil lawsuit.

Licensing agreements

Licensing agreements may govern anything from broadcast rights to product sales. As noted in earlier chapters, broadcast rights are complex agreements that may involve the local team or school, league, and media organizations. Leagues and conferences may also forge agreements related to control and distribution of profits for sale of franchise (league or school) materials.

Athletics administrators generally negotiate the agreements. They have little impact on the work of sports information specialists beyond the dictates of the agreement.

Ethics

Everyone agrees that both sports information professionals and journalists should go about their business ethically, but what does ethically mean in the context of sports? What kinds of ethical situations do SIDs and journalists face? To whom do they look for ethical guidance?

Ethics in sports, as well as in life itself, is a philosophy of morality. In practical application, ethics is a standard of conduct and moral values that governs the behavior and practices of a particular person or business. It is the sense of right and wrong. It is not what one does, but rather what one ought to do. Goodwin (1994) says the law determines what journalists are allowed to do, whereas ethics deals with what journalists ought to do. Ethics answers the question of why. It is the mental process through which an individual or a group makes value judgments on the proper course of action to take in a given situation. Consistent judgments and behavior compose a moral standard.

The moral standards that guide personal and business decisions in the United States are based on a number of factors, including religious foundations, societal concepts of right and wrong, and personal beliefs and attitudes. Societal concepts of right and wrong are an outgrowth of ideas presented by religious leaders, philosophers, poets, and prophets on the nature of humankind and the role of the individual in society. Because some of the religious ideas, philosophies, and treatises on society do not agree, no universal set of ethical rules exists. Countries, corporations, and individuals formulate their own ethical principles based on the factors mentioned previously.

Goodwin (1994) titled his book on the subject *Groping for Ethics in Journalism* because he believes the profession in the United States—relatively young at an age of 200 years—has not settled on an ethical posture suitable to all. Ethical standards are evolving as journalists sort through various ethical constructs as those constructs relate to the concept of democracy. Buzzwords such as "the public's right to know," "social responsibility," and "situational ethics" fill the air when the media take different stances on ethical questions and support their positions with ideas from different philosophies.

At the root of the idea of a public's right to know are the foundations of democratic government. The framers of the United States Constitution were heavily influenced by thinkers of the English Enlightenment, particularly John Milton, a 17th-century poet and philosopher. Milton believed in individual rights, and that the individual had the ability to discern the truth. The way to truth was knowledge or information. The best way to obtain knowledge was through "a marketplace of ideas," that is, an examination of the ideas presented by as many people as possible. He advocated a free press as a means for people to express their ideas and to contribute to the common knowledge. The press represented a partner in the "marketplace of ideas" and served as a watchdog on government abuses of the people. Journalists who ascribe to Milton's philosophy therefore believe that all information is good, even negative information, because it leads to the truth. They justify printing or broadcasting any kind of information, including pictures, on the grounds that it presents a real or truthful account of the event.

Other journalists rely on common sense or a sense of what best serves society, an approach based on the utilitarian principles espoused by Jeremy Bentham and John Stuart Mill in the late 1700s and early 1800s. Bentham and Mill believed that societal decisions should reflect the "greatest good for the greatest number of people." Utilitarians weigh the benefits or harm to society against the benefits or harm to individuals in making decisions, and Utilitarians judge each case on its own merits using those criteria. Making decisions based on the merits of a particular situation is called *situational ethics*. Those who embrace situational ethics might print the name of an athlete charged with sexual battery in one case and, in another, decide not to use the name.

Inconsistencies in media ethics and the sensationalistic practices of the early 1900s gave rise to the concept of *social responsibility*. The term grew out of a study of the media by a commission headed by Robert Hutchins, chancellor of the University of Chicago in the 1940s. The Hutchins Commission, composed of scholars, political scientists, and politicians, concluded that the media had strayed from the purpose envisioned for it by America's founders; that is, providing information the public needs to make wise decisions about operation of the government. The commission recommended that the press strive to provide the following:

- A truthful, comprehensive, and intelligent account of the news of the day in a context which gives them meaning

- A forum for the exchange of comment and criticism

- A representative picture of the constituent groups in the society

- The presentation and clarification of the goals and values of society

- Full access to the day's intelligence (Goodwin, 1994, p. 15, from Peterson, 1956, p. 88)

The right to know, situational ethics, and social responsibility are part of a loose conglomeration of philosophical concepts applied to American journalism by publishers and broadcasters. Some believe the media do not have the moral right to pry into the private affairs of people, even if those people are public officials.

Others view prying as a public responsibility of journalists. One newspaper or TV station may print rumors and sordid details of an orgy involving members of an athletics team based on the belief that the media serve an information-gathering role in the public's right to know. Another newspaper or TV station may withhold such details until formal charges are filed, out of a sense of social responsibility. One may play the story prominently—on the front page or at the top of the newscast; the other may mention the story only briefly in the sports section or sports news at the end of the newscast. Both approaches can be justified ethically, but inconsistencies in the behavior of different media in the same situations give the impression that media in the United States, collectively, possess neither moral values nor professional ethical standards.

The ethical practices of public relations professionals and journalists fall at various points between two poles. At one end are those who believe in no government restrictions on the media and no restraints on content. They argue that such freedom serves society well, because it peels away every layer of government secrecy. They also believe the individual nature of the media creates a wide range of information and opinion that serves the public well. At the other pole are those who believe freedom of the press carries enormous societal responsibilities. They contend the media must be accountable to the public and act responsibly. They believe the way to serve the public well is to act with constraint and compassion on matters that intrude on individual privacy, while vigorously examining the workings of government. Sometimes those responsibilities conflict, as in, for instance, the public's right to know about the firing of a coach and the coach's right to privacy in dealing with a drinking problem.

No universal set of guidelines exists because journalism is not a profession in the purest sense of the word. True professions, such as medicine, require aspiring practitioners to complete a prescribed educational curriculum or training program. The student must pass a licensing or certification test to gain entry into the profession, and the tests are designed to weed out those who are incompetent. Professions create standards of conduct, with penalties for violations. The punishment for serious violations is revocation of the individual's license and banishment from the profession.

Journalists in the United States have long resisted licensing or any form of regulation. Journalists, on the whole, value individuality. They resist any constraints on freedom of the press, and they view freedom and individuality as strengths—the diversity an effective "marketplace of ideas" demands. Still, journalists have initiated a number of serious efforts to bring some order and ethical consistency to their work in the 20th century. Professional trade associations, such as the Public Relations Society of America (PRSA) and the Society of Professional Journalists (SPJ), have developed codes of conduct for members. The problem is that these organizations serve only members of the association, not the profession as a whole. Furthermore, only the PRSA code includes an enforcement mechanism to penalize members who violate the standards. As a result, ethical standards remain an individual concern (Goodwin, 1994). Each media organization is free to adopt its own standards. Some do impose penalties, including dismissal, for violation of company policies; for others, the ethical standard is the individual conscience of the journalist on the scene.

The lack of a licensing system and universal set of guidelines does not mean the journalism professions are amoral or immoral. Inherent in their self-concept or sense of professionalism is an unwritten, widely accepted set of standards such as honesty, accuracy, objectivity, fairness, and so on. The preceding chapters have consistently echoed those themes in discussions of the working relationships and practices of both sports information professionals and sports journalists. The overwhelming majority of practitioners in both professions would say that ethics is equal in importance to writing skills when it comes to their chosen careers. One cannot succeed without either, because credibility as a journalist is built on honesty and fair play. Likewise, school athletics administrators and representatives of professional sport franchises must be ethical in all dealings with the media. If a practitioner does not lie, then he or she does not have to remember what he or she said. If a practitioner does lie and does not remember, he or she will expose the deceit eventually. Deceit damages a practitioner's reputation.

Administrators must be consistent in all dealings with members of the media, and ties should never let the personality of media personnel influence their decisions in disseminating information to the media. They must make consistent decisions and live with the consequences, regardless of public reaction. If the sport organization adopts an open communication policy, administrators will have to acknowledge NCAA violations and other mistakes made by athletes and coaches. However, they can be secure in the knowledge that from an ethical standpoint such acknowledgement is the right course of action.

Although working practitioners may not be able to recite the PRSA or SPJ code of ethics, they probably can express what it means to be a professional. Here are some of the broad characteristics professionals have emphasized throughout this text:

Ethical Guidelines
Honesty
Truthfulness
Respect
Compassion
Fairness
Accuracy
Professional distance
Ethical models

Ethical Guidelines

Honesty

Honesty tops the list. Members of sport organizations and the media should deal honestly with one another and should expect the same treatment in return. Without compromising values, each can take action that exposes or penalizes an unethical member. Unethical members do not last long in either profession, because both put such a high premium on honesty.

Truthfulness

Truthfulness is allied with honesty. Honesty applies to the working relationship, whereas truthfulness relates to the actual practices of sports information directors and sports journalists. The sports information director does not put false or misleading information in a news release or call a press conference just to get media attention. The SID or public relations director also tells journalists when he or she cannot disclose information. In turn, the journalist does not fabricate or exaggerate the facts, nor does he or she mislead sports information personnel or athletics officials about the purpose of an interview or inquiry.

Respect

An effective working relationship depends on mutual respect. Each party should respect that the other is a professional trying to do a difficult job. Out of respect, each party overlooks trivial complaints and forgives unintentional mistakes.

Respect also applies to sources and to the public. The journalist should not badger or browbeat sources for information. Athletes and administrators should not carp; members of sports organizations and media companies must remember that they are public servants of sorts in the information business. They should put public interest before self-interest in all that they do.

Compassion

The nature of news throws journalists and sports information specialists together in many difficult situations. Both parties deal with athletes at emotional extremes—the heights of success and the depths of defeat. They also deal with people in the most agonizing of personal situations, from firings to deaths in the family. All such professionals should take care to treat people with concern and compassion in difficult emotional times.

Fairness

A professional working relationship also demands fairness. The sports information director must try to give all the media the same information, the same access to members of the sport organization, and the same considerations for special requests. The SID cannot play favorites. Neither can the journalist. The journalist should treat all members of the sport organization fairly, both in personal relationships and in story and broadcast.

Accuracy

Both sports information specialists and sports journalists are in the business of providing information to the public. If the information cannot be trusted, neither can the sport organization or the journalist. From the public perspective, accuracy is an anchor in the foundation of honesty.

Professional Distance

Mutual respect goes too far if it extends to practices that compromise the professional distance essential to an effective working relationship. Sports information personnel should avoid sponsoring junkets or parties for the media or giving them lavish gifts. Journalists should not accept lavish gifts or free trips. Today, most sports journalists pay for their own airline tickets instead of flying for free on a team or school charter. In short, they pay their own way to avoid the appearance of a conflict of interest or favoritism. Journalists also should avoid cheering in the press box or showing any hint of support for a team, even if they are beat reporters assigned to one of the teams. Reporters cannot help secretly pulling for teams they cover regularly; showing it, however, is a breach of ethics.

Ethical Models

Within the broad characteristics of professionalism, journalists find a lot of room to wiggle and little help in making decisions. They sometimes must rely on their sense of right and wrong. In the Summer 1989 issue of *Hiram* [College] *Magazine*, Ellen Potter of television station WKYC in Cleveland addressed the dilemma, saying that people are guided by their own definitions of ethics.

In addition, people's definitions may vary slightly because of the unique nature of the medium in which they work. Print reporters and broadcast journalists frequently make different decisions regarding sensitive pictures because of differences in the impact of their work. A printed picture has a lasting impact, because people can look at it over and over. The impact of a TV video clip is more shocking at first glance, but the image disappears quickly. Therefore, television reporters are far more likely to use a shocking picture, such as the victim of an accident, than are print journalists. Furthermore, print journalists do not have to worry about ratings. The TV journalist must deal with ratings pressure constantly because of the need for advertising revenue, and that puts greater pressure on the TV journalist to come up with an exclusive, to beat the competition.

In the *Hiram Magazine*, David Arnold, a photojournalist at WEWS in Cleveland, said he refuses to photograph victims without permission. Cleveland TV personality Robin Swoboda was asked if she ever refused an assignment because she found the guidelines given to her to be unethical. She replied, "I'll just look for a different angle."

Still, journalists feel pressured to meet deadlines at the expense of accuracy. Potter resists, and never lets facts go unconfirmed. "Anything that is unclear doesn't go on the air," she said in the magazine. Added former Channel 8 news director Virgil Dominnic, "Because of the impact of television, there is reason to be careful of what is on the air."

Trying to be fair also is difficult under deadline pressure. "True objectivity is possible when reporting on some subjects, the one I'm ambivalent about, it's tough, sometimes, but it's possible," Potter said in the same publication. She said a reporter can achieve true objectivity by sticking to the facts and turning off personal feelings.

Tom Gaffney, sportswriter for the Akron *Beacon Journal*, said ethics should be a reflex action, drawing from the unconscious of a reporter rather than the conscious (Nichols, 1996). Reporters should not have to think ethically, but rather should do their entire job as both writers and editors. Accuracy should be an everyday goal, and privacy should be respected. Reporters should treat sources as sources, not as friends.

David Glasier of the Lake County *News Herald* covered Division I college basketball for several years and is both a movie and television critic. He recommends "an atmosphere of mutual candor with the sports media" (Nichols, 1996).

"Deal straight with busy reporters, and they will deal straight with you," he said. "Do not favor one reporter over another in distribution of basic information.

"On the other hand, if a reporter exhibits enterprise in coming up with a story or angle on a story other reporters do not have access to, do not share that information and ruin the exclusive. Also, make judicious use of requests to go 'off the record' with reporters."

These reflections from working journalists illustrate the difficulty in applying general guidelines endorsed by all. In light of this, where does the journalist turn when his or her conscience says two options are right choices or the only options are bad ones? What does the journalist do when personal moral principles conflict? Philosopher Sissela Bok offers a three-step model for ethical decision making in *Lying: Moral Choice in Public and Private Life:*

1. Consult your own conscience first. How do you feel about the action?

2. Seek expert advice for alternatives to the act creating the ethical problem. Is there another way to achieve the same goal that will not raise ethical issues?

3. Conduct an ethical discussion with the parties involved in the dispute. The discussion can include those directly and indirectly influenced by the decision. How will my action affect others? (quoted in Patterson & Wilkins, 1991, p. 4)

Talking to the parties involved might shed a different light on how an ethical decision might affect these parties. The Paducah (KY) *Sun* once elected not to run a story in the 1970s about a married coach accused of having an affair with a student, because the newspaper's editors did not want to invade the coach's private life and perhaps damage his reputation. The coach had told a sports reporter that school officials had offered to keep the matter quiet if he would resign. He chose not to resign, insisting the accusation was a lie. He wanted to see a story in the newspaper, because the community was rife with rumors. He wanted to voice his innocence, and he feared the board would remove him arbitrarily if the public was not aware of the controversy. The coach's viewpoint relieved ethical concerns about the impact of the story on his family and his reputation, but editors still opted to wait until the board took some action. The board never acted, he remained coach, and no story about the accusations appeared.

Expert advice also can help, in two respects. First, expert help can suggest alternatives. It also can provide direction on what course of action peers usually take in similar circumstances. Expert advice is readily available from the codes of conduct developed by professional associations. Most professional associations—e.g., the Public Relations Society of America, the Society of Professional Journalists, the American Society of Newspaper Editors and Radio and Television News Directors Association—have codes of conduct.

Summary

The general public often views members of the media as ruthless people who play loose with the facts and purposely invade people's private lives to damage their reputations. They regard journalists as immoral people with no compassion for others and no respect for traditional American values.

On the contrary, most journalists are not so different from other members of society. The public myth exists largely because of the complexities and ambiguities of legal and ethical principles in the United States. To be sure, journalists tenaciously collect as much information as possible, as quickly as possible, on stories to which they are assigned. State and federal open-records and open-meetings laws help them dig out information germane to the public's business. By the same token, federal statutes, state laws, regulatory agencies, and institutional policies make it possible to keep certain personal information private.

The law that has perhaps the greatest impact on the work of sports information directors and sports journalists is an amendment to the 1974 federal Family Educational Rights and Privacy Act. It limits the amount of personal information public educational institutions can reveal. In addition, private businesses and private schools can close virtually all information to public and press inspection, because they do not depend on expenditure of public tax monies; that is, they are not the public's business.

The law provides civil remedies for people and businesses when the media overstep their rights. Libel and slander laws protect an individual's right to a good reputation. Individuals can recover damages from members of the media who defame their character through publication or broadcast of false statements. Private individuals must prove negligence or carelessness to win a libel suit. Public officials and public figures must prove actual malice, a tougher standard in that the plaintiff must show that the media knew the information was false or that they "recklessly disregarded the truth."

Invasion-of-privacy statutes protect a citizen's right to be left alone. Journalists can invade privacy by intruding on someone's private property, printing sensational personal facts, portraying someone in a "false light" by distorting the facts, or using a person's name or likeness for personal gain. Copyright laws protect an individual's work, whether it be printed word, a musical composition, a film, or a recording. The owner of a copyright can sell rights to use the work, rent it, or give it away, but no one else legally can use the material without permission.

Journalists are constantly alerted to the dangers of libel and the invasion of privacy. Most errors occur due to carelessness, dependence on unreliable sources or failure to check and confirm facts.

Although the law prescribes what journalists can do, ethics addresses what they *ought* to do. This a moral philosophy of right and wrong. Such philosophies are based on religious foundations, personal beliefs and attitudes, and theories about the relationship between humankind and society. The primary ethical concepts at work in American journalism today are the public's right to know, situational ethics, and social responsibility.

Proponents of the public's right to know see the media as a public watchdog, a check on abuses by government. They believe the public is best served by exposure to all information, even negative information. Those who favor situational ethics are pragmatic. They make judgments based on the special circumstances of a given situation. As a result, they may take different action in similar situations. The third group contends the press has a responsibility to society to protect as well as to inform. They may exercise restraint in publication of personal facts or graphic pictures of violence out of a sense or of responsibility to protect the individual as much as possible.

Unlike other professions, journalism does not prescribe educational requirements and licensing or certification for those pursuing careers in the field. In fact, journalists resist efforts to take away their individuality. As a result, each organization is free to follow the ethical dictates of the principles to which it adheres. In some cases, individual members of an organization make decisions based on personal conscience and moral values. Different media responses to the same ethical questions suggest to the public a lack of consistency or a lack of moral principles.

Both sports information professionals and sports journalists adhere to unwritten but widely accepted standards of conduct. Among them are honesty, truthfulness, mutual respect, compassion, fairness, accuracy, and professional distance. Professionals may differ in how they apply those concepts to specific situations. For direction, they can discuss alternatives with people affected by the situation or seek advice from experts. The major professional journalism associations have developed codes of conduct for members to follow. Many media organizations also have created their own codes, and they penalize employees who violate those codes.

DISCUSSION QUESTIONS

1. What is the Sunshine Law, and where does it apply?
2. What are the Family Education and Rights of Privacy Act and the Buckley Amendment? Explain each.

SUGGESTED EXERCISES

1. List five examples each of possible acts of libel and slander.
2. List and discuss all forms of defense against libel or slander. Give five illustrations.

Chapter Fourteen

THE FUTURE: THE IMPACT OF MEDIA AND TECHNOLOGY

The day after the University of Kentucky won the 1998 NCAA Division I Men's Basketball Championship, a 14-year-old Wildcat fan gathered a thick pile of stories about the title game against the University of Utah from newspapers in Kentucky, Utah, Texas, Illinois, Michigan, and Pennsylvania, as well as from the *Associated Press* and *Knight Ridder* news services.

Chapter 14 of this text examines the impact of economics and technology on the principal players in Wenner's "sports production complex" summarized in Chapter 1; that is, sport organizations and media industries. The first section of Chapter 14 examines the economics of sport programming, its impact on the game, and its effect on the sport organizations. It looks at changes in the structure of sport organization and administration of sporting activities and explores the effect of the changes on sport offerings and scheduling decisions. The chapter addresses changes in the relationship between sport information specialists and journalists that result from such economic factors.

Chapter 14 also summarizes the industry enhancements through computer technology that continues to advance and change the professional practices of sport information specialists and journalists. The second section of the chapter summarizes new types of information-delivery systems and their connections to the work of journalists and sport information professionals. It also surveys the influence of technology on the scope and speed of information delivery to audiences.

The scrapbook collection did not cost her much—less than a penny per story, the cost of copy paper. She did not have to go far to get the copies, either. In fact, she did not have to go anywhere. She printed all the stories from online versions of newspapers on the World Wide Web. She could have copied stories from online versions of sport magazines, too, but the family already subscribed to *Sports Illustrated* and *Sports Illustrated for Kids*. They arrived by mail several days after the tournament.

She did not have to go to the library to catch up on stories she had failed to collect earlier in the tournament; all she had to do was type a telephone number into a designated blank on her computer, link up with another computer, and start reading through archives of newspaper and magazine stories stored in a database (a computer library). She also gleaned personal data on the players—everything from basketball statistics to favorite movies—and more stories from the University of Kentucky Athletics Department site on the web.

Finished with UK, she switched to the University of Tennessee athletics page to pick up similar information on the Lady Volunteers (another of her favorite teams) and their march to a third consecutive NCAA Division I Women's Basketball Championship. By the time Tennessee coach Pat Summitt made an appearance at a local mall in April to sign copies of her biography, the 14-year-old fan was a flesh-and-blood database of information on Summitt, former Lady Vols, current stars, and future recruiting prospects.

At that time, basketball season was not yet over for the teenage sports enthusiast. She still had teams alive in two online National Basketball Association fantasy leagues sponsored by *Sports Illustrated for Kids*. She was also keeping up with pre-draft news on the recruiting battle between the now-defunct American Basketball League and the Women's National Basketball Association for the top collegiate talent. The women's basketball league websites provided an opportunity to send email questions to players in both leagues, participate in chat room discussions with players and other fans, and enter a contest to name the two new teams in the ABL. The young fan could order clothing, memorabilia, and other team items from both the college and the professional teams without leaving the comfort of her home by using her credit card (with her parents' permission) at online team shops.

The 14-year-old's immersion in basketball through the media—she watched most of the UK men's and UT women's tournament games on television—illustrates the two primary factors shaping the future of sports and sport communication: economics and technology. Each is inseparable from the media. As noted in previous chapters, sporting events, particularly major championships, generate enormous advertising revenues for television because they enable major corporations and local companies to pitch their products to large audiences. Because of the competition for exclusive rights to broadcast sporting events, the TV media share huge portions of the largess with professional teams, college conferences, college and university teams, and some amateur organizations.

To attain a share of the television money, colleges and professional sport organizations put pressure on executives, coaches, and players to win. Winning compounds the gains. Winning teams appear on television more often than losing teams do. Television exposure gives a sport organization more viability and visibility, and viability and visibility translate into additional fan support, media support, and revenues.

Technological advancements during the past two decades, of course, have made it easier for TV to deliver larger and larger audiences to advertisers and greater exposure to sport organizations. Satellite technology has made it possible for graduates in Germany or in the Atlantic Ocean on a cruise ship to watch Division II Northern Kentucky University play in a men's national championship game (1996) as easily they may watch the University of Kentucky play in the Division I title game.

Technology has improved the speed of delivery as well as the range. Both radio and television can broadcast a game, live, around the world. Computer users can pick up broadcasts through electronic/telephone connections and built-in audio equipment; so can the print media now, thanks to advances in personal computers and telephone communication systems. In fact, the print media can deliver pictures, action, and sound on computer networks, much the same as the TV networks do.

In the mid-1990s, such technological improvements began to blur the lines distinguishing the traditional forms of the media and to change the working relationship between sport organizations and the media. Prior to the 1990s, the media served as the middle parties, delivering messages between sport organizations and their audiences. However, the media presented their own interpretations of the messages, setting the agenda and offering a modified view of reality or, at least, a different perspective. The new technology made it possible for a sport organization to communicate directly with corporations, boosters, fans, *and* the media electronically, thus eliminating the media's translation of the message. By creating their own websites, sport organizations began to deliver information directly to the sporting public; consequently, the sport organizations' dependence on the traditional media for visibility began to decrease.

Economic Influences

The high-stakes financial wheelings and dealings involving major corporations demonstrate the impact of economics on the future of sport entertainment and sports organizations. The century closed with two stunning, billion-dollar deals for TV rights totaling nearly $8.5 billion—one for college men's basketball and one for auto racing.

On November 18, 1999, CBS agreed to pay $6 billion for rights to broadcast the National Collegiate Athletic Association men's basketball tournament for 11 years, through 2013 (*Cincinnati Enquirer*, Nov. 19, 1999). The deal included rights for marketing, corporate sponsorship, promotion, licensing, Internet, radio, satellite, digital TV, and other NCAA sporting events. CBS outbid FOX and ABC-ESPN (both owned by Disney). Only a week before, CBS had lost a bid for rights to broadcast the two premier series of the National Association of Stock Car Racing—the Winston Cup and Busch Grand National races. FOX, NBC, and its cable partner, TBS, won that battle for the six-year packages of broadcast and cable rights by offering $2.4 billion, or about $400 million a year (*Cincinnati Post*, Nov. 13, 1999). The deal marked the first time NASCAR sold rights to all races. Previously, individual tracks sold rights to the events they staged. The consolidation under the NASCAR umbrella knocked ABC, ESPN, CBS, and TNN out of the NASCAR picture. All had previously broadcast some NASCAR events through deals with the tracks. FOX immediately began promoting the deal, and NASCAR races on its weekend pregame National Football League program.

The NASCAR deal represented a 400% increase in right fees over 1985, when the auto-racing organization received $3 million for TV rights to 28 races (*Cincinnati Post*, Nov. 11, 1999). The increase resulted from dramatic rises in the TV ratings, that is, dramatic increases in the number of people watching NASCAR. At the time of the deal, NASCAR ranked as the second-highest-rated sport on television, behind the National Football League. The NCAA basketball deal more than tripled the contract CBS signed for rights to the men's tournament for seven years ending in 2002. Former CBS Sports president Neal Pilson said the new package illustrated the increasing value of sports properties (*Cincinnati Enquirer*, Nov. 11, 1999).

In 1993, the FOX Network took away CBS's share of pro football for four years for a bid of $1.6 billion (Black, 1995). FOX got the rights to National Football Conference games and the 1997 Super Bowl as part of the deal. Sean McManus of CBS Sports vowed then to fight for a share of subsequent NFL packages, as well as National Basketball Association games (Kiesetter, 1997) and later proved successful in reacquiring rights to broadcast NFL games by the turn of the century. McManus also expressed hope that the NBA would spread games over several networks, as the NFL and Major League Baseball did, but the NBA still is televised on three networks—ABC, ESPN, and TNT.

Why would a television network guarantee such huge sums of money for rights to broadcast sporting events? Prestige and money.

FOX gained credibility as a major network after it paid $100 million more than CBS offered for the NFL rights in 1993. At the time, FOX was struggling to gain equal footing with the three original television networks (ABC, CBS, and NBC) with a limited schedule of prime-time entertainment programs. Most of the programs were mired near the bottom of the ratings, so the purchase of rights to NFL games was a financially sound gamble, even if FOX lost money on the deal. Improvement in image might lure more viewers to FOX, boost ratings, and increase advertising revenues both directly and indirectly, the analysts reasoned.

Seattle Seahawks running back Shaun Alexander tapes an intro for Monday Night Football. ESPN acquired the rights in 2006 to broadcast the NFL's Monday night matchup.

It is important to remember that higher ratings translate into higher advertising rates. Higher rates mean more revenue. Furthermore, NFL games attract greater numbers of younger viewers, an audience all the networks continue to scramble for. More viewers, a broader audience base, and an enhanced image might lure more producers with pilots to FOX and improve the entertainment lineup. At the least, football would provide an alternative to Sunday-afternoon movies and syndicated shows, a break from situation comedies and dramas in the evening. John Kiesewetter (1997), the media critic for the *Cincinnati Enquirer*, speculated that the Thursday- and Sunday-night telecasts mentioned by McManus might serve ratings objectives. Sports events might draw viewers away from top-rated programs on NBC.

How can television networks pay so much for rights to broadcast sports events? Power and money.

In the corporate climate of the 1990s, big business began competing—with big sponsorship dollars—for positions of rank in the public (media) spotlight. They began sponsoring major sporting events, from the Rose Bowl to the 24 Hours of Daytona, just to get their corporate names and banners on the TV screen. For the same reason, they invested in stadiums, among them the RCA Dome in Indianapolis (formerly the Hoosier Dome) and Quicken Loans Arena (formerly Gund Arena). Quicken Loans officials publicly admitted they paid a premium to put their name atop the arena in Cleveland in order to enhance the corporation's image. Everything from shoes to shirts to hats began carrying corporate emblems, too.

To promote products, corporations invested ever-larger sums in advertising during sporting events in the last quarter of the 20th century. No other form of advertising reached so many potential buyers instantly. The FOX deal for NFL football telecasts was far from a financial write-off because of the advertising revenues sports telecasts produced. FOX sold the 29 minutes of commercial time for the 1999 Super Bowl for an average of $1.6 million for a 30-second spot, according to Jon Nesvig, president of sales for the network ("29 Minutes," 1999). That totals to $92.8 million, without adding advertising revenues from the pregame show and related telecasts leading up to the event.

Television networks and other media industries underwent a major restructuring in the 1990s. They became subsidiaries of giant conglomerations, business divisions within diverse corporations. Walt Disney bought ABC, which held a share of ESPN. General Electric purchased RCA, which owned NBC. Ironically, GE was among the original owners of NBC. The Westinghouse Company took over CBS. An international conglomerate, News Corp., owned by Australian Rupert Murdock, started the FOX Network in 1987. Murdoch's company also bought 20th Century Fox film studio, newspapers, a European satellite service, and Asia's only satellite TV network (Dominick, 1996). Murdoch's attempts to control several types of media and capitalize on the public's appetite for news and entertainment (including sports) mimicked Ted Turner's pioneering entrepreneurship of the 1970s and 1980s. Turner turned a struggling UHF station into a "superstation" that could reach every city in America; bought the Atlanta Braves and Atlanta Hawks for programming; and he then started launching cable channels, including Cable News Network, CNN Headline News, and Turner Network Television (a movie channel) to pick off target audience segments. Murdoch's News Corp. purchased the Los Angeles Dodgers in 1998, and the corporation's FOX media division controlled the local broadcast rights for all but six Major League teams that season (Verducci, 1998).

The conglomerates turned the media into big businesses—big financial businesses in general and big entertainment businesses in particular. As the networks transformed into financial units of larger corporations, the bottom line gained in importance to broadcast executives. Sport programs proved to be a consistently popular and lucrative form of entertainment—a moneymaker far more predictable than movies, situation comedies, and syndicated shows—as the ratings for Super Bowl broadcasts illustrate (see Chapter 1).

The evolution of the television networks, coupled with the rapid growth of cable channels, changed the economic power structure. Competition among networks and cable suppliers for sport programming drove up the value of broadcast rights. Sale of broadcast rights provided an answer to the problem of shrinking gate receipts and escalating player salaries for professional teams. Sale of broadcast rights also promised a solution to shrinking gate receipts and governmental financial support for colleges and universities. Rights fees represented a revenue guarantee, immune to the vagaries of ticket sales, alumni donations, and corporate contributions.

Competition for shares of this relatively new and recently rich revenue source shifted power and control from sport organizations to the media. The money dangled by TV could buy a lot of uniforms and pay a lot of travel costs, and professional teams and colleges could not buy the kind of audience exposure that came along with the check. Professional teams moved playoff games and championships to nights to accommodate TV. They expanded the playoffs to provide more games and more telecasts. Major League Baseball opened the league playoffs to wild-card teams in 1997. Colleges put up lights on football fields, rescheduled football games to be televised at nights on Wednesdays, Thursdays, and even Fridays (a night typically reserved for high school football), and created conference tournaments in both football and basketball to decide playoff qualifiers. Of course, conference tournaments added more games to the TV menu, as well. Sport organizations did whatever TV asked, in many cases, to ensure they would get a share of the largess.

Competition for media dollars and exposure also altered the power structure within professional and collegiate athletics organizations. This alteration included the migration of professional teams to cities that represented "major media markets," that is, cities that offered more lucrative "rights fees" markets. The breakup of traditional conferences and the creation of "super conferences"—the collegiate equivalent of conglomerates—to improve marketability of league members was also part of the change, as were the modifications in scheduling prompted by the rush to get a share of the TV package. Conference basketball games once followed a rotation dictated by classroom and travel concerns—Thursday-Saturday, Saturday-Monday, and so on. Now, a conference may align with ESPN for Big Monday or Conference USA Thursday, then permit teams to play interconference games on Sunday afternoon, at midnight Friday, or any other time they can find a TV slot—never mind that the time may be inconvenient for fans or student-athletes. That's entertainment.

Athletics administrators, coaches, and sports information professionals agree the economic dynamics of sports changed markedly in the last two decades of the 20th century primarily because of TV revenues. "Competition for the sports dollar is greater every year, and there is no indication that it will ease up in the future," said Merle Levin, a retired sports information director and assistant athletics director at Cleveland State University (Nichols, 1996).

Unquestionably, television has become the engine driving sports. Jane Meier, athletics director at Northern Kentucky, called it "the sole reason" for the restructuring of sport from the top level of the professional ranks to the lowest division of collegiate sport. She said expectations created by the media trickle down to every division. "It's not just money . . . it's visibility," she said (Moynahan, 1996).

Levin and Meier witnessed the transformation from the inside. Levin was at Cleveland State when the university attempted to capitalize on the changes. The university built a 13,000-seat convocation center on campus to take the sport program to that "next level" coaches are fond of discussing. "Next level" is a buzz-word or phrase that means a higher level of visibility. Cleveland State's basketball teams play in the convocation center (an attractive stage for TV cameras, it should be noted). In addition, the 13,000-seat center would appear to be more attractive to future, high-profile, Division I opponents than its predecessor, 3,000-seat Woodling Gym. CSU seldom lost in Woodling, but it perhaps missed out on opportunities to increase the quality of its schedule. Because of added ticket revenues in the new venue, Cleveland State could afford to offer the elite in Division I considerably more attractive financial guarantees. Now it needs those teams—large teams with big fan followings—to help fill those seats on a regular basis. In

1996, the university hired a high-profile coach, Rollie Massimino, to direct the men's basketball team, another move with the potential to increase viability and visibility. Massimino was replaced in 2003 by Michigan State University assistant Mike Garland after Massimino failed to turn CSU into a winner, compiling a 90-113 record from 1996 to 2003.

The plan in hiring a high-profile coach like Massimino and erecting a new playing facility was that Cleveland State would then be able to beef up its non-conference schedule with high-visibility teams. It was hoped that the high-visibility visiting teams, high-profile coach, and attractive stage would lead to more TV appearances. The additional TV appearances would increase both the visibility of the men's basketball team and the revenues for the athletics program. The additional revenue would make it possible to increase contract guarantees and to schedule even more top-rated teams. It also might help to elevate the status of CSU's conference. Cleveland State played in the Midwestern Collegiate Conference in 1997–1998, along with eight other colleges in Northern Ohio, Illinois, Indiana, Michigan, and Wisconsin.

The step-up plan required CSU to increase efforts to schedule the nation's elite teams. The university built up its promotion and merchandising departments to help in the task, according to Levin. Athletics officials worked to arrange additional TV exposure through cable outlets. Of course, the plan demanded that Cleveland State win at basketball. Losing teams do not attract large crowds or TV audiences. That's entertainment. And unfortunately for Cleveland State, the team did not win often enough under Massimino, so most of the university's efforts went unrewarded.

Entertainment is the sports imperative of the future, according to Meier. She has worked at Northern Kentucky University for more than two decades and has led teams in three sports (volleyball, softball, and baseball) to national tournaments. She moved up from coach to athletics director in 1988. In recent years, the impact of the media on sports in general has begun to affect schools at the Division II level, she said. For example, some Division II conferences started cutting their own TV deals. Furthermore, all Division II teams had to work harder at promotions to attract people away from the TV set to home games.

"I used to say we're in the E-game—the education game," Meier said. "Now, I say we're in the E-game—the entertainment game. People used to come to the gym to see quality. Now, we have to do more things in connection with games." These things include contests and promotions during timeouts and halftime.

The value of another E-game—television exposure—was evident at Northern Kentucky University. Thirty-four million people watched the Norse play Fort Hays State (KS) in the championship game of the NCAA Division II Men's Basketball Tournament in 1996, according to Meier. The viewing audience included a basketball fan in Germany and graduates on a cruise ship.

Prior to the TV appearance, NKU struggled to fill a 1,800-seat gymnasium, primarily because the Norse played in the deep shadows of a geographical region rich in big-time basketball. Northern Kentucky University is right across the Ohio River from the University of Cincinnati and Xavier University. The University of Kentucky is 70 miles to the south. The University of Louisville and Indiana University are 90 miles to the west. Following the TV appearance, NKU's corporate support increased substantially, as did its community support. The enthusiasm and local pride generated by the success of the men's basketball team spurred community interest in a football team. The momentum culminated in January 1997 in passage of a "sports enhancement" proposal designed to double the athletics budget and to add football and four women's sports by the year 2003. Although the football plan was subsequently tabled due to financial and gender-equity concerns, NKU moved ahead in steps to add the four women's sports. The Norse women's soccer team made its debut in the fall of 1997 and enjoyed immediate success. The Norse women advanced to the NCAA Division II Final Four in November 1999.

Without the viability and visibility generated by the basketball team's success and television appearance, however, the expansion of the athletics program likely would not have begun to blossom so rapidly. The NKU athletics budget did not increase substantially between 1984 and 1996, even though the women's basketball team made several appearances in the Division II tournament. The success of the 1995–96 men's basketball team spawned optimism that NKU could raise enough money to double the size and cost of the athletics program over a seven-year period. Lining up corporate donors was difficult prior to the Norse appearance in the NCAA finals on TV. "Since we won, it's been incredible," Meier said. "Corporate support is much easier to get" (Moynahan, 1996).

It also is much easier to lose. The changing economic dynamics put a higher value on winning than at any previous time in history—that is one reason coaches whose teams fail to make the playoffs do not last long, even if they string together winning seasons. One year off a 10-2 season, including a win in the Cotton Bowl, the University of Alabama fired football coach Mike Shula after going 6-6 in 2006. Steve Lavin was fired as the men's basketball coach at UCLA in March of 2003 after his Bruins went 10-19 that season. The previous six seasons, he had compiled a 135-59 record and led UCLA to the Sweet 16 of the NCAA Tournament five times. Lavin is now a college basketball analyst for ESPN.

"If you don't win, you're not viewed as credible," Meier said in the Moynahan interview three months earlier. "If you're not credible, no one wants to put money in your program. Some (in the community) still want to put money in your program to help. But winning is what brings in the fan base and corporate support. If you don't get into this business to win now, you are wasting your money."

The Structure of Sports

Athletics administrators, sports information specialists, and media experts do not all agree on the long-term impact of the economic shift on the structure of sport organizations. No one knows whether television contracts will continue to grow at astronomical rates. No one is certain the battle for sports programming will spread from the professional ranks to amateur sports or trickle down through all levels of collegiate sports. No one can predict whether the round-the-clock feast of athletics events on the TV menu eventually will satiate the public appetite for sport programming, and no one can foretell whether a new technology will come along to alter the economic dynamics of sports communication to the same degree as television has changed them.

However, many of those in media and sport organizations questioned about the changing dynamics of sport agree on factors that will dictate whether individual teams and leagues will survive well into this 21st century. The economic, media, and sport trends of the 1990s suggest the future belongs to sport organizations that identify their target audiences effectively, put together entertaining promotional packages, and market them successfully through multiple media outlets. Organizations that build spectator interest, maintain high media visibility, and sustain corporate and graduate support likely will flourish.

The expansion, reorganization, and realignment of professional and collegiate sport leagues appear likely to continue for years. Believing a professional franchise would bring higher visibility and economic benefits, American cities showed a willingness in the mid-1990s to build plush stadiums and to offer lush financial incentives to attract NFL teams. Baltimore lured the Browns away from Cleveland, and they became the Ravens. Oakland got back the Raiders, and the Rams went to St. Louis. The Oilers plotted a move to Nashville and became the Tennessee Titans. Cincinnati residents voted a sales-tax increase of 1/2% to build new stadiums for both the baseball Reds (Great American Ballpark) and the football Bengals (Paul Brown Stadium). The NFL moved to fill markets that promised strong fan and media bases. The Carolina Panthers and the Jacksonville Jaguars thrived in the early years of operation, with the Panthers advancing to Super Bowl XXXVIII in 2004. On the other hand, citizens and municipal governments in Minneapolis and Miami previously rejected plans to use public money to expand or replace sport facilities, although Dolphin Stadium in Miami was undergoing a major facelift in 2006–07.

Nonetheless, the combination of new cities and new stadiums increased the revenue-sharing prospects for all teams, not just the teams in those cities. Larger stadiums, of course, boost ticket sales because they offer more seats. New stadiums boost corporate income. Most of the new stadiums include suites that companies can lease for a healthy price. A new stadium with corporate suites (renting for $45,000 to $134,000 per year) and the increased revenues they would generate was instrumental in owner Mike Brown's decision to stay in Cincinnati, according to local media reports. The Bengals also sold "charter ownership agreements." For a one-time cost of $300 to $1,500 per seat, Bengal fans could guarantee they would get the first chance to reserve or "own" the same seats each year. In addition, the Bengals forged a radio contract with a new station with only a slightly higher financial bid than WLW, but with big plans for game promotions.

Broadcast/promotional packages were one strategy professional teams and leagues employed to improve the entertainment value of their "products." Both attendance and TV viewership of Major League Baseball games dropped off significantly following the labor strike in 1994 that canceled the playoffs and World Series. Baseball owners added another round of playoffs in 1995, but the 1996 World Series between the Atlanta Braves and the New York Yankees played to low ratings. The owners approved interleague games for 1997, hoping to generate additional interest. With two expansion teams joining Major League Baseball in 1998, league owners also realigned divisions to create new rivalries and fresh interest.

Whereas television opportunities increased with the expansion of cable networks, so did competition for media exposure. Professional baseball, football, and basketball ceased to rule the airways in the 1990s. Auto racing took a big bite out of the media dollar. NASCAR scattered its Winston Cup series across networks, worked up a deal for the stock-car minor league (Grand National Series), and started a truck series that opened with a TV contract worth $400 million ("TV Deal," Nov. 13, 1999). Predictably, new auto-racing tracks popped up in Florida, Texas, Nevada, and California. Other racing associations, such as the National Hot Rod Association, the American Speed Association, and World of Outlaws also landed spots on the TV menu. The National Hockey League and the North American Soccer League got deals, as did each of the two women's professional basketball leagues that arose in 1997—the American Basketball League and Women's National Basketball Association. Games played by the latter, backed by the NBA, appeared on both network (NBC) and cable (Lifetime and ESPN) TV.

The proliferation of sports on TV is likely to continue for the foreseeable future. Golf everywhere. Tennis everywhere. Even figure skating everywhere. Professional skating competitions, many of them made for TV, popped up all over the broadcast and cable system in the late 1990s. TV made up its own sports, too. Ted Turner played a major role in the development of the Goodwill Games, international competition during non-Olympic years that was broadcast on his WTBS cable network. ESPN created and promoted the Extreme Games, a collection of out-of-the-mainstream events such as ice climbing and skateboarding. They helped to fill airtime on the cable network's two around-the-clock channels, ESPN and ESPN2.

Like their professional counterparts, college and university athletics departments maneuvered to put themselves in power positions for media negotiations. The major postseason bowls lined up corporate sponsors to boost the kitty and attract high-profile teams. They also collaborated with the nation's football powers to create a bowl format involving the top-rated teams and designed to crown a national champion, known as the Bowl Championship Series (BCS). The plan went awry in 1996 and 1997 when one of the two top-ranked teams in the country, Arizona State in 1996 and Michigan in 1997, went to the Rose Bowl, which was not in the alliance. Consequently, the plan was altered to pull the Rose Bowl into the deal in the future, to ensure a meeting between the top two teams in the BCS rankings. The alliance then came up with a plan to choose the participants in the major bowls through a combination of various computer polls and rankings by sport journalists and coaches.

Likewise, the major holiday basketball tournaments lined up corporate sponsors to increase incentives to attract the nation's top teams and TV deals; one of the last holdouts on postseason conference tournaments, the Big Ten, launched a playoff in 1998 to determine its automatic qualifier for the NCAA tournament.

In the late 20th and early 21st century, a major reorganization of conferences was under way. The Southwest Conference disappeared, whereas the Big Eight swelled to the Big 12 by absorbing some of the teams from the old Southwest Athletic Conference. Conference USA was born in 1995 but the makeup of the teams in that league has changed dramatically since its inception. Cincinnati (which changed conferences four times in a little more than a decade), DePaul, Louisville, Marquette, and South Florida all left Conference USA for the Big East Conference in 2005–06. The Big East was forced to pilfer those teams when the Atlantic Coast Conference lured football powers Boston College, Miami (Fla.), and Virginia Tech away from the Big East. In the continuing domino effect, Conference USA replaced its void by taking two schools from the Mid-American Conference (Central Florida and Marshall) and four teams from the Western Athletic Conference (Rice, Southern Methodist, Tulsa, and the University of Texas at El Paso). Even Notre Dame, a staunch independent, gave in and aligned with the Big East except for football, where the Fighting Irish remain an independent.

Meier, the NKU athletics director, expects realignments to continue as colleges and universities jockey to improve their visibility through TV exposure.

> The restructuring of conferences is about control of money. Each division is guaranteed so much money. The conferences are about control of resources—how big a part of the country you can control. The bigger share of the country you control, the greater the potential TV audience you can deliver for conference games and the stronger your bargaining power with TV executives. (Moynahan, 1996)

In addition, the more teams in the conference, the better the revenue prospects. Each participating school gets a share of the revenues from postseason bowls and tournaments. The more teams in the conference, the greater the odds for multiple postseason appearances. Furthermore, conferences require members to share a portion of their take from tournaments with others in the conference, so teams that fail to make the playoffs get a revenue boost from their more successful brothers and sisters. That makes alignment with a major conference a plus. A team struggling to get to the "next level" can improve both its visibility and its revenue through the right conference alignment. The right alignment, said Meier, is an association of similar institutions with the same athletics mission; in other words, the odds of success are poor unless a school picks a conference in which organizational and operational criteria are compatible.

Athletics administrators differ in their opinions on how deeply the power dynamics will dip into collegiate levels in the future. Television clearly has some influence at all levels. The Division II and Division III playoffs in major sports now are telecast. Some Division II conferences have arranged TV packages, Meier said. Previously, corporate money was not viewed as a major revenue source. "Now it is," she said.

There is evidence that Division II is following the example of Division I, particularly in formation of power conferences. The Great Lakes Valley Conference, which includes Northern Kentucky University, sent a team to the Division II championship game five years in a row (1994–98). Two or more teams qualified for the playoffs through most of the 1990s. As a result, interest in aligning with the conference to enhance playoff prospects and visibility increased. Ashland University and Kentucky State University dropped out in the mid-1990s. But the conference grew to 12 teams with the addition of Quincy College (Illinois), University of Wisconsin-Parkside, University of Missouri-St. Louis, and Southern Illinois University-Edwardsville. Geographically, the conference spread across Kentucky, Ohio, Indiana, Illinois, Wisconsin, and Missouri.

However, NKU's athletics director expects to see more autonomy within divisions than "follow the leader" efforts because of the wide disparity in revenues between Division I and lower levels. Said Meier:

> You're going to see Division I do its own thing. You're going to see Division II do its thing. And you're going to see Division III do its thing. There won't be as much trickle down. In the past five years (1992–97), I've seen a move in that direction. You see rules more conducive to your situation . . . I see that as better. (Moynahan, 1996)

Changes in Division II and Division III required Division I approval initially. Schools in all three divisions had to follow many of the same rules on recruiting, scholarships, grants, and so on. That put schools at the lower levels at a disadvantage. Greater autonomy will enable each Division to adapt the rules to the realities of the division, Meier believes. For example, Division II athletics grants might pay for tuition and books but not meals.

Debby Ghezzi, former athletics director at Notre Dame College of Ohio, told author Nichols (1996) that she did not expect to see a trickle-down effect, either. She believes the educational aspects of athletics will continue to receive more emphasis at the "small college" level. Notre Dame College is a private, women's college with six intercollegiate sports under the National Association of Intercollegiate Athletics umbrella. Decisions on issues, such as scheduling, that are dictated by television producers do not always take into account what is best for students from the standpoint of educational preparation, according to Ghezzi. "The future—our future—will be controlled by the educated," she said. "On all college campuses we have the responsibility to educate. It is this viewpoint that will account for all of college sports returning to a grassroots level of sport—as a means of education."

Although television revenues drive high-profile college sports, their impact on the makeup of athletics programs may vary from school to school and division to division. At the Division I level, football and men's basketball have developed into huge sources of revenue for the most successful universities. But because of the high expense, football is a drain on a lot of budgets. Only two of the eight state-supported universities in Kentucky made money on their athletics programs in 1995, the University of Kentucky and University of Louisville. The major source of income for both was basketball. Neither made money on its football program, according to information gathered by a Northern Kentucky University committee exploring football. Nor did the Division I-A football teams at Eastern Kentucky University, Morehead State University, Murray State University, and Western Kentucky University. In an effort to slow the drain on its budget, Morehead decided not to offer football scholarships.

Some schools are cutting back on sports because of the expense. Gymnastics and wrestling programs, in particular, fell frequently to the budget axe in the 1990s. Julie Dalpiaz, the former SID at John Carroll University in University Heights, Ohio, predicted declines in the number of sports offered by colleges, because of decreases in budgets, college-age students, and students interested in athletics. "Many schools simply cannot afford to fund many athletics programs anymore," said Dalpiaz, who later moved to the University of Illinois to take a position as editor of sports publications. "Therefore, many schools are dropping their so-called 'minor sports.' This will mean less to cover for the media organization and probably greater coverage of the sports that are left" (Nichols, 1996).

Kevin Ruple, the SID at Baldwin-Wallace College in Berea, Ohio, is not convinced sports with little media exposure will perish. "Probably the biggest development that will occur in sports in the next 10 years is the continued development of women's athletics programs and the development of some of the so-called 'small sport' teams and programs," he predicted. "Coaches, athletics directors, athletes, and 'Joe Average Guy' have all realized that you can benefit financially in sport with the proper following and promotion." Women's sports will continue to grow "if they continue to cultivate an audience that will be interested" (Nichols, 1996).

Ruple points out that volleyball, hockey, track and field, softball, swimming, golf, tennis, and soccer showed signs of gaining media and spectator followings, in part because of television coverage in connection with the 1996 Olympic Games in Atlanta. Those sports can prosper if administrators can identify an audience and promote themselves effectively, the formula utilized by figure-skating promoters, he said.

By the middle of the decade, all signs indicated that women's sport in general would make the greatest advances in sport as the 20th century closed. Women's basketball appeared to be capitalizing on two of the elements essential to growth in the economic dynamic of the 1990s—visibility and media/corporate interest. More than 35,000 people watched the women's basketball team play in the 1996 Olympic Games in Atlanta. The Division I women's basketball Final Four was a sellout and a television hit in 1996, too. ESPN and ESPN2 planned to televise 22 women's games during the 1996–1997 season (*Sports Illustrated,* Dec. 2, 1996), not counting NCAA tournament games.

"The growth and opportunity for young women to participate in intercollegiate athletics has been tremendous," said Mary Masters, assistant commissioner of the Big Ten Conference. "The promotion and television exposure provided by the NCAA has led to broader acceptance and supports for girl's and women's sports" (Hall, 1996).

Women's basketball attendance ran ahead of projections in the first year of the professional American Basketball League. At the end of 1996, attendance was averaging "several hundred fans" more than the league estimate of 3,000 per game (Wolff, 1996, p. 126). More significantly, TV producers were taking notice. ABL games appeared on regional cable outlets, such as Sports Channel (now FOX Sports) before the league folded. WNBA games were telecast on the USA cable network as well as NBC.

Meier said women's basketball scored higher in the TV ratings than NFL exhibitions. True to the economic equation, advertisers and corporate sponsors took notice, too. ABL cofounder Gary Cavalli told *Sports Illustrated* that the early ticket success generated calls from corporate sponsors (cited in Wolff, 1996). Meier said the media's bias toward male sports showed in the Olympic coverage. The TV schedule focused on gymnastics—"a feminine sport," noted Meier—instead of soccer and softball. Nonetheless, the media coverage helped to attract corporate interest. "Companies are now sensitive to female products in advertising," she said. "They're smarter with their advertising dollars. They're going with the teams that are most visible and credible. That is what built men's sports" (Moynahan, 1996).

That helped to build women's sports in the 1990s. The level of play in the Olympics answered the harshest of critics. Virginia Stahr, a former All-American volleyball player at Nebraska, noted that most high school coaches now are former players who understand the techniques of the game well. So there has been a natural progression in skill level and quality of play.

Donna Lopiano, executive director of the Women's Sports Foundation, suggested that the key to success is slow growth, one sport at a time. When one sport is on solid ground, in perhaps six or seven years, sport organizers move on to the next. "But you must put the same energies and talents toward making women's athletics as successful as you do for the men," she said (Hall, 1996).

Judith R. Holland, chair of the NCAA Women's Basketball Committee, concurred. To maintain the growth, administrators must develop a mission and a plan to accomplish it, she said (Hall, 1996). For example, women's basketball could shoot for its own contract, separate from men's basketball.

Lopiano believes women's sports need print and electronic media coverage for seven reasons:

1. To establish media credibility.
2. To advertise the availability of product.
3. To reap recruiting benefits.
4. To increase gate receipts and donations.
5. To acquire television rights fees.
6. To enhance corporate sponsor packages.
7. To create athlete income benefits for professional sports.

Increased growth in women's athletics will depend on marketing in the media world of the 21st century, according to Tracy Ellis, a two-time All Big Eight basketball player from the University of Missouri. The successful women's teams in the country must receive the same kind of support base and promotion as the men's teams receive, she said (Nichols, 1996).

The entertainment focus, promotional demands, and high visibility of sport also are changing the administration of sport organizations. In addition to increased pressure to win in every sport, there is closer media scrutiny and, by extension, public

Administration of Athletics

scrutiny of owners, athletics directors, coaches, and players. Journalists and fans have a chance to see more coaches and make comparisons among them. The fans are more knowledgeable because they see more games and hear more analysis by former players and coaches. They develop more ways to evaluate coaches and players.

Because of the high stakes and close, critical scrutiny, college presidents began playing a more active role in the administration of athletics in the 1990s. The president now wants to be in the middle of every significant decision in the athletics department. The president wants to make sure that athletics are a part of the student's education, not apart from it. The president also wants to know where the revenues are coming from and what expenses are incurred in operating athletics programs, and administrators want to make certain that the athletics program reflects the same image as the university's academic programs.

In response to criticism about academic deficiencies among student-athletes, college and university presidents acted to take control of the situation. To make clear that academics transcend athletics, in April 2004 the NCAA unanimously approved an academics reform package to help hold schools accountable for the academic progress of student-athletes. An academic-progress rate (APR) calculates the graduation success rate of all of a school's scholarship student-athletes over a six-year period. If a team falls below a certain mark on its APR score, a reduction of scholarships and limitations on recruiting can be imposed. The legislation was passed because university presidents were determined to make sure that athletics did not damage academic integrity.

In an attempt to better track the academic progress and assist in the academic support of student-athletes, athletic directors have created positions with the specific duty of overseeing an athletic department's tutoring and academic counseling program. Mark Shook, the assistant athletics director for student-athlete services at Bowling Green State University, pointed out that most universities believe that their role is to assist all student-athletes in becoming independent and self-reliant members of society. The use of technology has made it easier to accomplish these goals. Shook said, "Technology has certainly changed the ways in which were able to communicate, monitor, and support the academic progress of each student-athlete" (Hall, 2003). He outlined the various ways the student-athlete is given support as the advisor is able to access a number of computer-based records from various campus departments that are connected to a general server, which allows the advisors to effectively monitor the range of needs of each student-athlete. The use of email enables Shook to keep in touch with instructors in order to get feedback on classroom performances, and then quickly relay that feedback to coaches.

The trend in selection of athletics directors shifted toward people with master's degrees in sports administration and previous experience. Fewer coaches and more professional administrators moved into the top leadership positions, according to Dalpiaz. No longer does the football or men's basketball coach automatically move up to athletics director, although there are some recent exceptions to the rule, including Barry Alvarez, who went from head football coach to athletic director at the University of Wisconsin in 2006. Professionals in marketing, sales, promotion, and sports information are joining the ranks. On the whole, athletics departments are run more effectively, resulting in fewer problems, Dalpiaz said. More and more graduates of sport administration programs are moving into the work place. This will make for more knowledgeable and experienced sports administration from the athletics director all the way down. It also should bolster the relationship between sport organizations and the media. Reporters should be able to get knowledgeable answers to questions and quick attention to problems. Better management should result in fewer problems and less negative press.

The coach-to-administrator connection is still viable in some circumstances. Division I coaches often go to Division II for administrative experience, then return to Division I, Meier said. The athletics director must deal with bigger budgets, fundraising, and compliance with NCAA regulations. Meier oversees 200 athletes and a staff of 40. In both jobs, however, "the ability to lead and motivate" is the key to success.

Serving as coach and athletics director at the same time is not recommended for the future, although Alvarez balanced both duties for a short time before fully committing himself to his athletic director duties. Parks and Zanger (1990) point out the athletics director is responsible for administering the budget, scheduling, running events, complying with conference and national rules, paying referees and officials, running facilities (at times), and taking care of any differences that arise. It is illogical to think one person can handle such a large responsibility and coach, too. The demands of handling both positions can be a strain on the entire program. Over the past decade, the stress on coaches has increased. The workload has increased. The responsibilities of maintaining a clean program have increased. Add the time it takes to build a successful overall athletics program, and administrators who would assign both positions to a single person are asking that person to take on an overwhelming task.

A division of responsibilities between men's and women's sports is one option some colleges are pursuing, but in today's integrated world, the division of men's and women's programs might not be the wisest approach. Some conferences moved from a mostly male-oriented administrative staff to a cooperative situation for both sexes. In most large universities, however, there is an athletic director and several associate or assistant athletic directors that help balance the workload of managing an athletic department. For example, in 2006 The Ohio State University had an athletic director, three senior associate athletic directors, an associate athletic director, and an assistant athletic director.

The restructuring of sport also is changing the roles of other people in the athletics department, including the sports information director. Sports information personnel are involved in the decision-making process at many colleges today because of their training in crisis management and promotions. A communications expert, the SID can offer perspective on a problem from the point of view of both the institution and the media. The SID can provide guidance on scheduling in regard to media deadlines and other factors that affect coverage. Furthermore, the SID can contribute to promotional brainstorming and marketing, that is, identifying target audiences and crafting strategies to reach them.

Many schools, like Cleveland State University, have built large multipurpose centers for physical education instruction, athletics competition, practices, and recreation purposes to fit the diverse needs of the student body. At small schools the facility also is available to all students, not just the student-athletes. The athletics director must coordinate scheduling with the facility director to avoid problems. The facility director has to juggle between the physical education, athletics, and recreation needs of the entire student body. That can cause conflict and strained relations at times. Previously, athletics directors usually ran the facility. The AD dictated when a team could practice.

Some smaller schools are hiring both a recruiting coordinator and an academic counselor. This person helps find student-athletes who best fit the profile of that particular institution. Once the recruit arrives on campus, the athletics department wants to keep the prospect in school. An academic counselor can help coaches, athletics directors, and other interested faculty keep an eye on a particular student or group of students. More important, the school can better monitor progress and offer help when needed. Athletics officials can spot potential academic problems much more quickly.

The recruiting coordinator/academic counselor also can assume some of the duties of part-time coaches. The athlete will have someone to talk to all the time. When a student-athlete needs help, it is available much more quickly. An unbiased observer whom the student-athlete can trust and come to in time of need, when the coach is not on campus and the athletics director is not available, can be a valuable asset.

Sports information, promotion, and marketing have seen great changes in the past 10 years. In the next 10 years, the changes may be even more dramatic. With the ever-increasing use of television, the possibilities for exposing the public to more games and more sports are endless. One promotional strategy is to play doubleheaders, such as men's and women's soccer, basketball, baseball, and softball. This approach would also cut travel, reduce meal costs by half, and offer a chance for men and women to play alongside each other in a competitive learning environment.

Administrators can be expected to continue to schedule events around the needs of the media to increase visibility. John Carroll University moved men's basketball games one-half hour earlier to accommodate newspaper and TV deadlines. Small colleges in geographical areas with professional teams are arranging schedules to avoid conflicts. Northern Kentucky University plays some basketball games at 3:15 P.M. on Saturday afternoons. Some colleges are even scheduling multiple events on one day, though not at the same time. That way one media person can cover a variety of events on the same day and at the same place, such as covering a football game early Saturday afternoon, and a volleyball game that evening.

Tom Bochenek, public relations aide with the Cleveland Indians and former SID at Mount Union College in Alliance, Ohio, cautions against alienating one's spectator audience in scheduling decisions, regardless of the promotional benefits. "Based on my traditional way of thinking, I think it is important that the SID in the ad marketing operation of an athletics department express concern about scheduling and time of games," he said (Nichols, 1996). At Kent State, for example, athletics officials decided to move Saturday home basketball games from afternoon starts to 7:30 P.M. for one year, then switched to 8 P.M. The strategy did not work well because the games ended too near media deadlines. The trend these days is toward scheduling that helps morning newspapers, because the number of afternoon newspapers is dwindling.

"I am leery about 7:30 P.M. Saturday night games, no matter the sport," Bochenek said. "I would suggest, if that is the decision of the department to play at night, 6:30 P.M. or 7:00 P.M. starts."

The athletics director must balance the needs of TV, athletes, and spectators. Some athletics departments are hiring specialists for promotions and marketing to help with the entertainment aspect of athletics events. The promotions director can bring company representatives to campus to show the campus off. Games, events, community affairs, projects, and promotions can bring in many people throughout the community, area, state, and possibly, the nation. It does not do a school any good to be "The Best Kept Secret in the Area," as Northern Kentucky University officials were fond of saying in the early 1990s.

The marketing director can do the same. The marketing professional will take the promotion person's idea, find an audience, and go after it. A good marketing approach often will enhance the sales pitch, and a good sales pitch is essential in sport today. Athletics administrators say advertising and promotion will continue to be powerful influences on sport. Meier said the biggest change she observed in two decades at Northern Kentucky University was "the sophistication of promotion and marketing"—strategies for getting fans into the stands (Moynahan, 1996).

"We're constantly trying to build a fan base and a friend base," she said. "Coaching is no longer tied to education. Athletics is no longer tied to education. It's entertainment-based."

Expansion of Media

Sports fans are getting more coverage of athletics events than ever before, and there is no sign of a slowdown. Sports fans are getting more data, more pictures, and more information of better quality faster than ever before and all signs point to a speed-up. Fans also are getting sports information and sports entertainment from more different media sources than ever before. The options probably will continue to expand rapidly before inventors exhaust the media uses of satellite transmission, digital technology, computer chip development, and fiber optic cable.

No one is quite sure how long the "Information Age" will last. But the history of technological advancement, from the invention of movable type to the Industrial Revolution, would suggest that it is still in its infancy. The "Information Age" appears to be in the "tinkering" stage. Historically, the discovery of a new technological process or invention of a new mechanical or electrical device has sparked a great burst of experimentation. First, the tinkerers or inventors try to determine how many different uses they can find for the new creation. Some of the inventions turn out to be impractical and unfeasible. Others prove useful for purposes other than those originally imagined. Over a period of time, the inventors find out how to use the technology to best advantage and what chores it does best. Often the chore is something entirely different from the tinkerer's original vision.

Consider the development of new media during and following the Industrial Revolution. The pioneers in the development of radio set out to develop a method of communication that could send a message without wires, so-called *wireless telegraphy*. Foremost among them was Guglielmo Marconi, a young Italian who figured out how to send Morse code via an electromagnetic signal. The obvious practical application was ship-to-shore communication for vessels in the ocean. At the same time, however, Thomas Edison was creating a machine that could record and play back sounds. What if someone could send sounds as well as Morse code? Not a good idea, said Heinrich Hertz, the man who discovered the electromagnetic waves. Hertz did not believe the waves would be useful for communication (Dominick, 1996, p. 176). But the marriage of sound and signal produced radio, which became a source of news and entertainment.

Edison's phonograph laid the groundwork for musical recordings, which now provide a programming staple for radio. Someone else decided adding pictures to the sound would be even better, and television soon followed. It was not simply radio with pictures, although TV executives initially copied radio's programming formats.

So it is with computer technology. The personal computer is part printing press—arranging information in linear form on pages and printing it—and part phonograph—a CD player. It is part radio and television, audio and pictures. It also can be a combination of media and communication devices: A telegraph with messages delivered via telephone lines (email messages), for example. Or, a CD encyclopedia with film or TV clips and sound/voices. Or a video game. Or an interactive movie. If a computer chip can provide all those possibilities, why not TV? Turn TV into a giant computer. Oh yes, throw in a fax machine and hook up the telephone and ham radio, too. It is all possible, but is it all useful and feasible?

The tinkerers are finding out. An early marriage of film and computer technology proved largely unpopular. It sounded like a great idea. If you like interactive video games, you'll love interactive movies in which you get to play a character. But what the experimenters discovered was that games are games and movies are . . . well, relaxing entertainment. If you have to make plot decisions to save the universe, perhaps they aren't so relaxing after all—they are work! In the mid-1990s, electronic manufacturers began to market devices that would connect the television with the Internet. So the viewer could get the Internet and entertainment on a big-screen TV with a couple of additional clicks on a remote control device. But how often do people *read* a TV screen? Will they use the TV for intellectual stimulation as well as entertainment? It remains to be seen.

So it is with much of the innovation and experimentation in the media. No one can predict with any degree of certainty what directions the new technology will take. What one can say with a high degree of certainty is that computer technology is not likely to eliminate any of the existing media. If anything, it probably will create new forms of media and new methods of communication. Shezaif Rafaeli (1996, p. 9) contended that the evolution of communication rarely leads to extinction of media. Both Newhagen and Rafaeli agree that the Internet and World Wide Web are not likely to put newspapers or TV out of business. Said Rafaeli: "Some technologies, such as the telegraph, have withered. On the whole, however, niches in our communication ecology have developed, with media adapting to the niches more often than niches responding to media abilities" (p. 10).

The death of newspapers has been predicted each time a new medium has blossomed, but newspapers, the oldest of the media, still survive. They struggled to find their niche in the last quarter of the 20th century, but the rapid rise of suburban newspapers and online editions indicates they are finding their way. Likewise, radio seemed to be in trouble when TV took away its soap operas and serials, but radio found an audience for music—numerous audiences, to be exact. Every radio station now sticks closely to a particular format, a niche within a niche. The higher quality of sound reproduction pushed FM radio to the forefront in the early 1990s, leaving AM searching for a niche. By the middle of the decade, "talk radio" was flourishing on AM. So were sport broadcasts.

What is most likely to occur as the 21st century progresses is the rise of a new medium, or several new media, as the tinkerers identify the practical new uses for the technology. The existing media will adapt, identifying new audiences and developing strategies to serve them just as newspapers adapted to TV. Given the diversity of the mass audience, different demographic groups may turn to different media as their first choice for news or entertainment. The explosion of narrowly targeted cable offerings, such as the Home and Garden Network, offer further evidence of media targeting to a niche audience.

The most popular new medium, or combination of media, in the late 1990s was online communication, that is, communication among computer networks or personal computers linked electronically through telephone connections. Technological advancements made it possible for anyone with a personal computer and a modem—a device that translates computer language into an electronic signal—to hook into the Internet and World Wide Web. The Internet and World Wide Web are unstructured networks of computer users and computer databases—in simplest terms, a worldwide party line and library rolled into a complex "web" of electronic linkages.

Newspapers, radio and TV stations, and broadcast networks rushed to create online versions of their work in the mid-1990s. So did numerous corporations and businesses, including sport organizations. Most major corporations, colleges, and universities were connected to the web by 1998. So were millions of individuals. Anyone who owns a computer can create a site—called a *home page, address,* or *URL* in computer terminology—on the network and become a miniature media mogul for a small fee. In recent years there has been an explosion of *bloggers,* that is, authors of a personal on-line web page. Some bloggers have actually begun to serve as a sort of watchdog or competition for the mainstream media.

Anyone who owns a computer with a modem can get onto the Internet and the World Wide Web by subscribing to a service that provides a telephone, cable, or wireless link to the network. Subscribers typically pay a monthly fee for the service based on the speed of the subscriber's connection. Some Internet providers charge additional fees per hour for usage beyond a set amount of time each month, although that is less and less common. In most cases, subscribers also get electronic mail (email) software, a way to send text messages to other network-connected computer users individually or collectively. Computer users can utilize web browsing software that enables them to link with the World Wide Web, a network that links them to large libraries of text, graphics, audio, and visual information.

Brian S. Brooks (1997) of the University of Missouri believes such computer-based information delivery methods constitute "an entirely new form of communication" because of three unique capabilities: (a) linking, (b) layering, and (c) research (p. 81). The World Wide Web makes it possible to create links from one site (computer or computer network) to another with related material. Consequently, a person perusing the World Wide Web site for the WNBA on May 19, 1998, could jump directly to the NBA site, which included the announcement of the selection of Michael Jordan as 1998 Most Valuable Player. The NBA website provided connections to newspaper articles about Jordan in the *Chicago Sun-Times* and *Hoop Magazine*. It also offered NBA statistics, plus links to individual teams, including the Chicago Bulls, and all of the Bulls' promotional material on Jordan. That means consumers or fans no longer are limited to the media version of an event or the sport-organization version of an event. They can examine multiple news and promotional sources and form their own conclusions, creating their own version of reality by drawing from both the media and the sport organization. "No longer is the consumer limited to what the newspaper wants to write about the subject" (Brooks, 1997, p. 81).

The links facilitate layering, providing connections to other stories, statistics, and related information. The consumer can decide whether just to scan headlines, read a page or two about a topic, or examine a hundred related subjects among various sport organization or media-operated computer sites. The layering provides a systematic process and directory to help one move from headline to in-depth collections of information. The layering makes in-depth research much easier because millions of documents, databases, media sources, scholarly papers and journals, and government data sources, such as the U.S. Census, are available online. The sport fan can explore a topic thoroughly with less expense, less time expenditure (because the links are provided), and less effort. The computer user does not have to go to a bookstore or library. On most sites, the consumer can even ask questions electronically and request additional information. Sound, pictures, and motion also may accompany the information. For example, a computer user could listen to an audio replay of a news conference interview conducted by the media with Kobe Bryant following an NBA playoff game.

Brooks (1997) expects the new medium to flourish deep into the 21st century because of its advertising and subscription potential. Whereas the early advertising efforts on the World Wide Web have proven inconclusive, Brooks believes online advertising has a significant advantage over other media forms. Computer-based media can give clients specific demographic information on who reads the advertisement and how long, whereas the best the traditional media can offer are scientific estimates, such as Neilsen samples or readership surveys. The precise data available in online communication will enable businesses to target advertising more effectively, according to Brooks. Randy Reddick of FACS, an online service for journalists, and Elliot King of Loyola College cited sources in *The Online Journalist* that estimated advertising revenues could jump $312 million in 1996 and observed that "online advertising could continue that upward trend for several years" (Reddick & King, 1997, p. 225).

Brooks (1997) did not anticipate that the new medium will lead to the extinction of any existing medium because each enjoys a significant strength related to delivery of information. The print media boast large staffs of reporters who can churn out large volumes of information. The broadcast industry brings to online communication the sound and picture qualities that enhance written information, but broadcast journalists lack the information-gathering expertise and the large staffs of the print media. Brooks attributed the rush to media conglomeration in the past decade, in part, to an attempt to form partnerships of experts and multiply strengths. For example, Time Warner, which owns Warner Brothers studio as well as *Sports Illustrated*, also bought into Cable News Network (Brooks) and in 2000 bought into American Oline (AOL).

Reddick and King (1997) concluded that computer-based communication networks have developed into "dynamic, widespread, accessible new channels of communication" (p. v). They attributed the changes to technological advances in the Information Age, much as improvements in papermaking and printing technology sparked newspaper expansion during the Industrial Revolution of the mid- and late-19th century. However, more people have gained access to the World Wide Web "in a shorter period of time than have adopted any new media technology in previous history" (p. 222). That is because the new technology made it possible for anyone to become a publisher or member of the media at relatively low cost—most certainly at far less cost than building a printing plant or television station. In 1995, the cost for maintaining a web page was as low as $125 for 50 megabytes of information through a service provider or as high as $30,000 for startup costs for a professional site with its own access to the Internet (p. 223).

Reddick and King (1997) found that most major companies were using the Internet and the World Wide Web to reach computer users. More than 1,115 commercial newspapers or news services were online by 1995. Radio stations, television stations, and magazines were flocking to online communication. Statistics, such as those recorded by the *News & Observer* of Raleigh, North Carolina, would seem to encourage even more participation by traditional media. The Raleigh newspaper reported more than 8 million contacts—"hits" in computer jargon—in a week (Reddick & King, p. 225). Although the contacts may represent anywhere from 80,000 to 250,000 readers because of multiple connections to different web pages by some users, the numbers are impressive. In addition, the growth of the Internet would suggest that the number of readers interested in online editions will increase. A study by ZD Market Intelligence, which collects information about the Internet, reported a 140% increase in personal computers that regularly used the Internet in the two-year period. The numbers jumped from 18.6 million in 1996 to 44.6 million in January 1998. Furthermore, a ZD study of 150,000 households indicated one of every three computers in the workplace and one of every two home computers utilized Internet access (Brewer, 1998).

Although no one can predict the number or forms of new media that may evolve, what is certain to occur is continued increases in speed of delivery of information.

The fax machine made it possible to deliver written communication to someone on the other side of the world in a matter of four to five minutes. Satellite technology made it possible to transmit a television picture or videotape clip anywhere in the world with similar speed. The development of faster computer chips and technologies that can deliver larger quantities of information over fewer or smaller lines, such as fiber optic cable, will increase the speed of delivery even more.

One of the ways in which the advances in computer technology has had an impact on the sports media and sports information professionals is that software programs have revolutionized the keeping of statistics. Sports information directors as well as sports reporters now have a virtual storage facility for statistics that can be immediately updated upon the completion of a game and easily accessed by reporters and fans alike.

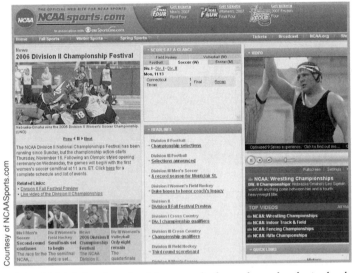

The NCAA has benefited immensely from the technological advances made regarding the recording of statistics. The NCAA utilizes the STAT CREW software for its statistical services.

The software programs used by the National Collegiate Athletic Association (NCAA) statistical services are from STAT CREW out of Cincinnati, Ohio. An early advocate of the electronic statistical programs in athletics, STAT CREW has provided the NCAA with electronic capabilities for more than 10 years. Jim Wright, the chief statistician for the NCAA, has seen the NCAA statistics department go from tons of paper to no paper. Wright, who has been with the NCAA for 30 years, heads a staff of 12 people, eight of whom are in statistics. He points out that the NCAA has been electronically reporting athletic statistics for more than 10 years. "The great thing about electronic reporting is that statistics must agree," Wright said. "If there are errors, they can be quickly found in the computer program and corrected" (Hall, 2003).

In football, the NCAA services Division I and Division I-AA. The schools in these divisions report to the NCAA and by using statistical programs that can produce, accumulate, and sort leaders in various football categories, the NCAA is able to manage team and individual statistics for both divisions. Division II and Division III football statistics are garnered from the various conferences throughout the country. "We rely on other sports information directors at the Division II and III institutions and the conference sports information directors to compile the top individuals and teams in their league and then electronically send the information to the NCAA," Wright said. "This method of reporting Division II and Division III statistics by conferences has worked quite well."

The NCAA has a website, NCAAsports.com, where statistics are accessible so that the media as well as individuals can quickly see the individual and team leaders in various statistical categories. "We keep the different sports by season," Wright said. "Our next project is to start establishing an archives where different leaders through the years can be recalled." At the conclusion of the 2006 football season, the NCAA had established archives for the past seven years, dating back to 1999. The NCAA's website has all but eliminated the need to send out press release and to mail statistics. "*USA Today* is one of the top users of our statistics and they have easy access as do other media to the leaders among the NCAA institutions," Wright said. "We use very little paper anymore."

Mike Ranieri has developed STAT CREW over the past two decades. He was looking for an avenue to develop a new company and by working with Dave Young at Miami (Ohio) University was able to produce a statistical software program for use with basketball. At the CoSIDA Convention in Kansas City in 1988, Ranieri found that many people wanted information about his product. Georgetown University and Loyola University of Chicago were early users of STAT CREW. In 1992, the NCAA became a user of STAT CREW. "The sports information director goes into the software, creates a statistics file, then gets on the Internet to the NCAA website and sends the file to the NCAA," Ranieri said. "No telephone calls are involved" (Hall, 2003). With STAT CREW, the computer guarantees correct statistics plus speed and accuracy. STAT CREW programs are used in various women's and men's athletic programs. "We focused on higher educational institutions as our market," Ranieri said. "The data can be used in the press box and on the scoreboard at the stadium." STAT CREW is now developing programs for colleges and universities that will show career statistics for individuals and teams.

Tony Hamilton of the Mid-Continent Conference uses STAT CREW to total his conference statistics. "Our statistics cover all aspects of our conference schools' basketball programs," Hamilton said. "We even include attendance in our statistics" (Hall, 2003). Bill Rogers, a former assistant athletic director of media relations at Valparaiso University, also pointed out the advantages of the computer program. "We have a complete and easily available file for the game and the season as soon as the contest is completed," Rogers said (Hall, 2003). Al King, an assistant athletic director and the sports information director at Ashland University, echoed Rogers' praise of statistical software programs. King said, "We can update career statistics for individuals almost immediately and keep those in attendance apprised of records set and broken and help the media in reporting about the contest" (Hall, 2003).

While updating statistics has become increasingly easier thanks to new software, another manner in which software and computers have impacted sports is computerized rankings. In fact, the participants in the national championship football game in NCAA Division I are determined in large part by computerized rankings. The Bowl Championship Series (BCS) computes its standings based on three components: the coaches' poll, Harris Interactive poll, and the average of six computer rankings ("BCS standings," 2006). Much controversy has been created in recent years regarding the BCS standings and how computers have played a role in selecting the matchup for the national championship game.

But computerized rankings aren't relegated to the collegiate level. In fact, some amateur organizations were using computerized rankings to determine postseason matchups long before the existence of the BCS. An athletic association that has become attached to the electronic base is the Ohio High School Athletic Associa-

Ohio High School Athletic Association
Football Computer Rankings

The following is an example of how the points are awarded and how to read the OHSAA Computer Rankings:

KEY

Wins over a Division I school — 6.0 points

Wins over a Division II school — 5.5 points

Wins over a Division III school — 5.0 points

Wins over a Division IV school — 4.5 points

Wins over a Division V school — 4.0 points

Wins over a Division VI school — 3.5 points

COMPUTER RANKINGS EXAMPLE

- Team A, a Division III school, is 3-0.
- Each opponent Team A has defeated is Division III.
- Opponents 1 and 2, which Team A has defeated, are each 2-1, with their victories coming over Division III schools.
- Opponent 3, which Team A has defeated, is 1-1, with its victory coming over a Division III school. Opponent 3 has had one open date.

First level points: 15.0 points {3 wins times 5.0 points (for defeating Division III opponents)} divided by 3 (the number of games Team A has played thus far) = **5.0000 first level points**.

Second level points: 10.0 from Opponent 1 {2 wins times 5.0 (for defeating Division III opponents)}, 10.0 from Opponent 2 {2 wins times 5.0 (for defeating Division III opponents)} and 5.0 from Opponent 3 {1 win times 5.0 (for defeating a Division III opponent)} for 25.0 points. These 25 points are then divided by 99 (since Opponent 3 thus far has had an open date) and multiplied by 10 = **2.5253 second level points.**

Total Points: 5.0000 (first level points) plus 2.5253 (second level points) = **7.5253**

NOTE: Say during week four, Opponent 1 has an open date. Then the second level points divisor for Team A after week four becomes 98, since Opponent 3 has had one open date and now Opponent 1 has had one open date.

HOW TO READ YOUR OHSAA COMPUTER RANKINGS

Level-1	Level-2	Average	Rank	City	High School Name
15.0000	25.0000	7.5253	1	A-TOWN	TEAM A

- To find out what the first level average is, divide the 15 points by the number of games Team A has played to date (15 divided by 3 = 5.0000)
- Next, subtract the 5.0000 from the total average of 7.5253. This number (2.5253) shows what the second level average is.
- So, 5.0000 first level points plus 2.5253 second level points = 7.5253 total points.
- To find out what divisor was used to determine second level points, divide the total level-2 points (25.0000) by the second level average (2.5253). So, 25.0000 divided by 2.5253 = 9.8998138. This means the divisor used was 99, which shows that one of Team A's opponents has had an open date.

Source: http://www.ohsaa.org/sports/ft/boys/rankcalc.htm

tion (OHSAA). The ranking system for football was adopted in 1972 and is used for selecting teams to participate in the OHSAA football playoffs. The original computer system was established by Jack Harbin of Cleveland and has been modified by the Board of Control of the OHSAA and the Ohio High School Football Coaches Association.

The football rating system is based on a point compilation that is established by the following system. Points are awarded for each game won, ranging from six points for a victory over a Division I opponent to 3.5 points for a win over a team in Division VI. Points are also earned for each game a defeated opponent wins. The points awarded for winning games are considered Level One points; those points awarded from defeated opponents are called Level Two points. Level One points and Level Two points are then added together and given an average based on the number of games played. (See table for further explanation of the point system.)

Bob Goldring, the director of information services of the OHSAA, pointed out that the OHSAA wanted to ensure that the computerized rankings do not promote teams "running up the score" on a weaker opponent in order to earn additional points in the standings. "The margin of victory is not a factor," Goldring said. "A win by one point or 10 points counts only as a win" (Hall, 2003). The OHSAA relies on reporters from the news media throughout Ohio to assist in reporting scores of football games played, and the rankings do not begin until the fourth week of the system. Weekly ratings are available on Tuesdays on the OHSAA website or through the *Associated Press*. The game opponents and sites for the first round of playoff football games are also available on the website and *Associated Press* after the close of the season. The sections or classifications of schools grouped together in football throughout the state are established to keep the same approximate number of schools in each section. Divisions (currently there are six) are examined, and sections are changed year-by-year based on geography and the enrollment of male students in grades 9–11 from the previous year.

The OHSAA uses its website to distribute information on all of its sports. The website is used by the media particularly for the girls and boys basketball tournaments. All high schools are eligible to participate in the state basketball tournament. The tournament parings are drawn locally but are put on the OHSAA website to show the brackets. "We are also updating our website by showing former teams, past champions, former events and histories of the events," Goldring said. "Electronics has certainly opened up the information venue for our high school events."

The aspiring sports information professional who keeps up with the technological advances and adjustments within existing media may find new outlets for promoting the sport organization. Here is a summary of changes in existing media and new directions they are pursuing because of technological evolution:

Newspapers and Magazines

Newspapers still are struggling to separate themselves from television and to compete with TV in the delivery of news and information. The answers may lie in specialization, regionalization, and collaboration with other types of information delivery.

All kinds of special-interest publications are popping up around the country: business publications, sport publications, and entertainment publications. Advances in computer technology make it possible for anyone to get into the publishing business at a much lower cost. For example, Pat Lense, a soccer enthusiast in Petersburg, Kentucky, started a local newspaper on the sport in the mid-1990s. He produced the stories and designed the pages on a home computer with desktop publishing software. Then he took the pages to a printer. The publication was so successful, he planned to expand into a wider region with an eye toward starting a statewide publication, and due in part to its success he began hosting a weeknight radio show called "The Soccer Pitch", which focused on the local soccer scene in the Cincinnati area

In addition, small-town newspapers and community weeklies showed gains in circulation in the 1990s. Circulation in dailies in cities with 100,000 or fewer residents jumped 19% from 1979 to 1994, and subscriptions to weekly newspapers increased from 29 million to 55 million (Dominick, 1996). The small dailies and weeklies put more emphasis on community events and local news, consistent with Newhagen and Rafaeli's (1996) views on niche markets.

In the mid-1990s, newspapers and magazines began to explore other niches including online editions on the Internet, fax newspapers, and call-in services. Some newspapers, such as the *Wall Street Journal,* began charging a subscription price for access to an online edition. Some also charged a fee for specific information from archives or for other subscriber services, but access to the bulk of newspapers on the Internet was free. Most of the sites offered selected stories from the current edition, classified advertising and connections to display advertisers, and other services ranging from archive searches and genealogy searches to copies of pictures and reprints of daily editions or commemorative issues.

Subscription-based Internet websites such as Rivals.com now play a large role in the dissemination of information, competing with the more traditional print and broadcast sports media outlets.

In addition, professional publications and organizations, such as the *American Journalism Review,* offered listings of newspapers and magazines online by geographical region (within the United States), country, and topic (AJR News Link, newslink.org/news.html). A reader anywhere in the world could call up the online edition of any newspaper or magazine on the link simply by clicking the computer pointer on the name of a publication on the list. The AJR site also provided a job bank for journalists and research guides.

Subscribers to fax newspapers could get delivery of a miniversion of the day's news via a facsimile machine in their homes or offices for a special fee. Call-in services enabled readers to get up-to-date information on sports scores, election results, stock market quotations, weather forecasts, and so on. The information usually was free, unless the call was long distance. The Internet, however, has made both of these forms of media virtually obsolete.

Online editions make it possible for newspapers and magazines to provide up-to-date information. A newspaper can update a developing story as it unfolds, much as radio and TV reports can. In other words, connections to the World Wide Web enable newspapers to counter the advantage of immediacy long enjoyed by radio and TV. Online editions also enable newspaper editors to interact with readers. Some online newspapers and magazines encourage users to send questions, compliments, or complaints by email, and the editors respond to them. Some services create computer bulletin boards, on which readers can discuss a story by sending messages to a common area where all who view the site can read them. Online editions also may help newspapers tap into the younger market, because a high percentage of computer users fall into younger age groups. A survey funded in part by *Parade Magazine* found online information was fairly or very important to 78% of the teenagers (13–17 years old) interviewed, while 35% said they never picked up a newspaper (Reddick & King, 1997).

Newspapers traditionally have attracted readers who tended to be middle aged and middle income. The potential for interactivity and new demographic audiences ultimately may help newspapers regain a share of the niche audiences they lost to the broadcast media. That is one reason the online editions often are free. They may attract computer users to the printed editions. They also provide another outlet for advertisers, thereby introducing another revenue source.

However, a study conducted by the Radio and Television News Directors Foundation in 1997 concluded that online newspapers will be forced to adapt television technologies and consider alliances with TV stations, such as the alliance between the *Sacramento Bee* and KXTV-TV, an ABC affiliate. Each promotes the other's websites online in print and on air (Noack, 1997). The study also suggested that online publications will have to add more sound and video to continue to maintain the edge they enjoyed at the outset of the latest computer craze.

Radio

Interactive opportunities are bringing AM radio back to life, both on traditional radio stations and through computer linkages. Talk show formats of all types are flourishing. Sport talk stations and shows are popular from coast to coast. Like small dailies and weekly newspapers, talk shows have a distinctly local flavor. So does radio broadcast of sports events. Although the major radio networks cover major sporting events, local stations follow specific teams.

Agreements with Internet and multimedia companies led radio into the world of computer delivery, too. Computer users now can pick up radio broadcasts of their favorite teams via audio hardware and software programs available commercially and online. Radio stations began to collaborate with Internet companies to feed their programming to computer users. Two sports fans and entrepreneurs launched AudioNet in 1995 to offer sports, talk and music radio, television shows, business events, CDs, news, commentary, and full-length audio books on the Internet around the clock seven days a week. Mark Cuban, a pioneer in multimedia technology as early as 1983 with MicroSolutions, and Todd Wagner, an attorney specializing in corporate and securities law, cut partnerships with companies such as

Motorola, a leading manufacturer of electronic equipment; Intel, the world's largest computer chip maker; Yahoo!, Inc., a global Internet media company; Premiere Radio Networks, which produces and distributes network radio programming; Host Communications, which holds rights to numerous sports broadcasts, including the NCAA Final Four; Capital Broadcast Company, a company that owns radio and television stations as well as the rights to both NCAA and professional sports teams; and Hicks, Muse, Tate & Furst, Inc., a private investment firm with interests in more than 100 radio and TV stations ("About Broadcast .com," 1998). The entrepreneurs also arranged distribution agreements with Yahoo!, RealNetworks, and Microsoft Corp. The interconnections enabled the company, renamed Broadcast.com in 1998, to deliver or "stream" live audio and video to computer users. AudioNet also offered Internet and intranet broadcasting services to businesses as well as Internet advertising services.

By mid-1998, Broadcast.com boasted live, continuous broadcasts of more than 310 radio stations, broadcasts of 17 television stations and cable networks, game broadcasts and other programs from more than 350 college and professional sports teams, live and on-demand broadcasts of corporate and special events, on-demand music from more than 2,100 CDs, and more than 360 full-length books. The "About Broadcast.com" website (1998) said the company had delivered 11,000 live events, including three straight Super Bowls and NCAA basketball tournaments as well as the entire 1997–98 season for 24 of the 26 National Hockey League teams by April 1998. Broadcast.com signed a three-year contract that month to broadcast live every New York Yankees baseball game. In addition to the live broadcasts, computer users could get the weekly *Yankees Magazine* television show, Yankees Online "insider information from the experts," live chats with Yankee coaches and players in a monthly question/answer forum, and replays of great Yankees games from the past. In an online news release announcing the agreement, Tim Wood, Yankees director of publications and multimedia, said, "This landmark deal with AudioNet is a gift to Yankee fans worldwide who now have access to the most comprehensive broadcast coverage and exclusive content not previously available" ("Press Room," broadcast.com, June 4, 1998).

The creators organized Broadcast.com into channels like television and turned the home page into an electronic TV guide. Each guide page (such as Sports Channel) listed programs and topic channels by sport. The computer user also could find a specific program by typing in a key word and clicking the computer's "search" function. Furthermore, the computer user could pull transcripts of earlier programs from the website's archive database ("Frequently Asked Questions," Broadcast.com, June 4, 1998). To tune in to the radio broadcasts, the computer user needed only to install special computer software that could be downloaded simply by clicking on a link on the website and following directions.

Because of the nature of computer technology and lack of federal regulation, there was no limit on how many programs Broadcast.com could deliver at one time. In addition, the reach of the "broadcast" was not limited by the power of the signal of the originating station. That was one of the primary attractions to sport organizations, such as the New York Yankees, who want to expand their audience reach worldwide. That also was one of the attractions to radio stations, which could break free from FCC assignment of broadcast bands and limitations on power. Broadcast.com could take the signal around the world and introduce the station to listeners everywhere.

Broadcast.com was later sold to Yahoo.com in a deal that made Cuban and Wagner billionaires and allowed Cuban the luxury of purchasing the NBA's Dallas Mavericks, becoming the franchise's majority owner in January 2000. The online broadcast of sporting events of the major professional leagues and high-profile college athletic teams has become increasingly popular, with the professional leagues and colleges offering a yearly subscription for access to the online radio broadcast of games.

Television

Television can be expected to continue to reign as king of the entertainment world for the foreseeable future. Digital technology (computer based) and high-definition TV (more lines per screen) are improving the quality of the picture. New production techniques are enhancing the entertainment value of telecasts. Instant replay is a staple. Gimmicks such as chalkboards that enable an analyst to pinpoint key moves, tackles, and so on, further add to the package. Dirigibles (blimps) provide aerial views of the action. Moving cameras follow the athlete down the field or court as the action unfolds. In other words, the viewer can see much more of the game in greater detail by watching it on TV than by attending the game, even though baseball teams have installed huge TV monitors within their scoreboards for selected replays.

Lou Holtz, a former college football coach, is one of countless coaches who have been lured from the sidelines to the broadcast booths by networks offering hefty financial packages made available by television stations' economic success.

Microwave and satellite technology are increasing the reach of TV viewers, that is, the number of networks (signals) or channels a viewer can see. A television viewer no longer is limited by an antenna on top of the house. Viewers can subscribe to a cable provider that delivers a package of channels via coaxial cable. They can contract with a company that delivers a package of stations via microwave dish. They can buy a satellite dish and hook up with a company that provides a link to transmissions from one or more communication satellites. Such links make it possible to get hundreds of channels from around the world. Finally, viewers can subscribe to pay-TV services that offer access to selected movies and selected sporting events for a fee for each event.

TV stations also are catching up with the print media in online delivery of information, according to the 1997 study by the Radio and Television News Directors Foundation (Noack, 1997). The study predicts the gap between online newspapers and TV will disappear as bandwidth increases and technologies such as real-time streaming video continue to become more popular. "When it takes just a few seconds to download a full-motion video news clip on the Internet, TV newsrooms will gain the edge over their counterparts," the study concluded (Noack, 1997). Downloading can be slowed by technology geared to text-based systems designed for standard telephone lines, but the personal use of high-speed Internet connections are becoming increasingly more popular, allowing users to quickly download and then view video highlights of their favorite team.

The proliferation of technologies, networks, and cable-oriented channels is at the root at the competition for broadcast rates. All of these information-delivery possibilities are also creating concern over saturation of sport programming and costs to the consumer. Professional wrestling, prize fights, and college sports are among the offerings on pay TV. Dominick (1996) said networks fear that subscription services will take away some sports that viewers have previously watched for free. For example, the Madison Square Garden Network held exclusive rights to all New York Yankees games from 1991 to 2002. However, some Yankee games still appeared on other networks through deals cut by MSGN.

Television producers are capitalizing on the same content innovations and interactive opportunities as radio and the print media are using. Local talk shows are making their way onto television, too. Coaches' shows have been a staple for a couple of decades. In recent years, stations have started their own local talk shows, many of them staffed by a panel of experts who respond to viewers' calls. Four television stations in Cincinnati offered such shows after the late Sunday news during the pro football season in 1996. Three of them continued the shows through the basketball season.

TV stations and networks also have moved online, providing news and information drawn from the telecasts. The sites allowed viewers to send in questions, compliments, complaints, or other comments much like the communications sent to their print counterparts. Like radio, TV stations began signing up with companies like AudioNet for live computer links to telecasts of games and other programs. Some local news stations place video from their evening news broadcasts on their websites so that the newscasts are not limited to being viewed by people living only in that market.

Television networks and TV stations added information in largely printed form, and newspapers and magazines provided audio and video components via the Internet. In some cases, they combined their efforts. As noted earlier, Time Warner owns interests in *Sports Illustrated* and Cable News Network. The cable network and magazine shared a site on the World Wide Web.

Sport Organizations

The new technologies are making sport organizations equal partners with the media in the delivery of information. The World Wide Web provides not only a new outlet for dissemination of information, but also a new vehicle through which sport organizations can communicate directly with fans and supporters.

Sport organizations likely will continue to utilize the traditional media for dissemination of information through news releases, features, and so on. Sport organization will continue to produce media guides for journalists and programs for spectators who attend the games, but they also can be expected to utilize the World Wide Web as a complementary link to both media and sport audiences. For example, sports information specialists can post news releases, statistical updates, rosters, and game previews on the web for round-the-clock access by both reporters and fans. They also can arrange email contacts and computer "chat room" interviews for media and fans to increase interaction with coaches, athletes, and sports information personnel, and they can add promotional and advertising materials to the website to enhance marketing efforts.

Professional sport organizations began to appear on the Internet in the mid-1990s. Some sport organizations hired computer technicians to create and operate sites in-house. Others forged service agreements with companies with either Internet technology experience or mass communication expertise. For example, Medius Interactive claims to have created the first official professional sport site in 1994 ("Company Info," 1998). Medius Interactive is a subsidiary of Medius Communications, Inc., a Canadian company incorporated in August 1994 to provide Internet expertise to business clients. Medius Interactive calls itself a one-stop full-service resource that provides "web design, backend programming, advertising representation, consulting, database creation and integration, maintenance tools and services for both external and internal sites" ("Company Info," 1998). Clients in the late 1990s ranged from such sport organizations as the American Basketball League, New York Yankees, and Professional Sports Car to such corporations as Northwestern Mutual Life, Coca-Cola Japan, and radio station KIRO 710. Starwave Corporation bills itself as "the premiere Internet technology company and creator and producer of the leading online sports, news and entertainment services" ("About Starwave," 1998). The company was founded in 1993 by Microsoft investor Paul Allen, who shared ownership with The Walt Disney Company, which bought interests in ABC and ESPN in the 1990s. In 1997, Starwave entered into partnerships with ESPN and ABC to create subsidiaries to produce original interactive programming and online services. Among Starwave-created sites were ABC News, ESPN.com, the National Basketball Association and Women's National Basketball Association, NASCAR, *Mr. Showbiz* magazine, and Wall of Sound (a musical entertainment site).

In May 1998, the website for the now-defunct American Basketball League, created by Medius Interactive, offered league and team news briefs, schedules and results, standings, and statistics from the most recent season, and league records. The site provided links to each team, complete with team news, team statistics, a team directory, a roster with pictures and personal information on each player, and ticket information. The information and pictures in both areas were virtually identical to traditional news release, media brochure, and program materials. However, the site also contained a Gear page that offered clothing and publications for sale, and a fan club that provided opportunities to interact with the league, teams, and players. For example, computer users could submit pictures of themselves wearing ABL gear for display on the site. They could chat at a prescribed time

• KEY TECHNOLOGY TERMS •

bandwidth—the capacity of a network to handle data traffic

bookmark—a computer tool through which the user can "mark" a home page on the World Wide Web and return to it with a single keystroke or click of the computer mouse

bulletin board—computerized information services that can be accessed using a computer, modem, and telephone line

chat room—a functional equivalent of a telephone conversation. People who are online at the same time can communicate with each other simultaneously. A large number of people can participate at the same time

commercial information services—commercial enterprises that provide information online for a fee, such as America Online

cyberspace—the collective environments or "place" created by computer networks

database—a body of facts, usually focused on a predefined topic, and gathered together in a computer. Organized into meaningful patterns, data (facts) in a database becomes information

discussion list—a method by which individuals can communicate easily with many people by using email. People subscribe to discussion lists, then automatically receive all messages other subscribers send to the list. A discussion list functions like a conversation among hundreds of people interested in the same topic. More commonly known as a *listserve*

download—to retrieve a file from a server or any other online computer

email—electronic mail; text messages sent across computer networks to digital mail boxes where they can be retrieved and read at leisure

E-zine—electronic magazine on a website

home page—applied to HTTP (HyperText Transfer Protocol) documents on the World Wide Web; generally, the top page (welcome or index page) of websites and to personal pages placed on web servers by many individuals

HTML—HyperText Markup Language, a text-based scripting language (like words on paper) used to create documents served on the World Wide Web

HTTP—HyperText Transfer Protocol, the network data communication specification used on the World Wide Web

hypertext—a means of linking information

Internet—the network of computer networks that used the TCP/IP communication language and can communicate with each other. Some people see the Internet as the prototype of the information superhighway

listserv—software for managing an email discussion list. A *listserv* takes messages sent to a list and distributes those messages to all who are subscribed

modem—a device through which a computer links to the network through telephone lines. Most personal computers today come equipped with a modem

network—computers linked in order to transfer information and share other resources

news group—a discussion forum with the Usenet news system; functions like a *discussion list* but operates differently technologically

online—connected to the Internet and World Wide Web via personal computer, a modem, and a service provider

program—a set of instructions written in binary code, telling a computer how to perform certain tasks

search engine—a computer "robot" that searches through sites on the World Wide Web to locate and list pages with a specified key word

server—a machine on which resides software designed to deliver information across a network in a manner specifically recognized by another computer; also described as the software that delivers information

TCP/IP—Transmission Control Protocol/Internet Protocol, the set of communication rules by which computers connected to the Internet talk to one another

World Wide Web—allows for information located on many different computers to be linked through key terms. This approach is called hypertext or hypermedia. The Web is accessed through client programs, such as Internet Explorer and Netscape.

Source: Adapted from *The Online Journalist* (Reddick & King, 1997)

with Danielle McCulley, a player from the Portland Power. They could send questions or comments to the ABL Fan Forum via email as well as read the questions and responses of other computer users. They also could enter a contest to name and design the logos for two new ABL teams.

The Women's National Basketball Association site provided similar basic information on teams and players. It offered a store and interactive opportunities, too. In addition, the WNBA site included a theater link, which featured audio and video highlights of key events such as the presentation of the first-place award in the 2-on-2 competition during NBA All-Star Weekend to Cynthia Cooper of the Houston Comets and Clyde Drexler of the Houston Rockets. A "What's Next" page invited computer users to sign up for a weekly email message from the WNBA complete with notes and facts from around the league, excerpts from upcoming features, updated broadcast information, and previews of key matchups—in other words, the kind of data sport information professionals typically put into an advance or game preview package.

Most colleges and universities affiliated with the National College Athletic Association maintained sites on the web by 1998. Many simply piggybacked onto academic or administrative sites created and maintained by the college or university. Several universities with large, Division I sport programs signed up with professional groups, such as University Netcasting, Inc., (UNI) a conglomeration of companies that provided college sport services including Collegiate Licensing Company and Stella Interactive ("Company Info"). Collegiate Licensing manages collegiate licensing for more than 150 institutions, bowl games and athletics conferences, according to information on the site. University Netcasting built its first website for the University of Southern California in August 1996 ("Company history," 2003). Later that year the company had added five more schools to its list, calling the collection FANSonly Network. All of the schools' webpages in the FANSonly Network were linked and maintained some type of consistent design. FANSonly was later rebranded and called Official College Sports Network (OCSN). The OCSN network was later turned over to College Sports Television (CSTV), and CSTV.com boasted of more than 250 official university athletic sites in 2005 ("About us," 2006). CSTV.com provides a basic "shell" for a school's website, with each university offering information and features unique to that particular school. For example, the University of Kentucky site includes pages for all of the school's athletic teams, but it would be more likely to feature men's basketball more prominently on the front page than a school such as the University of Notre Dame, which is known more for its football program than for its men's basketball team. Much of the information available on the team websites is similar to that available in a media guide.

Many smaller schools simply add a page(s) to a site created and maintained by a department or unit within the university. The site for the University of North Dakota, which won the Division II women's basketball championship, devoted a section to athletics in the 1997–1998 academic year. The athletics page linked consumer users to each UND team with information on the roster, schedule, coaches, statistics, and brief summaries of recent news releases. Southern Indiana University's site incorporated news releases, varsity club news, season ticket information, general information about the teams and coaches, and a composite schedule. The site also provided a connection to the radio broadcasts of basketball games, so fans could listen to games through the audio components of their personal computers.

Six of 22 Division II conferences also maintained Internet sites by the end of the 1997–1998 academic year. The Great Lakes Valley Conference (GLVC), in which Southern Indiana competes, gave readers news briefs, a rundown on the All-Sports Trophy competition, and information on the history of the league, officers, championships, and major awards. Links on the site enabled consumer users to jump to pages on each GLVC sport as well as the home pages of member teams and NCAA Division II home.

As the 20th century approached its end, such technological innovations blurred the lines between sports and entertainment, between entertainment and information, and between news and public relations. The sports information specialist of the 21st century must keep abreast of the evolution of computer technology and melding of media to capitalize on new opportunities to reach the organization's primary audiences. The scope and speed of communication on the World Wide Web expanded the reach and the potential audience for all.

The Sport Information Challenge

So where should a sports information specialist look for guidance through this maze of overlapping technologies, interconnecting media, and expanding audiences? Look to content, say the Internet pioneers. Representatives of Starwave Corporation went to the Collegiate Press Association national convention in 1995 looking for young people who could write well. Jim Albrecht of *Mr. Showbiz* magazine told a seminar group that content gives a website staying power when the bells and whistles and gimmicks of technology on the Internet cease to fascinate. "If you can write good, clean English, there are jobs for you on the Internet," he told prospective journalists. There will be jobs that put amps of sound with stories to combine words and pictures into a single, entertaining package. The Starwave representatives also dismissed suggestions that newspapers are dying. The Internet pioneers are finding that "35 cents a day is a tough price to beat," said Geoff Reiss of ESPN.com. "You get a lot of value for the money."

The most practical uses of the Internet and communication technology for journalists and sports information personnel are storage and retrieval of information. Because they provide access to everyone almost instantaneously, however, they will forever change the media habits and relationships among journalists, sport organizations, and sport audiences. For journalists, the Internet puts sources of information from around the world at their fingertips. They can search for data and other information in libraries and network systems throughout the world. They also can store all their materials in the computer system, for instant retrieval and review. For sports information directors, computer technology provides a storehouse for records and information used frequently. The word processing and design capabilities of computers make it possible to produce a news release or picture in a variety of forms quickly, and an Internet storage site can open access to all kinds of records to both media and fans. For fans, the Internet provides a home library. The personal computer user can plug into a newspaper and read all the stories on a favorite topic, no matter the publication date. Likewise, a computer user can plug into a sport organization site and get almost any information on the team from its inception through the current date.

The new technology provides new tools for packaging and delivering information, not new kinds of content. Although new tools and new techniques are emerging, the essential elements of sport communication remain the same, that is, words, sound, and pictures. The foundation for success will continue to be mastery of the fundamentals of written, verbal, and visual communication. However, the prospective sport communication professional will need to understand the basic tools of Information Age technology—from CD-ROMs to the World Wide Web—to craft messages effectively for various types of media audiences. That does not mean a sports information director will have to learn how to create a CD or construct a web page. What it does mean is that the information professional will have to learn the strengths and weaknesses of evolving new media as they relate to the message and the audience. The journalist and sports information specialist will have to adapt the fundamentals to new kinds of presentation. The shelves at public libraries, bookstores, and computer stories are filled with guides to online communication, publications that translate the language of computer technicians into terms the layperson can understand.

The primary challenges to the sports information professional of the 21st century are threefold:

First, the sports communication professional will have to gather information and craft messages effectively, that is, create informative and entertaining content whether written, verbal, visual, or a combination of forms.

Although research on the Internet is still in its infancy, mass communication scholars suspect people process information viewed on a computer monitor in different ways than they process words on paper. A short feature on paper may appear to be very long on a computer screen, and therefore less effective in holding audience interest. To be most effective, the communicators of the 21st century need to learn how to adapt a news release for online readers instead of using a single release for both a website and for the print media. Likewise, sports information specialists likely will have to adapt to differences in audio and video presentation instead of simply delivering the same highlights on the computer screen as on videotape for television.

As noted earlier, computer technology provides the tools to gather and analyze information quickly from a worldwide range of sources. For journalists, computer applications may facilitate finding story ideas, gathering background information, identifying and contacting sources, verifying and confirming facts, and analyzing information. For example, a journalist might decide to explore the changes in the number and types of sports offered by NCAA Division I universities in the wake of Title IX. The reporter could gather background information on gender equity from Internet and library sources. Websites maintained by professional journalism organizations could lead the journalist to expert sources, university officials, and athletes affected by the changes. The reporter might even conduct an interview electronically, either in real time or by email. Internet sites also might link the journalist to databases of information on the topic created by athletics organizations or academic researchers. Finally, computer programs that sort numbers, analyze data, and perform calculations could help the reporter identify trends and patterns resulting from the implementation of Title IX.

Lisa Miller (1998) of the University of New Hampshire emphasizes in *Power Journalism: Computer-Assisted Reporting* that technology supplements the basics of good journalism. The data helps the reporter conduct better interviews, add greater detail to the story and improve the context—in other words, improve the content. Said Miller:

> Computer-assisted reporting (CAR) doesn't replace the other techniques you already use; it gives you more tools for doing your job well. And it won't do stories for you; in fact, CAR is often only the beginning of your reporting work. After you've done your online research, after you've crunched all the numbers, you still have to go out and talk to and observe people. Their stories give meaning and life to the numbers and the facts. It's also important to treat information gathered through CAR the same way you would any information, verifying and attributing it when necessary, and to plan and craft stories carefully. (Miller, 1998, p. v)

Both CD-ROMs and the Internet represent enormous research assets for both the journalist and the sports information specialist because of the volume of data/information on the Internet and speed in collecting it. In 1997, reporters at the *Evansville* (Ind.) *Courier* could draw from CDs containing

> millions of business and residential listing, including addresses and telephone numbers; encyclopedias; electronic atlases that include street-level maps for the United States; information about toxic substances released into air, water and land by manufacturing plants; census information; data about over-the-counter and prescriptions drugs; the complete text of hundreds of literary works; the budget of the United States; criminal justice statistics; stories from daily newspapers across the country; and databases concerning music, sports, cinema, historical government documents, U.S. foreign affairs, marriage records and businesses. (Miller, 1998, p. 151)

In addition, research tools incorporated in computer software enable one to explore the Internet for information on a specific topic. The researcher does not have to know the Internet address for specific organizations or databases. The computer user literally can hunt for information on a topic using Internet tools called "search engines"—Ask.com, Google, and Yahoo, for example—that automatically list all the stories on a given topic. That means one might find thousands of sites with information on Title IX simply by typing the words into a blank field on the search engine website. Furthermore, some websites provide indexes that lead/link the computer researcher to databases on a given topic.

One such site is maintained by the Foundation for American Communications (FACS), which was founded in 1976 as an independent education institution to help journalists gather knowledge, perspectives, and resources "to effectively communicate, through the news, information about important public issues" ("Mission," 1998). The organization conducts journalism education programs for the media, corporations, nonprofit executives, and academics. It also produces a wide range of support materials, including the *Media Resource Guide*, *Academic Media Handbook*, *NewsBackgrounders*, audio and videotapes, and regular newsletters. FACSNET, a website created in collaboration with the San Diego Supercomputer Center, gives journalists Internet assistance in four ways. The Top Issues link provides insight, background, and sources on current issues. The Internet Resources section provides annotated links to resources useful to journalists on specific topic areas. For example, the Sports area includes a list of sports. The researcher also can search for more narrow topics within individual sports by using a keyword search. The Reporting Tools option links the computer user to background information and both reporting and Internet guides. Finally, the Sources Online area lists names, telephone numbers, and email connections for sources of expert information.

Computer technology makes it possible for the sports information professional to deliver information in different ways. The SID not only can deliver news, features, and game previews to the media, but also can put copies on a website for access by journalists not on the mailing list and by computer users (fans and potential fans). The sports information professional can create databases with rosters, schedules, statistics, and the like that both journalists and fans can use. In addition, the sport organization can use the site to market products, call attention to game promotions, and link fans to sponsors' sites as the WNBA has done.

Second, the 21st-century sports information professional will have to develop new ways to interact with the organization's fans and supporters.

Of all the advances in the Information Age, the interactive capabilities of computer technology will play perhaps the most significant role in changing the relationship between the sport organization and the audience. That is because these capabilities connect the spectators to Lawrence Wenner's sports production complex in ways no one could imagine when he wrote his book *Media, Sports and Society* in 1989 (see Chapter 1). Interactive communication enables spectators to challenge the views of sportswriters, sportscasters, and talk show "experts," as well as to offer their own views. In other words, it allows the spectator to become commentator on a sporting event and correspond directly with the sport organization—to join the media in an individual way. Interactive communication makes it possible for sport organizations to communicate directly with the audience, too, and cut the media out of the middle.

The most successful sport organizations in the future may well be those that develop new ways to serve audiences directly. Sport information and public relations personnel already are sending news releases instantly to the media over facsimile machines and via email. The fax has replaced the U.S. Mail in a lot of cases, although the use of email is beginning to lead to the extinction of fax machines. Sports information staffs are beginning to experiment with sending information to fans who subscribe to an email service or sign up on the Internet at URLs like the WNBA's "What Next?" page. They also are looking for new ways to connect the audience to the excitement of the event itself. NASCAR literally puts computer users in the driver's seat with a subscription to its Nextel TrackPass available on its website, NASCAR.com. With the service, online racing fans can listen to in-car radio feeds, the communication between drivers and their teams, during the race.

The rapidly expanding technology available with cellular telephones is another avenue in which sports information specialists have begun to experiment. Some professional teams and major universities have a subscription service for fans that allows the users to receive breaking news and timely updates by getting text messages from the organization. Real-time scores, in-game statistics, and audio and video clips are other items being offered to cell phone users.

How much does that add to the excitement? How much does that add to the bond between spectator and sport? Remember, sport creates a sense of belonging among audience members (see Chapter 11). Interactive communication with fans may help to cement the bonds between the two. Consider the interaction opportunities and potential benefits on the professional and collegiate sites mentioned earlier in this chapter. What would it mean to a young fan to get an email message from a star player, or to appear on the team's computer site for all the world to see? The 14-year-old basketball fan mentioned in the introduction to the chapter entered the contest to name the two new American Basketball League teams. She felt connected to the league, a participant in one small way. She also checked the ABL site frequently, which exposed her to new information and opportunities. She created a "bookmark" for the league, a computer link that took her directly to the site with a single keystroke upon logging onto the Internet. So the interactive connection and bookmark took her back again and again to the ABL website. She did not have to wait for a newspaper or television newscast to provide information on scores and statistics. She could go get it herself any day . . . and she did, frequently.

The savvy sport organization explores new ways to increase such interaction. Email, bulletin boards, chat rooms, and contests multiply the opportunities to connect and bond with fans, both literally and figuratively. The return for an email interview or one-hour chat room session with a player or coach might pay enormous benefits. Not only does it facilitate bonding, but it also enables the sport organization to control the message to a greater extent. Fans would not have to depend entirely on the media to tell them what kind of person Alex Rodriguez or Mia Hamm is. They could draw their own conclusions based on personal email and chat room interactions.

Furthermore, the sport organization can influence the interpretation of the message. The sports information staff could put news, features, statistics, and pictures (with audio and video) on its own home site that collectively create the desired message. The computer-connected fan would be introduced to the same, consistent message with each visit to the site. The sports information staff also could choose selected quotations from email and chat room interactions to reinforce the image the sport organization wants to project.

Third, the sports information professional will have to identify specific target audiences and the media that serve those audiences.

In an age of specialization, the SID will have to know the special interests of each media representative. No longer will all newspapers seek the same kind of information for a general audience. Sports information directors will have to cultivate the right messengers to reach a specific niche audience and achieve predetermined goals.

Sport administrators and sports information directors also will have to continue to find ways to help the media do their job. They may have more media and more ways to consider. Email makes it possible for journalists to correspond with sports information personnel from any location at any time. The journalist and SID do not have to be in the office at the same time to "converse"—one of the limitations of telephone contact. The reporter or SID can send an email message and the other can respond to "calls" simply by checking the email upon returning to the office. Curtis Danburg, manager of media relations for the Cleveland Indians, uses email almost exclusively to communicate with the media (Nichols, 2002). "Email has vastly improved communications between the team and the media," Danburg said. "It has improved the efficiency in communicating, not only with the media, but with other ball clubs, Major League Baseball, and the Elias Statistical Bureau."

Likewise, sports information professionals can schedule email or chat room interviews with coaches and players that do not require everyone to be in the same location at the same time. A reporter might submit questions to a designated email address, and the coach or athlete could respond by email, or the SID could arrange a chat room interview with a player or coach for all reporters at a designated time. The SID could provide a link to a transcribed version of a chat room interview for other journalists or fans. Remember, however, that online interviews lose the benefits of interpersonal communication attached to one-on-one interviews.

Email also enables the sports information specialist to reach a large number of reporters with the push of a button. Sports information specialists are no longer limited to mail, fax, or telephone in getting a press release out to the media. The Cleveland Indians have two media lists. The local list includes approximately 200 members, including television, radio, and print media. The Cleveland Indians national list of about 150 members includes the accredited journalists for Major League Baseball, key employees at other clubs, and contacts with ballparks around the Major Leagues. The Indians use email to forward news releases on announcements regarding player movement and then follow up with a telephone call to the key local media. A member of the Indians staff pushes a button and the email will immediately go to everyone on the local contact list. Another button is pushed and the message goes to everyone on the national contact list. Game notes are also sent to a select list of 30 people, including local beat writers, via email. When the Indians are at home (Jacobs Field), hard copies of the news release are put in the pressbox. "This is how we communicate with the other teams and the media," Danburg said. "This saves time and there is less telephone interaction. However, there is not as much personal interaction as before" (Nichols, 2002).

The Cleveland Browns of the National Football League use telephone calls to make important announcements. Email is used for roster moves and for weekly releases, which are sent on Monday to a local list of approximately 200 and a national list of approximately 400. Notes and statistics of the previous game are sent to 25–30 newspapers and NFL beat writers. A weekly review/preview is sent through email to arrive on Wednesday of each week to all teams and beat writers. Ken Mather, manager of publicity and media for the Browns, points out that within 10 minutes after each game a play-by-play (Game Statistics Information System) is available online (Nichols, 2002). This package includes play-by-play, individual statistics, team statistics, defensive statistics, and drive charts. "We provide all the statistics along with quotes from coaches and key players in our postgame notes," Mather said. "These interviews are shown in the pressbox on television monitors and also are given to the opposing team."

The National Basketball Association (NBA) has a master list of all league teams and beat writers. The NBA also has a website for media only. The Cleveland Cavaliers website is part of the NBA network. The Cavaliers have a local contact list that numbers approximately 200, and email can reach these members very quickly. According to Bob Price, former senior director of communications and public relations with the Cavaliers, email is used because of expediency and economy (Nichols, 2002). "You can get information disseminated much quicker by email," Price said. "You can pull up a game summary on the website immediately."

The access and convenience created by online communication potentially will enable reporters to gather more information on deadline quicker, resulting in more complete and more entertaining information. Access and convenience will also help the sport organization reach fans and journalists who do not even attend the game with information and audio and video highlights quickly delivered on web pages or through bulletin boards. The sports information staff could put pregame and postgame data on the site for journalists and fans. Newspapers, radio, and TV stations could plug into the information themselves, reducing the number of telephone calls SID staffers must make after a game and speeding up delivery time to the media (all can get the information at the same time). Furthermore, computer connections would enable journalists unable to attend a news conference to get the information quickly or even participate in the news conference.

Videoconferences are possible for sport organizations with access to interactive video technology. Many colleges are offering interactive classes through video systems. A professor in one location can lecture to students at any number of remote locations equipped with the same technology. The instructor can see each classroom on a large screen. Each class can see the instructor, and students can talk to the instructor, much like a live television interview. In the future, a coach may be able to conduct a pregame videoconference with the media, much like the postgame news conference. Journalists would not have to leave their offices to participate.

Because of technology, speed of information delivery will be one of the criteria by which journalists and sports information professionals will be judged in the future. Sports information directors will have to stock media areas with state-of-the-art equipment to ensure that reporters have access to up-to-date information and can recycle it quickly. Tom Gamble (1997), a reporter for *The Kentucky Post*, scoffed at Northern Kentucky University's proposal to start a football program in 1995 because of limitations in computer technology. He wondered in print how a university with "sports information phones that don't work properly and a computer system one step ahead of Bedrock" could afford to launch a football program (p. K-6).

Professional golf offers an example of how to deliver up-to-date information quickly. Golf is difficult to telecast because the game action is spread across several acres of terrain. Spectators cannot see all of the action at the same time. Television gives them a chance to see most of it, with cuts from one tee or green to another. An elaborate communication system makes it work. Information from each camera location is relayed immediately to a central communication point. When a player sinks a putt, the information goes to the central communication point, which distributes it to other locations throughout the course. Computers compile information on the status of every player after every hole, and the up-to-date numbers flow to all points on the course.

If content remains the bedrock of sport communication, the advances in technology and evolution of new delivery techniques offer clues to content directions in the future. "Print reporters must know that readers have heard about the event on television or radio and thus look for narrative leads with unusual angles or takes on a story," said Gaffney, of the Akron *Beacon Journal* (Nichols, 1996). Newspapers first turned to more depth, analysis, and comment from participants to meet the challenge of TV. Now, they are trying to put a human face on stories. This will mean sports information directors will have to be more alert to feature angles about their athletes and programs so they can help direct media attention to those areas.

A picture is still worth a thousand words, and the methods and speed of delivery improved dramatically in the 1990s. Software programs enable a journalist or sports information professional to "scan" or copy a picture into a computer system. The journalist or SID also can incorporate stories and pictures into a page design. Journalists can prepare pages more quickly, and SIDs can put together pamphlets and brochures more quickly. Instant photo shops can eliminate the need for darkrooms. Some campus and small professional newspapers contract their photography processing to speedy commercial businesses. More and more, however, the technology of digital cameras has begun to eliminate the film development process entirely. Journalists and sports information directors can transfer the image directly from the camera to the computer. This allows them to deliver game photos within minutes of the end of a contest. And if the sports information department can deliver a strong action photo or headshot to print journalists, they can facilitate better media coverage. Sports information directors are also beginning to branch out from simple photographs and may also put video highlights on the Internet shortly after the completion of a contest.

Whereas technological advances are widening the scope of sports' international proportions, specialization is turning the focus inward. Yes, sports fans want to see soccer in Africa and South America, horse racing in England and Japan, and golf and tennis around the world, but their allegiance remains with the hometown team. The success of rural and urban dailies and weeklies and the popularity of talk radio make clear the importance of local audiences to the media. The spread of cable TV and development of local channels by cable operators have opened more media opportunities to sport organizations. Some media watchers expect high school coverage to increase dramatically in the near future (Mencher, 1991). The more effectively sports information professionals can capitalize on such regionalization, the better.

Ruple, the SID at Baldwin-Wallace, advises sports communication professionals to "make stories as localized as you can" (Nichols, 1996). That means, for instance, that for the metropolitan newspapers, the SID should emphasize athletes from the geographic area; for the local daily, establish local identification, such as a local high school graduate. For the weekly, the SID can do basically the same but with different deadline considerations.

Summary

Changes in the delivery of information and entertainment through the print and broadcast media are taking place almost daily. The development of existing media technologies and evolution of new ones are profoundly changing the economic foundations, structure, and administration of sports. All are creating new demands for the sports information specialist and adjustments in the relationships among media industries, sport organizations, and sports fans.

Sport communication evolved into big business in the 1990s. Media organizations were swallowed up in the corporate expansions and movement toward conglomeration that dominated the economic landscape. In many cases, the shift in ownership put more emphasis on watching the bottom line and making profits. Giant media corporations found a popular source of entertainment and lucrative source of revenue in sport programming on television. American corporations invested in media corporations to gain prestige and increase revenues. They poured money into stadiums, shoes, and shirts—anything that afforded an opportunity to keep their names and images in front of the television cameras and the public eye.

The large sums of advertising money available for sport programming created enormous competition for broadcast rights among the ever increasing numbers of TV networks, cable channels, and independent producers. The competition provided a rich source of income for sport organizations. From a positive standpoint, the relatively new source of revenue helped to offset dwindling allotments of public money. It also provided visibility to sport organizations, exposure that translated into increased spectator interest and corporate support. From a negative standpoint, the pot of TV money shifted some control over sport organizations to television producers.

TV provided a regional, national, and sometimes international stage for sport organizations. In return, sport organizations relinquished the right to manage the stage. The demands of the media forced many organizations to schedule events to meet production needs. Sport organizations now change starting times to meet deadlines, set up schedules to avoid conflicts with other athletics events, and package two or three sports events together on the same day.

TV revenues contributed to changes in the structure and administration of sport organizations. Professional teams gravitated toward major media markets that offered greater revenues. Colleges and universities formed power conferences across wide geographic expanses to try to garner a greater share of the revenues. The influence trickled into the Division II ranks during the 1990s but journalists, athletics administrators, and sports information professionals do not agree on whether the money and influence with seep into Division III and colleges affiliated with the National Association of Intercollegiate Athletics. Though clearly, the high visibility and link to revenues put greater importance on winning and maintaining a positive image.

The high visibility and TV revenues led college presidents to take a greater role in governance of athletics. The economic shift also shuffled the roles and duties of other personnel in sport organizations. College presidents started looking for administrators with experience or training in marketing and promotions. Sports information directors began to play a greater role in decision making because of their expertise in dealing with the media as well as their marketing and promotional skills.

The developments of the 1990s suggest the future belongs to sport organizations that can put a quality product on the field of play and market it effectively. Successful marketing depends on building a winning program, increasing spectator interest, and tapping corporate financial resources. All help to attract media interest, especially television. That formula has pushed women's sports into the high-visibility spotlight. Increased coverage of women's sports represented the most significant change in programming as the decade of the 1990s neared its end. Administrators and sports information personnel held out hope that other sports could be marketed successfully following the same model.

There is no sign of a slowdown in the demand for sports programming, nor is there a letup in the development and evolution of media technologies. The last decade of the 20th century provided more information of better quality to the sports public than any previous decade in history. It also produced significant changes in the types and number of media sources. Satellite technology created new methods of delivering TV programs and videos. Computer technology made it possible to send words, pictures, audio, and video around the world in a matter of minutes. Computer technology also led to creation of computer libraries housed by businesses, colleges and universities, and media industries. Software programs provided links between computer networks, enabling users to travel from library to library without leaving their seats at home or office.

The technological revolution altered the makeup of the media and added to the methods of delivery. Connections to the Internet gave the print media an opportunity to eliminate the time advantage enjoyed by the broadcast media. The print media now can offer words, pictures, and sounds instantly over the Internet. The

Internet gave the broadcast media an opportunity to provide printed text with the audio and video. Online versions of traditional media and new media employing aspects of various media created opportunities for both sport organizations and the media to interact with their audiences.

Interactive communication online represents perhaps the most significant influence on sport communication and media relations. Interactive applications of the new technology by journalists and sport administrators alike have changed the relationship between the sport industries and fans. Email, bulletin boards, and talk shows that give sports fans an opportunity to participate in the dialogue foster the sense of belonging coveted by sport organizations. Interactive communication also helps both journalists and sport organizations deliver information more quickly. Both can update information rapidly on the Internet.

The greatest challenge to the sports information professional of the 21st century will be to develop the right message for a specific audience and cultivate the messengers that deliver it most effectively. The sports information specialist will have to adapt basic storytelling techniques to the peculiarities of different media and new media. The explosion of sports coverage and media technology in the second half of the 20th century has had the effect of making the world of sport communication both larger and smaller. The media can transmit a message, a story, or a picture to all parts of the world at the same time. The number and types of media that can deliver information have increased rapidly, but the media's need to find a niche has turned coverage decisions inward, in many cases. Coverage of local sports was on the rise at the end of the last decade, and the interactive capabilities of new technologies were pulling the relationship among spectators, the media, and sport organizations together more tightly.

So coverage of the sports world is contracting at the same time it is expanding. New technologies are creating new methods of communication, but the media are looking more like each other as they evolve. Each is finding new ways to provide information through words, sound, and pictures. The sports information professional who keeps that in mind will not stray too far, however the technology changes. Athletics events are human dramas. The sports information professional is still in the business of telling stories. The techniques have changed; the tools have changed. The audiences are more diverse and more demanding, but the demands of the job have not changed. Sports information demands a specialist who can adapt the tools of various media to tell a story effectively to the particular audience tuned to a specific medium. The effective storyteller always will survive. As the pioneers of the Internet media have discovered, "Content is still king."

As the 21st century begins, the window on the world of sports is wide open. Spectators can see more sports events and accumulate more sports information than ever before. When CBS-TV elected not to renew the contract of well-known sportscaster Brent Musberger, he made his final appearance with the network at the NCAA Division I championship game. He closed his final telecast this way: "I've had a front row seat for 20 years. Thanks for sharing it with me."

One day soon we all may have a front-row seat for almost any game of our choice.

DISCUSSION QUESTIONS

1. Why did the Women's National Basketball Association in its first year of operation receive high visibility?
2. How can sports information departments create greater audience interest using new technologies? How can they increase visibility?
3. For sports information specialists, what are some of the benefits of using email instead of the telephone to communicate with the media?

SUGGESTED EXERCISES

1. Check with the A. C. Nielsen Co. or one of the major television networks to find out the trend of televising college basketball games. Has there been an increase or decrease?
2. Find the top five television markets in order in the United States. What determines the rankings?
3. Pick a professional sports league. Browse the Internet and each team's website and compare and contrast the sites.

References

29 minutes sold. (1997, Jan. 8). *Cincinnati Enquirer,* p. D-3.

About us. (2006). CSTV.com. Retrieved December 13, 2006, from http://www.cstv.com/online.

AJR News Link. *American Journalism Review and NewsLink Associates.* Retrieved June 4, 1998, from http://www.ajrnewslink.org

Altheide, D. (1985). *Media power.* Beverly Hills, CA: Sage Publications.

Altheide, D. L., & Snow, R. P. (1978). Sports versus the mass media. *Urban Life. 7,* 189–204.

Aprile, K. (1995, March 11). Ridgeville's Borsz new CSU volleyball coach. *Chronicle-Telegram,* p. 3-C.

Bailey, J. A., & Matthews, D. L. (1989). *Law and liability in athletics, physical education and recreation* (2nd ed.). Dubuque, IA: William C. Brown.

Baran, S. J., & Davis, D. K. (1995). *Mass communication theory.* Belmont, CA: Wadsworth Publishing Co.

Barone, J., & Switzer, J. (1995). *Interviewing art and skill.* Needham Heights, MA: Allyn & Bacon.

Baseball chiefs called in inquiry. (1920, Sept. 21). *New York Times, 70*(22,886), 8.

BCS standings. (2006). Bowl Championship Series. Retrieved December 12, 2006, from http://www.bcsfootball.org/bcsfb/standings.

Bellamy, R. V. (1988). Impact of the television marketplace on the structure of Major League Baseball. *Journal of Broadcasting and Electronic Media. 32*(1), 73–87.

Bensenhaver, A., & Emerson, T. (1996). *Protecting your right to know: The Kentucky open records and open meetings acts.* Frankfurt: Office of the Attorney General.

Biagi, S. (1992). *Media/Impact: An introduction to mass media.* Belmont, CA: Wadsworth Publishing Co.

Black, J., & Bryant J. (1995). *Introduction to communication* (4th ed.). Dubuque, IA: Wm. C. Brown Communications, Inc.

Blinde, E. M., Greendorfer, S., & Shanker, R. J. (1991). Differential media coverage of men's and women's intercollegiate basketball: Reflection of gender ideology. *Journal of Sport and Social Issues. 15*(2), 98–114.

Bodley, H. (1996, April 19). Scrap Iron polishes Brewers to a fine shine. *USA Today. 14*(153), 8-c.

Bok, S. (1978). Lying: Moral choice in public or private life. New York: Random House. In P. Patterson & L. Wilkins, *Media ethics: Issues and cases.* Dubuque: Wm. C. Brown Publishers.

Brewer, C. (1998, June 7). Internet use still growing like crazy. *The Cincinnati Enquirer,* p. E-4.

Broadcast.com. *About broadcast.com.* Retrieved June 4, 1998, from http://www.broadcast.com

Broadcast.com. *Fanscan.* Retrieved June 4, 1998, from http://www.broadcast.com

Broadcast.com. *Frequently asked questions.* Retrieved June 4, 1998, from http://www.broadcast.com

Broadcast.com. *Press room.* Retrieved June 4, 1998, from http://www.broadcast.com

Brooks, B. (1997). *Journalism in the information age.* Needham Heights, MA: Allyn and Bacon.

Burns, G. (1991). Production theory as administration research. In "Video Pedagogies of Production." *Journal of Film and Video. 43*(3), 30–41.

Chamberlin, A. (1990). Sports information. In J. B. Parks & B. R. K. Zanger (Eds.), *Sports and fitness management: Career strategies and professional content.* Champaign: Human Kinetics.

Coakley, J. J. (1986). *Sport in society: Issues and controversies* (3rd ed.). St. Louis: Times Mirror/Mosby College Publishing.

College Sports Information Directors of America. (1996–97). *CoSIDA Publications Committee Handbook.* Corpus Cristi, TX: Printers Unlimited Texas A & M.

Company history. (2003). OCSN.com. Retrieved December 13, 2006, from http://www.ocsn.com/about/ocsn-history.html.

Congressional Record, 75 stat 732, Sports Broadcasting Act, 1961, Public Law No. 87–331, vol. 75, p. 331.

Consol, J. (1996, June 22). Good news for newspapers. *Editor and publisher. 129*(25), 14.

Copyright Act of 1976, title 17 of the United States Code. (October, 1976): Government Printing Office.

Coulson, D. C., & Hansen, A. (1995, spring). The Louisville *Courier-Journal*'s news content after purchase by Gannett. *Journalism and Mass Communication Quarterly. 72*(1), 205.

Davis, H. M. (1978). *Basic concepts of sports information.* East Longmeadow, MA: Jeste.

DeFleur, M. I., & Ball-Rokeach, S. (1989).

Theories of mass communication (5th ed.). New York: Longman.

Dominick, J. (1996). *The dynamics of mass communication* (5th ed.). New York: The McGraw-Hill Companies, Inc.

Doyle, J. E. (1934, Feb. 12). The sport trail. *The Plain Dealer*, p. 16.

Duncan, M. D., & Hasbrook, C. A. (1988). Denial of power in televised women's sports. *Sociology of Sport Journal. 5*(1), 1–21.

Editor & Publisher yearbook. (1995). *Editor and Publisher*. Part 1, p. 4.

FACS. Mission. *FACSNET*. Retrieved June 4, 1998, from http://www.facsnet.org

Federal Educational Rights and Privacy Act. (1974). 20 U.S.C. § 552.

Fedler, F., Bender, R., Davenport, L, & Kostoyu, P. (1997). *Reporting for the media*. Fort Worth: Harcourt Brace & Company.

Foley, D. H. (1992). Making the familiar strange: Writing critical sports narratives. *Sociology of Sport Journal. 9*, 36–47.

For NCAA, the address remains CBS. (1999, Nov. 19). *The Cincinnati Enquirer*, p. B-3.

Gamble, T. (1997, Jan. 30). Football at NKU: Gimme a break. *The Kentucky Post*, p. K-6.

Gertz v. Welch. 418 U.S. 323 (1974).

Goodman, M. (Ed.). (1990). *Access to campus crime reports*. Washington, DC: Student Press Law Center.

Goodwin, H. (1994). *Groping for ethics in journalism*. Ames: Iowa State University Press.

Government and Sunshine Act. 5 U.S.C. § 552b (1976, Sept. 13).

Hall, A. (1996, July). Interview with Donna Lopianao, executive director of the Women's Sports Foundation.

Hall, A. (1996, July). Interview with Judith Holland, chair of the NCAA Women's Basketball Committee.

Hall, A. (1996, July). Interview with Mary Masters, assistant commissioner of the Big Ten Conference.

Hall, A. (2003, July). Interview with Jim Wright, chief statistician for the NCAA.

Hall, A. (2003, July). Interview with Mike Ranieri, STAT CREW.

Hall, A. (2003, July). Interview with Bob Goldring, director of information services of the OHSAA.

Hall, A. (2003, October). Interview with Tony Hamilton, Mid-Continent Conference.

Hall, A. (2003, October). Interview with Bill Rogers, former assistant athletic director of media relations at Valparaiso University.

Hall, A. (2003, October). Interview with Al King, sports information director at Ashland University.

Hall, A. (2003, October). Interview with Mark Shook, assistant athletics director for student-athlete services at Bowling Green State University.

Hammer, J. (1989, Dec. 11). Betting billions on TV sports. *Newsweek. 114*(24), p. 66.

Helitzer, M. (1992). *The dream job: Sports publicity, promotion and public relations*. Athens, OH: University Sports Press.

Hiebert, R. E. (1966). *Courtiers to the crowd*. Ames: Iowa State University Press.

Hiebert, R. E., Ungurait, D. F., & Bohn, T. W. (1991). *Mass media IV*. NY: Longman Publishing Group.

Hiebert, R. E., Ungurait, D. F., & Bohn, T.W. (1991). *Mass media VI*. NY: Longman Publishing Group.

Hoffarth, T. (1996, Feb. 29). CBS bets $1.725 billion investment brings big dividends. *LA Daily News*, p. 2.

Horowitz, I. (1978). Market entrenchment and the sports broadcasting act. *American Behavioral Scientist. 21*, 415–430.

Howard, D. R., & Crompton, J. L. (1995). *Financing sport*. Morgantown, WV: Fitness Information Technology.

Huggins, S. (1996, Oct. 21). Study shows that women's sports lag behind men's in terms of media coverage. *The NCAA news*, 3(37), 1.

Hunt, T., & Ruben, B. (1993). *Mass communication producers and consumers*. New York: HarperCollins.

Infante, D. A., Rancer, A. S., & Womack, D. F. (1990). *Building communication theory*. Prospect Heights, IL: Waveland Press, Inc.

Itule, B., & Anderson, A. (1987). *News writing and reporting for today's media*. NY. McGraw Hill.

Keith, J. (1985). Tough public relations problems. In *NCAA public relations and promotional manual* (NCAA, Ed., p. 69). Mission, KS: The National Collegiate Athletic Association.

Kiesewetter, J. (1997, Jan.9). Play ball. *Cincinnati Enquirer*, p. D-1.

King, A. (1987). *Power and communication*. Prospect Heights, IL: Waveland Press, Inc.

Koch, B. (1997, Feb. 3). Finch's ouster a sign of the times. *The Cincinnati Post*, p. B-1.

Kohler, D. (1994). *Broadcast journalism: A guide for the presentation of radio and television news*. Englewood Cliffs, NJ: Prentice-Hall, Inc.

Lambert, P. (1989, Nov. 27). Billion-dollar basketball for CBS. *Broadcasting*.

Lebowitz, H. (1996, April 22). Let's hear it for nice guys like Lucarelli. *News Herald. 118*(5), 9, 12.

Lee, J. (1992). Media portrayals of male and female Olympic athletes: Analyses of newspaper accounts of the 1984 and the 1988 Summer Games. Review for *Sociology of Sport. 27*(3), 197–222.

Littlejohn, S. W. (1989). *Theories of human communication* (3rd ed.). Belmont, CA: Wadsworth Publishing Co.

Local Organizing Committee. (1993, July 8). *Indianapolis lands another final four* [news release].

Manasseh, P. (1985). Football press-box operations. In *NCAA public relations and promotion manual*. Mission, KS: The National Collegiate Athletic Association.

Martze, R. (1996, April 19). All systems go at ESPN for NFL draft weekend. *USA Today. 14*(153), 2-C.

McCombs, M. E., & Shaw, D. L. (1972). Agenda setting. In S. J. Baran & D. K. Davis (Eds.). *Mass communication theory*. Belmont, CA: Wadsworth Publishing Company.

McKay, J., & Huber, D. (1992). Anchoring media images of technology and sport. *Women's Studies International Forum. 15*(2), 205–218.

McQuail, D. (1987). *Mass communication theory: An introduction* (2nd ed.). Newberry Park, CA: Sage Publications.

Medius Interactive. *Company info.* Retrieved May 30, 1998 from http://www.medius.net

Mencher, M. (1991). *News reporting and writing* (5th ed.). Dubuque, IA: Wm. C. Brown Publishers.

Middleton, K., & Chamberlin, B. (1991). The law of public communication (2nd ed.). White Plains, NY: Longham Publishing Group.

Miller, L. (1998). *Power journalism: Computer assisted reporting*. Orlando, FL: Harcourt Brace College Publishers.

Min, G. (1987). Over-commercialization of the Olympics 1988: The role of the U.S. television networks. *International Review for the Sociology of Sport, 22*(2), 137–142.

Morgan, B. (1985). Brochures: What the media wants. *In NCAA public relations and promotional manual.* Mission, KS: The National Collegiate Athletic Association.

Moynahan, P. (1996, November). Interview with Jane Meier, athletic director at Northern Kentucky University.

NASCAR joins majors with TV deal. (1999, Nov. 13). *The Cincinnati Enquirer*, B-3.

NASCAR signs with NBS, Fox. (1999, Nov. 11). *The Cincinnati Enquirer*, C-5.

National Collegiate Athletic Association. (1992). *Gender equity study*. Overland Park, KS.

National Collegiate Athletic Association. *NCAA championship: promotion concepts for NCAA championships*. Overland Park, KS.

NCAA Board of Directors adopts landmark academic reform package. (2004, April 29). NCAA.com. Retrieved December 13, 2006, from http://www.ncaa.org/releases/divi/2004/2004042901d1.htm.

Newhagen, J., & Rafaeli, S. (1996, winter). Why communication researchers should study the Internet: A dialogue. *Journal of Communication, 46*(1), 4–13.

Newspaper Association of America. *Number of U.S. daily newspapers.* Retrieved November 17, 1999, from http://www.naa.org.info/info/facts/11/html

Newspaper Association of America. *U.S. advertising expenditures.* Retrieved November 17, 1999, from http://www.naa.org.info/info/facts/09/html

Newspaper Association of America. *U.S. daily and Sunday/weekend newspaper reading audience.* Retrieved November 17, 1999, from http://www.naa.org.info/info/facts/02/html

Newspaper Association of America. *U.S. daily newspapers in circulation.* Retrieved November 17, 1999, from http://www.naa.org.info/info/facts/12/html

Nichols, W. (1993, November). Interview with Dale Gallagher, former Kent SID.

Nichols, W. (1996). Interview with David Glasier, sports reporter for the *Lake County News.*

Nichols, W. (1996). Interview with Tom Gaffney, sports reporter for the *Akron Beakon Journal.*

Nichols, W. (1996, February). Interview with Julie Dalpaiz, editor of sports publications at University of Illinois.

Nichols, W. (1996, July 7). Interview with Kevin Ruple, sports information director at Baldwin-Wallace College.

Nichols, W. (1996, July 20). Interview with Merle Levin, retired sports information director at Cleveland State University.

Nichols, W. (1996, July). Interview with Debby Ghezzi, former athletics director at Notre Dame College of Ohio.

Nichols, W. (1996, July). Interview with Tom Bochenek, public relations aide with the Cleveland Indians.

Nichols, W. (1996, July). Interview with Tracy Ellis, former basketball player at the University of Missouri.

Nichols, W. (1996). Interview with Chris Wenzler, SID at John Carrol.

Nichols, W. (2002, May). Interview with Curtis Danburg, manager of media relations for the Cleveland Indians.

Nichols, W. (2002, May). Interview with Ken Mather, manager of media and publicity for the Cleveland Browns.

Nichols, W. (2002, May). Interview with Bob Price, former senior director of communication and public relations for the Cleveland Cavaliers.

Noack, D. (1997, Sept. 13). Online newspapers as TV stations? *Editor and Publisher.* p. 35.

Olson, J., Hirsch, E., Breitenbach, O., &

Saunders, K. (1987). *Administration of high school and collegiate athletic programs.* Philadelphia: Saunders College Publishing.

Overbeck, W., & Pullen, R. (1991). *Major principles of media law.* Fort Worth: Holt, Rinehart and Winston, Inc.

Parks, J. B., & Zanger, B. R. K. (1990). Definition and direction. In J. B. Parks & B. R. K. Zanger (Eds.), *Sport and fitness management: career strategies and professional content.* (pp. 2–12). Champaign, IL: Human Kinetics Books.

Patterson, P., & Wilkins, L. (1991). *Media ethics: Issues and cases.* Dubuque: Wm. C. Brown Publishers.

Perkins, D. R. (1985). The SID seen as a specialist. In *NCAA Public Relations and Promotions and Promotional Manual.* Mission, KS: The National Collegiate Athletic Association.

Pratt, C. A. (1990). Sports journalism. In J. B. Parks & B. R. K. Zanger (Eds.). *Sport and fitness management: career strategies and professional content.* Champaign, IL: Human Kinetics Books.

RADAR Report, (Spring, 1998). Statistical Research, Inc. Retrieved November 18, 1999, from http://prplace.com/mds_guide/medstat.html

Reddick, R., & King, E. (1997). *The online journalist* (2nd ed). Orlando, FL: Harcourt Brace College Publishers.

Reggie Warford v. *Lexington Herald Leader,* et al. 789 S. W. sd 758, 17, Med.L.Rptr. 1785 (KY 1990). cert. denied, 111 S. Ct. 754 (1991).

Sanford, B. (1984). *Synopsis of the law of libel and the right of privacy.* New York: Pharos Books.

Sanford, B. (1990, August/Sept.). Wrestling with libel in the 1990s. *Scripps-Howard News, 46*(5), 2–4.

Sayer, J., & Hoehn, L. (1994). *Interviewing skills and applications.* Scottsdale, AR: Gorsuch Scarisbrick, Publishers.

Schudson, M. (1987). The new validation of popular culture: Sense and sentimentality in academia. *Critical Studies in Mass Communications. 4,* 51–68.

Schulte, H., & Dufresne, A. (1994). *Getting the story: An advanced reporting guide to beats, records, and sources.* New York: Macmillan.

Slack, J. D., & Allor, M. (1983). The political and epistemological constituents of critical communication research. In *Ferment in the field. Journal of Communication. 33*(3), 212–218.

Smith, R. (1996). *Becoming a public relations writer.* New York: HarperCollins College Publishers.

Starwave Corporation. *About Starwave/Infoseek.* Retrieved May 30, 1998, from http://www.starwave.com/jobs/aboutsw/index.html

Stewart, C., & Cash, W. (1994). *Interviewing principles and practices* (7th ed.). Dubuque, IA: WCB Brown and Benchmark.

Stovall, J. (1994). *Writing for the mass media.* Englewood Cliffs, NJ: Prentice-Hall, Inc.

Television Bureau of Advertising. Trends in television. In *Television Bureau of Advertising.* Retrieved August 13, 1998, from http://www.tvv.org/researchreports/trends

Television Bureau of Advertising. Time spent viewing per television home per day. In *TV basics.* Retrieved November 17, 1999, from http://www.tvb.org/tvfacts/tvbasics5/html

Television Bureau of Advertising. Multi-set and color television households. In *TV basics.* Retrieved November 17, 1999, from http://www.tvb.org/tvfacts/tvbasics2/html

Television Bureau of Advertising. Time spent and daily reach by major media. In *TV basics.* Retrieved November 17, 1999, from http://www.tvb.org/tvfacts/tvbasics21/html

Television Bureau of Advertising. Top 25 network telecasts ranked by household ratings. In *TV basics.* Retrieved November 17, 1999, from http://www.tvb.org/tvfacts/tvbasics11/html

The United States Golf Association. (1997a). *Publicity handbook for USGA championships.* Far Hills, NJ: Author.

The United States Golf Association. (1997b). Questions and answers. In *USGA championship programs.* Far Hills, NJ: Author.

Trenholm, S. (1991). *Human communication theory* (2nd ed.). Englewood Cliffs, NJ: Prentice Hall.

Tuchman, G., Daniels, A., Benet, J. (Eds.). (1978). *Hearth and home: Images of women in the mass media.* NY: Oxford University Press.

TV deal worth $400 million. (1999, Nov. 11). *The Cincinnati Post,* B-7.

TV sports: The $3.5 Billion Ticket. (1996, May 13). *Broadcasting and cable, 26*(21), 34.

University Netcasting. *Company info.* Retrieved May 19, 1998, from http://www.uninc.com

University Netcasting. *Fansonly.com.* Retrieved May 30, 1998, from http://www.uninc.com

Valdiserri, R. (1985). Duties of a modern SID as viewed by an SID. In *NCAA Public Relations and Promotions and Promotional Manual.* Mission, KS: The National Collegiate Athletic Association.

VanderZwaag, J. J. (1988). *Policy development in sport management.* Indianapolis, IN: Benchmark Press.

Verducci, T. (1998, May 25). Fox is in the hunt. *Sports Illustrated, 88*(21), 44.

Vivian, J. (1995). *The media of mass communication* (3rd ed). Needham Heights, MASS: Allyn & Bacon.

Vruggink, R. (1985). Release and mailing. In *NCAA public relations and promotions manual*. Mission, KS: The National Collegiate Athletic Association.

Wang, P., & Irwin, R. L. (1993). An assessment of economic impact techniques for small sporting events. *Sport Marketing Quarterly*, *2*(3), 33–37.

Watkins, B. (1991). Communications. In B. L. Parkhouse (Ed.), *The management of sport: Its foundation and application*. St. Louis: Mosby Year Book.

Webster, J. G., & Lichty, L. W. (1992). *Ratings analysis: Theory and practice*. Hillsdale, NJ: Lawrence Erlbaum.

Wenner, L. A. (1989). Media, sports and society: The research agenda. In L. A. Wenner (Ed.), *Media, sports and society*. Newberry Park, CA: Sage Publications, Inc.

West, M. (1985). Duties of the modern SID as viewed by the sportswriter. In *NCAA public relations and promotion manual*. Mission, KS: The National Collegiate Athletic Association.

Whiteside, T. (1985, May 20). Onward and upward with the arts. In *Cable television: Part 1, 61*(13), 78.

Wilcox, D. L., Ault, P. H., & Agee, W. K. (1992). *Public relations: Strategies and tactics*. (3rd ed.). New York: Harper Collins.

Willis, J., & Willis, D. B. (1993). *New directions in media management*. Boston: Allyn & Bacon.

Wolff, A. (1996, Dec. 23). A survival guide. *Sports Illustrated*, *85*(26), 128.

Wong, G. M. (1991). Sports law: The theoretical aspects. In B. L. Parkhouse (Ed.), *The management of sport: Its foundation and application*. St. Louis: MO: Mosby-Year Book. p. 74–95.

Wonsek, P. L. (1992). College basketball television: A study of racism in the media. *Media, Culture and Society, 14*(3), 449–461.

Zeigler, E. F., & Bowie, G. W. (1983). *Management competency development in sport and physical education*. Philadelphia, PA: Lea and Fibizer.

Index

About the Authors

Allan W. Hall

Dr. Allan W. Hall spent 42 years in university athletics. He is retired from Ashland University, where he was Director of the Sports Communication major and Assistant Athletic Director. He also served as Athletic Director at Edinboro University of Pennsylvania and was an athletic administrator and the cross country coach at the University of Akron. Hall is a member of the the University of Akron Sports Hall of Fame, Summit County (Ohio) Sports Hall of Fame, and Edinboro University of Pennsylvania Sports Hall of Fame.

Hall is past president of the Ohio United Methodist Historical Society and is chair of the Commission on Archives and History of the East Ohio Conference of the United Methodist Church. He also served as President of the Pennsylvania State Athletic Conference and President of the Tri-State Athletic Officials Association.

Hall is a graduate of Baldwin-Wallace College and has two master's degrees and a doctorate from the University of Akron. He and his wife, Pam, live in Wadsworth, Ohio, and have two grown children, Beth and Dale.

William E. Nichols

William E. Nichols has taught media relations in sport administration and related journalism courses at Baldwin-Wallace College, John Carroll University, Hiram College, and Notre Dame College Of Ohio, since 1988. As a freelance writer, Nichols has written for *The Sporting News*, *Football Digest*, *Basketball Digest*, *Golf World*, *Street & Smith College Basketball Annual*, and *Street & Smith Pro Basketball Annual*.

Nichols has received recognition as The Sportswriter of the Year (Cleveland Press Club, 1981), runner-up author of sports story of the year (Akron Press Club, 1981), Western Tennis Association Writer of the Year (1988), Ohio Track Writer of the Year (1988), Associated Press Award for Excellence (1987), and Lakewood High School Distinguished Alumni Award for Journalism (1991). He was a sportswriter at *The Plain Dealer* in Cleveland, Ohio, for 30 years, covering professional basketball, college sports, golf, tennis, bowling, and harness racing. He was also an official scorer for the Cleveland Indians for six years.

Nichols has a BBA from Baldwin-Wallace College and an MA from Kent State University. A native of Greater Cleveland, Nichols and his wife of 48 years, Jean, have a son, Wade, and a daughter, Lee Anne Chambers.

J. Patrick Moynahan

J. Patrick Moynahan serves as associate professor of journalism and vice provost at Northern Kentucky University in Highland Heights, Kentucky. His responsibilities include international programs, curriculum assessment, faculty development, and enrollment planning. He works with the Dean's Council on instruction, research, and scholarly activity as well as public engagement and information technology, and serves as acting provost in the absence of the provost.

Moynahan joined the NKU faculty in 1990 after 20 years in the journalism profession, 14 of them in sports writing and sports editing positions. He previously served as adviser to the campus newspaper, chair of the Department of Communication, and dean of the College of Professional Studies. He oversaw the creation of the College of Informatics, a merger of Communication, Computer Science, and Information Systems, for a year prior to accepting the vice provost position in July 2006.

Before moving to academia, Moynahan worked as night city editor, city editor, and assistant managing editor at *The Kentucky Post* from 1984–90. He has also worked as executive sports editor at *The Sunday Courier & Press* (Evansville, Ind.) and as sports editor at *The Paducah Sun* (Paducah, Ky.). At *The Sunday Courier & Press*, the sports section was judged the best in Indiana for five consecutive years (1978–83), and Moynahan received the top award for sports reporting from UPI. At *The Kentucky Post*, teams he directed won regional and nationals awards in news and investigative reporting.

A native of Kentucky, Moynahan holds a BS in journalism and speech/theater and an MS in mass communication from Murray State University. He and his wife of 37 years, Anita, have three daughters: Kristie, Kori, and Kelli.

Janis L. Taylor

Dr. Janis L. Taylor retired from teaching in 1988 after a 25-year career as a college educator and documentary filmmaker. Her teaching career included full-time appointments at Barat College in Lake Forest, Illinois; Northwestern University in Evanston, Illinois; and Northern Kentucky University in Highland Heights, Kentucky. Throughout her career in academia, Taylor produced and directed her own independent documentaries. Her two most noted ones are "When Diamonds Were a Girl's Best Friend" (1987), which won first place in the documentary category of the Chicago Access Corporation Video Festival, and "When Dreams Come True" (1989), which received honorable mention at the same Chicago Access competition. Both documentaries are about the All American Girls' Professional Baseball League that existed in the Midwest from 1943–1954. Since retirement, she has continued to work on independent documentaries with nonprofit organizations.